UNDERSTANDING CRIMINAL LAW

UNDERSTANDING CRIMINAL LAW

JAY A. SIGLER
Rutgers University

Little, Brown and Company
Boston Toronto

Library of Congress Catalog Card No. 80-83078

ISBN 0-316-790540

9 8 7 6 5 4 3 2 1

HAL

Published simultaneously in Canada by Little, Brown & Company (Canada) Limited

Printed in the United States of America

For Niall, Ian, Georgianna, and Alysson

Preface

Criminal law holds a peculiar fascination for Americans. Jesse James, the Dalton gang, and John Dillinger have been portrayed on our movie screens. Truman Capote and Norman Mailer, two of our finest novelists, have depicted the life and times of mass murderers. Yet the romance that crime holds for our moviemakers and fiction writers is mixed with fear and loathing. Crime is a great and growing problem in America. Steps must be taken to meet the very real threat of crime to the quality of our lives. This book attempts to examine the criminal law in America so that it may be better understood. Beyond that the book strives to provide a perspective on the policies underlying criminal law and the new approaches to criminal law policy that are now emerging.

There are many books about American criminal law. The inadequacies of our criminal law system were dramatically and effectively described by James Q. Wilson in his important book *Thinking About Crime,* written in 1977. Wilson believes that there are no simple causes for crime which can be alleviated to reduce its incidence. He says we "must think instead of what it is feasible for a government or a community to do, and then to try to discover by experimentation and observation" just which techniques may help reduce the incidence of victimization. Pumping tens of billions of dollars into crime control has not worked, as Wilson predicted. In the belief that we must reexamine the goals and purposes of American criminal law as one means of dealing more effectively with crime, this book attempts to explain the basic elements of the criminal law and to indicate what is being done to bring that law into greater conformity with the experience of the past two decades.

The standard criminal law topics are considered. The elements of crime, criminal defenses, crimes against property, crimes against the person, and various economic crimes are given ample attention. Highlighting these and other materials are exhibits drawn from statutes, case decisions, newspapers, journal articles, government studies, and scholarly sources. These materials are intended as illustrations of important aspects of criminal law, and most are accompanied with a probing question about the meaning or implication of the document. Juvenile offenses are not covered in this text because they tend to be treated professionally as a separate type of noncriminal conduct.

This is not a criminal law casebook. Many excellent casebooks are available, and there is no need for another one. Some cases do appear in this book, but they are meant to illustrate or highlight a difficult point rather than to serve as precedent for a basic legal principle. As a result this book can be profitably used to supplement a case-by-case approach, but it is meant to stand on its own as a text.

Most of the current textbooks in criminal law are careful, accurate summaries of the current state of the law. Little analysis or criticism is provided in these texts because the authors set out to provide useful thumbnail summaries of current doctrines in criminal law. In contrast this book puts the criminal law into a social, cultural, and political context generally ignored by other books.

This book contains material not to be found in any other text. Space is given to administrative, political, and judicial crimes, topics not usually treated elsewhere. Victimless crimes are given special attention, as are certain newer crimes of a white-collar variety. Then the terms *victimless crime* and *white-collar crime* are themselves questioned.

Because this book is devoted to examining American criminal law rather than simply describing it, considerable attention is given to the purported goals and purposes of existing laws and doctrines. A questioning, probing attitude is adopted which many will find controversial or at least stimulating. Teachers should find the text provocative and useful as a basis for classroom debate.

The final chapter tries to draw the various trends of criminal law development into a patterned order. Considerable attention is given to legal codification, the Model Penal Code, and other recent efforts to renew and reform American criminal law. This material points the way toward the future growth of American criminal law.

Because this book is intended for those who are not trained in the law, a glossary is provided as well as a section on locating and working with legal materials. For the generalist just entering into the criminal law this book should serve as both a compass and a roadmap. For teachers, students, and general readers these sections should provide a permanent reference source.

This book, then, aims to provide a clear, succinct, modern statement of the current condition of American criminal law. The approach is more comprehensive and balanced than that of other texts. Although violent crimes are discussed, other more prevalent crimes are given prominent positions too. I hope the readers of this book will acquire a questioning, critical attitude about American criminal law. Much still needs changing, but first students and the public must understand the criminal law as it is.

The author is indebted to those writers and thinkers who have peered deeply into these questions before him. Roscoe Pound, the legal philosopher who so profoundly shaped American law, also led the way into our understanding of criminal law. Herbert Packer gave us a new image of criminal law when he wrote *The Limits of the Criminal Sanction.* Ramsey Clark alerted the nation to the need for a new approach to crime in his book *Crime in America.* Professor Herbert Wechsler has been the guiding genius of criminal law reform in America. However, in spite of the debt to these legal scholars, I must remind the reader that little is known about the social and political processes that lead to the enactment of new criminal laws. For some hints the author is indebted to *A Measure of Justice,* an excellent study of changes in the California Penal Code written by Richard A. Berk, Harold Brachman, and Selma Lesser.

This book could not have been written without the help of several typists, a secretary, and a small army of technical supporters provided by Rutgers University. But I employed no graduate assistants, no researchers, no library hounds, no student laborers or other unfortunates who might have been helpful, perhaps, but who would not have seen things I wanted to see for myself. No foundation underwrote my efforts. No released time was sought or provided. This was a labor of love and an effort to answer some questions that have long disturbed me. My editors were patient and kind, but my greatest assistance came from the advice received from colleagues at other institutions who saw the manuscript at various stages of preparation and gave valuable suggestions for changes and improvements. They are Thomas Barker, Jacksonville State University; Jerry L. Dowling, Sam Houston State University; David A. Jones, University of Pittsburgh; and Susette M. Talarico, University of Georgia. Special thanks to Jane Hardwick and Jesse Matthews.

Jay Sigler
Philadelphia, Pennsylvania

Contents

1

THE NATURE AND FUNCTIONS OF CRIMINAL LAW

American criminal law is passing through a period of reconstruction and revision. Many of the familiar and well-accepted practices of the criminal process have been brought into question. The reforms of the early years of this century are now seen as inadequate to cope with deviant behavior. Parole, probation, the indeterminate sentence, juvenile courts, and the creation of penitentiaries and low-security prisons have all been tried, but with limited success. Many experts question whether the ideal of rehabilitating lawbreakers really works. Indeed, the attempt to treat convicted persons as sick is losing ground as crime figures mount. At the heart of the problem of contemporary American criminal law is the realization that there is no longer any general agreement about the purposes of criminal punishment.

If American criminal law lacks a general theory of punishment it still has a more or less coherent shape. Our criminal law derives from English and American common law as modified by the acts of state legislatures or by Congress. Increasingly, the common law, the judge-made aspects of American criminal law, is being replaced by consciously constructed criminal legislation. Like other legislation, criminal laws are the end result of political compromises and the work of various interest groups, a fact highlighted in subsequent chapters. Sometimes lawmaking is a complex and time-consuming task, as exemplified by the decade-long effort to revise and codify the federal criminal law. Sometimes the process is less deliberate and less carefully considered.

There are experts in criminal policy, but their expertise is limited. Criminologists and sociologists have long attempted to locate the cause or causes of criminal behavior. Cultural, economic, demographic, social, and psychological explanations are available, but they tend to be inconclusive or even contradictory. The experts no longer are confident of their ability to locate criminal causes, to identify criminal types, or to find criminal personalities. They do not agree on which kinds of behavior ought to be within the scope of the criminal law, so legislators have made these choices. Consequently, social scientists have had little impact upon the construction of American criminal law, leaving the field to lawyers and legal philosophers. For good or ill American criminal law is the handiwork of lawyers, judges, and politicians.

WHAT IS LAW?

To many people the law seems to be a body of powerful, abstract rules that hovers over our everyday lives. Mysterious technical jargon known and understood by lawyers and judges helps shape our lives in ways that ordinary lay persons can only dimly grasp. Whether justice or merely some means of exerting social power is the end in view is not clear. But the law surrounds us, protects us, and controls us, attempting to bring order, at least, to the confusion and conflict produced by people pursuing private goals in a mass society.

Much law is neither unjust nor just. In America the law is generated by our legislators, executives, judges, and administrators, guided, to some extent, by the will of the people. Their enactments, orders, and rulings are not merely the product of an isolated elite but responses to the claims, demands, and pressures of competing groups and influential individuals. Whether we like it or not, the law our governments produce reflects the tensions and cleavages of our society. The law does not derive from any divine source or from some inspired group of self-serving leaders. It is the law our leaders think we want, even if we do not ourselves give much thought to what it contains.

Criminal law is easier to understand than most other kinds of law. Orderly group life requires some means of social control. Criminal law may be defined as "a formal means of social control [that] involves the use of rules that are interpreted, and are enforceable, by the courts of a political community."[1] The rules themselves are generally made in our legislatures. The function of the rules is to set limits to the conduct of the citizens, to guide the officials (police and other administrators), and to define conditions of deviance or unacceptable behavior.

Law is divided roughly into two parts: criminal and civil (noncriminal). Civil law is essentially private law governing the relationships among persons or groups. Its primary role is to resolve and regulate disputes among private parties. The subject matter of the dispute may be money, property, a contract, or a personal injury. The state attempts to be the neutral umpire among disputants. In the criminal law the state is directly involved and may bring a legal suit against an offender, in the name of the government. The decision to arrest or to prosecute for violation of the criminal law is a public act. The criminal law brings the weight of the whole society into the legal arena.

There are, of course, overlapping situations. A single act may

[1] F. James Davis, Henry H. Tooster, Jr., C. Ray Jeffery, and E. Eugene Davis, *Society and the Law: New Meanings for an Old Profession* (New York: Free Press of Glencoe, 1962), pp. 42-43. This quotation has been adapted and applied here to the criminal law, rather than accepted as a general definition of law.

constitute the basis for both public and private legal treatment. If so, American law usually requires two separate trials, one for the criminal case and the other for the civil case. In the criminal action the state will be the complaining party. Victims can privately institute their own action. But the purpose of the private case is to repay the victim for injuries, while the criminal case is aimed at control of antipublic behavior, regardless of the victim's attitudes or desires. The two cases will be considered under two separate kinds of procedures, resulting in different kinds of consequences. Criminal sanctions may include fine, imprisonment, or even death. Civil sanctions are much more flexible, but they cannot be as severe as criminal sanctions because the state alone has a monopoly of the use of legitimate force.

Rape provides a vivid illustration of an overlapping criminal and civil proceeding. A rape is a tort, a civil wrong done to a person, for which the victim may seek damages in a court. But rape is also a violation of the criminal law. The police and the public prosecuting attorney may decide to act or not to act after receiving a rape complaint. They may choose their course of action without regard to the feelings of the victim, and the punishment imposed, if any, is solely on behalf of the state. In America crime victims cannot compel police to make arrests or prosecutors to prosecute. Prosecution for crime is a public monopoly and (with few exceptions) private prosecution is almost unknown.

The criminal law can be found in many legal sources. It derives from the following sources.

Distinctions between crimes and civil offenses are sometimes small.

Because the elements of both civil and criminal fraud are seemingly identical, the courts have concluded that the only significant difference between the sanctions is to be found in the varying burdens of proof. In a prosecution for tax evasion the Government must prove the defendant guilty beyond a reasonable doubt, while in a civil case fraud need only be established by clear and convincing evidence.

Source: Paul P. Lipton, "The Relationship Between Civil and Criminal Penalties for Tax Frauds," *University of Illinois Law Forum,* 68 (1968), p. 528.

1. The Constitution of the United States and the constitutions of each of the 50 states
2. National legislation
3. State legislation
4. Municipal legislation
5. Judicial decisions of federal and state courts interpreting constitutions of legislation
6. From the common law in the states, which is judge-made criminal policy resting upon precedent or upon the older English common law (Some states, such as New York and California, have abolished the common law of crimes.)

Under the "void for vagueness" doctrine that has been developed by the United States Supreme Court, a statute may be declared unconstitutional whenever the meaning of a criminal statute cannot be arrived at without speculation and guesswork. Mere ambiguity may or may not create undue vagueness. Failure to describe the persons within the scope of the statute, the conduct deemed criminal, or the punishment to be imposed may cause a criminal statute or an administratively defined crime to be declared unconstitutional as violating the Fifth Amendment due process clause (federal) or the Fourteenth Amendment due process clause (state). Judges retain the authority to determine whether to invoke the void for vagueness doctrine.

Under the Constitution the states have general jurisdiction over crimes committed within their territorial limits. The federal government, however, has exclusive criminal jurisdiction over crimes committed on federal lands. Crimes committed on federal lands or federal enclaves may resemble crimes defined in state law by virtue of the Federal Assimilative Crimes Act, which provides for the applicability of state criminal statutes to crimes not punishable under federal law that are committed on federal enclaves. The act adopts appropriate state laws by reference, but these laws are incorporated within the federal law, and offenses committed within federal enclaves must be tried in federal courts.

Most federal criminal statutes are enacted by Congress under its powers over interstate commerce, but many statutes derive from other powers listed in the enumerated powers section of Article One of the Constitution. The same act may constitute an offense against both the national and state governments as a result of federalism, which gives both levels of government sovereign powers to define and declare policy concerning criminal law. Neither the double jeopardy clause of the federal Constitution nor similar clauses of state constitutions bars two separate prosecutions before federal and state courts, even though the offense is but a single event or occurrence.

Certain offenses, such as piracy and treason, are exclusively federal crimes under the Constitution. But states are free to create any other crimes referring to events that take place within their territory. A state probably has no jurisdiction to punish for acts committed beyond its territorial limits by persons other than its own citizens. Municipalities may enact ordinances having criminal characteristics only to the extent permitted by state law, and such ordinances may not conflict with either state or federal law. A single act may constitute both a crime under a state statute and a violation of a municipal ordinance, which would give both the municipal courts and state courts jurisdiction over the offense.

American criminal law is quite unintegrated. Towns, cities, states, and the federal government may each have similar or diverse versions of criminal law. The federal system of government and a tradition of local autonomy encourage a looseness and an inconsistency in criminal law policy.

Defining criminal law can be a complex task. Criminologists have long grappled with the task of determining the nature of deviant behavior. Rather than entering into some difficult sociological or philosophical issues, we can say that a crime is "any defined social harm made punishable by law."[2] This definition does not tell us what ought to be criminalized, nor does it describe the necessary elements of a crime. We shall postpone discussion of those matters to later chapters. We should emphasize at the outset one of the chief characteristics of the criminal law—its politicality.[3] Only the rules made by public agencies, especially legislatures and courts, comprise the criminal law. Union rules, Mafia orders, or college regulations are not part of the criminal law. Politicality does not mean that all of the criminal law is the result of partisan and pressure group politics, but it does mean that some of it is, and that all of it is part of the pattern of social power that Americans have come to accept.

[2] Rollin M. Perkins, *Cases on Criminal Law and Procedure* (Mineola, N.Y.: Foundation Press, Inc., 1966), p. 1.

[3] Part of a fourfold division of essential characteristics of criminal law as described in: Edwin H. Sutherland and Donald R. Cressey, *Principles of Criminology,* 8th ed. (Philadelphia: J. B. Lippincott Co., 1970), pp. 4–8. The other parts are specificity, uniformity, and penal sanction.

THE GOALS OF CRIMINAL LAW

Understanding criminal law requires attention to its underlying purposes. Unfortunately, these purposes have sometimes been assumed or neglected in the general pursuit of crime reduction. Most people—including most criminals—assume that crime is bad. The problem for law-abiding citizens seems to be to reduce the amount of badness in the society through the more or less coercive means of the criminal law. For many criminals the criminal law provides the rules of the game within which they can maneuver as they seek to advance their criminal careers. Both the law-abiding and the lawbreaking citizens seem to share a common agreement about the gamelike character of criminal law. Perhaps, in reflective moments, all citizens can discern the purposes of the rules of the criminal law game, while the goals of criminal law are less clear.

Surprisingly, criminology also accepts the game analogy of criminal law. Criminology as a social science attempts to analyze the causes, effects, and characteristics of deviant behavior. In an endeavor to explain and predict deviant behavior, classical criminology has developed sophisticated tools. Statistical studies abound. Single and multifactor explanations for criminal behavior have sometimes produced impressive scholarship.[4] Formidable case studies have been made.[5] But empirical criminological research is in its infancy and most studies lack precision, theoretical rigor, or consistent methodology.[6]

Professional criminologists have usually concerned themselves with causal explanations for crime in general. Serious criminal activity varies enormously from the bribe taker to the mugger to the bank embezzler; however, no general causative explanations have emerged. More fruitful are studies of particular crimes. Some evidence tends to provide explanations for embezzlement, forgery, and confidence games.[7] Some of this work is suggestive for the definition

[4] See Daniel Glaser and Kent Rice, "Crime, Age, and Employment," *American Sociological Review* 24 (October 1959): 679-686; and F. Ivan Nye, *Family Relationships and Delinquent Behavior* (New York: John Wiley & Sons, Inc., 1958).

[5] See Clifford R. Shaw, *The Jack-Roller* (Chicago: University of Chicago Press, 1970), a classic 6-year study of a young delinquent.

[6] Schlomo Shoham, "The Theoretical Boundaries of Criminology," *British Journal of Criminology* 31 (January 1963): 230-231.

[7] See Donald R. Cressey, "Criminological Research and the Definition of Crimes," *American Journal of Sociology* 56 (1951): 546-551; and for theft, Jerome Hall, *Theft, Law and Society,* 2d ed. (Indianapolis: Bobbs-Merrill, Inc., 1952).

of crimes, but no firm conclusions can yet be drawn from these efforts. When human behaviors are better understood, so, too, will criminal conduct be better regulated. We can only hope that future research in psychology, criminology, and sociology will yield more reliable results. Then criminal law can be guided more by social science than by political and other considerations.

A leading criminology text contends that universal causal explanations of crime may not be possible, especially since legal definitions of crime may confine the work of the criminologist who "should be completely free to push across the barriers of legal definitions whenever he sees noncriminal behavior which resembles criminal behavior."[8] As a result of the continuing linkages between criminal law violations and offenders' psychological or sociological characteristics and the lack of agreement upon the labels applied by the criminal law, other researchers have turned to a study of lawbreaking from the point of view of the efficiency of the law as a means of social control.[9] Unfortunately, causation is also a problem in that area of study, since the effectiveness of criminal law as a deterrent cannot be known until the connections between a law and its intended effects can be traced. This has been a recent focus of research.

Some criminologists hope to deter criminal activity through a deeper understanding of the criminal personality. Criminal law is constructed around notions of criminal responsibility. Personality theorists believe that criminals are deficient in self-understanding, are filled with self-disgust and are deficient in appreciating most of the world outside themselves. If this be so there may be therapeutic ways of enhancing self-regard and of enabling the criminal to learn responsibility and to act accordingly. Since most crimes are committed by people who have broken the law before, one task of criminal law may be to permit rehabilitation of those afflicted with a criminal personality. Criminal law that is focussed on personality change might actually reduce recidivism and crime rates generally, but this view assumes that a criminal is not only a person convicted of a crime, but also "a person whose pattern of thinking has led to arrestable behavior."[10] Few psychologists would claim the skill to

[8] Edwin H. Sutherland and Donald R. Cressey, *Criminology*, 9th ed. (Philadelphia: J. B. Lippincott Company, 1974), p. 21.

[9] See Marc Ancel, *Social Defense: A Modern Approach to Criminal Problems* (London: Routledge and Kegan Paul, 1965).

[10] Samuel Jochelson and Stanton E. Samenow, *The Criminal Personality* (New York: Jason Aronson, 1977), 2:3.

diagnose such incipient behavior, so the personality theorists may fairly be accused of assuming too much knowledge of human behavior.

Criminology may have been asking the wrong questions. Can we ever know the causes of deviant behavior? Can we ever identify in any individual's biography enough indicators to predict which youngsters are likely to become committed criminals? Even if we could know the causes of crime, what kinds of treatment or preventive actions can correct those personal or environmental factors that lead to crime? The ultimate question is whether those who commit criminal acts are essentially different from those who do not. Are not we all potential criminals? If the criminal law forbade the possession of private property, then many law-abiding citizens would be converted into criminals and some criminals might become leaders of a socialized society. Crime, then, is normal to all societies. This was a point made by sociologist Emile Durkheim, who believed that there would never be a sufficient unanimity of opinion or feeling in any society for criminality to be eliminated.[11] To say that crime is normal does not, of course, mean that all criminals are psychologically normal either.

The question of whether crime can be eliminated entirely must also be answered no, since humans are not angels and even angels can commit sins. But there is also some doubt whether crime is as bad a problem today as the media seem to indicate. Surprisingly, we have no reliable guide to the past that could reveal by comparison the dimensions of today's crime problem. There is one scholar who concluded that his data lent "no support to the hypothesis that the total amount of crime has increased with the complexity of modern living."[12] Another close study of the years 1854–1956 concludes that violent crimes reached their peak in America around the early 1870s.[13] Crime, then, seems to be the result of certain large-scale forces rather than merely the product of an individual defect. Professor James Q. Wilson reminds us that "what appears to be a crime explosion may in fact be a population explosion"[14] of the youth population, which always has a higher crime rate than adults.

[11] Emile Durkheim, *The Rules of Sociological Method* (Chicago: Free Press, 1950), first published in 1895.

[12] A. H. Hobbs, "Criminality in Philadelphia, 1790–1810 Compared with 1937," *American Sociological Review* 8 (1943): 198.

[13] Edwin H. Pavell, "Crime as a Function of Anomie," *Journal of Criminal Law, Criminology and Police Science* 57 (1966): 14.

[14] James Q. Wilson, "Crime in the Streets," *The Public Interest*, no. 5 (Fall 1966): 32.

Since the legislatures continue to invent new crimes every year, the public appears to believe that crime is a growing problem that requires new criminalizing statutes. Paradoxically, the effort to eliminate crime by creating new categories only tends to increase the statistical incidence of crime. We cannot reduce crime by creating new types of crimes. We might be better able to reduce crimes by eliminating some of them from the statute books, but this requires a realization that crime is a byproduct of society itself. Perhaps the best means of reducing crime is to remove some of the temptations to commit forbidden acts. If there were no cars, there would be no car thieves. If houses were better secured, there would be fewer robberies. But there will always be potential robbers.

Criminal laws resemble other statutes in that their sources are essentially political. Interest group activity is an important source of new criminal laws. Among the competing interests are law en-

---

Will this new bill be likely to discourage intruders if enacted into law?

Anti-intruder Bill Approved by Pennsylvania House

BY TERRY E. JOHNSON
Inquirer Harrisburg Bureau

HARRISBURG — A bill making minor changes in the law allowing a homeowner to use deadly force against an intruder was passed overwhelmingly by the House yesterday and sent to the Senate for consideration.

The bill is intended to put the burden on the intruder to prove that he did not enter a home illegally with the purpose of committing a felony. Under current law, a homeowner is required to justify the use of deadly force against an intruder.

Opponents of the bill charged that it would probably result in more accidental shootings and allow homeowners to be "the judge, jury and executioners."

The measure, sponsored by Rep. Joseph V. Grieco (R., Lycoming), had the backing of the National Rifle Association and most of the legislators who represent rural districts.

"What this bill does is allow every homeowner to decide when to use capital punishment," Rep. Mark Cohen (D., Phila.) said. "That's the job of the courts, not homeowners."

Although Democratic lawmakers had vowed to fight the bill or attempt to

forcement agencies themselves, including the police and prosecutors, who hope to simplify their tasks by creating criminal laws that are easier to apply and enforce. But many criminal laws are little more than legislative reflex actions—emotional outpourings of an overburdened public institution. Sometimes, as with some legislation concerning sexual psychopaths, the result is hopeless ambiguity.[15] Much of our drug control legislation came as a result of the policies of the Narcotics Bureau of the Treasury, which eventually led the crusade to include marijuana as a prohibited substance.[16] The passage of laws suppressing alcohol use was largely due to the

[15] Edwin H. Sutherland, "The Sexual Psychopath Laws," *Journal of Criminal Law and Criminology* 40 (1950): 543-554.

[16] See Howard S. Becker, *Outsiders* (New York: The Free Press, 1963); and Troy Duster, *The Legislation of Morality* (New York: The Free Press, 1970).

---

weaken it with amendments, House Republicans quickly called the proposal up for consideration shortly after the noon lunch break and passed it without debate by a 157-13 vote.

Rep. David Richardson (D., Phila.) said he had not expected the bill to be called up so quickly and was attending a meeting when the bill was called up for consideration.

Rep. John White (D., Phila.), who earlier had promised to offer an amendment to weaken the bill, said that he decided to withdraw his amendment and offer it later as a bill.

"It was just a PR (public relations) gesture," Rep. Stephen E. Levin (D., Phila.) said of the bill, which he voted for. "It doesn't make very dramatic changes in the existing law. Even if a homeowner shoots an intruder he still has to justify it to a judge if he is prosecuted."

"This bill is like the capital punishment bill," said Levin, who sits on the House Judiciary Committee, which approved the proposal. "It has overwhelming support and the only thing guys like us who are concerned about it can do is to try to change it before it gets out of committee."

Steven Goldblatt, Philadelphia deputy district attorney, said he doubted that the bill, if it becomes law, would significantly affect the way prosecutors determine whether to prosecute a homeowner for killing an intruder.

"What we have to do in any of these cases is to determine whether to prosecute based on the information we get from the police," Goldblatt said. "We are not opposed to the bill nor do we favor it."

Source: Reprinted by permission of *The Philadelphia Inquirer,* May 7, 1980, p. 1-B.

influence and power of white, rural Protestants who triumphed briefly over urban, non-Protestant groups.[17] Both the drug laws and the prohibition laws created whole new classes of criminals.

There are several theories of the origins of criminal law, ranging from finding its roots in the private law of torts through a conflict view of criminal law. There is probably no single historical explanation for the origins of criminal law, for contemporary laws stem from diverse conditions. Some criminal laws were passed in direct response to known evils, as in stock fraud statutes. Others emerged from moral or religious convictions, as in antiprostitution and Sunday closing laws. Some were originally intended to suppress labor unions or wandering unemployed persons. Since there is no single explanation for the historical basis of American criminal law, it may best be examined in terms of the functions it presently performs, remembering that the essential purpose is social control of unwanted behavior, even though the laws may serve other functions too.

The criminal law serves many functions, such as the following.

Law as Symbolic Action. In this function the passage of a criminal law may serve as a useful substitute for some more thorough means of attacking a social problem; example: laws incriminating the pollution of air or water. Typically, such laws are not enforced and may not be enforceable. The mere passage of the law provides a symbolic victory for the forces of environmental cleanliness.

Criminal Law as the Expression of Group Dominance. Such statutes are enacted when a dominant economic, religious, or other group wishes to discourage certain practices and make them subject to punishment; example: Sunday closing laws, which, while rarely enforced, show the social power of certain religious groups.

Crime as Impropriety: Enforcement of Moral Sentiments. These statutes express the community's grave concern over behavior that, while not dangerous, is irritating or embarrassing to many citizens; example: laws concerning drunkenness. At the furthest range within this category, laws on political corruption, when they do not involve outright theft of public property, give expression to a sense of outrage over possible unethical conduct by public officials.

[17] Joseph R. Gusfield, *Symbolic Crusade* (Urbana: University of Illinois Press, 1963).

Criminal Laws as Safety Techniques. The examples here are obvious: Motor vehicle laws that restrict speeding and various other traffic offenses are plainly aimed at promoting safety and convenience. The same can be said of health and labor codes that are intended to protect people's well-being rather than to punish evil-doers.

Criminal Laws as Regulations of Violent Physical Acts. This is the most familiar category. It covers assault, battery, murder, and other crimes against the person. Crimes such as burglary seem less violent than robbery because they often are committed when the victim is absent. Nonetheless, the physical entry element of burglary is close enough to violence to constitute a frightening quasi-physical episode for many people. Obviously fraud, embezzlement, and forgery do not fall into this category; for many people they are less serious because they are unlikely to result in physical harm.

Crime as Sin. A whole range of sexually related offenses fall under this heading. Although illicit sex and obscenity are declining as significant areas of social concern, most of the laws remain residually, an official reminder of our older standards of sexual conduct. Rape, of course, falls in the violent crime category, while prostitution is still, in a sense, sinful.

Crime as Property Violation. This category includes nonviolent larceny, fraud, embezzlement, and certain forms of official corruption. To it should be added various laws intended to protect businesses from credit frauds. Probably trespass laws fall into this category, as do criminal provisions of patent and copyright legislation (although these are rarely enforced).

Crime as an Administrative Convenience. Because of the severity of the sanctions as a potential deterrent, many social policies contain criminal features merely to serve the convenience of administrators. Many laws require filing information with administrators as a basis for reporting regulated activity (political campaign funds, registration of lobbyists). Failure to comply may result in criminal sanctions. Compliance could be achieved in other ways, but the threat of possible criminal action may be an inexpensive means of gaining cooperation with administrative requirements.

Criminal Law as a Form of Social Control. All law is a form of social control, since law applies state power to social behavior. In criminal law the most extreme form of social control is encountered. The possibility of social restraint (imprisonment) and other forms of punishment gives criminal law a greater coercive element than, say, the law of contracts. Contract violators are not regarded as antisocial in the same way as criminal law violators. It may be, however, that the coercive nature of criminal law may make it less effective as a means of social control than the more flexible, less threatening sanctions of civil law.

Criminal Law as a Form of Labeling. People need to locate themselves by religious, cultural, ethnic, sexual, racial, and class identity. This self-identification is reassuring and helps people sort out their value preferences and make personal choices. Men and women who are once labeled criminals usually fit a niche in society from which it is hard for them ever to escape. Even the white-collar embezzler and the corrupt politician are regarded with distrust and some fear. We try to avoid prematurely labeling young people as criminals by calling their offenses *delinquency.* We no longer brand or maim criminals to set them apart socially, but the impulse remains even in our enlightened society. Stigma and shame attach to violations of the criminal law.

We shall examine these functions again when we explore the substantive law of crimes. Bear in mind that particular criminal laws may serve several functions at one time. Remember, too, that the actual provisions of a criminal law may be ill-suited to the purported function.

EXTERNAL FACTORS IN CRIME

If crime is that kind of unacceptable behavior that is punishable by law, we should consider whether the coercive elements in criminal law are the only or best means of treating this behavior. There are certain factors that set criminal actions in motion. By examining those factors that are external and prior to the acts themselves we may examine the roots of criminality. This will be useful when evaluating the substantive provisions of criminal law. After all, when certain behavior is deemed unacceptable, there may be ways to reduce the incidence of crime by altering the conditions for its commission. Perhaps criminal laws can address some of these conditions more openly.

The oldest issue in criminology is the question of the criminal personality, touched upon previously. A leading criminologist finds "strong evidence [the data are now fairly overwhelming] that criminals and 'delinquents' do not possess personality characteristics significantly different from the rest of the population, and that the prevalence of psychoses, neuroses, and other disturbances among them is not significantly different from similarly matched samples of the rest of the population."[18] Traditional criminology has not thus far located a criminal type of individual or defined a criminal personality.

Most antisocial individuals are quite normal but some may be deemed psychopathic or sociopathic. Such individuals are not psychotic (insane); they indulge in antisocial behavior because of hidden, usually unconscious, drives. One guess places this group at from 10 to 15 percent of the criminal population (whatever is meant by that phrase).[19]

Truly insane, psychotic individuals who turn to criminal behavior are surprisingly rare, perhaps between 1 and 2 percent of our criminals. More typical are professional criminals who learn their criminal patterns early in life. They are schooled in criminal attitudes and conduct by their friends and often by their families. Professional thieves even develop a sort of code of behavior and technical skills.[20] Such individuals differ considerably from violent gang members or criminal thrill seekers who act from less rational motives.

Probably, certain kinds of crime are attractive to sociopaths and psychopaths. Rape and premeditated assaults generally proceed from rage and frustration. The drug pusher may have a personality structure quite different from that of the gambler or the loan shark. Personality differences between rapists and loan sharks are considerable and need to be taken into account.

We need to know more about the linkage between particular crimes and particular personality disturbances if we are to construct a more rational crimes policy. This linkage is exemplified by the

[18] Abraham Blumberg, *Criminal Justice* (New York: Quadrangle Books, Inc., 1967), p. 36.

[19] According to psychiatrist Manfried S. Guttmacher, "The Psychiatric Approach to Crime and Correction," *Law and Contemporary Problems* 23 (Autumn, 1958): 633-649.

[20] According to Edwin H. Sutherland, *Principles of Criminology* (Philadelphia: J. B. Lippincott Company, 1947), p. 213.

significant relationship between violent homicide and use of alcohol by the offender.[21] Nonfelonious assaults are as much as ten times more common among alcohol users as among nonusers.[22] Crimes involving physical violence are very frequently associated with intoxication, but violent crimes are never defined in terms of the offender's impaired state of mind as induced by alcohol. Public drunkenness, moreover, tends to be treated casually. Some states have no laws prohibiting drunkenness. Other states have harsh treatment policies. A presidential commission suggests that drunkenness should be prosecuted only when it involves disorderly conduct or

[21] Marvin F. Wolfgang, *Patterns in Criminal Homicide* (Philadelphia: University of Pennsylvania, 1958).

[22] Lloyd M. Shope, "Alcohol and Crime," *Journal of Criminal Law, Criminology, and Police Science* 44 (January-February, 1954): 661-665.

Predicting criminal careers may be impossible at our current state of knowledge.

This study has systematically examined the career development of a group of offenders about whom there is particular concern in public policy—habitual felons. Resolution of current debates about the crime-reducing potential of incarcerating a greater percentage of such persons for longer terms hinges on estimates of the amount of crime they actually commit and their probability of arrest and conviction. This study provides just such estimates, for a sample of 49 felons, by crime type and period in the criminal career, based on the offenders' own reports.

As to the other policy avenues for dealing with criminals—rehabilitation, deterrence, and prevention—even though our sample is too small and select to permit generalizing to the wider criminal population—this report provides new insight into why a group of serious habitual offenders remained undeterred and unrehabilitated after repeated incarceration and participation in a variety of treatment programs.

In this study, we sought to illuminate the birth and growth of serious criminal careers in the hope of identifying vulnerable times when appropriate interventions by the criminal justice system might best have reduced the offenders' threat to the community. Initially, we were optimistic that such points could be identified, for earlier research had suggested that habitual offenders tend to follow a common maturation process. We expected the interview data to reveal

some other criminal offense.[23] There is a growing tendency to regard drunkenness as a problem of personal health rather than of criminal law, but since there is an apparent connection between alcohol consumption and violent crime, should criminal law reflect this connection?

Dependent and weak personalities may tend to turn to alcohol and drug use as a source of solace and support. The imposition of severe penalties for such use has, however, proven ineffective.[24] Narcotics addiction has markedly increased in spite of increasingly

[23] President's Commission on Law Enforcement and the Administration of Justice, *Task Force Report: Drunkenness* (Washington, D.C.: U.S. Government Printing Office, 1967), pp. 1-9.

[24] See President's Commission on Law Enforcement and the Administration of Justice, *Task Force Report: Narcotic and Drug Abuse* (Washington, D.C.: U.S. Government Printing Office, 1967).

---

systematic development patterns in which juvenile offenders—peer-influenced, gang-related, and spontaneous—were transformed into adult professional criminals. Moreover, we expected them as adult professionals to pursue crime as a preferred occupation, continually developing their skills, increasing their profits, and becoming more specialized. It is now clear that this is too simplistic a notion of sustained criminal activity and criminal career development. The reality is much more complex and diverse than we imagined. Although some of our empirical findings were consistent with the traditional images, overall, even in an offender sample as small and select as this, the dominant finding was diversity—both in the offenders' personalities and in their conduct. Thus, a key conclusion of this study is that many of the traditional assumptions about the development of habitual offenders need to be reconsidered and restudied.

This section briefly reviews the most important study findings with regard to the nature and criminal activity of this sample. Then it turns to the implications of the findings for policies of rehabilitation, deterrence, crime prevention, and incapacitation. The latter discussion is too preliminary to be regarded as a proposal for changes in current policies; our observations should be substantiated by further study of habitual offenders. Nevertheless, these conclusions should enable policy-makers to expand their perspective on habitual felons.

Source: Joan Petersilia, Peter W. Greenwood, and Martin Lavin, *Criminal Careers of Habitual Felons* (Washington, D.C.: National Institute of Law Enforcement and Criminal Justice, 1978). Reprinted by permission.

severe criminal laws. Decriminalizing narcotics or alcohol abuse may not be the answer either. Since such dependent individuals may need some inducement to seek treatment, criminal law may provide that minimal function, if only to reduce incentives to commit other crimes.

If one of the problems of criminal law is to make the offense fit the offender, then account must be taken of the offender's personal-

---

Crime reduction may be accomplished by vigilant citizen activity.

Community Crime Prevention Program (CCPP), Seattle, Washington (January 1977)

The Seattle CCPP is demonstrating that crime rates can be lowered if the citizens of a community are willing to participate in crime prevention. The goals in Seattle are to mobilize citizen concern over a rapidly rising residential burglary rate and turn it into citizen action to attack the problem.

The four principal tactics used in organizing a neighborhood—residential security inspection, property marking, block watches, and informative materials—are not original. The CCPP's success in applying them has come from careful coordination, the commitment of full-time staff, the cooperation of the Seattle Police, and the cultivation of a sense of community in the neighborhoods.

A rigorous evaluation of the CCPP provides evidence of the project's success in meeting its goals.

- Two victimization surveys show burglary rate reductions in participating households ranging from 48% to 61%.
- Citizen reports of burglary have risen from 51% to 76% of actual burglaries committed.
- A higher proportion of calls made to police are burglary-in-progress calls.
- The decrease in burglaries among CCPP participants has not meant an increase among non-participants, or in adjacent neighborhoods.
- The program met or exceeded its goal of involving 30% of the households in each target neighborhood.

The CCPP was initially developed and directed by the city's Law and Justice Planning Office, using LEAA block grant funds. Its success has led to its incorporation into the city's Department of Community Development.

Source: National Institute of Law Enforcement and Criminal Justice, *Exemplary Justice* (Washington, D.C.: Government Printing Office, 1979), p. 4.

---

ity and career. Apparently social deviance takes many forms. Shoplifters play roles different from those of automobile thieves. Embezzlers satisfy needs different from those of assaultists. Successful criminal laws may make a better match between a chosen personality role and the offense category. Criminologists have sought in vain to link human biology and psychological types to crime in general, regarding crime as essentially abnormal. To the contrary, it appears that many crimes are part of the normal career of some individuals, given the right circumstances and environment.[25] A rational crimes policy must be adjusted to meet our best understanding of reality.

An optimal environment also encourages criminal activity. Most big city criminal homicides are likely (according to one study) to occur during the weekend, especially on Saturday nights. In London one-half of all the recorded violent crimes from 1950 to 1960 involved attacks in and around bars, cafes, and/or streets. The majority of these violent crimes were committed among working-class people in slum neighborhoods.[26] There is little proof, however, that working-class people are exceptionally violent.

Physical environment has a great deal to do with crime. In large American cities many big buildings are unoccupied nights and weekends, thereby virtually attracting crime. The police cannot maintain adequate surveillance of large urban buildings. Different building design could reduce the incidence of crimes against property.[27] Evidence suggests that physical changes at the site can significantly reduce robberies.[28] We have reason to believe that better environmental design can lead to crime reduction.[29]

Police have long known that better lighting is an effective deterrent to robbery and many other street crimes. Similarly, better locks, warning systems, and tamper-proof devices discourage break-ins. Traveling alone is an invitation to victimization, particularly at night in urban areas. Better physical controls not only discourage potential criminals, they create a general environment en-

[25] Wolfgang, *Patterns,* pp. 106-119.

[26] See Julian Roebuck, *Criminal Typology* (Springfield, Ill.: Charles C. Thomas, Publisher, 1967), p. 159.

[27] C. Lepage, "Crime and Urbanism," *Revue Internationale de Criminologie et de Police Technique* 28 (1975): 289-292.

[28] W. J. Crow and J. L. Bull, *Robbery Deterrence: An Applied Behavioral Science Demonstration* (La Jolla, Calif.: Western Behavioral Sciences Institute, 1975).

[29] See Clarence R. Jeffery, *Crime Prevention Through Environmental Design* (London: Sage Publications, 1977).

couraging law-abiding behavior. Filthy slums are centers of crime and vice. Neat neighborhoods are not crime-free, but they are less crime-prone.

Criminal geography is another aspect of crime control. Maps can be drawn to indicate the prevalence of certain kinds of crimes in certain sections of communities.[30] Crimes are unevenly distributed in space and time. Patterns of crime emerge clearly from close studies of crime sites. In Philadelphia, according to one study, 82 percent of the rape cases involved offenders and victims living in the same area, and most occurred between 6 P.M. and 2 A.M.[31] Violent crimes appear to follow specific spatial arrangements in major cities.[32] Nonviolent crimes can also be area-specific, since wealthy neighborhoods attract burglars.

Certain environmental features seem to breed crimes. Tunnels,

[30] Gerald Pyle et al., *The Spatial Dynamics of Crime* (Chicago: University of Chicago Department of Geography Research Paper no. 159, 1974).

[31] Figures almost identical to those found by the National Commission on the Causes and Prevention of Violence.

[32] Lynn A. Curtis, *Criminal Violence* (Lexington, Mass.: D. C. Heath, 1974).

Do hidden cameras reduce crime or merely increase conviction rates?

Hidden Cameras Project, Seattle, Washington (August 1978)

Like many urban areas, Seattle recorded a dramatic increase in robbery during the last decade. Between 1966 and 1975, the number of reported robberies jumped from 650 to more than 2,000—a 224 percent increase. At the same time, clearance rates remained consistently low—approximately 25 percent. Because robbery often results in injury as well as financial loss to the victim, the City made it a priority "target crime."

The Seattle Law and Justice Planning Office decided to focus on commercial robbery for three reasons: First, potential targets could be readily identified through police crime reports. Second, commercial robbers were believed to be repeat offenders, so that any arrests would have a telling effect on robbery rates. Third, since commercial robberies were widely publicized, they engendered a disproportionate amount of fear among the public.

In 1975 the Seattle Police Department installed cameras in 75 commercial establishments that had been identified as high risk robbery locations. The cameras were hidden in stereo speaker boxes and activated by removing a

dark parks, alleys, and narrow streets seem to invite criminal encounters. Expressways often divide urban areas and induce high crime rates on either side. Space that is hidden from surveillance tends to be dangerous. Residents of New York City are aware of the risks of entering Central Park at night, but other cities have similar crime centers. Better urban planning could discourage crime.[33]

WHAT'S WRONG WITH AMERICAN CRIMINAL LAW?

If the chief function of criminal law and of the criminal justice system is to control deviant behavior, then criminal law has been a failure in America. There is no clear indication that criminalizing certain kinds of conduct actually deters unwanted behavior. Puni-

[33] Shlomo Angel, *Discouraging Crime Through City Planning* (Berkeley: Institute of Urban and Regional Development, University of California, 1968). See Patricia L. Brantingham and Paul J. Brantingham, "Residential Burglary and Urban Form," *Urban Studies* 12 (1975): 273-284.

---

dollar "trip" bill from the cash drawer. The project director, who is on call 24 hours a day, seven days a week, immediately retrieves the film, develops prints, and distributes them to police within hours to aid in the identification, apprehension and prosecution of robbery suspects.

The City's Law and Justice Planning Office conducted a rigorously controlled experiment to measure the project's impact on arrests, convictions, and the overall commercial robbery rate in Seattle. The results are compelling:

- The overall clearance rate for robberies of businesses equipped with hidden cameras was 68 percent, compared to a 34 percent clearance rate for the control group of businesses without the hidden cameras.
- Fifty-five percent of all hidden camera cases were cleared by arrest, compared to only 25 percent of control group cases.
- Forty-eight percent of the robbers at hidden camera sites were eventually identified, arrested and convicted, compared to only 19 percent of control group robbers.

Source: National Institute of Law Enforcement and Criminal Justice, *Exemplary Justice* (Washington, D.C.: Government Printing Office, 1977), p. 7.

tive techniques have in general failed, although there are many people who believe, with Professor James Q. Wilson, that crime can be managed best by swift execution of short-term prison sentences for criminal violations.[34] Heavy police enforcement, compulsory treatment of drug addicts, and other means of reinforcing current criminal laws may yield better crime control, but the lessons of history seem to suggest that these, too, will prove futile. There should be a fresh analysis of the purpose and the effectiveness of our current criminal law, and this means that a reexamination of our current laws is appropriate at this time.

Criminal law, with all its punitive or retributionist aspects, is essentially only one means, and not a particularly effective means, of redirecting human behavior. The lawyer's view of human behavior has rested on the idea that human beings are free moral agents, making their own individual choices. According to Jeremy Bentham and others who laid the groundwork for current criminal law policies, lawbreaking could be deterred and discouraged best by making the pain (punishment) more severe than the pleasure derived from committing the offense. The law would seek to do this by defining both the crime and the punishment which would flow from its commission. This is becoming a prevalent ideology that undergirds American criminal law.[35] This trend toward coupling the punishments with the substantive offense has increased greatly in the past decade and is part of the movement toward a more determinate sentencing. The other effect of this utilitarian view is to reduce the judge's discretionary powers over sentencing. Some regard this approach as a "just desert" for criminal conduct. But having many criminal laws does not deter of itself. Consider the new crime of skyjacking: The act of seizing control of an airplane and coercing its pilot to change course was criminalized in the United States and in other countries after a rash of air piracy incidents in the late 1960s and early 1970s. Actually skyjacking is not very different as an offense from piracy, one of the most ancient of all crimes, but it was felt that a legal description of a new crime coupled with unusually severe penalties would discourage this kind of behavior. It did not. The mere passage of laws had little impact upon the incidence of skyjacking. Only the placing of armed guards in airplanes and improved inspection/surveillance techniques seemed to do the job.

[34] James Q. Wilson, *Thinking About Crime* (New York: Basic Books, 1975).

[35] See Leon Radzinowicz, *Ideology and Crime* (New York: Columbia University Press, 1966).

Skyjacking virtually disappeared in those places using intense physical security measures.[36]

Better locks may be stronger crime deterrents than new criminal laws protecting property. If cars were not so readily available many crimes could not be committed at all. There would be fewer violent crimes if there were fewer guns. Laws can require better locks, less access to cars and to guns. Such laws may be much more effective at crime control than criminal laws as we have known them in the past. As another example of this fundamental insight, consider the problem of parking meter slugs. In 1970 New York City lost over $11 million from the use of slugs in city parking meters. An experiment was run in several parts of the city in which labels were placed on parking meters, stating either "violation of city ordinance—$50 fine," "violation of state law—3 months imprisonment and $500 fine," or "violation of federal law—1 year imprisonment and $1,000 fine." In none of the test areas was there a reduction in the use of slugs. Only when a new type of parking meter was installed which rejected slugs and displayed the last coin in a window was the problem effectively reduced.[37]

As we shall see, American criminal law has been largely derived from the English historical tradition. While the English criminal law was adapted to the frontier conditions of early America, the general outlook remains much the same, causing the criminal categories to be similar to those of a prescientific, pretechnological age. Numerous modifications have been made in American criminal law, but, with some exceptions, they rest upon the same basic assumptions regarding individual choice, individual responsibility, and the manipulation of individual behavior through threats of punishment. Whether this is consistent with current knowledge of human psychology is doubtful.[38] Nonetheless, the criminal law continues to multiply and prosper, creating new subdivisions and variations with every passing year. Meanwhile crime rates steadily increase, fed in some small part by the continuous criminalization of behavior that was not previously criminal.

[36] W. William Minor, "Skyjacking Crime Control Models," *Journal of Criminal Law and Criminology* 55 (March, 1975): 94-105.

[37] John Decrer, "Curbside Deterrence," *Criminology: An Interdisciplinary Journal* 8 (August, 1972): 127-242.

[38] See James D. Baker, "On the Criminal Justice System," in *Law Enforcement, Science and Technology,* ed. S. I. Cohn (Chicago: ITT Research Institute, 1969), 2: 230-235.

Rational criminal laws would be geared to preventing or discouraging crime rather than to punishment. Even the rehabilitation of offenders, a worthy if probably unattainable goal, is really only incidental to this main and overriding goal of reducing crime. Crime prevention is concerned with placing direct controls on behavior or on the environment that fosters the behavior. As we explore the various substantive areas of American criminal law we should bear in mind what it is we want the law to accomplish. Sadly, we may have to accept the law as it is, but we can hope to understand it better, warts and all.

Rational criminal law policy would grasp the basic fact that most crimes go undetected and unpunished. The criminal population is much larger than the prison population or the population of those arrested. Consequently the crime problem exists largely outside the criminal justice system, beyond the reach of police, judges, prosecutors, probation officers, and social workers. The crime problem cannot be met merely by hiring more police, judges, and prosecutors. We shall simply stuff the jails, which are themselves known breeding grounds for more future crimes.

To understand American criminal law is to understand its shortcomings. Our laws do define unacceptable behavior, but they do not effectively regulate or control that behavior. Increasing the effectiveness of criminal law requires a fresh and critical attitude. Improving the criminal law may mean the elimination of some of it, the clearer statement of many of its provisions, and some scientific, empirical proof of its effectiveness. In the pages that follow we shall attempt to view our system of criminal law critically.

NEW FRONTIERS IN PSYCHOLOGICAL CONDITIONING

Law and psychology seem to have much in common, but in practice they do not. Criminal law is concerned with intentions, attitudes, and states of mind. For the most part criminality is based upon mental outlook as much as upon the commission of criminal acts. Mental incompetence, infirmity, immaturity, and insanity are often defenses against charges of criminal conduct. Yet the lawyer's views of mental condition and the psychologist's views rarely coincide. Volition and free will are the central ideas of criminal law, while psychological predisposition or inclination is generally neglected.

Has there been a need for the continual expansion of criminal justice payrolls?

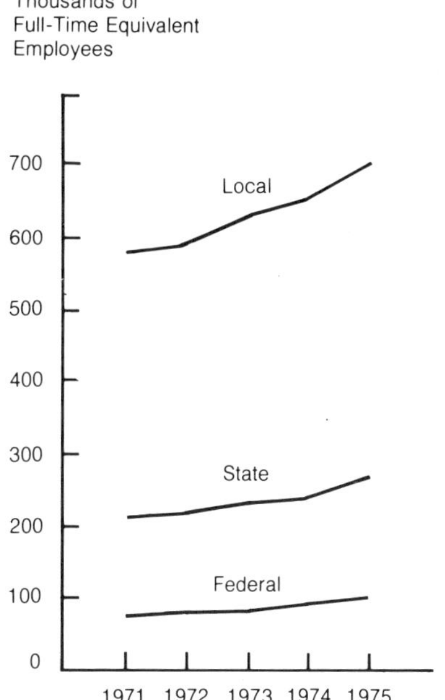

Figure 1. Trends in criminal justice full-time equivalent employment by level of government, October 1971–October 1975

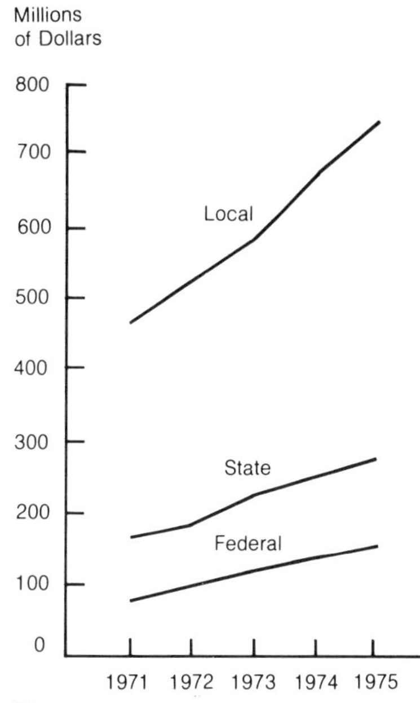

Figure 2. Trends in criminal justice payroll by level of government, October 1971–October 1975

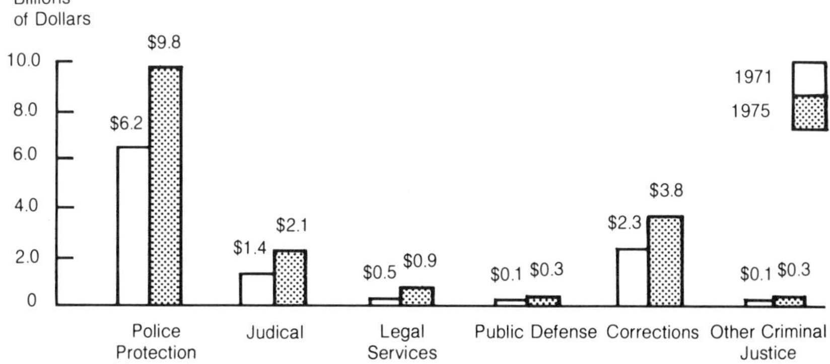

Figure 3. Total criminal justice system expenditure by activity for all levels of government, FY 1971 and FY 1975

Source: U.S. Department of Justice, *Trends in Expenditure and Employment Data for the Criminal Justice System* (Washington, D.C.: 1977).

The criminal trial process itself depends upon certain psychological assumptions. The perceptions of witnesses, their ability to recall events, and the rules of evidence are all based upon notions about the human nervous system and the brain. Most of these legal doctrines and procedures do not square with the findings of modern psychology.[39] The trial process itself, with its adversarial combat, is not conducive to fact-finding, since it relies upon the clash of the parties and the witnesses and on the emotional state of the jurors.

Most psychological findings are not used in the legal process in a direct way. Even when psychiatrists are called in as expert witnesses on the issue of a party's sanity, the tendency is to convert science into legal combat, so that there are usually disputes among the expert witnesses that the jury or judge must resolve. Thus, determinations that a defendent is a sexual psychopath are usually unscientific.

If Freudian and other schools of psychology have proven inappropriate for regular use in the criminal law, one variety, behavior modification, holds more promise of utility. If crime is to be discouraged then potential criminals must be encouraged to adhere to accepted principles of conduct. Conditioning of behavior to create optimum behavior patterns is a complex and difficult enterprise, but it suggests a fresh approach for criminal law. Behavioral conditioning requires a broader approach than simple threats of punishment. Reward mechanisms and other stimuli may also produce desired behavior and discourage antisocial behavior. Obviously such behavioral engineering carries with it risks of personality manipulation and excessive control. At the worst, *1984* or *Brave New World* situations might be established. At its best, behavior modification could reduce the cruelty implicit in criminal law threats of sanction, replacing them with positive reinforcement devices that make individuals feel better while making society safer.

Psychological behaviorism was pioneered by scientists Pavlov, Watson, and Skinner, among others. Their approach was essentially an environmental explanation of learning and behavior. They believed that antisocial behavior is learned, not innate. If the environmental factors that feed, build, and reinforce antisocial behavior can be detected—a big if—then the reduction of such environmental factors should result in a reduction of undesired behavior.

[39] James Marshall, *Law and Psychology in Conflict* (Indianapolis, Indiana: Bobbs-Merrill Co., Inc., 1966).

The brain itself is structured so as to receive and process information from the environment. The complex biology of the brain is beyond the reach of legal regulation, but the environment itself is not. Research is still continuing to discover the linkage between environmental stimuli and actual behavior. Criminals differ from noncriminals in the way they act, which depends in turn upon what they have learned by interaction with their environment.

Criminal behavior is learned behavior. Behavior therapy is intended to produce new learning through pleasure and pain conditioning. A large number of behavior therapies have been developed, some of them suggesting the basis for a different kind of criminal law.[40] Experiments with juvenile delinquents suggest that early intervention with behavioral therapies can discourage antisocial tendencies.[41] Aversion therapy using chemical or electrical simulation has been used to discourage unwanted behavior with alcoholics and sex offenders.[42]

The study of behavior modification is still quite new. But the traditional reliance of criminal law upon punishment as therapy is very much in question. The issues of freedom or control that are raised by critics of behavior therapy certainly have some validity. If acceptable behavior could be induced by compelling individuals to swallow a do-good pill, there would be a certain loss of freedom. On the other hand, if the criminal law relies upon the free choice of individuals to commit antisocial acts that are then punished after the fact, there may be no end to the spiral of criminality. We must remember that criminal law, as traditionally conceived, is intended to change the behavior of potential criminals (all of us) by making us aware of our ability to choose either to abide by the law or to break it. But punishment as deterrence seems not to work very well. The cruel sanctions of criminal law often encourage further cruel reactions on the part of those branded criminals. Worse yet, once jailed the criminal is exposed to a learning environment that is a virtual school for crime. There must be a better way. Although behavior therapy is in its infancy, it holds the hope of a better way.

[40] See Cyril Franks, ed., *Behavior Therapy: Appraisal and Status* (New York: McGraw-Hill Book Co., 1969); and Harold Leitenberg, ed., *Handbook of Behavior Modification and Behavior Therapy* (Englewood Cliffs, N.J.: Prentice-Hall, Inc., 1976).

[41] John D. Burchand and Paul T. Hanig, "Behavior Modification and Juvenile Delinquency," in *Handbook of Behavior Modification and Behavior Therapy*, ed. Harold Leitenberg (New York: McGraw-Hill, 1976), pp. 408–448.

[42] Franks, ed., *Behavior Therapy*, pp. 279 ff.

SUMMARY

Criminal law is simply one type of social control in that it defines behavior deemed by society to be deviant and unacceptable. The criminal law, like other law, is the product of a political process in which legislators and judges play a major role in proscribing unwanted behavior. Interest groups are sometimes active participants in the creation of criminal law. The causes of criminal behavior are only dimly understood and a truly rational crime policy cannot be constructed until the causal factors can be managed and treated. Until criminology provides greater insight into the roots of crime, the reduction of the incidence of crime can be achieved only by physical and environmental preventative techniques. Criminal law itself cannot alter the attitudes that lead to the commission of crime, and there is little evidence that most criminal conduct is discouraged by the risks of criminal sanctions.

2

THE SOURCES AND SETTING OF AMERICAN CRIMINAL LAW

THE EUROPEAN ORIGINS OF AMERICAN CRIMINAL LAW

American criminal law is derived from European, especially English, law. Borrowings from French, German, Dutch, and other continental laws and practices exist, but they are relatively insignificant. The Norman conquest introduced some continental notions into the British Isles, but these were superimposed on a structure that was well rooted in tribal law.

The Anglo-Saxon legal system was essentially tribal. Crime was perceived as an act against the family, not against the state. Family members sought retribution against members of the offending family, for the guilt of the individual was transferred to his or her family. Retribution at first led to blood feuds, but later there came to be a system of payments of money for particular injuries. Offenders could also be ignored or exiled.

There were three forms of money payments for criminal harm under feudalism. The *wergild* was paid to a family group if a member of the family was killed or injured. The *bot* was a general kind of payment for lesser injuries than death. The *wite* was the only public fine and was payable to the local lord or to the king. The *wite* is the germ of the idea of public concern with deviant behavior, an idea that later became the chief feature of criminal law.

A transformation in English criminal law took place in the twelfth century when, especially during the reign of Henry II (1154–1189), the *wergild, bot,* and *wite* were gradually replaced with a more modern, more humane version of criminal law. The old criminal rules made little distinction between accidental injury and intentional harm while those of the church made no distinction between crime and sin. A more civilized idea of crime emerged.

The influence of the rediscovered Roman law, of contacts with the Near East during the Crusades, and of a revival of ethical thought all helped to develop a more modern idea of criminal law. Murder, arson, theft, and rape were no longer merely "regrettable torts which should be compensated by payment to the family"[1]; they became crimes against society at large. Six centuries after Henry II, Blackstone, the English authority on common law, was able to define a crime as essentially a public, not a private, wrong. The dis-

[1] J. W. Jeudwine, *Tort, Crime and the Police in Medieval England* (London: Williams and Norgate, 1917), p. 14.

tinction holds to this day, and is especially meaningful in America, where the public prosecutor has a near monopoly of the task of proceeding against crime in the courts. Blackstone is still appropriate today for America:

> The distinction of public wrongs from private, of crimes and misdemeanors from civil injuries, seems principally to consist of this: that private wrongs, or civil injuries, are an infringement or privation of the civil rights which belong to individuals, considered merely as individuals; public wrongs, or crimes and misdemeanors, are a breach and violation of the public rights and duties due to the whole community, considered as a community, in its social aggregate capacity.[2]

However clear this distinction between crime and private injury has become, a great ambiguity was introduced into criminal law policy at much the same time, and is incorporated in Blackstone's writings as well. Blackstone stated that there were some acts so terrible that, "if there were no criminal law at all, would be judged by the public at large much as they are judged. . . ."[3] He included murder, theft, and rape in the category of *mala in se* (acts bad in themselves). All other acts were merely *mala prohibita* (crimes only because the law had defined them as such). This distinction has haunted the criminal law ever since, creating an artificial distinc-

[2] William Blackstone, *Commentaries on the Laws of England,* 8th ed. (Oxford: Clarendon Press, 1778), 4: 5.

[3] Ibid., p. 9.

Civil rights violations may give rise to civil as well as criminal actions.

Civil action for deprivation of rights

Every person who, under color of any statute, ordinance, regulation, custom, or usage, of any State or Territory, subjects, or causes to be subjected, any citizen of the United States or other person within the jurisdiction thereof to the deprivation of any rights, privileges, or immunities secured by the Constitution and laws, shall be liable to the party injured in an action at law, suit in equity, or other proper proceeding for redress.

Source: 18 U.S.C. sec. 1983.

---

tion in the formulation of criminal law.[4] Some acts are more anti-social than others only because the legal organs of society have decided that they should be—this is the bedrock of a conscious criminal law policy, not some nebulous notion about innate evil.

THE ENGLISH COMMON LAW

The English common law is the major source of American criminal law, even though seventeen American states reject the traditional common law offenses. The original thirteen colonies were nurtured in English common law and retained parts of it after independence, although major modifications were made. As the nation expanded, the common law was transported to the new states and territories. In Louisiana French law was, at first, more important than the English traditions of the eastern seaboard. Criminal law in parts of the Southwest formerly governed by Spain exhibits some Spanish influence. Hawaii and Alaska also were subject to other non-common law elements.

At common law all crimes were either evil in themselves (*mala in se*) or prohibited by law (*mala prohibita*). *Mala in se* offenses were often subject to capital punishment, whereas *mala prohibita* offenses were not. There were nine *mala in se* offenses: murder, manslaughter, rape, sodomy, robbery, larceny, arson, burglary, and mayhem. All other crimes, save treason, were misdemeanors, which were much less severely punished. Misdemeanors were the products of positive legislation, while felonies were, supposedly, more funda-

[4] C. Ray Jeffery, "Crime, Law, and Social Structure," *Journal of Criminal Law, Criminology, and Police Science* 47 (1956): 4–9.

European notions differ from ours.

While Europeans have a long tradition of legal codification, running back to the Code Napolean [*sic*] of 1804, in the United States true codification is still a relatively new notion. Lack of familiarity with codification still causes problems in jurisdictions adopting codes.

Source: Jerry E. Norton, "Criminal Law Codification: Three Hazards," *Loyola University Law Journal* 10 (1978): 61.

---

mental wrongs. Today the line between felony and misdemeanor is still the basic division in American criminal law.

Most common law crimes have been defined by legislation in the American states. There is no federal common law of crimes. Common law definitions are preserved insofar as they are not inconsistent with statutes, posing difficult questions of the scope of a statute in the face of the common law. The common law is of most direct importance in conspiracy and common law misdemeanors, especially public mischief and indecency offenses.[5]

The distinction between a misdemeanor and a felony still retains much force. In many states misdemeanor sentences are limited to 1 year. Misdemeanor offenses, unlike felonies, often result in fines rather than imprisonment. Conviction of a felony usually results in a loss of the franchise or the privilege of holding office, which misdemeanor convictions do not entail. Formerly felons at common law often had their property seized and were banished or executed, but these punishments have been largely eliminated, except for the vestigial use of the death penalty.

In most states there are other very minor crimes; these are usually called violations and embrace traffic infractions, jaywalk-

[5] See, e.g., State v. Benson, 144 Wash. 170 (1927); State v. Severns, 158 Kan. 453 (1944).

Has the need for this statute diminished?

Desertion; withholding support; proviso

(1) Any man who shall in this state desert his wife and children, or either of them, or his wife where there are no children or child, or who shall willfully withhold from them or either of them, the means of support, or any mother, who shall desert her child or children, or who shall willfully withhold from them the means of support, shall be guilty of a felony of the third degree, punishable as provided in § 775.082, § 775.083, or § 775.084. However, no husband shall be prosecuted under this section for the desertion of his wife, or for withholding from his wife the means of supporting her where there is existing, at the time of such desertion or withholding, such cause or causes as are recognized as ground or grounds for dissolution of marriage, by statute, in this state, if such person shall have provided for the support of his children, if there be any.

Source: Florida Statutes Annotated sec. 856.04.

ing, and illegal parking. There are also many quasi-criminal laws, rules, and regulations unknown to the common law, which stem from the twentieth-century growth of the modern administrative state.

EMERGENT AMERICAN POLICIES ABOUT CRIMINAL LAW

After the American Revolution some portions of the English common law of crimes were rejected on the grounds that they were monarchical and antirepublican. Certainly the notions of treason and criminal libel were modified. Then, too, American criminal law tended to be concerned more with crime as sin than with crime as assaults on individuals and their property. This was especially true in Puritan-influenced Massachusetts, where "two-thirds of all prosecutions were for immorality and crime was pictured as sin."[6] Gradually this vision of crime receded in America, but the approach is sometimes evident in liquor control laws, gambling and drug possession laws, and laws regulating sexual behavior.

"The common law of England," wrote lawyer John Dickenson in 1768, "is generally received . . . but our courts exercise a sovereign authority, in determining what parts of the common and statute law ought to be extended: For it must be admitted, that the difference in circumstances necessary requires us, in some cases, to reject the determination of both. . . ."[7] The adaptation of the English common law to American conditions is an important story, but for criminal law it is one not yet fully told or understood. Throughout the eighteenth and nineteenth centuries, American judges reshaped the common law of England, including the criminal law. Unfortunately, no one has detailed the judicial development of criminal law policy in that period. This gap in historical scholarship does not mean that we cannot understand the roots of twentieth-century criminal law policy. It means rather that our evaluations at this time must be tentative.

There is some evidence that criminal law was used for essen-

[6] William E. Nelson, "Emerging Notions of Modern Criminal Law in the Revolutionary Era," *New York University Law Review* 42 (1967): 461.

[7] John Dickenson, *Letters from a Farmer in Pennsylvania to the British Colonies* (Boston: Mein & Fleming, 1768), p. 46.

tially economic purposes. A New York law of 1715 made it unlawful to rake oysters from May 1 to September 1, and also criminalized the sale of oysters in New York City by "any Negro, Indian, or Maletto [*sic*] slave" at any time.[8] Our current list of economic crimes goes far beyond oyster (and slave) regulation, but the nature of the changes that have been made between this early statute and the modern criminal laws and quasi-criminal regulatory devices used to control the American economy today is not generally understood.

New crimes have been added to American statute books continually, shrinking the domain of the common law. Some frontier states criminalized the alteration of animal brands; others attempted to control new chemical substances. A survey of nineteenth-century criminal legislation suggests a continuation of the movement away from defining crime as sin toward using criminal law to protect property and promote economic prosperity.[9]

The notion of a federal common law was discarded in 1812 when a Supreme Court decision held that federal judges could not define crimes for themselves.[10] Federal courts could have jurisdiction and power only over acts defined as crimes by congressional legislation.

Many states specifically abolished the concept of common law crime, although most still recognized the technical possibility of a common law crime. Yet nineteenth-century criminal law was notoriously ambiguous, seeming to sweep away vestiges of the common law while still leaving substantial power over criminal policy to the judiciary. Consider this 1881 New York criminal law:

> ... no act ... shall be deemed criminal or punishable, except as prescribed or authorized by this Code, or by some statute of this state not repealed by it [but] ... a person who wilfully and wrongly commits any act, which seriously injures the person or property of another, or which openly outrages public decency or is injurious to public morals ... is guilty of a misdemeanor.[11]

Vigilantes, lynch mobs, Ku Klux Klanners, and other "self-help" groups sprang up in America during the nineteenth century.

[8] *Colonial Laws of New York,* 1: 845 (Law of May 19, 1715).

[9] This is the lightly supported view of Lawrence Friedman in his *History of American Law* (New York: Simon and Schuster, 1973), p. 258. Friedman also points out that criminal laws for economic regulation were rarely enforced in the nineteenth century.

[10] United States v. Hudson and Goodwin, 7 Cranch 32 (1812).

[11] N.Y. Penal Code (1881), secs. 2, 675.

By virtue of their violent actions, they established a sort of private version of the criminal law.[12] Vigilante crime flourished in Texas, Montana, and other parts of the West, but the southern lynch mobs were probably the most vicious of these groups. This kind of private criminal law has almost disappeared in America, an aspect of our heritage for which we need feel no loss.

Legislative dominance over criminal law policymaking gradually emerged during the nineteenth century. In most states this meant a proliferation of offense categories and the creation of numerous crimes unknown to the common law. Indiana statutes tacked onto the familiar crime of embezzlement a number of variations: there was embezzlement of public funds, embezzlement by officers, by employees, by railroad employees, by lawyers, by bailees, by agricultural tenants, by treasurers, and by other kinds of individuals. Trivial crimes were invented, such as maliciously or mischievously injuring telephone or telegraph poles. Public morality was regulated in familiar ways, but pimping, "bunkosteering," dealing in obscene literature, and selling drugs purporting to induce abortions were added to the statute books. The legislature saw fit to criminalize the killing or injuring of tagged dogs and the selling of intoxicating liquors to inmates of the Soldier's Home.[13] The common law was being replaced hastily with an ill-conceived laundry list of crimes that defined previously innocent behavior as criminal.

Confusion abounded concerning the goals of criminal policy. The expansion of government regulatory power over railroads, banks, and corporations brought in its wake a host of new crimes. Sharp business behavior and electoral fraud were criminalized, although a large element of piety existed in the criminal statutes since prosecutions for economic or electoral crimes were rare. The costs of criminal lawsuits were usually too high to justify this form of prosecution. Nonetheless, so far as the statute books were concerned, these activities were denoted as crimes. As Professor Friedman wryly suggests, there was more crime in America in 1900 than in 1850 or 1800, if only because there were more crimes on the statute books, but there has probably been a decrease in violent

[12] See Richard Maxwell Brown, "The American Vigilante Tradition," in *Violence in America: Historical and Comparative Perspectives,* eds. Hugh D. Graham and Ted R. Gurr (New York: Praeger, 1969), pp. 31-66. See also William E. Hollen, *Frontier Violence: Another Look* (New York: Oxford University Press, 1974).

[13] All cited as examples in Friedman, *History of American Law,* pp. 508-509.

crimes with the passage of time, a trend that has continued, more or less, to the present.[14]

Legislatures not only invented new crimes, they also dispensed with some of the mental elements required under the older common law crimes. The motives or attitudes of the wrongdoer, long the major feature of crime, were sometimes reduced or eliminated as factors in the criminal law. The intention in the mind of the wrongdoer often became less significant than the outcome of his or her action.

During the past hundred years or so, there has been a marked decline in the specific intent requirements in criminal law. The common law typically required proof of a specific intent to act illegally. Statute after statute has dispensed with this requirement or modified it sharply. Passing bad checks, selling mortgaged property, embezzlement, and similar crimes no longer require a specific intent to defraud in most states. Injuries to property formerly required a proof of malicious intention to cause the injury. Generally this has been eliminated by statute.[15] The elimination of elements of malice, hatred, revenge, cruelty, and other kinds of specific intent to cause injury only enhances the protection of property and makes property crimes easier to prove.

There has been a widespread trend toward the creation of new crimes in America. At the turn of the twentieth century, almost every state had a penal code of about 350 sections in length that eliminated a few of the common law crimes but retained many of them by incorporation. Within a few years crimes were added in virtually every state touching upon railroads, banking, corporations, and other forms of business. Penal codes have doubled and tripled in length since 1900. Whole areas of behavior have been criminalized that once were unregulated. This expansion can be partly explained by the desire to cope with changing patterns of economic life, but another explanation may rest in an undue reliance upon the criminal law as a means of dealing with social unrest.

Blue laws, blasphemy laws, laws regulating sexual behavior and drunkenness generally have tended to languish or disappear. The invention of the automobile, the radio, the Xerox machine, the

[14] Ibid., p. 513; Friedman's argument is more complex, but this is the essence of it.

[15] These trends are summarized in Livingston Hall, "The Substantive Law of Crimes, 1887-1936," *Harvard Law Review* 50 (1937): 616-653.

airplane, and other new modes of transportation and communication has multiplied the varieties of individual contacts and conducts. Accordingly, a host of new criminal categories dealing with automobiles, airplanes, and other devices have been created. Drug regulation has proliferated, for special reasons to be mentioned shortly.

A good example of the interaction between economic maturation and criminal law is provided by banking and finance laws. Until the twentieth century, neither the federal government nor the states were much concerned with the regulation of banking. Except for a few laws on embezzlement, false entries, and check certification, the criminal law was almost silent. But often following bank failures and money panics popular demand for new laws bursts out vigorously. Criminal laws were passed in complex detail to mete out justice to careless bankers. Laws regulating insolvency, fraud, and negligence blossomed. Punishment of bank officers (rarely invoked) was made a feature of these laws. Security selling, after the 1929 crash, came under similar criminal laws. In both cases the criminal law was seen as a means of changing the behavior of unpopular groups—bankers and brokers. In neither case has criminal law had much impact. Still, more criminal laws are being passed all the time to improve the conduct of bankers, business executives, and brokers and to protect the public from the risks of a mature industrial society.

THE POLITICAL SETTING OF AMERICAN CRIMINAL LAW

The American criminal law is a product of the social and political systems. The central feature of the political system is the constitutional order that impinges directly upon criminal law through the restrictions on governmental power found in the Constitution. Then, too, politics in the sense of group struggles for influence over policies also marks the American system of government. For criminal law an understanding of the constitutional features of policymaking is indispensable. But the politics of policy formation cannot be understood solely by gaining familiarity with the Constitution.

Federalism, the constitutional division of powers between the national and state governments, has enormous significance for criminal law in America. The constitutional foundation for criminal law is the assumption that the states are the principal sources of policy. The national government has no general power to decide which kinds of social acts should be tolerated and which criminalized. The jurisdiction of the national courts is limited to the application of federal criminal laws. Federal criminal laws, while numerous, are largely of a special nature, linked either in interstate commerce or some other source of national government power under the Constitution.

Federal criminal laws exist defining kidnapping, extortion, bank robbery, burglary, and larceny. Although these are similar to state laws, some kind of interstate event is an element in the crime or, at the very least, there is a national regulatory connection. Postal, customs, and internal revenue violations are exclusively federal crimes. Treason and threats to internal security are also regarded as national concerns. The FBI, the major agency for investigation of the violation of federal law, has jurisdiction over about 170 crimes, most of them exclusively federal in nature. Nonetheless, considerable overlap exists between major federal and state criminal laws. As a result of the federal principle, both sovereign powers are free to prosecute for the same event because the crimes are regarded as entirely separate in law, if not in fact. Double jeopardy has been ruled out.[16]

Since much of American criminal law is a branch of regulatory policy, there are numerous federal and state laws intended to protect the public and to regulate industry. These will be examined later in greater detail. Again, federalism often results in dual criminal laws managing the same conduct.

The national Constitution also sets up limitations on the criminal justice system. Much of the Bill of Rights is a virtual handbook for criminal procedure. The familiar Fifth Amendment privilege against self-incrimination is an example. Criminal law, too, is restrained by constitutional provisions. Two provisions directly bear upon criminal law: the prohibition upon bills of attainder and the *ex post facto* clause. A bill of attainder is a legislative adjudication of guilt, a statutory declaration that particular individuals are criminal. An *ex post facto* law is retroactive criminal legislation. An act cannot be criminalized after it has occurred. An individual must be capable of knowing in advance that an act is criminalized. Both kinds of legislation are unconstitutional at the national, state, or local levels.

[16] Bartkus v. United States, 359 U.S. 121 (1959).

The Bill of Rights itself is an important constraint upon criminal legislation; for example, First Amendment rights of freedom of speech may not be infringed by the criminal law. The right to speak freely may not ordinarily be restrained. By virtue of judicial interpretation, libel and obscene speech are excluded from First Amendment protection. Also, breaches of the peace may be punished and fighting words are unprotected. But short of these situations, the criminal law may not invade freedom of speech.

Other portions of the Bill of Rights also apply to criminal law. Freedom of the press, freedom of assembly, freedom of religion, and other major individual rights may not be infringed by criminal law either by the states or the national government. For practical purposes the boundaries of legitimate criminal laws are set by the United States Supreme Court, which constantly alters the contours of individual rights. In some cases recently discovered individual rights have emerged. When they do, as with criminal laws affecting abortion, the state criminal laws must give way.[17]

Constitutional limitations are the most significant political features of American criminal law. However, most criminal laws are enacted by legislatures, created by administrative rules, or interpreted by courts in a fashion similar to other political decisions. Criminal law is a part of the political process. Criminal laws are created through the process of bargaining and compromise so typical of democratic politics. However, some scholars contend that criminal laws represent the victory of some groups and interests over others. From this point of view, criminal law is not the product of the compromise of competing groups, but the result of the superior position of certain groups or classes that dominate the process of criminal law formulation.[18] If criminal laws are produced by dominant groups, rather than by group struggle and accommodation, then criminal law can best be understood as a reflection of the values held by elite groups. As we shall see, the politics of criminal law are not as simple as either model would suggest. Indeed, criminal laws sometimes seem to have resulted from a kind of vacuum of political power and a widespread indifference to the criminal law.

There are many explanations of the origins of American criminal law. One school of thought contends that American criminal legislation is itself a weapon of prey. It is, for some, a tool of class exploitation. In this view the criminal law is merely a method of the

[17] Roe v. Wade, 410 U.S. 113 (1973).

[18] Richard Quinney, *The Social Reality of Crime* (Boston: Little, Brown, 1970).

Generally the public is not aroused by changes in the criminal law.

Jersey Hearing on Anti-Homosexual Bill Disrupted

BY MARTIN WALDRON
Special to The New York Times

TRENTON, Nov. 20. — A State Senate hearing on a proposal to make homosexual acts a crime in New Jersey—instead of decriminalizing them, which would happen next September under a recently passed measure—was disrupted today by an elderly woman who called homosexuality a sin.

The woman fell to her knees to pray that the 50 or so homosexuals waiting to testify would not be allowed to recruit children "into this abomination."

After almost half an hour, the woman, Catherine Crilley of Newark, was asked to leave the Judiciary Committee's public hearing by Senator Martin L. Greenberg, Democrat of East Orange and chairman of the committee, but she refused to do so.

When sergeants-at-arms tried to carry her from the room on a chair, Mrs. Crilley said that she feared she might have a heart attack. She was finally persuaded by a hastily summoned nurse to leave the crowded committee room to rest.

Hearing to Reconvene

The disruption came during the testimony of the first witness, State Attorney General John J. Degnan, who opposes the bill. After some hostile cross-examination of Mr. Degnan from several committee members backing the bill, Senator Greenberg adjourned the hearing and said it would be reconvened on a day when the Legislature was not in session.

Legislative leaders have been trying to keep the bill from coming up for a vote. It is believed that the bill, if it came to the floor, would pass because of strong pressure from organized groups supporting it.

These groups, dominated by older persons, have put on demonstrations on several occasions when the subject of eliminating criminal penalties for homosexual acts has been broached.

When the State Senate was passing a model penal code last summer, members of these groups shouted "sodomites" from the balcony as Senators passed the new code, which legalizes all sexual behavior between consenting adults.

A Matter of Priorities

The code becomes effective Sept. 1. The current law prohibits all sodomy, but Mr. Degnan—the state's top law enforcement official—said that the police and courts had better things to do than to try to police the sexual habits of adults, and that no one had ever been prosecuted under the current law.

If the proposed measure on homosexual acts should pass the Legislature, Mr. Degnan said, he would advise Governor Byrne that there is some question as to its constitutionality. Mr. Degnan said the bill as written probably would not apply to female homosexuals. It would make "deviate sexual conduct" a crime punishable by a fine up to $7,500 and a prison term up to 10 years.

The bill is being pushed by Senator Joseph A. Maressa, Democrat of Blackwood, who has said he introduced it to "drive homosexuals back into the closet."

Author's Note: The law passed in 1979, without making homosexuality a crime.

Source: The New York Times, November 21, 1978, p. B3. © 1978 by The New York Times Company. Reprinted by permission.

ruling class exercising control over the working class.[19] Obviously this suggests that legislatures merely respond to the needs and demands of big business interests when they enact criminal legislation. If this view is correct, the politics of criminal law is merely the politics of class dominance.

However, there is considerable evidence to the contrary. Early American law was responsive to the religious and ethical needs of the community. Values commonly shared were the source of criminal legislation.[20] More recent studies, such as Sutherland's classic investigation of sexual psychopath legislation, also show that broadly held community attitudes strongly influenced criminal legislation, together with professional judgments.[21]

Some criminal laws emanate from bureaucratic interests; for example, the Federal Narcotics Bureau has been chiefly responsible for the enactment of federal drug legislation.[22] Bureaucratic agencies may use the criminal law as a means of increasing their span of authority. The tangled history of marijuana legislation began at the

[19] Richard Quinney, *Crime Control in a Capitalist Society* (Boston: Little, Brown, 1974); Anthony M. Platt, *The Child Savers: The Invention of Delinquency* (Chicago: University of Chicago Press, 1969); Ian Taylor, Paul Walton, and Jack Young, *The New Criminology* (New York: Harper and Row, 1973).

[20] See George Lee Haskins, *Law and Authority in Early Massachusetts* (New York: Macmillan, 1960).

[21] Edwin H. Sutherland, "The Diffusion of Sexual Psychopath Laws," *American Journal of Sociology* 56 (September 1950): 142-148.

[22] Alfred R. Lindesmith, *The Addict and the Law* (New York: Vintage, 1965); Howard Becker, *The Outsiders: Studies in the Sociology of Deviance* (Glencoe, Ill.: The Free Press, 1963); D. F. Musto, *The American Disease: Origins of Narcotics Control* (New Haven: Yale University Press, 1973).

federal bureaucratic level, and the federal bureaucracy still retains an interest in the preservation of criminal laws in this area. Doubtless many administrative agencies sponsor criminal legislation at both the federal and state levels, but most criminal laws are not created in this way.

Most criminal law derives from legislative politics. Even as sensitive a social matter as prostitution can be defined as a result of a struggle in legislative committees conducted by various interest groups.[23] A careful legislative case study of criminal law reveals that important decisions are made exclusively by negotiating lobbies and a few members of key legislative committees.[24] Floor debates are relatively unimportant. Votes on criminal law legislation are usually near-unanimous—rubber-stamping deals concluded behind the scenes in committee chambers and hotel rooms. Criminal legislation is usually created by a handful of groups, including police and prosecutor organizations in many states.

Not surprisingly, the inner workings of legislative politics are little understood in the criminal law. The real origin of criminal law is hidden behind a facade of near-unanimous voting. On some issues, such as capital punishment, obscenity, or election reform legislation, politicians may take a clear stand in order to influence voters. For the most part, though, criminal law is the product of a small range of interest groups, with no one representing organized crime, and few people concerned with the interests of potential lawbreakers. Lawbreakers have no lobby.

In 1977 a detailed, empirical study of the criminal laws in California was published. The authors examined the changes made in the California Penal Code from 1955 until 1971, a period of major substantive change in criminal law.[25] Among their conclusions, the authors noted that public opinion had little or no impact upon criminal legislation. Newspaper coverage of criminal justice did produce an effect, resulting in more stringent criminal laws. The law enforcement lobby (police and prosecutor groups mainly) was both active and effective. The Democrats in the California legislature tended to vote for increases in criminalization. Statistical reports on

[23] See Pamela A. Roby, "Politics and Criminal Law: Revision of the New York State Law on Prostitution," *Social Problems* 17 (1969): 83–108.

[24] John P. Heinz, Robert W. Gettleman, and Harris A. Seeskin, "Legislative Politics and the Criminal Law," *Northwestern University Law Review* 64 (1969): 277–356.

[25] Richard A. Berk, Harold Brackman, and Selma Lesser, *A Measure of Justice* (New York: Academic Press, 1977).

the commission of crime probably had little impact. The general conclusion seems to be that criminal legislation is responsive to highly organized groups and to newspaper editorials. There is a constant tendency to increase rather than to reduce criminalization, probably because the forces that might resist are not usually active or represented.

The politics of criminal law do not appear to resemble other legislative politics. Liberal and conservative ideologies are largely irrelevant. Competing and balancing interest groups are largely absent. Almost all the significant forces seem to agree upon increased state powers over private conduct. No coherent policy approaches to deviant behavior would seem to be operative. As the California study concludes, "at least in terms of criminalization, perhaps the real winner was state power."[26] This does not mean that capitalists or big business interests were involved; they seem to have been inactive and uninterested in criminal law.

[26] Ibid., p. 186.

An unusual position for the Republican party?

G.O.P. Seeks Softer Juvenile Law

BY SELWYN RAAB

A leading Republican state legislator on criminal justice matters called yesterday for a "fundamental" change in the state's new juvenile-justice law to prevent many teen-agers from being treated initially as adults in the criminal courts.

Assemblyman Dominick L. DiCarlo, a Republican-Conservative from Brooklyn who is the deputy minority leader in the Assembly, said the Republican Party would press for a revision in the law that would restrict the criminal-court proceedings only to youngsters who are accused of committing violent crimes. Mr. DiCarlo said the law has led to unnecessary and expensive criminal-court proceedings against 13-, 14- and 15-year olds who are arrested on minor charges before their cases are transferred to Family or Juvenile Court.

Mr. DiCarlo's announcement followed a report in The New York Times yesterday disclosing that, in the first two months of the law, charges against three of every four teen-agers arrested in the city were dismissed or transferred from the adult Criminal Court to the Family Court, where all matters are confidential.

THE JUDICIAL ROLE IN CRIMINAL LAW

In spite of the encroachment of legislation upon criminal law, judges still retain an important role in the formulation of the criminal law. Interpretation of statutes has become more significant than application of ancient principles of common law, but these interpretations form a body of case law that in some ways resembles the heyday of common law judicial power. Legislatures are often confronted with a variety of judicial interpretations that modify the basic criminal statute. Of course, legislatures are always free to erase judge-made precedents by simply passing new legislation, but the process of judicial interpretation is never-ending and wisdom may suggest that allowing the judges to work with an old statute is better than starting afresh.

The most basic principle of judicial interpretation of criminal law is that criminal statutes be strictly defined. Conduct may not be treated as criminal unless it has been properly described by a criminal statute. People are entitled to know what is forbidden so that

---

Lawyers of the Legal Aid Society who represent most of the arrested youngsters contend that many of them are being held for such things as trivial theft, which are then wrongfully described as "robbery." As examples, the lawyers have cited the cases of two boys held in Criminal Court for stealing five candy bars and of another jailed overnight for a schoolyard fight with a classmate.

"The law as it is presently written has such a broad definition of what crimes should go into criminal court that it is catching in its net a lot of kids who shouldn't be tried as adults," Mr. DiCarlo said. "We are going to introduce legislation to narrow the kinds of crime, especially robbery, which belong in the criminal courts."

The law which treats juvenile offenders more severely than before went into effect on Sept. 1. With a goal of reducing violent crime by teen-agers, the law permits 13-, 14- and 15-year-olds to be tried publicly for felonies in the Criminal and Supreme Courts where they face longer prison sentences than could be given in Family Court.

An aide to Governor Carey, a Democrat, said the Governor had no immediate response to the proposed revisions by the Republicans.

Source: The New York Times, November 17, 1978, p. B3.

---

they can choose to shape their conduct. Another reason for this basic principle is to regulate the police and the prosecutors so that they pursue only offenses that are described in a law. In the absence of prohibition by law (statute or common law) no act is a crime, and it is the task of the judges to avoid stretching statutory language by inferences to include conduct that may have been outside the strict ambit of the law.

Acts of a legislature may be voided by courts on constitutional grounds of vagueness and excessive scope under the Fifth and Fourteenth Amendments' provisions requiring due process of law. A vague statute is one that does not give adequate advance notice of what conduct is prescribed.[27] "Loitering" may be too vague a phrase to constitute criminal conduct. So, too, "obscene," "nightwalking," "loafing," or even "vagrancy."[28] This means that if public authorities wish to regulate suspicious behavior they must describe in some clear way what aspect of the conduct is wrongful, or else risk the possibility of judicial rejection of the statute or regulation.

Many statutes invite considerable judicial intervention because they adopt terminology previously developed by courts. Since most states retain property acquisition offense definitions derived from common law categories, judicial activity is often anticipated. The distinctions among robbery, theft, swindling, embezzlement, extortion, and receiving stolen property are sometimes based on very fine factual issues. Appellate courts are often used to discover whether or not appropriate crime categories have been employed. The same is true for crimes against the person in which assault, kidnapping, and other kinds of forceful conduct may be very similarly defined. In such cases the courts are called upon to clarify imprecise crime categories because legislatures have neglected to repeal overlapping laws or to logically codify the laws.

Words such as "willful" or "malicious" are sure to provoke judicial scrutiny. Any word that attempts to define subjective intent in emotive terms is bound to result in judicial controversy. Sometimes these words have, with the accumulation of numerous precedents, acquired judicial meaning. In such situations the legislation has effectively adopted long-standing judicial usage of language.

Double jeopardy poses special problems for the judiciary. Because of the overlapping offense categories that sometimes create the possibility of multiple prosecutions, prohibition against double

[27] United States v. Harriss, 347 U.S. 612 (1954).

[28] See People v. Berck, 32 N.Y. 2d 567, 347 N.Y.S. 2d 33 (1973).

jeopardy is severely strained. The decision to permit multiple prosecution and multiple charges hinges upon an interpretation of the intent of the legislature. Did the legislature intend to repeal all or part of an overlapping criminal statute? Did the legislature mean to criminalize the same behavior in several ways? Courts are compelled to grapple with such issues when statute books are crammed with similar offenses.[29]

Both the void for vagueness doctrine and the strict construction of penal statutes doctrine provide substantial judicial power to help shape the criminal law. But even beyond these instruments of judicial power, the courts must of necessity refine the crude categories created by the legislatures. There is no simple separation between lawmaking and law application. Those who interpret the law help to make it. If the legislature does not like what the courts have done, its members can easily correct it. The fact is that the criminal law of today rests upon the older body of judge-made law. Much of the common law of crimes has been abandoned, but its major categories, its methods, and its approaches remain. Judges, trained in the analytical technique of reasoning from similar cases, still resort to the method of the common law, even when the statute in question rejects the formal rules of the common law.

SELECTIVE ENFORCEMENT OF THE CRIMINAL LAW

None of the criminal laws on the statute books is ever fully enforced. Police, prosecutors, and judges are the main actors in the criminal justice system, and each has a great deal of discretion in the implementation of the law. For a variety of reasons, criminal law is only selectively enforced. Some crimes are virtually overlooked while others consume vast amounts of time and energy. Those who write the criminal law must realize that the law alone does not assure the desired social ends. This awareness should, but rarely does, discourage the proliferation of criminal law.

Police discretion controls entry into the criminal justice system. If the police do not arrest an offender, there can be no further processing of most crimes. If the police overlook an offense, the offender

[29] See Gore v. United States, 357 U.S. 386 (1958) and Irby v. United States, 390 F. 2d 432 (D.C. 1967).

gets off scot-free. Once an arrest has been made, the authorities are obliged to at least consider the filing of formal criminal charges.

Police discretion extends more fully to minor crimes. Police have less freedom to ignore serious crimes than trivial ones.[30] Murder cannot be ignored. Gambling and bicycle theft can be. Similarly,

[30] Donald J. Black, "Production of Crime Rates," *American Sociological Review* 35 (1970): 733-747.

Even extremely selective use of prosecutorial discretion is supported by the courts.

Petitioner, convicted of murder, unsuccessfully petitioned for state habeas corpus on the basis of respondent prosecuting attorney's revelation of newly discovered evidence, and charged that respondent had knowingly used false testimony and suppressed material evidence at petitioner's trial. Petitioner thereafter filed a federal habeas corpus petition based on the same allegations, and utlimately obtained his release. He then brought an action against respondent and others under 42 U.S.C. § 1983, seeking damages for loss of liberty allegedly caused by unlawful prosecution, but the District Court held that respondent was immune from liability under § 1983, and the Court of Appeals affirmed.

The ultimate fairness of the operation of the system itself could be weakened by subjecting prosecutors to § 1983 liability. Various post-trial procedures are available to determine whether an accused has received a fair trial. These procedures include the remedial powers of the trial judge, appellate review, and state and federal post-conviction collateral remedies. In all of these the attention of the reviewing judge or tribunal is focused primarily on whether there was a fair trial under law. This focus should not be blurred by even the subconscious knowledge that a post-trial decision in favor of the accused might result in the prosecutor's being called upon to respond in damages for his error or mistaken judgment.

We conclude that the considerations outlined above dictate the same absolute immunity under § 1983 that the prosecutor enjoys at common law. To be sure, this immunity does leave the genuinely wronged defendant without civil redress against a prosecutor whose malicious or dishonest action deprives him of liberty. But the alternative of qualifying a prosecutor's immunity would disserve the broader public interest. It would prevent the vigorous and fearless performance of the prosecutor's duty that is essential to the proper functioning of the criminal justice system and would often prejudice criminal defendants by skewing post-conviction judicial decisions that should be made with the sole purpose of insuring justice.

Source: Imbler v. Pachtman, 424 U.S. 409 (1975).

---

highly public lawbreaking cannot easily be overlooked, while discreet lawbreaking (i.e., the distinction between the streetwalking prostitute and the expensive call girl) may be.

The exercise of police discretion is controlled somewhat by chiefs of police. The enforcement policies of the chief and of the chief's boss, the mayor, are part of the working environment of the police officer. James Q. Wilson has identified several types of police behavior that flow from the policies of the chief. Wilson writes of: the watchperson style, the legalistic style, and the service style. The watchperson style emphasizes the maintenance of order. Arrests are

---

Prosecutorial discretion is exercised according to secret policies.

Disparity Reported in U.S. Prosecutions
Survey Tells of Differing Criteria on Which Crimes to Attack

BY ROBERT PEAR
Special to The New York Times

WASHINGTON, JAN. 6. — A survey of Federal prosecutors shows that most of them refuse to prosecute certain crimes because of secret written criteria that vary substantially from one prosecutor's office to another.

Eighty-three of the 94 United States Attorneys have written guidelines under which they regularly decline to prosecute certain violations of Federal law, the survey by the Justice Department reported. Where one district may prosecute, another may decide that such a case is not serious enough or does not involve a large enough loss of money to merit inclusion in its bulging load of cases.

The study dramatizes the lack of any uniform national policy in an important area of criminal justice. The disparities in the sentences that different judges impose for similar crimes have been recognized for years. The new survey is the first to document the nationwide variation in Federal prosecution policies, which presumably are tailored to local needs in each district.

Variations Are Wide

The survey reported wide variation in prosecution policies regarding narcotics violations, bank fraud and embezzlement, theft from interstate shipment, illegal aliens, fraud against the Government, forgery of Treasury checks and 30 other offenses.

Source: The New York Times, January 7, 1980, p. 1.

---

usually made when incidents occur that disrupt public order. Under the legalistic style, almost any infraction of the criminal law may result in an arrest. In a police force guided by the service style, technical infractions are often overlooked as the police tend to be concerned with responding to calls and complaints from citizens, rather than seeking out all offenders. Wilson found dramatic differences in arrest rates according to the dominant style of a city police force.[31]

A major problem faced by police is that of enforcement created by the multiplicity of criminal statutes with which they are confronted. If police concentrate on traffic offenses, they have less time to pursue thieves. If they enforce Sunday closing laws, they have less ability to pursue drug offenders. For this reason a reduction in criminal law offenses should lead to a greater degree of enforcement of the remaining offenses.

[31] James Q. Wilson, *Varieties of Police Behavior* (Cambridge, Mass.: Harvard University Press, 1968), pp. 274–277.

A rare example of an explicit policy on selective enforcement of the criminal law.

It is the Department's view that generally no useful purpose is served by a felony conviction of individuals who have willingly exchanged private letters, although obscene. This is not to say that prosecution may never be instituted in such cases. Rather, prosecution should be the exception and confined to those cases involving repeated offenders or other circumstances which may fairly be characterized as aggravated.

. . . United States Attorneys should give careful consideration to all of the surrounding circumstances, such as the subject's prior record, particularly with respect to his involvement with obscene materials and sex related offenses, his employment, including his opportunity for close association with young people; and his educational level. . . .

The United States Attorney should determine initially whether a strong warning and declination of prosecution is adequate in the particular case. This disposition should suffice in the routine cases of consensual obscene private correspondence. In other cases, the United States Attorney should give serious consideration to exploring with defense counsel voluntary submission by the accused to psychiatric evaluation.

Source: United States Attorney's Manual, Section 9-75.630 (January 17, 1977).

Administrative enforcement at the arrest level is also hampered by a surplus of laws and regulations. In addition many law enforcement agencies (aside from local police) are severely understaffed. Enforcement of the immigration laws is made very difficult because of the small numbers of officials who patrol our borders. The same problem exists at the federal level in the criminal division of the Department of Justice, which simply lacks enough staff to fully enforce federal criminal laws. These staff inadequacies inevitably lead to selective law enforcement.

Public prosecutors are also overworked. As a result there is a strong tendency not to fully enforce the criminal laws in the making of charging decisions. The chief feature of the American criminal justice system is the negotiated guilty plea. Fully 80 to 95 percent of all convictions flow from plea negotiations between public prosecutors and criminal defendants.

The decisions of prosecutors have low visibility, but their performances tend to be judged in gross terms. Their conviction rate is the normal scale of prosecutorial effectiveness. Consequently most prosecutors are anxious to obtain large numbers of guilty pleas, even if defendants escape full enforcement of the criminal law in the process. At times the public becomes aroused about a particular crime. Then a politically sensitive prosecutor will commit many of his or her resources to that crime category.

Ironically, the proliferation of criminal law is well suited to the performance needs of the public prosecutor. The vast array of potential criminal charges presented by a loaded statute book makes the prosecutor a powerful figure. Criminal defendants and their lawyers are cognizant of the wide-ranging discretion of the prosecutor in bringing charges. Very often the bargain to plead guilty is struck on a basis of dropping some of the potential charges against a defendant while retaining other, lesser ones.

Thus prosecutors are often intent on improving the criminal law by adding new offense categories. Their job is made easier every time a statute removes an element of proof to constitute a crime. Their job is made more difficult when (as very rarely happens) large numbers of overlapping statutes are consolidated. Small wonder that prosecutors have little interest in the "simplification" of the criminal law. Their power stems from the complexity and confusion of the criminal law.

Judges usually cooperate with prosecutors in the processes of bail setting, plea bargaining, and sentencing. At each stage the judge is theoretically in charge. Very often the prosecutor's advice and opinion are sought. Often this advice is followed.[32] In some communities judges are quite independent of prosecutorial influence, but in many places they welcome it. Failure to post bond means that a defendant remains in jail until the date set for trial. In many American cities this has become a major means of deterring crime, although only poor defendants are unable to post bail. This kind of punishment of the unconvicted is regrettable, but the more or less compelled plea bargain is much more justifiable since the bargaining defendant is almost certainly guilty of some crime, even if it is not the one with which he or she is formally charged. At least, this is the usual justification for this kind of discretionary detention practice.

Selective enforcement of the criminal law seems to be a permanent fixture of American criminal law.[33] Selective enforcement is not inherently unjust or undesirable, however. Since the prime purpose of the criminal law is to discourage antisocial or deviant behavior, that purpose is not necessarily advanced by full, literal enforcement of every criminal law. Some people are discouraged from lawbreaking by signs, such as those that proscribe spitting in public places. Only certain kinds of crimes require regular police enforcement to drive home the message to would-be lawbreakers. Even so, divergent treatment of similar offenders (as after the notorious Watergate scandal) may create widespread disillusion with the criminal justice process.

SUMMARY

American criminal law is derived from English law, with some borrowings from other European sources. It is important to understand the common law crime concepts since so many of them form the basis of modern American criminal law. Yet American criminal law is now primarily statutory. It has changed a great deal in the past hundred years, in response to social and political forces that

[32] See James Eisenstein and Herbert Jacob, *Felony Justice* (Boston: Little, Brown, 1977).

[33] Police and prosecutors may not enforce the criminal law in a discriminatory fashion, singling out only members of a religious or racial group as targets of their discretion to invoke the criminal law. However, proving the existence of a pattern of discriminatory enforcement is difficult, given the judicial tolerance of selective enforcement.

accompanied industrialization and urbanization. There has been a tendency for new crimes to emerge in reaction to newly perceived problems. As a result American statute books became filled with more and more criminal statutes, many of them overlapping and highly specific. The penalties attached to criminal law violations became quite harsh, to be modified by the discretionary decisions of American prosecutors. Today, most American criminal law derives from legislative politics but in a distinctive manner. American judges retain a large role in the interpretation and application of criminal law, and the loose interactions among police, prosecutors, defense counsel, and judges allow great discretion in the actual implementation of American criminal law.

3

ESSENTIAL ELEMENTS OF CRIMINAL LAW

THE *CORPUS DELECTI*

Murder mystery fans may be familiar with the term *corpus delecti*. In homicide cases the law formerly held that the corpse had to be seen or discovered in order to prove that the death was the result of a criminal deed. No body, no crime. While a few states still have statutes requiring some sort of "direct evidence" of murder, most now permit the use of purely circumstantial evidence to establish the existence of any crime at all. So, even if the body of the victim is never found, strong circumstantial evidence may be sufficient.[1]

But the term *corpus delecti* does not refer to corpses particularly. The corpus in question is the *body* of the offense. For example, in a larceny offense the *corpus delecti* consists of the actual taking away of the property of another. There must be a criminal event as the starting point for the analysis of a criminal law problem. For practical purposes, the *corpus delecti* requirement means that the public prosecutor must prove that a crime has been committed by someone.

One of the peculiar rules that has grown up around the *corpus delecti* requirement is the idea that an out-of-court confession by the accused is insufficient. The *corpus delecti* must be proven before confessions or admissions by the accused can be considered. In the absence of independent proof of the existence of a crime, there is no way to proceed with a criminal prosecution.[2] The only kind of confession that would satisfy the *corpus delecti* requirement is an in-court confession, presumably because this is more reliable.

MENS REA

One of the most important elements of crime, in the traditional view, is the *mens rea* ("guilty mind"). This is the subjective condition that must accompany an act (*actus reus*) in order for it to constitute a true crime. A general *mens rea* is a willing, conscious decision to do a prohibited act. It is not necessary that the wrongdoer intend to commit a crime, only that he or she intend to do something that is defined as a crime.

This subjective aspect of a crime, the necessary element of criminal intention, is difficult to define, but in a criminal trial the prose-

[1] People v. Scott, 176 Cal. App. 2d 458 (1959).

[2] Hicks v. Sheriff, Clark County, 86 Nev. 67, 464 P. 2d 462 (1970).

cution must prove that the defendant had the requisite degree of intention. Since there is no way to prove directly what anyone actually intends, other than by the person's own testimony, *mens rea* must be established by circumstantial evidence surrounding the event.

Some criminal statutes require more than merely a wrongful state of mind. To prove a case of burglary, there must be a showing of *specific intent.* There must be breaking into and entry of a home (general *mens rea*) plus an intent to commit a felony within the dwelling. This latter is a specific element of intention. Specific intention is also required for charges of abortion, assault, extortion, robbery, and many other crimes. Because specific intent is difficult for prosecutors to prove, there has been a tendency for legislatures to remove some of the specific intent requirements as part of a general attack upon crime.

Courts tend to impose only a general *mens rea* requirement unless there is a clear statutory mandate to the contrary. Hence such words as "willful" or "deliberate" when attached to crimes are usually construed to add nothing to a general criminal intention.[3] The special mental element of malice is sometimes a necessary part of such crimes as malicious mischief or mayhem. So, if someone hits another with a brick causing the person to lose the sight in one eye,

[3] Fields v. United States, 164 F. 2d 97 (D.C. 1947).

How is the mens rea *requirement met?*

Use of motor vehicle without authority but without intent to steal

Any person who takes or uses without authority any motor vehicle without intent to steal the same, or who shall be a party to such unauthorized taking or using, shall upon conviction thereof be guilty of a misdemeanor, punishable by imprisonment in the state prison for not more than 2 years or by a fine or [of] not more than 1,000 dollars: Provided, That in case of first offense the court may in its discretion reduce the punishment to imprisonment in the county jail for a term of not more than 3 months or a fine of not more than 100 dollars: Provided further, That the provisions of this section shall be construed to apply to any person or persons employed by the owner of said motor vehicle or any one else, who, by the nature of his employment, shall have the charge of or the authority to drive said motor vehicle if said motor vehicle is driven or used without the owner's knowledge or consent.

Source: Michigan Compiled Laws Annotated sec. 750.414.

proof of basic malice is sufficient for a mayhem charge, even if there was no specific intent to cause blindness.[4]

Of course, the significance of the *mens rea* requirement is that the accused may be found innocent if it can be shown that the accused did not have a guilty mind. If a college student were seen standing nude in front of his dormitory window, he could escape prosecution for indecent exposure by showing that he had no intention of displaying himself or causing embarrassment to anyone.[5]

On the other hand, if one does have a guilty mind and intends to commit a particular unlawful act, one is guilty of any other criminal conduct that may result from the state of mind. So, if someone intends to commit murder and inadvertently commits arson instead, the intent to commit murder, even if the murder is prevented by the absence of the intended victim, will suffice for the guilty mind element in an arson charge.

A legislature may eliminate the requirement of *mens rea*. Statutes can prohibit acts regardless of the subjective intention of the actor. Such offenses, called *mala prohibita* or "strict liability offenses," are regarded as exceptional within the criminal law. They are limited to public welfare offenses such as traffic violations, hunting and fishing violations, liquor violations, and the sale of adulterated foodstuffs. Even purely accidental violations are punishable, though not by imprisonment. Unlike other crimes, strict liability offenses can result in punishment of an employer for acts committed by an employee. This vicarious liability is an important means of regulating improper business activity.[6]

Incidentally, murder mystery fans should realize that motive and intention are vastly different. Motive is irrelevant in criminal law, although it seems to have been significant for Charlie Chan and Hercule Poirot. Motive may be important to establish the reason a wrongdoer decides to commit the crime, but only criminal psychologists and armchair detectives are concerned with it. All that is necessary for the criminal law is to find some sort of criminal state of mind coupled with the actual commission of a criminal act.

Mens rea requirements are undergoing radical change and

[4] Terrell v. State, 86 Tenn. 523 (1888). Actually there are many types of malice, dependent upon the type of crime. The malice required for a murder conviction is different from the malice needed in criminal libel cases. More complicated still are the requirements of actual knowledge, or *scienter,* in such offenses as false pretenses and uttering.

[5] State v. Perry, 244 Minn. 346 (1947).

[6] See Commonwealth v. Koczwara, 397 Pa. 575 (1959).

modernization. The accretion of terms and phrases intended to measure the degree of wrongfulness and type of mental state created inconsistencies and contradictions within the criminal law. One of the major accomplishments of the drafting of the Model Penal Code was the elimination of many of the terms that had been used to establish culpability. Some states have patterned their revised penal codes after the Model Penal Code. As a result vague phrases such as "unlawfully" and "maliciously" have been dropped in favor of a fourfold division of *mens rea* into categories such as "purposefully," "knowingly," "recklessly," and "negligently." However, many states still retain a much larger list of statutory words describing culpable mental conditions and still employ "presumed intent," a rebuttable presumption of general criminal conduct. The rebuttable presumption places a burden upon the defendant in simple "cause-and-result" crimes to show that he or she did not intend to produce the result.

The drafters of the Model Penal Code favor the *"sine qua non,"* or "but for" test, in determining whether a defendant's act is a contributing proximate cause of the wrongful result. Under this test the finder of fact must make a determination as to whether "but for" the defendant's conduct the harm would not have happened. In homicides the "year and a day" rule applies as a test of causation. Under this rule if a death occurs later than a year and a day after the date of the act in question, the causation is deemed too remote to constitute a proximate cause of death. Of course, deaths that occur within a year and a day may not be linked to the defendant's conduct, but the state is not barred from attempting to establish a causal connection.

ACTUS REUS

There can be no crime without a criminal act, or *actus reus*. A criminal act may be conscious, voluntary conduct or it may be a voluntary omission to do something required by law. Murder cannot exist only in the mind. Someone must commit the murder. Failure to pay income taxes is an example of an omission that amounts to a crime.

Certain kinds of acts are not voluntary and may not be crimes. Acts committed while asleep or while under hypnotic suggestion are not crimes, even if many people are injured by them. Similarly, acts performed while in an epileptic fit or as simple reflexes are also not crimes.

However, if you were to kill someone as a result of your having fallen asleep at the wheel of your car, you may be held accountable if you knew you were sleepy when you first started out in the car. Drug addicts and alcoholics are criminally responsible for their acts because they know that they are susceptible to irrational or dangerous conduct when under the influence of drugs or alcohol.

All that is required to satisfy the *actus reus* rule is that the accused voluntarily moved his or her body in such a way as to set the crime in motion; pulling a trigger, setting a fire, punching another's face are, in themselves, conduct sufficient to be made criminal. Even verbal acts can be crimes, as when someone commits blackmail over the telephone.

There has to be a concurrence of the *actus reus* with the *mens rea* to constitute a crime. Criminal intent and criminal conduct must be joined together. They need not occur at exactly the same time and place, but they should be so connected as to constitute a single criminal event. If a gangster in Chicago orders the death the following Tuesday of a victim in Miami, there is a sufficient connection of *actus reus* and *mens rea* to constitute a crime.

An omission to act may also constitute a crime. The commission

---

Is the actus reus *requirement satisfied?*

False personation; willful wearing of lodge badge; using purported receipt for payment of dues; penalty; exceptions.

Whoever willfully wears or uses the badge, insignia, jewel or badge of recognition or any instrument in writing or printing purporting to be an official receipt for dues of any society, lodge, guild or association, fraternal or otherwise, who is not a member in good standing, or entitled to wear or use the same, under the laws, rules and regulations of such society, lodge, guild or association, fraternal or otherwise, shall be deemed guilty of a misdemeanor, and shall be fined in any sum not to exceed fifty dollars, or be imprisoned in the county jail for a term not to exceed ninety days; *Provided,* nothing contained in this section shall be construed to prohibit the mother, wife, sister, daughter or affianced wife of a member in good standing from wearing a badge, insignia, jewel or badge of recognition of the lodge, society, guild or association, fraternal or otherwise, of which the husband, son, brother, father or affianced husband is a member in good standing.

Source: Revised Statutes of Nebraska sec. 28-1220.

of a crime by failure to act may be difficult to understand since many people believe that crime is based upon willful movements of the body, not just standing still or ignoring an event. The law does not draw a line between acts and nonacts; nonacts too may cause harm and injury to others.

The clearest examples of criminal omissions to act happen in situations where the law creates an obligation to act. The failure to meet the legal obligation may constitute a crime. Americans are under a legal obligation to file an income tax form, to report a crime, to obtain a license to drive a car. The failure to carry out these legal obligations is a crime. In many states there is a legal duty to render aid at the scene of an accident. To flee from the scene, or merely to stand and watch passively, increases the risk of harm. Many states have criminalized such an omission. Our legislatures may penalize acts *or* omissions. They tend to penalize acts rather than omissions because of the common expectation that harm is more likely to be caused by an act than by an omission.

There may be good reasons for extending the criminal law in extreme circumstances. How much difference is there between killing and letting someone die? Today physicians must sometimes choose whether or not to provide life-sustaining treatments and mechanisms to seriously ill patients. Ultimately the public and the legislatures will have to decide whether a failure to supply such treatment is a criminal act. We shall have to decide whether the law should create a duty to preserve life. Beyond that problem lies the more difficult issue of whether the law should create a duty to intervene to protect the life or safety of another. Criminal law might make better citizens and neighbors of us by criminalizing our failure to aid a person in danger. But do we want to coerce decent behavior? Perhaps not.

CAUSATION

In addition to all other requirements for crime, it must be shown that the act of the accused was the legal cause of the injury for which criminal charges are being brought. Even if X intended to harm another and tried to hurt him, if the injury was actually the result of a third person's action, no criminal wrong has been committed by X.[7]

[7] Bush v. Commonwealth, 78 Ky. 268 (1880).

A landmark case dealing with failure of physicians to sustain treatment or life.

Karen is described as emaciated, having suffered a weight loss of at least 40 pounds, and undergoing a continuing deteriorative process. Her posture is described as fetal-like and grotesque; there is extreme flexion-rigidity of the arms, legs and related muscles and her joints are severely rigid and deformed.

From all of this evidence, and including the whole testimonial record, several basic findings in the physical area are mandated. Severe brain and associated damage, albeit of uncertain etiology, has left Karen in a chronic and persistent vegetative state. No form of treatment which can cure or improve that condition is known or available. As nearly as may be determined, considering the guarded area of remote uncertainties characteristic of most medical science predictions, she can *never* be restored to cognitive or sapient life. Even with regard to the vegetative level and improvement therein (if such it may be called) the prognosis is extremely poor and the extent unknown if it should in fact occur.

She is debilitated and moribund and although fairly stable at the time of argument before us (no new information having been filed in the meanwhile in expansion of the record), no physician risked the opinion that she could live more than a year and indeed she may die much earlier. Excellent medical and nursing care so far has been able to ward off the constant threat of infection, to which she is peculiarly susceptible because of the respirator, the tracheal tube and other incidents of care in her vulnerable condition. Her life accordingly is sustained by the respirator and tubal feeding, and removal from the respirator would cause her death soon, although the time cannot be stated with more precision.

V. Alleged Criminal Liability

Having concluded that there is a right of privacy that might permit termination of treatment in the circumstances of this case, we turn to consider the relationship of the exercise of that right to the criminal law. We are aware that such termination of treatment would accelerate Karen's death. The County Prosecutor and the Attorney General maintain that there would be criminal liability for such acceleration. Under the statutes of this State, the unlawful killing of another human being is criminal homicide. *N. J. S. A.* 2A:113–1, 2, 5. We conclude that there would be no criminal homicide in the circumstances of this case. We believe, first, that the ensuing death would not be homicide but rather expiration from existing natural causes. Secondly, even if it were to be regarded as homicide, it would not be unlawful.

These conclusions rest upon definitional and constitutional bases. The termination of treatment pursuant to the right of privacy is, within the limitations of this case, *ipso facto* lawful. Thus, a death resulting from such an act would not come within the scope of the homicide statutes proscribing only the unlawful killing of another. There is a real and in this case determinative distinction between the unlawful taking of the life of another and the ending of artificial life-support systems as a matter of self-determination.

Furthermore, the exercise of a constitutional right such as we have here found is protected from criminal prosecution. *See Stanley v. Georgia, supra,* 394 *U.S.* at 559, 89 *S. Ct.* at 1245, 22 *L. Ed.* 2d at 546. We do not question the State's undoubted power to punish the taking of human life, but that power does not encompass individuals terminating medical treatment pursuant to their right of privacy. *See id.* at 568, 89 *S. Ct.* at 1250, 22 *L. Ed.* 2d at 551. The constitutional protection extends to third parties whose action is necessary to effectuate the exercise of that right where the individuals themselves would not be subject to prosecution or the third parties are charged as accessories to an act which could not be a crime. *Eisenstadt v. Baird, supra,* 405 *U.S.* at 445–46, 92 *S. Ct.* at 1034–35, 31 *L. Ed.* 2d at 357–58; *Griswold v. Connecticut, supra,* 381 *U.S.* at 481, 85 *S. Ct.* at 1679–80, 14 *L. Ed.* 2d at 512–13. And, under the circumstances of this case, these same principles would apply to and negate a valid prosecution for attempted suicide were there still such a crime in this State. . . .

Declaratory Relief

We thus arrive at the formulation of the declaratory relief which we have concluded is appropriate to this case. Some time has passed since Karen's physical and mental condition was described to the Court. At that time her continuing deterioration was plainly projected. Since the record has not been expanded we assume that she is now even more fragile and nearer to death than she was then. Since her present treating physicians may give reconsideration to her present posture in the light of this opinion, and since we are transferring to the plaintiff as guardian the choice of the attending physician and therefore other physicians may be in charge of the case who may take a different view from that of the present attending physicians, we herewith declare the following affirmative relief on behalf of the plaintiff. Upon the concurrence of the guardian and family of Karen, should the responsible attending physicians conclude that there is no reasonable possibility of Karen's ever emerging from her present comatose condition to a cognitive, sapient state and that the life-support apparatus now being administered to Karen should be discontinued, they shall consult with the hospital "Ethics Committee" or like body of the institution in which Karen is then hospitalized. If that consultative body agrees that there is no reasonable possibility of Karen's ever emerging from her present comatose condition to a cognitive, sapient state, the present life-support system may be withdrawn and said action shall be without any civil or criminal liability therefor on the part of any participant, whether guardian, physician, hospital or others. We herewith specifically so hold.

Source: In re Quinlan, 70 N.J. 10, 355 A. 2d 647 (1976). Reprinted by permission of West Publishing Company.

In a criminal case the prosecution must always show that the defendant's action (or inaction) caused the injury that resulted. There is not sufficient criminal causation if the injury occurred independently of the accused's acts. If Y, while spiriting her intended victim away, is caught in an earthquake and the victim dies, there is no action for the death—although there is enough for a kidnapping charge. Logic may suggest that the victim would not have died unless she had been kidnapped, but the law in this regard does not hold to the rules of logic.

The doctrine of criminal conspiracy creates special problems of causation. Under most modern statutes an agreement of two or more persons to effect an unlawful purpose is a criminal conspiracy. The agreement itself constitutes the offense regardless of the actual harm caused, if any. A conspiracy is a kind of criminal partnership in which each conspirator is held accountable for the acts of others. Since the element of causation is diminished or absent in criminal conspiracy, the charge is a favorite of prosecutors seeking easy convictions. By emphasizing the intention of the conspirators rather than the outcome of the conspiracy, causation of harm need not be proven as strictly as for other offenses. Some states require an overt act by one of the conspirators that leads toward the accomplishment of the plot, a definition that adds to the common law.

There are a number of complicated legal doctrines that surround the issue of causation. No one can ever be certain whether an unforeseen harm to a victim could have been foreseen in fact. When there are intervening forces or factors involved in an injury, one cannot be quite certain which one actually caused the injury. But as a practical matter most courts hold defendants responsible for almost any harm that might have been or should have been foreseeable.[8] The causation issue is a matter of fact, left to the judgment of criminal juries or to judges when they serve as finders of fact in certain kinds of criminal cases.

IMPUTED LIABILITY

In some circumstances individuals will be held criminally responsible for acts in which they took no part at all. Employers may be held strictly accountable for the acts of their employees, and

[8] The Model Penal Code distinguishes between causation in cases of recklessness or negligence and in other kinds of criminal acts, setting different standards for each (Mod. Pen. C., sec. 203 (2) (a) and (b).

corporations can be convicted of crimes directed or authorized by their boards of directors.

The policy behind this apparent exception to normal rules of criminal responsibility is to hold businesses liable for acts committed as a result of business activity. At the same time victims of such criminal conduct can gain the satisfaction of knowing that the business setting that made the crime possible will not be ignored.

In general, if employees commit minor crimes within the course and scope of their employment, the employer is criminally responsible. Typical offenses are sales of alcohol to minors and various traffic violations. Offenses requiring a *mens rea* do not fall under the doctrine of imputed liability, although such crimes, when committed by corporate officers for a corporate purpose, may result in prosecution of the corporation if within the course of corporate employment.[9] However, corporations cannot of course be imprisoned. If corporations and businesses were immune from criminal prosecution, there would be less control over harmful business practices.

CRIMINAL NEGLIGENCE

Criminal negligence is on the borderline between criminal law and the civil law of torts. Ordinary negligence that is not subject to criminal punishment consists of a departure from a reasonable standard of conduct resulting in injury to the person or property of another. The failure to act with due care and the subsequent unintentional exposure of others to an unreasonable risk of harm is the central element in negligence. Negligent conduct is conduct that falls below the standard of care that reasonable persons expect and anticipate. But the central notion in negligence is the absence of deliberation and intention, so there is no *mens rea* element whatsoever in the idea of criminal negligence. Criminal negligence is more than civil tort negligence, involving a reckless or indifferent disregard for the health or safety of others.

In criminal negligence cases a mere failure to observe proper caution or a breach of a legally imposed existing duty will often constitute an offense. Child neglect cases reveal such a policy because the abuse of the child may be obvious to the eye and, standing alone, supply the element of a lack of due care owed by parents to their children. Of course, in such cases the defendant should know that he or she has a legal duty to perform. But even were a defen-

[9] W. T. Grant Co. v. Superior Ct., 23 Cal. App. 3d 284 (1972).

dant not to know the legal obligation, if a fact finder believed that the defendant reasonably should know of it, then failure to perform his or her duty would constitute criminal negligence. The standard of care is that expected of a "reasonably prudent person," a legal fiction that encourages a jury to apply its common sense to the fact situation.

Other statutes define criminal negligence in terms such as "wantonness" or "flagrant" or "reckless" disregard of the safety of others or "willful indifference." However, when statutes use such terms, or even stronger ones such as "gross negligence," the lines between criminal negligence and intentional crime blur considerably. So some courts have found extreme forms of negligence to be tantamount to intentional crime. Players of "Russian roulette" may find themselves involved in murder, even if no one deliberately intended to hurt another.[10] Courts have flip-flopped on this delicate issue, often leaving to the jury the question of whether or not extreme forms of negligence can be equated with intentional injury.[11]

CRIMES WITHOUT OVERT CRIMINAL ACTION

It was mentioned earlier that there can be no crime without an *actus reus,* a criminal act. In a broad sense this is a safe guide to understanding the criminal law. Nonetheless, there are a number of criminal statutes that criminalize general patterns of behavior or a combination of passive conditions, seeming to depart from this general rule. Social control may seem to require punishment before serious harm has occurred. As a result, merely behaving differently or oddly or simply holding items in one's possession may be made elements of crime. Such laws test the very limits of criminal law and of the state's coercive powers over individuals.

Classic examples have been "vagrancy," "loitering," and "suspicion" offenses, used by police to "nip crime in the bud." Courts have recognized that such laws serve a preventive function.[12] Police perceive a need for such laws because they permit removal of suspects from the areas of anticipated crimes and because arrest prevents crime, at least during confinement. In 1975 the police made a recorded 40,000 arrests for vagrancy and 146,000 arrests for loitering

[10] See Commonwealth v. Malone, 354 Pa. 180, 47 A. 2d 445 (1948).

[11] State v. Chalmers, 100 Ariz. 70, 411 P. 2d 448 (1966).

[12] See Fenster v. Leary, 20 N.Y. 2d 309, 229 N.E. 2d 426, 428, 282 N.Y.S. 2d 739, 742 (1967).

and curfew violations.[13] Of course, some of these arrests may be pure harassment as much as crime prevention.

The United States Supreme Court has cast doubts on the constitutionality of such statutes when grounded upon mere suspicion of "future criminality."[14] In a 1972 decision the Court declared a law invalid because it failed to give notive of the prohibited conduct, thus inviting arbitrary police enforcement. A number of vagrancy and loitering statutes have been invalidated since the 1972 Supreme Court decision, but state legislatures have been trying valiantly to define and limit vagrancy and loitering laws in order to save them from constitutional challenge.

One approach is to forbid anyone to be in particular places at particular times; thus parks and schools are off limits and violators are put on notice of this absolute prohibition.[15] Another approach is to prohibit loitering committed with the "specific intent" to perform some other, usually criminal, act. Thus the California Penal Code forbids loitering near a public toilet "for the purpose of engaging in

[13] United States Federal Bureau of Investigation, *Uniform Crime Reports for the United States* (Washington, D.C.: Government Printing Office, 1976), p. 179.

[14] Papachristou v. City of Jacksonville, 405 U.S. 156, 169 (1972).

[15] See Peters v. Brier, 322 F. Supp. 1171 (E.D. Wis. 1971).

Tramps are defined differently from vagrants in Nebraska.

28-1115. Tramp, defined

Whoever shall go about from place to place, asking or subsisting on charity, minors under the age of sixteen years, females and blind persons excepted, shall be taken and deemed to be a tramp.

28-1116. Begging by tramp; refusal to labor; penalty

Any tramp who shall ask and receive from any person of any precinct, village or city within this state any food, clothing, lodging or other assistance, may be requested by such person, in his or her discretion, to perform a reasonable amount of labor therefor; and any such tramp who shall refuse to perform any such labor when so requested shall be deemed guilty of a misdemeanor, and upon conviction thereof shall be fined not less than three dollars nor more than twenty dollars and cost of prosecution, and shall stand committed until the same is paid.

Source: Revised Statutes of Nebraska secs. 28-1115, 28-1116.

---

or soliciting any lewd or lascivious or any unlawful act."[16] Similar laws have been stricken down in other states for failure to provide adequate notice or for vagueness,[17] but generally they have been sustained by the courts because they limit the police officer's discretion somewhat by requiring the suspect to say or do something beyond merely standing around.

Vagrancy and loitering laws cannot serve the purpose of crime prevention if held to strict tests of constitutionality. The idea that crimes should be discouraged before they fully begin seems sound enough, but it goes beyond classic ideas of the role of criminal law. Some have proposed that statutes be drawn up that would allow police officers to issue orders for a suspect to "move on" when the officer is alarmed by the suspect's conduct and after the suspect has been asked for an explanation of his or her presence.[18] Such statutes would specify an offense, that is, the failure to obey a lawful order. Potential criminals would be arrested and detained in the station house. Unfortunately, this suggestion can also lead to police harassment or illegal orders, but at least it defines a specific piece of conduct—disobedience—as a criminal act.

Another legislative technique for nipping crime in the bud is to criminalize the mere act of possession of the tools of crime, such as burglar's tools. A suspect could be apprehended before the actual break-in. A Connecticut statute provides that mere possession of burglar tools is a crime if "under circumstances manifesting an intent to use . . . in the commission of an offense."[19] Texas, more generous toward potential burglars, makes possession of such instruments "under circumstances evincing an intent to use . . . in the commission of burglary" a felony if the possessor has been convicted of a felony before.[20] This statute was upheld against a claim of unconstitutional vagueness.[21]

ATTEMPTS TO COMMIT A CRIME

Preliminary crimes are also prevalent in America. Events and actions that are not complete commissions of a crime have been

[16] Cal. Penal Code, sec. 647 (d) West Supp. (1977).

[17] See People v. Gibson, 184 Colo. 444, 521 P. 2d 774 (1974).

[18] Note "Orders to Move On and the Prevention of Crime," *Yale Law Journal* 87 (1978): 603-626.

[19] Conn. Gen. Stat. Ann., sec. 53a-106.

[20] Vernon's Ann. Tex. P.C., art. 1402 (6) (Penal Code) (1953).

[21] Logan v. State, 448 S.W. 2d 462 (Tex. Crim. App. 1970).

criminalized. The best example is the crime of attempting to commit a crime. Although a naked intention to commit a crime may not in itself be criminalized, steps taken toward the completion of a crime might be. This approach does not violate the rule regarding an *actus reus* because some kind of perpetrating act is required, together with specific intent. But attempts are always peculiar kinds of crimes because the antisocial act in question has been only partially completed.

The law of attempted crimes is relatively new. Until recently there was no general doctrine that an attempt to commit a crime without the completion of an act could be criminalized. Now in most states any crime may be the object of a criminal attempt. This development may be attributable to the desire to obtain easier arrests and convictions, since a wholly completed act need not be proven. There is also an evident preventive purpose; obviously if the crime in question is never fully completed, it has been thwarted.

The intent required for attempts must be a specific intent to perform an act that would, if committed, be a crime. So if a person passes a ten dollar bill he or she believes to be counterfeit, the person may not be tried for a crime if the bill turns out to be genuine.[22] Attempts must relate to a specific known crime, using the same intention requirement as for a completed crime.

The main problem in attempt law is determining how much beyond mere preparation for a crime must take place to constitute an attempt. Is the strapping on of a silencer an attempted armed robbery? Is the drawing of a floor plan or a map an attempted robbery? Acts of preparation are always equivocal, but when the conduct is a direct step toward the commission of the act and is a "substantial step" in bringing about the injury intended, then it is a criminal intent.

Examples of "substantial steps" to make out a criminal attempt are given in the Model Penal Code. They are:

1. lying in wait, searching for, or following the contemplated victim;
2. enticing the victim to go to the place contemplated for commission of the crime;
3. reconnoitering the place contemplated for commission of the crime;
4. unlawful entry of a vehicle or structure where the commission of the crime is contemplated;

[22] Wilson v. State, 85 Miss. 687 (1904).

5. possession of materials to be used in the commission of the crime, which can serve no lawful purpose under the circumstance; or
6. soliciting an innocent agent to engage in conduct constituting an element of the crime.[23]

Only a few states have adopted the categories of the Model Penal Code, but the code expresses a policy of broadening the reach of criminal law. The same can be said of the defense of "impossibility" that is rejected by the drafters of the Model Penal Code. Under this defense, available in many states, to be punishable an act committed by an accused must have an apparent chance of success. If a person pays money to another believing it to be a bribe to a juror, the legal impossibility acts as a defense when it turns out that the bribed person is not a juror. Similarly, at common law a youth under the age of 14 could not be accused of attempted rape because of a presumed impossibility.[24] Death by voodoo curse being inherently impossible, no charge of attempted murder can be made against the witch doctor.[25] The Model Penal Code avoids the sticky problem of determining what is impossible by making a defendant guilty of an attempt to commit a crime when the person engages in intentional

[23] Model Penal Code, sec. 5.01 (2).

[24] Duchett v. State, 191 S.W. 2d 879 (Texas, 1946).

[25] Attorney General v. Sillem, 159 Eng. Rep. 178 (1863).

Possessory offenses discount the intentions of the defendant.

Possession of implements of crime—Penalty

No person shall have in his possession in the District any instrument, tool, or other implement for picking locks or pockets, or that is usually employed, or reasonably may be employed in the commission of any crime, if he is unable satisfactorily to account for the possession of the implement. Whoever violates this section shall be imprisoned for not more than one year and may be fined not more than $1,000, unless the violation occurs after he has been convicted in the District of a violation of this section or of a felony, either in the District or in another jurisdiction, in which case he shall be imprisoned for not less than one nor more than ten years.

Source: District of Columbia Code sec. 22-3601.

conduct that would constitute a crime if "the attendant circumstances were as he believed them to be."[26]

The law of attempts raises some of the most fundamental policy issues in the criminal law. Underlying the formal rules is the nagging question of whether an incomplete crime deserves punishment, which depends upon whether the accused him/herself deserves punishment. After all, society has not been harmed if the crime was never committed. The protection of society is not accomplished by the law of attempts unless the crime was close to completion. Under one policy perspective, the conduct of the accused is not a proper concern of society if there is no risk of harm to society. However, if the criminal law is retributive—aimed at the punishment of morally flawed individuals—then the law of attempts should include conduct that falls far short of a completed crime. For the most part these policy considerations lie buried in the language of judicial decisions.

There is a modern trend to permit attempts to be excused if the actor repents or abandons the plans. Some statutes recognize renunciation as a defense to a charge of criminal attempt.[27] Any such renunciation or abandonment would have to be both voluntary (not coerced by fear of arrest) and permanent. This reform of the law of attempts rests upon a recognition that repentance by the accused eliminates any proper social interest in punishment.

The laws of solicitation and of conspiracy resemble the law of attempts in that the crime consists of some preparatory activity that precedes a completed act. In all three the social injury has not yet occurred and the concern is with the moral attitude of the actors. The incomplete criminal act is sometimes called an "inchoate crime," suggesting that the criminal act is still unripe. We shall examine the laws of solicitation and of conspiracy as an aspect of the problem of the parties participating in criminal acts, but we should recall that all three rest upon some ostensible retributive policy.

Another way to look upon the laws of inchoate crimes is to regard them as administrative conveniences. It is easier for the police to arrest arsonists when they are caught with kerosene-soaked rags than to find them in the midst of a conflagration. It is easier for a prosecutor to prove an attempt or a conspiracy than a completed crime. The evidence required is much less. While the punishment for inchoate crimes is much less than for completed crimes, the ease of arrest and prosecution more than compensates

[26] Model Penal Code, sec. 5.01 (1)(a).

[27] See New York Penal Code, sec. 35.45.

for the deficiency. Police and prosecutors bent upon preventive (some would say repressive) practices toward crime may turn frequently to the inchoate crimes, rather than vigorously pursuing completed crimes.

THE CRIMINAL JUSTICE MODEL

Jurisprudence, legal philosophy, is full of speculation about the purposes of criminal law. Although the elements of crime in America are generally understood, the purposes of the criminal law are not agreed upon. The British legal philosopher H. L. A. Hart has proposed that retribution is the true foundation of criminal law.[28] The application of pain to a person who is morally wrong is an appropriate purpose of criminal law. If this is true, then the criminal intent, the *mens rea,* is the most essential element of crime. Since people are to be punished for their wickedness, then "punishment must match the wickedness of the offense, and the justification for punishing men is that the return of suffering for moral evil voluntarily done is itself just or morally good."[29]

If criminal law is aimed mostly at deterrence rather than repayment of wrongdoers for their wickedness, the policy problems shift. Herbert Packer believes that the principal purpose of punishment is to prevent the recurrence of offending conduct.[30] Society has a right to protect itself from repeated criminal conduct. Under this policy imperative, the *actus reus,* the criminal act itself, is the main concern. Inchoate crimes are of indifferent importance since society has not actually been harmed.

Packer also described two models of the criminal justice system that still serve to guide thinking in the field: a crime control model and a due process model. Under the first, upheld mostly by police and legislators, emphasis is placed upon administrative efficiency, suppression of crime, and quick apprehension of criminals with little attention given to the formal processes that lead to quick convictions. The due process model is favored by lawyers and is based upon a concern with adherence to formal procedures. Safeguards for the

[28] H. L. A. Hart, *Punishment and Responsibility* (New York: Oxford University Press, 1968).

[29] Ibid., p. 231.

[30] Herbert Packer, *The Limits of the Criminal Sanction* (Stanford, Cal.: Stanford University Press, 1971).

protection of the individual are often derived from the constitutions of the states and federal government. However, these safeguards, such as the right not to incriminate oneself, make the criminal justice system less speedy and efficient, even if a premium is placed upon the adversary process.

The crime control model suggests that crimes should be easier to prove for the sake of efficiency. Under such a policy perspective, strict liability offenses that eliminate the requirement of intent are most desirable because they are most efficient. Traffic offenses are a prime example because the courts could be clogged forever if *mens rea* were an important factor in such offenses. Any violation of the law, even an accidental one, is a crime.

Some crimes, such as statutory rape, are strict liability offenses for questionable reasons. Why should the age of the female sex partner automatically result in a conviction? Should the defendant's knowledge of the true age of the woman be a factor in determining whether or not a crime has been committed? This issue has been much debated recently, but unless pure administrative convenience and crime control are sufficient justification, the state of mind of the defendant should be considered also, not merely the act itself.

Obviously strict liability is a powerful and dangerous tool for crime control. Fortunately only extremists have attempted to employ this weapon frequently. In drug control, selling narcotics is usually a strict liability offense, while possession of narcotics (or other contraband) is construed to require a knowing or conscious possession.[31] At this margin of the criminal law, the limits of the crime control model can be seen.

Repression of crime through stricter criminal laws is always a possibility. However, to achieve such control may require the abandonment of many of the traditional elements of American criminal law. Moreover, stricter criminal laws will result in more arrests, more trials, and more convictions, requiring more prisons, a very high social cost.

We need pay little attention to the theory that criminal law can lead to the treatment and rehabilitation of criminals. Except for alcoholism and, more limitedly, drug abuse, the treatment model has been little used. Few people today can regard prisons or reformatories as centers of education and rehabilitation. The best we can hope for on this score is that fewer people will be drawn into our prisons, which seem to be schools for crime.

[31] People v. Gory, 28 Cal. 2d 450 (1946).

Lastly, we should consider whether criminal law can be preventive. Can we reach criminal attitudes before they result in criminal actions? Can we intervene between the criminal intent and the deed? Here the law of inchoate crimes holds some possibility of help. However, unless punishment for inchoate crimes is virtually eliminated, the prospects for reducing crime are dim. After all, nowadays, the attempted burglar only goes to jail, where he or she learns how not to get caught next time.

SUMMARY

The criminal law in all American jurisdictions bears the marks of English legal theory. Such concepts as *corpus delecti, mens rea,* specific intent, *actus reus,* and criminal causation generally have been widely regarded as basic building blocks of crimes policy. Unresolved issues of imputed and vicarious liability still trouble criminal law writers, but there is surprising consistency in these areas, too. Recently these basic concepts have been reexamined by the American Law Institute and by many state legislatures in an effort to clarify the mental states that must accompany the commission of criminal conduct. At the same time legislators, in an effort to prevent crime, have expanded the area of attempted crimes, raising delicate issues of the proper limits of crimes policy. The warning of Professor Herbert Packer suggests that inchoate crimes or incomplete crimes may be peripheral to a crimes policy that rests upon traditional due process ideals.

4

CRIMES OF FORCE AND STEALTH

Violent behavior is part of everyday life. Football and hockey fans are familiar with the controlled violence in sports arenas. Military service involves training in violence. American labor history has been marked by violent episodes. Violence sometimes erupts within family units. Without doubt, there are some kinds of violence that are accepted as tolerable, abortion being a disputed example. But one of the most consistent tendencies in criminal law is to regard some violent behaviors as deviant, and criminal law has long had as its central purpose the reduction and discouragement of physical harm to individuals and their property.

It is impossible to determine whether American life is more or less violent today than in the past. Given the frontier conditions that prevailed in the early years of our history, violence probably was more common in our past.[1] What is known is that criminal violence varies according to geography, race, and age. Violent crimes by strangers tend to be committed outdoors, those by acquaintances, indoors. Weapons used in violent crimes are a function of their availability. Most urban criminal violence takes place in poverty areas, but violent crimes also occur frequently in suburbs, small cities, and rural areas.[2]

WHY TREAT VIOLENT CRIMES AND CRIMES OF STEALTH TOGETHER?

Crimes of stealth have been grouped with crimes of force because they often are related to violent incidents. True, the burglar may be very different from the murderer, but the risk of a violent encounter is inherent in burglary, and violence may occur whenever there is a victim-offender encounter. Kidnapping always carries the risk of physical harm to the victim. Crimes involving property do not present the same threat of physical violence as direct attacks on other human beings, but the pickpocket sometimes resembles the mugger, and the arsonist surely anticipates that people may be hurt as a result of his or her deeds. Fire fighters certainly can be innocent victims of arsonists.

Any grouping of criminal offenses is more or less arbitrary, but combining crimes of force and crimes of stealth fairly reflects popu-

[1] For the most recent information on this interesting subject, see James A. Inciardi and Anne G. Pottinger, eds., *Violent Crimes: Historical and Contemporary Issues* (Beverly Hills, Calif.: Sage Publications, 1978).

[2] Lynn A. Curtis, *Criminal Violence* (Lexington, Mass.: D.C. Heath and Co., 1974) is based on a national violent crime survey.

lar attitudes toward crime. Victim survey research tends to be based upon this kind of grouping.[3] These offenses are usually denoted as "serious" in most analyses of crime, and they are probably what most people mean when they refer to the "crime problem" in America.

Of course we cannot equate the seriousness of murder with auto theft. Plainly we would want to deal with these undesirable behaviors in vastly different ways. All the same, the President's Commission on Law Enforcement and the Administration of Justice (1967) termed robbery the crime the public feared most, and the commission went on to state that robbery, along with burglary, is the most alarming kind of crime to most people, who fear being victims. Official government figures for 1973 indicate that there were 37 million victims of various forms of theft, including attempts.[4] Of these, approximately 15 percent involved violence or the threat of violence. The remainder did not overtly involve violence, but they are still regarded as serious by most victims.

The grouping of crimes of force with crimes of stealth does not agree with the categories of crime reported annually in the *Uniform Crime Reports*. This publication of the Federal Bureau of Investigation since 1930 is the basis of most statistics regarding crime in America. The *Uniform Crime Reports* are often used as an index to measure the trends and distribution of criminality in the United States, although their reliability has been seriously questioned by many experts.[5] Whatever their statistical shortcomings, the reports are built upon "crime known to the police" in seven categories: murder, forcible rape, aggravated assault, robbery, burglary, larceny-theft, and motor vehicle theft. This chapter expands the list somewhat, but is basically similar in its handling of serious crime.

THE SPECIAL PROBLEMS OF CRIMES OF PHYSICAL VIOLENCE

While only 15 percent of serious crime is deemed violent, the level of seriousness is obviously higher if the victim is killed, maimed, or injured than if property is taken. We know that some of

[3] See United States Department of Justice, *Criminal Victimization Surveys in 13 American Cities* (Washington, D.C.: U.S. Government Printing Office, 1976).

[4] United States Department of Justice, *Criminal Victimization in the United States, 1973 Advance Report* (Washington, D.C.: U.S. Government Printing Office, 1975), p. 1.

[5] See Marvin G. Wolfgang, "*Uniform Crime Reports:* A Criminal Appraisal," *University of Pennsylvania Law Review* 63 (1963): 408–38.

these crimes of violence are generically different from most other crimes, but the patterns of criminality are different among the violent crimes. Moreover, there are preventive steps to protect victims from losing property that will be quite ineffective in preserving their persons.

In 1979 approximately 22,000 murders were committed in America, accounting for about 2 percent of all crimes of violence. Murders tend to be committed by relatives or other people known to the victims. Killing within the family accounts for one-quarter of all murders. Strangers killing strangers is rather rare, but does happen. Handguns account for about one-half of all murders, and murders using firearms have more than doubled since 1964, demonstrating the ineffectiveness of legislation restricting handgun sale.

Aggravated assault occurred in more than 484,000 occasions in 1975 and seems to be increasing dramatically. Like murder, it is

---

An official view of violent crime.

1. Violent crime in the United States is primarily a phenomenon of large cities.
2. Violent crime in the city is overwhelmingly committed by males.
3. Violent crime in the city is concentrated especially among youths between the ages of 15 and 24.
4. Violent crime in the city is committed primarily by individuals at the lower end of the occupational scale.
5. Violent crime in the city stems disproportionately from the ghetto slum where most blacks live.
6. The victims of assaultive violence in the cities generally have the same characteristics as the offenders; victimization rates are generally highest for males, youths, poor persons, and blacks.
7. Unlike robbery, the violent crimes of homicide, assault, and rape tend to be acts of passion among intimates and acquaintances.
8. By far the greatest proportion of serious violence is committed by repeaters.
9. Americans generally are no strangers to violent crime; the homicide rate for the United States is more than twice that of our nearest competitor, Finland.

Source: National Commission on the Causes and Prevention of Violence: Final Report (New York: Praeger, 1970). Reprinted by permission.

---

most prevalent in the warm summer months and, like murder, often occurs within the family unit or among neighbors and acquaintances.

Murderers seem to be different from other violent criminals. They usually do not have a long history of criminal activity. Most

> kill on the spur of the moment, often during a heated quarrel. . . . These killers rarely try to escape; they are easily caught and readily confess. . . . [Such] actual killers have little to gain from their crimes, financially or otherwise.[6]

Most murders, then, involve some kind of rage between family members, friends, or acquaintances. Barroom brawls, neighborly disputes, and seething family resentments account for most murders.

Nearly one-third of all murders are related to the commission of other crimes; robbery, burglary, and sex offenses may lead to murder. Gangland-style killings also account for some murders, as do disputes over the distribution of drugs. In this type of murder, money is the motive. This is the stuff of murder mysteries, the kind of murder that may be planned, or at least anticipated by the perpetrator. Whether this form of homicide should be subject to the same criminal law as the majority of homicides is an important social issue.

Pathology or psychosis probably accounts for a few murders, which are often the most shocking and notorious. Mass murders differ from other murders. Typically, the mass murderer does not know the victims, who often belong to a group that torments the offender in his or her delusions. However, virtually every study of homicide ever made suggests that murderers, while they may be intoxicated, are very rarely insane.[7]

We know much less about assault and battery. Our best national survey indicated that 35 percent of victims of aggravated assault and 54 percent of victims of simple assault did not even report the incidents to the police.[8] Some of these victims simply did

[6] D. T. Lunde, "Hot Blood's Record Month: Our Murder Boom," *Psychology Today* 9 (1975): 35.

[7] The most thorough study was by Marvin G. Wolfgang, covering 558 cases in Philadelphia from 1948 to 1952. See Wolfgang, *Patterns in Criminal Homicide* (Philadelphia: University of Pennsylvania Press, 1958).

[8] President's Commission on Law Enforcement and Administration of Justice, *Challenge of Crime in a Free Society* (Washington, D.C.: U.S. Government Printing Office, 1967), p. 38.

not trust the police. Others, accustomed to such violence, did not regard the incident as serious enough to report it. Unlike murders, most assaults occur on the street. Also, unlike murder, neither the victim nor the offender is likely to be under the influence of alcohol.[9] Whether these differences between types of violent crime have a policy relevance is questionable. Violent crimes have a generic similarity since they all stem from basic aggressive tendencies.

Forcible rape is often an unreported crime. About one-half of all

[9] Based on findings of D. J. Pittman and W. J. Handy, "Patterns in Criminal Aggravated Assault," in *Crime in America,* ed. Bernard Cohen (Itasca, Ill.: F. G. Peacock Publishers, 1970), pp. 98-99.

A statute that takes account of emotional disturbance as a cause of violence.

Murder.—

(**1**) A person is guilty of murder when:

(a) With intent to cause the death of another person, he causes the death of such person or of a third person; except that in any prosecution a person shall not be guilty under this subsection if he acted under the influence of extreme emotional disturbance for which there was a reasonable explanation or excuse, the reasonableness of which is to be determined from the viewpoint of a person in the defendant's situation under the circumstances as the defendant believed them to be. However, nothing contained in this section shall constitute a defense to a prosecution for or preclude a conviction of manslaughter in the first degree or any other crime; or

(b) Under circumstances manifesting extreme indifference to human life, he wantonly engages in conduct which creates a grave risk of death to another person and thereby causes the death of another person.

(**2**) Murder is a Class A felony, except that in the following situations it is a capital offense:

(a) The defendant's act of killing was intentional and was for profit or hire;

(b) The defendant's act of killing was intentional, and occurred during the commission of arson in the first degree, robbery in the first degree, burglary in the first degree, or rape in the first degree.

(c) The defendant's act of killing was intentional and the defendant was a prisoner and the victim was a prison employe engaged at the time of the act in the performance of his duties.

Source: Kentucky Revised Statutes sec. 507.020.

---

arrested rapists are first offenders, and most rapists have not had a record of violent crime prior to arrest. About one-half of all rapes occur on the street or in a car and one-half in the victim's home.[10] Rape seems to be not so much a sexual crime as a crime of force against the victim. Some form of physical violence, beating, or roughness is involved in an overwhelming number of rapes.

Homicide, aggravated assault, and rape are the clearest examples of aggressive deviant behavior in American society. They are the kinds of conduct that result in the greatest irreversible personal losses. Property can be replaced, but never a life or a limb. There is little doubt that a well-organized society would criminalize such conduct. Whether criminalization actually reduces the incidence of such deviant behavior is another matter. These crimes of force seem to stem from impulsive or deeply felt urges, from aggressive propensities over which the offender may have incomplete control. In the long run psychobiological techniques may hold some hope for reduction of the frequency of such behavior.[11] In the short run the criminal law and the criminal process can do little more than contain such violent deeds, if that. If there are biological predispositions to violent, aggressive behavior, we may hope to anticipate such behavior before it occurs, but until that day dawns, the criminal law, with all its inadequacy, is all we have.

NONVIOLENT SERIOUS CRIME

Crime that is not so obviously based upon aggression may be treated differently. Since robbery, kidnapping, burglary, larceny, and similar offenses are usually part of a rational criminal calculation, they seem more appropriately dealt with by using concepts such as *mens rea,* criminal intention. There is some reason to believe that those persons committing such offenses do weigh the possibilities of gain against the risks of being caught and punished. In this calculation the criminal law itself may play a small role, since the issue is more of one of risking being detected than of one of incurring the sanctions possible under the criminal law.

Even if violent crimes are physiologically motivated (and that is

[10] M. Amir, *Patterns in Forcible Rape* (Chicago: The University of Chicago Press, 1971).

[11] Highly suggestive in this regard is Benson Ginsburg, "Biological Parameters of Aggressive Behavior and Possibilities for Therapeutic Intervention" (Paper delivered at meeting of American Society of Criminology, November 11, 1978).

dubious), most other serious crimes are products of a learned pattern of behavior, built upon past success or the possibility of success. Empirical studies of burglars show them to be deeply influenced by measurements of risk factors balanced against possible rewards. Burglar alarms, police patrol dogs, and complex locks are factors in the decision not to proceed with the offense. On the other hand, the risks are more worthwhile if the possible gain is high, as in affluent neighborhoods. Only regular drug users seem less calculating in deciding whether or not to break in.[12]

Ordinary career criminals comprise the major portion of the prison population. Typically these individuals commit the offenses of larceny, burglary, and robbery. Although they specialize in particular crimes, they spend a great deal of time in jail, a price accepted as part of their trade. Eventually most of their time is spent in jail because, with each subsequent conviction, they draw longer sentences and less parole.

There is a sharp distinction between ordinary criminals and professionals. The professionals, the elite of the criminal world, are seldom caught and rarely imprisoned.[13] Professional criminals, specially recruited and trained, tend to be drawn from the ranks of the legitimately employed: the "etcher becomes the counterfeiter; the skilled workman or foreman of a lock company becomes a safecracker; the worker in a stockbroker's office gets into 'hot' bonds."[14] Some are selected from legitimate jobs and trained to turn their skills to more "profitable" illegitimate ends; some are self-taught.

Professional offenders regard themselves as criminals. They accept the labels of the criminal law and try to evade the operation of that law to the best of their abilities; however, there are amateurs too. Many people have engaged in minor theft—shoplifting, vandalism, even check forgery—at some time in their lives. These little episodes are typically not repeated and may spring from sudden impulse or the immaturity of youth. Vandalism, the malicious destruction of property with no apparent purpose, is perhaps the most obnoxious such crime, but there is evidence that vandals are neither juvenile delinquents nor incipient ordinary criminals.[15] Vandalism

[12] Thomas A. Repetto, *Residential Crime* (New York: Ballinger Publishing, 1974).

[13] Marshall Clinard and Richard Quinney, *Criminal Behavior Systems: A Typology,* 3d ed. (New York: Holt, Rinehart & Winston, 1973).

[14] Walter C. Reckless, *The Crime Problem,* 5th ed. (New York: Appleton-Century-Crofts, 1973), pp. 258–59.

[15] Marshall Clinard, *Sociology of Deviant Behavior,* 4th ed. (New York: Holt, Rinehart & Winston, 1974), pp. 307–8.

and joyriding are the offenses of irresponsible youth, not of common criminals or professionals.

These types of offenders are all subject to the same criminal laws regarding property. If the criminal law is to be an effective deterrent to crime, some thought must be given to refining that law in light of the typical offenders. Maybe crimes committed by professional criminals (pickpocketing, safecracking, forgery) should be made easier to prove so that more perpetrators are punished if caught. Ordinary criminals perhaps should be made to serve still longer periods in prison just to keep them off the streets. On the other hand, the law should distinguish between amateur, casual offenders and those who are more calculating, or else force the amateurs into regarding and labeling themselves as criminal.

Also of note is the rise of the professional "heavy" criminal. This group of professionals usually engages in armed robbery, burglary, and auto theft, and stands ready to use force and the threat of force. Weapons are used, even though the professional hopes to obtain what he or she wants through skill rather than force.[16] Auto theft is an area in which both professionals and amateurs operate, but the professionals are almost never caught.

FELONY-MURDER

Homicide committed in the course of a felony has been regarded as more serious than murder itself. With the growing tendency of professional property offenders to use force, there is a decline in the usefulness of the distinction between violent and nonviolent crimes. This may justify resorting to the felony-murder doctrine, although the rule seems to be somewhat irrational in its foundation.

Felony-murder encompasses homicide that occurs in the perpetration of a felony, and may include acts committed before and after the actual felony. Felony-murder statutes treat a death occurring as a result of a serious felony in the same way as premeditated first-degree murder, even though the offender did not set out to kill anyone at the outset of the felonious deed. All those committing the felony are regarded as participants in a first-degree murder even though some of them were not armed. These who participate in dangerous felonies are held accountable for deaths that may occur.

The purpose of felony-murder statutes is to deter felons from killing negligently or by accident, by holding all participants in a

[16] James Inciardi, *Careers in Crime* (Chicago: Rand McNally, 1975).

crime responsible for any killing committed by the offenders in the course of the offense. Some courts have held that the accused's intent to kill is supplied by the intent to commit the felony,[17] but this is a patent fiction. The felony-murderer, by definition, is one who *does not* have an intention to commit homicide at the start of the offense; the intention is imputed (or supplied by legislative invention) and is contrary to the usual requirement of *mens rea* in criminal cases. However, there must be an intent to commit the underlying felony. The common law also recognized a felony-murder rule.

The felony-murder rule generally applies only where the felony is inherently dangerous to human life or is committed in a manner that is inherently dangerous; clearly it applies to rape, robbery, burglary, and arson. But if the felony does not normally involve risk to human life and no violent means are employed, felony-murder does not apply. Larceny is generally not considered inherently dangerous unless committed in a manner that is dangerous.[18]

The English Homicide Act of 1957 abolished the felony-murder rule. One American state, Ohio, does not recognize it.[19] The Model Penal Code does not recognize felony-murder, requiring proof of some kind of intention to kill or some indication of a "depraved-heart reckless" murder.[20] Before other states abandon the rule, it should be determined whether such statutes actually influence the criminal calculation of ordinary or professional criminals who contemplate a felony. If not, the rule, which is plainly irrational, serves no purpose. Otherwise, though irrational, it may actually discourage this most outrageous (because it affects innocents) form of killing.

HOMICIDE

Homicide is the unjustifiable and inexcusable killing of one human being by another. Killing by court executioners, by soldiers in combat, by peace officers suppressing a riot, or by an individual in legitimate self-defense are all justifiable and are not considered crimes. Killings resulting from accidents, without any intent to hurt, are excusable; therefore a hunting accident may not be a crime,

[17] Simpson v. Commonwealth, 293 Ky. 831 (1943).

[18] People v. Lopez, 6 Cal. 3d 45 (1971).

[19] Ohio: See Turk v. State, 48 Ohio App. 489 (1934).

[20] Model Penal Code, sec. 210.2.

unless committed negligently or recklessly. Killings by peace officers are not always justifiable, especially if the offense committed by the victim of the killing was not a felony.

Heated controversy surrounds the issue of what constitutes a human being. Is the abortion of an unborn child homicide? Most courts hold that a child is not a human being until it is born alive outside the mother's body.[21] Abortion may be a crime, but it is not a homicide in most states. Several states have adopted feticide statutes that redefine a homicide to include the killing of a fetus.[22] Abortion itself is a different offense and is treated later in this chapter.

Shortening a human life in any way is homicide. Mercy-killing (euthanasia), even at the request of the victim, is unjustifiable if one accepts the views of the criminal law. Nowadays there is some public sympathy for medical mercy killing of an individual who is suffering from a painful terminal illness, but the law still does not countenance self-slaughter or termination of life upon request, even though jurors may hesitate to find a homicide verdict under such circumstances. A few states no longer criminalize suicide, though. Apparently though, withdrawing life-support systems from a comatose patient when there is no hope for recovery may be justifiable if done at the request of the patient or a guardian.[23] This issue will continue to grow in importance as the sophistication and availability of life-support systems increase. It raises the additional question of what constitutes death, a medical-legal issue of enormous complexity faced by all physicians who treat terminally ill patients.

Murder is the unjustified, unexcused killing of one human being by another with malice aforethought. This term may be translated as an intention to kill, and does not mean that the offender need feel ill will toward the victim. So long as the offender intended to commit an act that creates a very high risk of death or serious bodily harm, he or she is responsible for the death of the victim. One need not have intended to kill. A killing that results from a wanton, conscious disregard for the life of another is murder, whether planned or not.

[21] See Shedd v. State, 178 Ga. 653 (1934).

[22] See California Penal Code, sec. 187, which is not applicable to lawful abortions. Obviously, the California law goes beyond the abortion controversy to make offenders responsible for injuries caused to pregnant women that result in the death of unborn children.

[23] At least, in New Jersey, under *In re Quinlan* (1976).

Most states have enacted statutes that classify murder according to the state of mind of the offender or the circumstances surrounding the crime. First-degree murder includes all killings with malice aforethought. Premeditation is a common requirement, meaning that some reflection must take place between the forming of the original intent to kill and the decision to kill. But no particular length of time is necessary, according to most states. Obviously though, a concept of "instantaneous premeditation" may "destroy the distinction between first- and second-degree murder."[24]

Other forms of first-degree murder are statutorily defined as felony-murder and killings committed with malice aforethought that are perpetrated by poison, bombing, torture, or lying in wait. This type of killing is usually regarded as equally wrongful as premeditated killing since the method is regarded as so bad as to eliminate the need to prove premeditation.

Second-degree murder includes all those killings not classified as first degree. Second-degree murders are less socially harmful than first-degree murders, with punishments less severe after conviction. Aggravated assault is a typical example. Also included are felony-murders not enumerated in first-degree felony-murder statutes.

Many states define the degrees of homicide in terms of the identity of the victim. The killing of prison guards may constitute first-degree murder. Killing police officers or fire fighters may elevate a murder from second to first degree. The policy underlying such statutes is to prize particularly the life of public servants, but placing a special premium on the lives of some citizens may not be equitable, even if rational. Plainly, police officers and correctional officials are particularly at risk in a violent society, but the lives of all citizens

[24] Bullock v. United States, 122 F. 2d 213 (D.C. Cir. 1941).

Felony-murder linked to first-degree murder.

All murder which shall be perpetrated by means of poison, or lying in wait, or any other kind of wilful, deliberate and premeditated killing, or which shall be committed in the perpetration, or attempt to perpetrate any arson, rape, robbery, * * * burglary, *larceny of any kind, extortion or kidnapping,* shall be murder of the first degree, and shall be punished by solitary confinement at hard labor in the state prison for life.

Source: Michigan Compiled Laws Annotated sec. 750.316.

ought to be of equal moral value. Apparently legislators are more concerned with the front-line risks of police officers and correctional officials than they are with the rest of the citizenry; indeed, in many states the death penalty is reserved for those who slay correctional officials or police officers.

Manslaughter is also homicide. Manslaughter differs from murder in that malice aforethought is absent in the killing. Manslaughter may be voluntary or involuntary. Voluntary manslaughter involves either an intent to kill or a wanton, willful, unreasonable disregard of the risk to human life. Voluntary manslaughter includes the key concept of adequate provocation. If the facts of the situation show that a reasonable person might respond passionately rather than thoughtfully, then what would otherwise be murder is deemed voluntary manslaughter.

If one strikes another with a very hard blow, inflicting great pain, provocation is probably adequate. But the killer must not strike the first blow. Catching one's spouse in the act of adultery is adequate provocation. Words alone are usually not sufficient provocation, but taunts might create a passionate reaction that is sufficient provocation.[25] The act of trespass upon private land is insufficient provocation. The acts of provocation must have resulted in the killing of the provoker.

Involuntary manslaughter is an unintentional killing while engaged in the commission of either an unlawfully dangerous act that is not a felony or criminally negligent conduct. Committing a minor crime (misdemeanor) that results in a death will constitute involuntary manslaughter even if there were no intent to kill. Criminal assault resulting in death is a typical example: If A shakes a fist at B in a threatening manner causing B to have a fatal heart attack, we have a case of involuntary manslaughter.

Criminal negligence consists of highly unreasonable behavior with very substantial indifference for the safety of others, resulting in death. A physician who ignores established medical procedures may be guilty of criminal negligence. Insufficient skill or a mistake that causes death is not adequate grounds for a criminal negligence charge. Some states have created a statutory category of "vehicular homicide" which, when a felony, is essentially criminally negligent killing committed with an automobile. Some lawmakers feel that negligent homicide should constitute a third, lower degree of homicide.[26]

[25] State v. Grugin, 147 Mo. 39 (1898).

[26] Model Penal Code, sec. 210.4.

ASSAULT AND BATTERY; SEXUAL ASSAULT

Battery is an unlawful application of force by one person on another. Battery is often confused with assault, which is a preparatory act. To make the distinction clear: Battery involves actual touching. Punching someone in the face is battery if the face is struck; otherwise it might be only assault. They often occur as one event comprising the assault and then the battery, but the law allows that only one may be charged.

No bodily harm need result to constitute battery, just unlawful touching is sufficient. Lack of the victim's consent to the touching will make it unlawful. Players in a football game have, by their participation, given effective consent to a great deal of touching. A punch in someone's face in the locker room, being without consent, is a battery. Tossing a loud customer out of a bar is not a battery if it is done gently, since those who frequent bars consent to some correction of their misbehavior by the bartender.

Any offensive, unconsented touching is sufficient for a battery. The touching may be of a person's clothes or of anything closely associated with the person, such as jewelry or eyeglasses. Many states have eliminated mere offensive touching as a ground for battery, requiring some showing of actual bodily injury.

Assault may constitute an attempt to commit a battery or a menacing of the victim, placing the person in apprehension of impending bodily harm. Waving a gun at someone is assault. Holding a knife may be assault if the intended victim is within striking distance. Words alone will not constitute an assault. There must at least be a threatening movement, gesture, or show of force. So long as the accused has the apparent ability to inflict bodily harm, an assault may have occurred when a victim is placed in fear of bodily

---

How is this different from assault?

Endangerment; classification

A. A person commits endangerment by recklessly endangering another person with a substantial risk of imminent death or physical injury.

B. Endangerment involving a substantial risk of imminent death is a class 6 felony. In all other cases, it is a class 1 misdemeanor.

Added Laws 1977, Ch. 142, § 61, eff. Oct. 1, 1978.

Source: Arizona Revised Statutes sec. 13-1201.

harm. Obviously both assault and battery raise substantial questions of fact for ultimate resolution by a jury.

Simple assault and battery are usually misdemeanors. Many states treat some assaults as much more serious than simple assaults. An assault with a deadly weapon may be treated as a felony, as may assaults with deadly drugs or poisons. Assaults on police officers or by convicts upon prison guards are often treated as felonies. Many states have created a felony of aggravated assault, attaching severe penalties; usually included are all assaults with intent to kill, to do bodily harm, to rob, or to rape. Other states separately criminalize each of these acts. Those accused of aggravated assault or some component offense must be shown to have had the specific intent to commit the act in question—that is, to rob, to kill, to rape, and so on.

Rape may be regarded as a separate crime or as an instance of assault. Under the common law, rape consisted of the unlawful, unconsented carnal knowledge of a female by a male. The slightest penetration of the female sexual organs is sufficient to constitute rape. The consensual aspects of rape law have concerned feminists and deeply disturbed many rape victims. While consent procured by force or fraud is no defense to a rape charge, the previous sexual experience of the victim and her prior relationship with an accused are often raised in rape trials. Rape victims are often subjected to pain and humiliation when they pursue charges against their attackers.

Recent statutes have changed the traditional approach to rape that treated the offense as unlawful sexual intercourse. Reforms in New Jersey law have virtually eliminated rape as an offense. In face, most consensual sexual activity has been decriminalized. Instead sexual activity based upon force, duress, or fraud is proscribed. The most serious offense is aggravated sexual assault, usually involving the use of force or duress. The offense has been defined as a type of assault, and the sex of the perpetrator has been rendered irrelevant. The question of the victim's resistance to the assault has also been eliminated from the criminal law. Other states have reformed the law of rape by including unconsented sexual contact between spouses and/or by limiting the use of evidence of a victim's previous sexual conduct to testimony directly relevant to the assault in question. Thus rape victims need no longer be exposed to shame, ridicule, and embarrassment when they choose to press charges, as the rape victim's privacy is gaining increased legislative respect.

The common law crime of rape has been expanded by most states so that females under a prescribed age, usually 18, are deemed incapable of consent to their sexual ravishment. Any sexual contact with an underage female is automatically rape, regardless of the consent question. Even an admitted prostitute can be raped if she is underage. This extreme policy has had little impact upon the sexual practices of young people, and many states have eliminated its harsher features, either by permitting the defendant to prove his mistake as to the victim's age or by allowing prosecution only if it appears that the woman had previously been "chaste and virtuous." Statutory rape policy here is simply out of phase with dominant sexual practices in most parts of the country. As a result such statutes are not usually enforced or are enforced only for much younger rape victims than 18-year-olds.

In many states the age of consent has been lowered: in New York, it is 17; in Massachusetts, 16; and in Pennsylvania, 14. The effect of these changes is to legalize sexual intercourse by younger females who consent to it. Similarly, males close in age to the consenting females may, under some state laws, be lawfully permitted to engage in consensual youthful sex acts. In many jurisdictions a male prosecuted for statutory rape may be permitted to raise as a defense the fact that the underage female acted as a prostitute and/or that she appeared to be the requisite age. For such a defense to prevail, the male defendant must show that he did not have actual knowledge of the female's true age.

Some of the sexist features that had been elements of rape have been removed by state legislatures. Unconsented homosexual acts, male or female, are sometimes included within the meaning of rape. The Model Penal Code (Sec. 213) makes deviate sexual acts, such as sodomy and bestiality, a form of rape. Probably the most important change in rape law concerns the admissibility of evidence of the victim's previous sexual conduct. Progressive states have tended to reduce the admissibility of such evidence as an unwarrented invasion of the victim's privacy. By limiting the use of evidence of a victim's previous sexual conduct to testimony directly relevant to the assault in question, the law has encouraged rape victims to prosecute their attackers. Since these and other changes are currently under consideration in many states, attention must be given to the latest versions of the law of rape in each jurisdiction to ensure accuracy.

Many states have abandoned the traditional distinctions among assault, threat, attempt, and battery when criminalizing nonconsensual touchings. Even the difference between assault and battery concerning touching has sometimes been eliminated. The use of a deadly weapon, the link with a more serious crime, the special nature of the victim (e.g., a police officer or fire fighter) may be regarded as more significant than the common law distinctions. For this reason generalizations about this body of law must be tempered with an awareness of changing versions of the law among the states.

ABORTION

At common law it was a crime intentionally to produce a miscarriage of a pregnant woman, with or without her consent, once the fetus had exhibited viability (signs of life), unless it was shown that the killing was believed reasonably necessary to save the life of the mother. Under most statutes today the crime consists mainly of the illegal operation. Whether or not there is a miscarriage is usually irrelevant, as is the issue of whether or not the woman is pregnant. Abortion is usually a felony, not a misdemeanor.

Under certain circumstances state antiabortion laws may be unconstitutional. During the first 3 months of pregnancy, an abortion decision must be left to the woman and to the medical judgment of the pregnant woman's attending physician.[27] Now some states allow "therapeutic" abortions beyond the first 3 months, but the meaning of a therapeutic abortion varies and the issue of the criminality of abortion has become a political issue, often involving women's interests groups in struggles with religious groups.

MAYHEM

At common law mayhem is the malicious maiming of another. Dismemberment, disfigurement, or acute disablement constitute the nature of the injury requisite for this felony. The injury must be permanent, but it need not involve the total loss of a body part. Biting off someone's ear is mayhem. Cutting off a hand or destroying sight are both mayhem.

Mayhem is the intentional dismemberment, disablement, or disfigurement of another's body. An intent (often including malice) is required. Intention to do any of these three acts of violence is sufficient, regardless of the specific results. State statutes have

[27] Roe v. Wade. 410 U.S. 113 (1973).

Abortion statutes tended to provide numerous procedural hurdles.

Termination of pregnancies [**Repealed by Laws 1976, c. 76-168, § 3, eff. July 1, 1979. See § 11.61**]

(1) Definitions.—As used in this section, unless the context clearly requires otherwise:

(a) "Physician" means a doctor of medicine or osteopathic medicine licensed by the state under chapter 458 or chapter 459 or a physician practicing medicine or osteopathy in the employment of the United States or this state.

(b) "Approved facility" means a hospital licensed by the state and accredited by the Joint Commission on Accreditation of Hospitals or approved by the American Osteopathic Hospital Association or a medical facility licensed by the [Department of Health and Rehabilitative Services] pursuant to rules and regulations adopted for that purpose, provided such rules and regulations shall require regular evaluation and review procedures.

(2) Termination of pregnancy.—It shall be unlawful to terminate the pregnancy of a human being unless the pregnancy is terminated in an approved facility by a physician who certifies in writing that:

(a) To a reasonable degree of medical certainty the continuation of the pregnancy would substantially impair the life or health of the female; or

(b) There is substantial risk that the continuation of the pregnancy would result in the birth of a child with a serious physical or mental defect; or

(c) There is reasonable cause to believe that the pregnancy resulted from rape or incest.

(3) Writings required.—One of the following shall be obtained by the physician prior to terminating a pregnancy:

(a) The written request of the pregnant woman and, if she is married, the written consent of her husband, unless the husband is voluntarily living apart from the wife, or

(b) If the pregnant woman is under eighteen years of age and unmarried, in addition to her written request, the written consent of a parent, custodian, or legal guardian must be obtained, or

(c) Notwithstanding paragraphs (a) and (b) of this subsection, a physician may terminate a pregnancy provided he has obtained at least one corroborative medical opinion attesting to the medical necessity for emergency medical procedures and to the fact that to a reasonable degree of medical certainty the continuation of the pregnancy would threaten the life of the pregnant woman.

(4) Reporting procedure.—

(a) The director of any medical facility in which a pregnancy is terminated pursuant to this section shall maintain a record of such procedures. Such record shall include the date the procedure was performed, the reason for same, and the period of gestation at the time the procedure was performed. A copy of such record shall be filed with the department of health and rehabilitative services, which shall be responsible for keeping such records in a central place from which statistical data and analysis can be made.

(b) Records maintained by an approved facility pursuant to this section shall be privileged information and deemed to be a confidential record and shall not be revealed except upon the order of a court of competent jurisdiction in a civil or criminal proceeding.

(5) Right of refusal.—Nothing in this section shall require any hospital or any person to participate in the termination of a pregnancy, nor shall any hospital or any person be liable for such refusal. No person who is a member of, or associated with, the staff of a hospital nor any employee of a hospital or physician in which or by whom the termination of a pregnancy has been authorized or performed, who shall state an objection to such procedure on moral or religious grounds, shall be required to participate in the procedure which will result in the termination of pregnancy. The refusal of any such person or employee to participate shall not form the basis for any disciplinary or other recriminatory action against such person.

(6) Penalties.—

(a) Any person who performs, or participates in, the termination of a pregnancy in violation of the requirements in subsection (2) of this section which does not result in the death of the woman shall be guilty of a felony of the third degree, punishable as provided in § 775.082, § 775.083 or § 775.084.

(b) Any person who performs, or participates in, the termination of a pregnancy in violation of the requirements in subsection (2) of this section which results in the death of the woman shall be guilty of a felony of the second degree, punishable as provided in § 775.082, § 775.083 or § 775.084.

(c) Any person who violates any provision of subsections (3) or (4) of this section shall be guilty of a misdemeanor of the first degree, punishable as provided in § 775.082 or § 775.083.

(7) Exception.—The provisions of this section shall not apply to the performance of a procedure which terminates a pregnancy in order to deliver a live child.

Laws 1972, c. 72-196, §§ 1 to 7, eff. April 12, 1972.

Source: Florida Statutes Annotated sec. 458.22.

often added disfigurement to the common law definition of mayhem. Disfigurement includes the loss of a tooth, the scarring of a face, or any other alteration in the ordinary appearance of the victim, so long as it is permanent. Biting off one-third of a victim's finger may be insufficient to constitute dismemberment, since the use of the finger is still available, but it may be deemed to constitute disfigurement. The loss involved need not be total, but it must be permanent. A substantial loss of vision may constitute disablement, as would a permanent limp. Many states prefer to treat mayhem-type injuries as instances of aggravated assault. In others the two offenses remain separate.

KIDNAPPING

Kidnapping tends to be described in statutes and is no longer defined by common law principles. Kidnapping has become so prevalent that it has become the object of legislative concern. Unlike most forceful crimes, kidnapping is both a federal and state offense. Kidnapping is usually defined as a secret confinement or movement of a person against his or her will. Federal law requires that the victim be transported across state lines.[28] This felony is often a capital offense when ransom is demanded.

Ransom is an element in the federal kidnapping law. While abduction of people against their will had long been a familiar offense, it was the holding of a person as a means of extracting money that became a special feature of kidnapping law. The law itself grew out of the 1932 kidnapping of the infant son of aviator Charles A. Lindbergh, who was then held for ransom by his abductor. Some statutes do not require ransom, emphasizing instead the compelled movement of the victims against their will while holding them in secret confinement. Ransom may result in an increase in the degree of the felony, in such states.

Statutes currently distinguish among child stealing, kidnapping for ransom, and other forms of kidnapping. The terminology used for these crimes differs from state to state, but in all states transportation of the victim, carrying away of the victim, is part of the offense.

Two aspects of kidnapping deserve special attention. The first, child stealing, frequently involves interference with the custody of children following a separation or divorce. The only way to justify this form of kidnapping is if the person doing it believed or reasonably could have believed that his or her conduct was necessary to preserve the child's health or physical welfare. The second situation involves holding people in involuntary servitude (for example, migratory laborers who are compelled to work). Under some state statutes this is defined as kidnapping.[29] Both situations are quite preva-

[28] 18 U.S.C. 1201.

[29] See Ohio Revised Code, sec. 2905.01.

lent and the use of kidnapping statutes to discourage them is an interesting development. False imprisonment, described in another chapter, differs from kidnapping in that unlawful restraint of the victim constitutes the offense, while kidnapping involves unlawful transportation of the victim.

ROBBERY

Robbery is the taking of property from persons by the use of force or intimidation. Robbery is a crime against property and the person. The elements of force and fear have always been part of robbery law. Pocket picking is not robbery because there is no force or intimidation involved. Robbery is a crime of force. Larceny (including pocket picking) is a crime of stealth. In effect, robbery is larceny aggravated by force or the threat of force.

Any force used to overcome the owner's resistance to loss of property is sufficient. Shoving and pushing are sufficient force. Breaking a chain secured to the victim's wrist is sufficient force.

In robbery the taking must be from the victim directly or it must take place in the victim's immediate presence. Many modern statutes have dispensed with this requirement.[30] Similarly, statutes have broadened the target of the threatened force so that it is often sufficient to show that the victim feared for personal safety and property or those of any relative or companion at the time of the robbery.[31]

There are other examples of stretching the limits of common law robbery. This particular crime is among the most feared in the public's perception. As a consequence the definitions of robbery are being extended to include behavior not previously criminalized as a felony. Moreover, there is a trend toward distinguishing between first- and second-degree robbery. In California, robbery by a person with a deadly weapon or by torture constitutes first-degree robbery, a crime carrying a more severe penalty than other forms of robbery, all of which are denoted second-degree robbery.[32] Whether these distinctions have had any impact upon styles of robbery is not known, but the notion of scaling robbery offenses in this way might discourage professional robbers from carrying guns.

Robbery must be contrasted with the much less serious offense

[30] See Model Penal Code, sec. 222.1.

[31] See California Penal Code, sec. 212.

[32] California Penal Code, sec. 211 (a).

of larceny from the person. Robbery is a misappropriation of property by threat of force. The combination of violence and theft is what concerns lawmakers the most. This concern reflects the public's legitimate fear of force. Larceny is more clearly a crime of stealth, committed against the victim's property. Robbery may be regarded as aggravated larceny, since it requires the use of force (or the threat of force) in addition to the taking or carrying away of property in the owner's presence. So a purse snatcher commits larceny unless the victim witnesses the act and feels the use of force, in which case it becomes robbery. Robbery is distinct from burglary in that burglary does not involve the use of force to the person of the victim nor need it be accompanied by a theft of property.

BURGLARY

Burglary is an old category of crime. Common law burglary consists of breaking and entering the dwelling house of another in the nighttime, with the intent to commit a felony within the premises. As we shall see, statutes have stretched the definition in almost every one of its elements until the crime has been fundamentally changed. All burglary requires both a general and a specific intent; there must be an intent to break and enter (general intent) and an intent to commit a crime within the dwelling place (specific intent). There need be no actual taking of property.

Many current statutes have eliminated either the breaking or the entry requirement for burglary. A *breaking* consists of any opening, with even the slightest use of force, that is not permitted by the occupant. If a window is left open and the thief enters, there is no breaking. *Entry* includes intrusion of a part of the burglar's body. Tools will not do, but the burglar's toe or fingernail will suffice.

The dwelling house requirement has been expanded by most statutes to include virtually any building, structure, tent, warehouse, store, mine, or aircraft. Motor vehicles have sometimes been included when the doors of the vehicle were locked. Of course, this expansion of definition represents a sharp departure from common law policy. Breaking into a person's home is quite different from breaking into a warehouse; yet the crime is still defined as burglary, though the protection of property is no longer exclusive to the dwelling place. In view of general public apprehension about home burglary, the older view still seems sensible for most people, in spite of legislative efforts to reach all sorts of theft behavior.

The common law also required that a burglary take place at night, which meant that period when it was too dark to distinguish a person's face. Most modern statutes define nighttime as the period between sunset and sunrise, or one hour in either direction.[33] Others eliminate the requirement altogether.[34] Daytime burglary is quite prevalent, especially in homes with two working spouses, so the daytime-nighttime distinction seems inappropriate to an age of extensive nighttime illumination and differing life-styles.

As with kidnapping and many other crimes, abandonment of the original plan may be to no avail. A person may be charged with burglary for merely breaking and entering with the requisite intent. If the person becomes frightened or decides to change his or her mind about the deed, it is too late to avoid liability. How, then, can a person be rewarded for reconsidering? Since the burglary was completed at its inception, abandonment is not encouraged. A person may calculate that the fruits of the crime might as well be gained, at that point.

ARSON

Another important crime of force is arson. Arson is a willful and malicious burning of the dwelling of another person. A mere careless or negligent burning is not arson. Accidental burning can never be arson because the intention to cause a burning is absent.

Because of the possible insurance benefits from arson to one's own property, some modern statutes cover any building or structure, including the accused's property. Setting fire to a factory or restaurant that is losing money would be arson under this modern view. Under the circumstances described, the arson would also constitute the crime of intent to defraud.

The loss of life that may be an aftermath of arson is not an element in this crime, although an arson and a homicide charge could result from a single burning. Perhaps legislators and policymakers generally should consider the difference between burning a dwelling place and any other building of social significance. Similarly, there would seem to be a great moral difference between setting fire to an unoccupied restaurant versus an occupied one.

[33] See Arizona Revised Statutes, sec. 13-301.

[34] See Model Penal Code, sec. 221.1 (1).

LARCENY

Larceny is a crime in which stealth, rather than force, is paramount. Larceny is trespassory taking and carrying away of the personal property of another person with the intent to permanently deprive the victim of that property. Each of the terms of this definition must be satisfied to constitute larceny: trespass (although this is very loosely defined); there must be a taking and a carrying away; personal property must be involved and it must belong to another; there must be a specific intent to deny the owner the possession of said property. Small wonder that classical common law larceny has been difficult to prove; consequently statutes have often greatly modified these requirements.

Larceny is different from criminal trespass, which requires an actual unpermitted entry upon the land of another. Larceny is distinct from burglary, which involves a use of force to obtain an entry into a dwelling place or similar structure. Larceny is not fraud because the fraud victim willingly parts with property.

Larceny at the common law did not include documents, records, deeds, contracts, or even banknotes, which were not regarded as personal property, merely evidence of property. Growing crops were not subject to larceny, nor were minerals in the ground. Abandoned goods could not be the subject of larceny, nor was it larceny to steal services (such as stowing away on a ship or sneaking into a theater).

Statutes have abandoned many of these limitations. Documents

Some burnings are not arson but are crimes.

Malicious burning of bridge or of thing not subject to arson; punishment

Every person who willfully and maliciously burns any bridge exceeding in value fifty dollars ($50), or any structure, snowshed, vessel, or boat, not the subject of arson, or any tent, or any stack of hay or grain or straw of any kind, or any pile or baled hay or straw, or any pile of potatoes, or beans, or vegetables, or produce, or fruit of any kind, whether sacked, boxed, crated, or not, or any fence, or any railroad car, lumber, cordwood, railroad ties, telegraph or telephone poles, or shakes, or any tuleland or peatground of the value of twenty-five dollars ($25) or over, not the property of such person is punishable by imprisonment in the state prison for not less than 1 year, nor more than 10 years.

Source: California Statutes Annotated sec. 449b.

that have an ascertainable value are covered, as are customer lists and secret formulas. Trade secrets, computer programming data, and similar intangible items (not printed documents) are also usually covered. Duplicating documents may not constitute larceny since the original document remains in the possession of the owner. In an age of copying machines this loophole seems an anachronism, and many legislators have tried to include document copying as a form of larceny.

Statutes have sometimes placed minerals and crops under the blanket of larceny.[35] Larceny of services, labor, or of the facilities of another are sometimes criminalized.[36] Possession obtained by fraud rather than trespass is treated by "larceny by trick" statutes that deal with the traditional confidence game depicted in the movie *The Sting*.[37] Numerous other versions of larceny exist, requiring some familiarity with the law in a given state.

The distinctions among larceny, false pretenses, embezzlement, and other crimes against personal property are breaking down. Many states have attempted to draw up general theft statutes that merge many of the old common law categories. Statutory theft is usually divided into degrees, based upon the kind of property stolen and the value of the items stolen. Automobile theft is often a separate crime category. Common law distinctions retain some significance, especially when criminal charges are pressed and a specification of the elements of the offenses is requested.

Receiving stolen property and concealing stolen goods are both often a part of the general theft statute. Usually the accused person must know the item was stolen; however, reflecting the vigorous campaign against property crimes, the Model Penal Code suggests that receiving stolen property should be criminalized so long as the accused believes that he or she is handling stolen property.[38] The effect of this provision is similar to most modern theft statutes, reducing the proof requirements. Prosecution in theft cases has been made easier by the elimination of common law restrictions and requirements.

[35] Recommended by Model Penal Code, sec. 223.0 (4).

[36] Recommended by Model Penal Code, sec. 223.7.

[37] This crime is often very similar to the offense known as false pretenses, which consists of obtaining the property of another by means of an untrue representation of fact with intent to defraud. In larceny by trick, only possession is required. In false pretenses, both title and possession must be obtained. Unauthorized use of a credit card may fall into one or the other category in different states.

[38] Section 206.8 calls the crime "theft by receiving."

MALICIOUS MISCHIEF

A less serious crime against property is the crime called malicious mischief. Malicious mischief was a misdemeanor at common law, and is still treated as a minor crime. Injury to or the destruction of the real or personal property of another are requisite elements. Given the rise of incidents in this category, some states have made this crime a felony, with attendant harsher punishment. Sometimes vandalism ordinances resemble state malicious mischief statutes, creating overlapping jurisdictional problems. Many offenses of this kind are committed by juveniles and are treated as noncriminal offenses. The lack of financial gain in such crimes suggests that professional criminals are rarely implicated.

SOME FEDERAL CRIMES OF FORCE

Some crimes, peculiarly federal in nature, are largely the concern of the national government. Armed rebellion or insurrection is such a crime. So is instigating overthrow or destruction of the government. Treason, sabotage, and espionage are all federal crimes, and each concerns the national defense. Impairing military effectiveness and evading military service have all been made crimes. Most of these national offenses contain elements of force, direct or indirect. However, speech is sometimes proscribed as well as actions, creating constitutional problems of great magnitude. The Su-

Why is this such a serious property offense?

Vessels, wilfully destroying

WILFULLY DESTROYING VESSELS, ETC.—

Any person who shall wilfully cast away, burn, sink or otherwise destroy any ship, boat or vessel within the body of any country, with intent to injure or defraud any owner of such ship, boat or vessel, or the owner of any property on board the same, or any insurer of such ship, boat or vessel or property or any part thereof, shall be guilty of a felony, punishable by imprisonment in the state prison not more than 10 years.

Source: Michigan Compiled Laws Annotated sec. 750.392.

preme Court has indicated that speech alone cannot be incriminating, but it can be incriminating when it comprises an incitement to imminent lawless action.[39]

Counterfeiting money is made a federal offense because of the national government's power to issue paper money and coins. Counterfeiting of works of art, antiques, rare books, and so on may constitute state or federal crimes. National criminal laws covering bank robbing, bombing threats, fraud, kidnapping, drug use, and a host of other offenses are less justifiable, since appropriate state laws exist. Overlapping state and federal criminal laws do not create double jeopardy problems because the Supreme Court has long held that two separate sovereign entities are offended by such violations.[40] Nonetheless, the prime explanation for the existence of parallel state and federal criminal offenses is that they supplement the law enforcement efforts of the states. Most of these criminal laws create federal violations when a criminal act involves the crossing of a state boundary line. As mentioned above, this dual set of laws is a result of the federal structure of the American political system. The use of force does not create a federal interest in crime.

SUMMARY

Crimes of violence command special attention. Fear of street violence ranks high among the concerns of average American citizens. Even crimes of stealth, such as robbery, burglary, and arson, often carry an element of threatened or implicit force. Victims of these crimes regard them all as serious. The assaultive crimes (rape, homicide, assault) are most prevalent in urban areas. Many of these crimes are committed by young people from ghetto slums. But robbery, burglary, arson, and vandalism are spread over both the cities and the countryside. In spite of great public concern with crimes of violence and stealth, little is known about methods of reducing their incidence. As a result serious crimes remain at a much higher level in the United States than in any other industrialized nation.

[39] Scales v. United States, 367 U.S. 203 (1961).

[40] United States v. Lanza, 260 U.S. 377 (1922); Bartkus v. Illinois, 359 U.S. 121 (1959).

5

ECONOMIC CRIMES

Crime is strongly related to the culture of a society, but it is also related to the economic and political structure of the society. Ours is a private property, modified capitalistic economy. This fact gives rise to certain crimes unknown to socialist regimes. Contrariwise our criminal laws do not criminalize the pursuit of private profits, unless extremely unpleasant means are used to acquire the profits.

According to some American scholars the whole criminal justice system is skewed toward the protection of capitalist property and profits. From this perspective American criminal law is becoming more and more punitive as the liberal welfare state decays.[1] Actually there is some truth in this approach, but it suffers from a doctrinaire Marxist interpretation. Capitalist laws are aimed at protecting life and limb primarily and property secondarily. Furthermore, corporations and businesses are subject to some of the constraints of criminal law. Business is not above the law, and there is a growing tendency to use criminal law sanctions to limit deviant business practices.

Crime among workers is a major cost of doing business in America. In 1976 crime cost American business at least $30 billion.[2] Some of this loss was caused by crimes of theft, arson, and vandalism committed by outsiders, but employees also were involved in many crimes against business. Bank frauds, claims frauds, bad checks, computer crime, and outright employee theft are growing by leaps and bounds. Embezzlement and other forms of management crimes are sometimes committed by executives. In the age of impersonal corporations with diffuse ownership of the assets, employees and managers alike are involved in "ripping off" business.

White-collar crime is prevalent in capitalist America. It is estimated that there is a better than 50 percent chance of sizable dishonesty in any business organization.[3] Conflicts of interest, corruption, kickbacks, industrial spying, price fixing, commercial bribery, payoffs, and monopoly practices have recently been subjects of newspaper headlines. These are employer crimes, often corporate crimes. They stem from personal greed and abuse of corporate power. The worker who steals tools from the owner is, of course, no less a criminal than the white-collar thief; both are indulging in

1 Richard Quinney, *Class, State and Crime: On the Theory and Practice of Criminal Justice* (New York: David McKay, 1977).

2 U.S. Domestic and International Business Administration, *Crime in Service Industries* (Washington, D.C.: U.S. Government Printing Office, 1977). The U.S. Chamber of Commerce opts for a figure of $41 billion annually.

3 See August Bequai, *White Collar Crime* (Lexington, Mass.: Lexington Books, 1978).

deviant behavior. The laws are being changed to make an employer/manager just as responsible for criminal conduct as an employee or even a hapless shoplifter.

USURY

Since capitalism depends upon the lending of money at interest to provide investment financing, then the laws regulating such loans closely reveal the relationship of capitalism to crime. In many societies the taking of interest for money loans has been regarded as criminal or sinful. Charging excessive interest was forbidden by early Chinese and Hindu laws, and is still forbidden by the Koran. Talmudic law prohibited Jews from charging fellow Jews any interest on loans, but permitted interest from gentiles.

During the European Middle Ages, money was considered merely a medium of exchange, naturally barren and unproductive. Therefore, to allow money to beget money was regarded as unnatural, sinful, and often criminal. In England, by the sixteenth century, this outlook began to change as a result of the slow rise of Protestantism and capitalism. By the nineteenth century interest charges were legal, and usury had become an almost forgotten crime.

Many American states have enacted statutes that regulate the maximum interest receivable for the use of money. The potential oppressiveness of moneylending has been recognized and limited in most American jurisdictions. In its most extreme form—"loan sharking"—charging exhorbitant rates of interest is quite clearly criminal. In general, interest limitation statutes are intended to protect the consumer against banks and powerful individuals. However, these laws are frequently evaded by such devices as charging money "points" to home buyers as a precondition for a loan agreement at the legal interest rate.

The crime of usury consists of several elements: (1) a loan of money or its equivalent; (2) an understanding that the principal is repayable; (3) the exaction of a greater profit than is allowed by law; and (4) an intent (*mens rea*) to violate the law. The determination of whether a given transaction is usurious is a question of fact for the jury. In some jurisdictions courts zealously enforce usury laws, but in most states usury violations are often lightly enforced, if prosecuted at all. Loaning money at high interest is not an unusual feature of capitalism. The law seems to touch only the most extreme

This verbose statute merely makes it easier for federal prosecutors to pursue loansharking. Note the last sentence in the quote, which eliminates (if the judge agrees) much of the need to prove that the debtor was threatened.

Making extortionate extensions of credit

(a) Whoever makes any extortionate extension of credit, or conspires to do so, shall be fined not more than $10,000 or imprisoned not more than 20 years, or both.

(b) In any prosecution under this section, if it is shown that all of the following factors were present in connection with the extension of credit in question, there is prima facie evidence that the extension of credit was extortionate, but this subsection is nonexclusive and in no way limits the effect or applicability of subsection (a):

(1) The repayment of the extension of credit, or the performance of any promise given in consideration thereof, would be unenforceable through civil judicial processes against the debtor

(A) in the jurisdiction within which the debtor, if a natural person, resided or

(B) in every jurisdiction within which the debtor, if other than a natural person, was incorporated or qualified to do business at the time the extension of credit was made.

(2) The extension of credit was made at a rate of interest in excess of an annual rate of 45 per centum calculated according to the actuarial method of allocating payments made on a debt between principal and interest, pursuant to which a payment is applied first to the accumulated interest and the balance is applied to the unpaid principal.

(3) At the time the extension of credit was made, the debtor reasonably believed that either

(A) one or more extensions of credit by the creditor had been collected or attempted to be collected by extortionate means, or the nonrepayment thereof had been punished by extortionate means; or

(B) the creditor had a reputation for the use of extortionate means to collect extensions of credit or to punish the nonrepayment thereof.

(4) Upon the making of the extension of credit, the total of the extensions of credit by the creditor to the debtor then outstanding, including any unpaid interest or similar charges, exceeded $100.

(c) In any prosecution under this section, if evidence has been introduced tending to show the existence of any of the circumstances described in subsection (b) (1) or (b) (2), and direct evidence of the actual belief of the debtor as to the creditor's collection practices is not available, then for the purpose of showing the understanding of the debtor and the creditor at the time the extension of credit was made, the court may in its discretion allow evidence to be introduced tending to show the reputation as to collection practices of the creditor in any community of which the debtor was a member at the time of the extension.

Source: 18 U.S.C. sec 892 (as of 1980).

abuses. Leniency toward economic activity under capitalism pervades much of the law on this subject.

Usury laws are generally evaded. One journal article describes twenty-four methods of circumventing these laws in California.[4] Since the usury rates are not linked to inflation or general market rates of return they often have the economic effect of dampening investment and, perhaps, helping to discourage productivity. Some banking experts contend that unless courts and legislatures treat high interest rates as relative to supply and demand in the money marketplace, the economy will be injured or the laws ignored.[5]

COUNTERFEITING

In a money economy false issuance of banknotes is highly disruptive. However, ours is not strictly a money economy. Documents, including stocks, bonds, and other valuable papers, also have great value. Under common law, counterfeiting was an offense strictly limited to the making of fake money. Statutes now extend counterfeiting to include faking any obligation or security of government. Counterfeiting is an economic crime. Copying works of art, antiques, or other valuable items is not counterfeiting, although passing fakes as the genuine article may also be a crime.

Counterfeiting consists of any forged or spurious imitation of money or things similar to money. Federal law makes it an offense to utter, pass, possess, or sell false money, bonds, or other securities

[4] Note, "A Comprehensive View of California Usury Law," *Southwestern University Law Review* 6 (1974): pp. 166–75.

[5] Geoffrey Giles, "The Effect of Usury Law on the Credit Marketplace," *The Banking Law Journal* 95 (1978): pp. 527–47.

of the United States or of private businesses, foreign bank notes, gold or silver bars, postal money orders, postage stamps, signatures of judges, military or naval discharge certificates, contracts, or public records. Obviously, federal law has sometimes gone beyond monetary items and included other kinds of valuable documents within the ambit of counterfeiting.

States also have counterfeiting statutes, which often resemble federal statutes. No double jeopardy problem is posed by such state statutes since the offenses are theoretically against different sovereign governments.

A counterfeit must be an imitation of an original. It must be sufficiently similar to deceive ordinary people. There must also be a guilty intent to deceive. Some statutes make it a crime merely to possess counterfeit money, as long as there is an intent to pass it.[6] Other statutes make it criminal even to possess counterfeiting instruments or to process paper of the same weight and appearance as the paper used for banknotes.[7]

Counterfeiting was once seen as a grave crime meriting capital punishment. Nowadays it is serious enough to constitute an infamous crime, requiring a grand jury. Punishment for counterfeiting is still rather severe, perhaps because this crime so endangers the structure of the business system. Traditionally, counterfeiters have been skilled artisans commissioned by other criminals, but they are still seen as a menace to the money economy.

[6] Commonwealth v. Price, 10 Gray (Mass.) 472 (1858).

[7] See United States v. Raynor, 302 U.S. 540 (1937).

Note overlap of forgery and counterfeiting.

Forgery or false use of passport

Whoever falsely makes, forges, counterfeits, mutilates, or alters any passport or instrument purporting to be a passport, with intent that the same may be used: or

Whoever willfully and knowingly uses, or attempts to use, or furnishes to another for use any such false, forged, counterfeited, mutilated, or altered passport or instrument purporting to be a passport, or any passport validly issued which has become void by the occurrence of any condition therein prescribed invalidating the same—

Source: 18 U.S.C. sec. 1543 (as of 1980).

FORGERY

Forgery is a crime somewhat similar to counterfeiting because it is an alteration of a document with an intent to defraud. False making of a writing is also forgery. Forgery is now defined by statute in most states, but the statutes merely extend the common law, rather than repealing it.

Under the common law, forgery was regarded as a misdemeanor. Now it is usually treated as a serious crime with consequent stringent punishment. In some states forgery is divided into degrees with different punishments assigned proportionate to the seriousness of the act. Since so many business transactions depend upon pieces of paper, there has been a marked tendency to treat forgery of business documents sternly.

Classic forgery consists of an alteration of a signed document to change the intention of the signer. False signatures are also examples of forgery. Altering receipts with fraudulent intent constitutes forgery. Raising the amount of a check is forgery. Even changing the dates on a document with the intention to deceive or defraud (as on income tax information) is forgery.

Fraudulent intent is the essence of forgery. It is immaterial whether anyone is actually deceived. Forgery takes place at the moment the alteration or faking occurs, even if the intended recipient never gets the document.

Forgery statutes have been extended to cover many kinds of writings, both public and private, including public records, railway tickets, letters of introduction, receipts, and bank deposits. Federal statutes define forgery of a wide variety of documents, also criminalizing counterfeiting of certain documents.[8]

CONSUMER FRAUD

Counterfeiting and forgery frequently involve individuals seeking to bilk businesses. Businesses, however, sometimes attempt to fool customers. To some extent existing larceny statutes may be used by clever prosecutors to pursue this kind of business fraud. But many states have attempted to refine this offense in order to regulate fraudulent business practices. Only 1.21 persons out of 1000 throughout the country have reported themselves as victims of consumer fraud, "a figure very far below what all evidence would indi-

[8] 17 U.S.C. sec. 471 et seq.

cate to be a true rate."[9] Currently, criminal statutes in this area are being developed that require simpler proofs and easier prosecution.

State legislatures are still groping for a viable policy toward consumer protection. Some statutes create civil liability for businesses; others use the sanctions of the criminal law. "Deceptive business practice" is the basis for some criminal legislation, while others treat business fraud as a special type of theft.[10]

In 1977 New York State passed a statute called the Scheme to Defraud Statute.[11] This statute, patterned after the federal mail fraud statute,[12] is the most far-reaching criminal legislation in the

[9] Norman Geis, "Criminal Penalties for Corporate Criminals," *Criminal Law Bulletin* 8 (1973): p. 385.

[10] Tex. Bus. Comm. Code Sec. 1741 et seq.; Texas Penal Code. Arts. 32, 42; Pa. Crimes Code sec. 3927.

[11] N.Y. Penal Law sec. 190.65.

[12] 18 U.S.C. sec. 1341 (1949).

Beyond the wildest dreams of a bank robber.

Wall St. Broker Pleads Guilty in $6 Million Fraud

BY ARNOLD H. LUBASCH

A Wall Street broker pleaded guilty yesterday to charges of defrauding hundreds of investors of $6 million in the sale of London commodity options, commodity pools and gold contracts.

The broker, Steven M. Arabatzis, admitted that his fees and commissions were so high that it was "virtually impossible" for investors to make any money in his ventures. He waived his right to a grand jury indictment and pleaded to fraud charges filed by United States Attorney Robert Fiske Jr. in Manhattan.

Mr. Fiske said he was conducting a continuing investigation into the rapidly growing area of commodity trading.

Audrey Strauss, the prosecutor in charge of the case, explained that Mr. Arabatzis had sold contracts giving customers the right to buy gold at a particular price at the end of a six-month period. She said he also sold participation in commodity pools, each consisting of $50,000 invested by up to 30 people, and offered investment in London commodity options that were "sold to the public with markups of up to 100 percent."

'Reaped Substantial Profits'

"While Arabatzis reaped substantial profits," the charges said, "almost all of the investors lost virtually all of their money."

consumer protection field. Under the New York law it is not necessary to name all victims, nor is the amount of actual dollar loss a significant element. The statute goes beyond the limits of the crime of larceny, and includes responsibility for a reckless disregard for the truth as well as for false representations. So, a seller who is careless or indifferent to the true quality of his or her product or service may be criminally liable even if no monetary loss has been proved, as long as basic business dishonesty is demonstrated.[13] Proving a criminal intent to defraud is much easier under this statute than under the long-standing rules regarding larceny.

Consumer protective civil actions with heavy civil penalties are also effective, particularly when coupled with injunctive relief. But the cost of mounting such suits is high. Criminal actions, especially for misdemeanors, are quicker and cheaper to maintain. Whether

[13] Using federal precedents for mail fraud, such as United States v. Isaacs, 493 F. 2d 1124 (7th Cir., 1974); United States v. George, 477 F. 2d 508 (7th Cir. 1973).

Two companies owned and used by Mr. Arabatzis to sell commodity investments were Fairchild, Arabatzis & Smith Inc. and Astor & Montcalm Inc., both at 63 Wall Street. They have gone out of business.

Mr. Arabatzis had employed a sales force of up to 60 at a time, who often, the charges alleged, used false names in dealing with customers.

Judge Kevin Thomas Duffy is to sentence Mr. Arabatzis on March 30 in Federal District Court in Manhattan. Mr. Arabatzis, who is 43 years old and lives in Manhattan, could face up to five years in prison and a maximum fine of $1,000 on each of four fraud counts.

According to the criminal charges, Mr. Arabatzis conducted his fraudulent operations from April 1977 through October 1978, using large-scale solicitation by telephone and mail directed at out-of-state investors throughout the United States.

"Relying on the aura of a Wall Street address," the charges said, "Arabatzis attempted to create the false impression of an established and reputable commodities brokerage house."

"This facade created by Arabatzis concealed what was in fact no more than a high-pressure telephone sales operation designed to push customers into hasty investments on the basis of misleading information and false impressions," the charges asserted.

Source: The New York Times, February 16, 1979, p. D3.

misrepresentations or misstatements by businesses are intrinsically criminal or not is an issue for legal philosophers. The experience of consumer protection units around the country suggest that criminalization is considered effective in discouraging business fraud.[14]

CRIMINAL ANTITRUST POLICY

Business abuse on a grand scale may take the form of monopoly formation. One company or a handful of companies in an industry can so dominate production, marketing, and consumption patterns that the public at large will be victimized. Monopoly price-fixing is akin to theft in that it coerces people to pay more for goods and services than they need to. Monopolies indirectly take money out of people's pockets.

The federal antitrust laws are geared to resist and sometimes to criminalize price fixing and other forms of monopolistic market control.[15] These laws are also intended to preserve the economic status of smaller producers, manufacturers, and merchants. Benefits to consumers also flow from effective antitrust activity.

The federal Sherman Antitrust Act of 1890 makes a violation a felony punishable by imprisonment not to exceed 3 years and/or a fine of up to one million dollars for a corporation or one hundred thousand dollars for an individual. Civil penalties are also provided.

The U.S. Department of Justice, which oversees the federal antitrust program, pursues certain kinds of cases through criminal actions. Price fixing, boycotts, and division of markets are high-priority items, especially if the department believes there is a specific intent to violate the law.[16]

Cases are often disposed of by consent decrees, by which businesses agree to change their practices. Others result in *nolo contendere* pleas, an admission of guilt that leads to a fine. Many cases are protracted struggles taking years of litigation. Crack criminal lawyers are hired by contesting businesses, consuming much of

[14] See John W. Witt and Dennis S. Avery, "Fraudless Fraud: A Misdemeanor Response to Consumer Protection," *Criminal Justice Journal* 1 (1977): pp. 233-50.

[15] The basic acts are: Sherman Antitrust Act of 1890, 15 U.S.C. sec. 1-7 (1973); Clayton Antitrust Act, 15 U.S.C. sec. 12-27 (1973); Federal Trade Commission Act, 15 U.S.C. sec. 41-51 (1953).

[16] Arthur D. Austin, *Antitrust: Law, Economics, Policy* (New York: Matthew Bender & Co., Inc., 1976).

the energy, time, and resources of the Antitrust Division of the Justice Department.

Manufacturers may not compel retailers to adhere to fixed resale prices of their products.[17] Exclusive franchise systems maintained by manufacturers may also violate the antitrust laws.[18] Business mergers that substantially lessen competition or tend to create a monopoly may be criminal practices.[19]

Federal antitrust laws exempt some groups. Excluded are agricultural cooperatives, labor unions, insurance companies, patents, export cooperatives, defense industries, and all public regulatory bodies. State antitrust laws cover some of these exempted areas, but not regulatory bodies.

INCOME TAX EVASION

Cheating on income tax forms has become almost a national pastime. But tax evasion is a form of deceit that has been criminalized. The loss of revenue to the state and national treasuries caused by tax evasion amounts to billions of dollars annually. How much tax evasion results from deliberate calculation rather than carelessness or ignorance cannot be known, but undoubtedly many well-to-do Americans flirt with the limits of those laws.

Wealthy persons may escape some tax liability by taking advantage of various provisions or loopholes in the tax laws. Capital gains schemes and incorporation devices are usually quite legitimate. Concealing income, hiding assets, and distorting facts to gain tax advantages, however, may be criminal behavior, even if most Americans do not see it that way.

Some estimates indicate that farmers fail to report two out of every three dollars earned. Self-employed workers and professional people alike often receive cash payments that they do not report as income. Some people use expense account monies for private affairs. Deductions from taxable income may also be fraudulent, fictitious, or exaggerated.

Tax evasion presents an opportunity for a dishonest gain that some people cannot resist. Middle-income taxpayers, who enjoy few

[17] United States v. Colgate & Co., 250 U.S. 300 (1919).

[18] United States v. Arnold, Schwin & Co., 388 U.S. 365 (1967).

[19] Brown Shoe Co. v. United States, 370 U.S. 294 (1962).

of the deductions available to the rich, are sorely tempted to cheat. Many citizens file honest returns, but those who do not are taking unfair advantage of those who do. Since only a small percentage of returns are audited, and since indictments for tax fraud are rare (less than 1500 annually), this is a kind of criminal conduct that some people are willing to risk, including even a former United States Commissioner of Internal Revenue, who was convicted and sentenced in 1967 to 5 years in prison for evading taxes on 5 years of income.

Other kinds of tax frauds are also commonly committed. Local and state sales taxes are often uncollected or unreported. Gross business taxes, inventory taxes, and excise taxes on cigarettes, liquor, and fuel are sometimes avoided. Billions of dollars in tax revenues are lost annually because of undetected tax fraud.

PROPERTY FRAUDS (CATCHALL WHITE-COLLAR CRIMES)

Every year people are defrauded of their savings and property by trusting these assets to white-collar thieves. There are several classic schemes for white-collar frauds: investment schemes based on bogus or questionable stocks, bonds, or other securities; Ponzi schemes, where old investors are paid off by new investors until the inevitable collapse of the house of cards takes place; and sales of nearly worthless property to gullible purchasers.

More sophisticated economic exploitation also take place. Bankruptcy frauds to conceal ill-gotten gains or to bilk the general public need the help of skilled lawyers.[20] Frauds by computers, involving unauthorized payouts, are possible when computer operators are corrupt. Violations of banking laws and of securities laws (discussed in another chapter) are also, typically, laced with fraud. Fraudulent use of credit cards is a newer crime. Home improvement frauds, mortgage milking, phony contests, medical frauds, charity frauds, FHA frauds, coupon redemption schemes, and merchandise swindles abound in our complex economic environment. Doubtless most business transactions in our country are quite legitimate, but the criminal law must be constructed in such a way as to discourage the unscrupulous.

In recent years there has been heightened consciousness of

[20] See Edward J. DeFranco, *Anatomy of a Scam: A Case Study of a Planned Bankruptcy by Organized Crime* (Washington: Government Printing Office, 1973).

these types of so-called white-collar crimes. In the past, the criminal justice system may have concentrated upon the poor street offender who commits classic types of offenses. The system may have been more lenient toward upper-class white-collar criminals. It is often difficult, however, to ascertain whether a particular case of economic exploitation actually constitutes a crime.

The problem of definition of white-collar crimes.

Definition of white-collar crime

The term "white-collar crime" is not subject to any one clear definition. Everyone believes he knows what the term means, but when definitions are compared there are usually sharp divergences as to whether one crime or another comes within the definition. It may well be that, as Humpty Dumpty said to Alice, "it means just what I choose it to mean—neither more nor less."

For the purpose of this paper, the term will be defined as *an illegal act or series of illegal acts committed by nonphysical means and by concealment or guile, to obtain money or property, to avoid the payment or loss of money or property, or to obtain business or personal advantage.*

The definition, in that it hinges on the modifying words "an illegal act or series of illegal acts," does not go to the question whether particular activities should be the subject of criminal proscriptions.

It is a definition which differs markedly from that advanced by Edwin H. Sutherland, who said that ". . . white-collar crime may be defined approximately as a crime committed by a person of respectability and high social status in the course of his occupation." Sutherland introduced this definition with the comment that these white-collar crimes are violations of law by persons in the "upper socio-economic class."

Sutherland's definition is far too restrictive. His view provided a rational basis for the economic determinism which was the underlying theme of his analysis, but did not comprehend the many crimes committed outside one's occupation. Ready examples of crimes falling outside one's occupation would be personal and nonbusiness false income tax returns, fraudulent claims for social security benefits, concealing assets in a personal bankruptcy, and use of large-scale buying on credit with no intention or capability to ever pay for purchases. His definition does not take into account crime as a business, such as a planned bankruptcy, or an old fashioned "con game" operated in a business milieu. Though these crimes fall outside Sutherland's definition, they were considered and discussed by him.

Source: Herbert Edelhertz, *The Nature, Impact and Prosecution of White-Collar Crime* (Washington, D.C.: Law Enforcement Assistance Administration, 1970), p. 3. Reprinted by permission.

Guile and deception are the hallmarks of most property frauds. According to one accepted definition, white-collar crime consists of "an illegal act or series of illegal acts committed by nonphysical means and by concealment or guile, to obtain money or property, or to obtain business or personal advantage."[21]

This definition is much better than the original definition by criminologist Edwin H. Sutherland, "white collar crime may be defined approximately as a crime, committed by a person of respectability and high social status in the course of his occupation."[22] The wrongfulness of the activity, not the social status of the offender, should define the crime. Moreover, some white-collar crimes are actually committed by organized criminal elements, who deal on the shadowy fringes of business. In fact, business itself is frequently a victim of white-collar crime.[23]

Experts do not agree on the meaning, scope, and extent of white-collar crime. Some use the term in a largely ideological, class-bound sense; others include a host of familiar crimes as well as newly created administrative crimes. The term itself tends to be confusing. In this section it is used to include a miscellany of frauds. The author believes the category of economic crime to be more appropriate to describe the range of societally disapproved behaviors, and confines the usage of white-collar crimes rather more than is customary.

Much white-collar crime falls in the criminal category known as *false pretences*. This offense consists of an untrue representation of fact used knowingly to obtain the property of another with an intent to defraud. A false representation may consist of words, silence, acts or an impersonation of another. To be convicted of false pretences, an offender must gain title to property and possession as well. Essentially, false pretences is a crime against another's title to property. For this reason, the crime category may not be adequate to deal with modern, sophisticated property frauds.

Under common law it was a crime to obtain the property of another through false weights and measures. But it was not criminal to obtain another's property by talking him or her out of it with

[21] Herbert Edelhertz, *The Nature, Impact and Prosecution of White-Collar Crime* (Washington: Government Printing Office, 1970), p. 3.

[22] Edwin H. Sutherland, *White-Collar Crime* (New York: Dryden Press, 1949), p. 9.

[23] This seems to be the position of the U.S. Department of Justice. See Law Enforcement Assistance Administration, *The Investigation of White-Collar Crime* (Washington: Government Printing Office, 1977), which emphasizes the connections between organized crime and white-collar crime.

false representations. This gap in criminal law policy toward property was partly cured by the passage of statutes. Some statutes have stretched the idea of property fraud to include "anything of value." Under such a statute it is criminal to obtain credit, board, lodging, services, or labor from another by means of false pretences.[24]

EMBEZZLEMENT

Embezzlement is also a statutory offense. Embezzlement statutes are designed to deal with situations in which property or goods are originally obtained lawfully by the offender, and are later taken by him or her. Possession is obtained legally and without felonious intent, so larceny and false pretences are absent. Embezzlement is a crime of betrayed trust. Victims allow the offender to deal with their property, but the offender converts it to personal use.

[24] State v. Snyder, 66 Ind. 203 (1879).

Compare this offense with embezzlement.

Diversion of funds received to obtain or pay for services, labor, materials or equipment

Any person who receives money for the purpose of obtaining or paying for services, labor, materials or equipment and willfully fails to apply such money for such purpose by either willfully failing to complete the improvements for which funds were provided or willfully failing to pay for services, labor, materials or equipment provided incident to such construction, and wrongfully diverts the funds to a use other than that for which the funds were received, shall be guilty of a public offense and punishable by a fine not exceeding five thousand dollars ($5,000), or by imprisonment in the state prison not exceeding five years, or in the county jail not exceeding one year, or by both such fine and such imprisonment if the amount diverted is in excess of ten thousand dollars ($10,000). If the amount diverted is less than ten thousand dollars ($10,000), the person shall be guilty of a misdemeanor. To constitute a diversion within the meaning of this section, the diversion must result in a reduction of the value of the owner's equity in his property or a reduction in the value of the security for the loan which provided such construction funds. (Added by Stats. 1965, c. 1145, p. 2890, § 1.)

Source: California Statutes Annotated sec. 484b.

Embezzlement is a type of theft. Some states have combined embezzlement with larceny and false pretences.[25] The element of trust and of permitting another to handle one's property is a peculiarly economic crime, however. Bank embezzlement by tellers, cashiers, or officers is the typical example. Since the intent to misappropriate property is formed after obtaining it, under most statutes, the social setting seems different than in larceny or false pretences. The decision to treat embezzlers as common thieves may be a sound public policy, but there are factual distinctions that could justify different treatment.

The concept of embezzlement is intended to protect employers from fraudulent taking of money and property by agents, clerks, and other employees who were intrusted with money or property. Embezzlement also covers employers and businesses entrusted with money or property by the general public. It does not cover those who are not in a position of trust, such as parking lot owners who receive a parked car in their lots or furriers who store valuable furs. Embezzlement is, however, often a useful means of discouraging deviant corporate officers who improperly manipulate corporate assets.

[25] California calls the offense "grand theft."

How does this differ from passing bad checks?

Theft of labor

(1) A person is guilty of theft of labor already rendered when, in payment of labor already rendered by another, he intentionally issues or passes a check or similar sight order for the payment of money, knowing that it will not be honored by the drawee.

(2) For purposes of subsection (1), an issuer of a check or similar sight order for the payment of money is presumed to know that the check or order, other than a postdated check or order, would not be paid, if:

(a) The issuer had no account with the drawee at the time the check or order was issued; or

(b) Payment was refused by the drawee for lack of funds, upon presentation within thirty (30) days after the issue, and the issuer failed to make good within ten (10) days after receiving notice of that refusal.

(3) Theft of labor already rendered is a Class A misdemeanor unless the value of the labor rendered is $100 or more, in which case it is a Class D felony. (Enact. Acts 1974, ch. 406, § 125.)

Source: Kentucky Statutes Annotated sec. 514.090.

EMPLOYEE THEFT

Employee theft is an economic crime of ancient vintage. Aristotle wrote about such thefts. In the Bible, the prophet Micah was made a victim of an employee theft by a priest who stole the temple ornaments. In our modern industrial, capitalist system, employee theft has become an important problem for business, a major cost of doing business in America.[26]

From a purely legal standpoint, employee theft may fit into established crime categories of theft or embezzlement. However, the social and economic behaviors involved are different from robbery or most other larcenies. Operationally speaking, employee theft has not been dealt with in a systematic fashion, although the law of theft generally was developed in response to changing economic development.[27]

Recently another definition has been proposed that clarifies the concept of employee theft. Such theft is "the unlawful taking, control, or transfer of an employer's property with the purpose of benefitting the employee or another not entitled to the property."[28] Although this definition is not derived from an existing statute, it may suggest a direction for future criminal legislation, if employee theft is to be spotlighted as a form of social deviance requiring precise policies.

Employees steal for many reasons, not just for gain. They may be frustrated on the job; they may dislike their employer; they may feel isolated from meaningful work. Whatever the psychological motivation, mass industry seems to have produced an epidemic of theft deriving from motives other than personal enrichment alone. Employees take home soap, towels, tools, scrap, parts of machines, furniture, and a lot of other things they may not particularly need. If this is to be treated as socially deviant behavior, there should be some way of dealing with it, but we have no reliable means of correcting such behavior. Criminal law is one approach, but not a sure cure.

[26] See Frederick Taylor, "Employee Thefts: They Rise Fast, Add to Problems of Stores Plagued by Slump," *Wall Street Journal,* April 29, 1958, p. 1. The best professional studies are the collection by Sheryl Leininger, ed., *Internal Theft Investigation and Control* (Los Angeles: Security World, 1975) and National Council on Crime and Delinquency (NCCD), *Workplace Crime: Systems in Conflict* (Hackensack, N.J.: NCCD, 1976).

[27] Jerome Hall, *Theft, Law and Society* (Indianapolis, Ind.: Bobbs-Merrill, 1952).

[28] Dwight H. Merriam, "Employee Theft," *Criminal Justice Abstracts* 9 (1977): pp. 375–376.

No one knows the extent of employee theft. A government survey observed, "perhaps the most difficult business crimes to detect or measure are those of employee theft and shoplifting . . . often it is difficult to separate employee from customer theft."[29] It is generally believed that internal theft exceeds external theft. This would mean that burglary and robbery account for less economic loss than employee theft. But it is far from certain, since most employee thefts are never detected. They are usually only treated as part of inventory shrinkage, which includes spoilage, breakage, honest bookkeeping errors, and shoplifting. The inventory shrinkage that is left unaccounted for is called employee theft.

There are lots of ways for employees to steal. They can get cash kickbacks from customers, overcharge customers and pocket the difference, doctor inventory lists, use company time and facilities (in-

[29] U.S. Small Business Administration, *Crime Against Small Business* (Washington, D.C.: U.S. Government Printing Office, 1969), p. 73.

A twentieth-century crime story.

A Weeping Tonelli Given 3 Years for Embezzling His Union's Funds

BY MAX H. SEIGEL

One of the nation's most powerful labor leaders, Joseph P. Tonelli, was sentenced yesterday to three years in prison for embezzlement of union funds, but the judge invited him to challenge the sentence.

Judge Jack B. Weinstein told the head of the 350,000-member United Paper Workers International Union in Federal District Court in Brooklyn that he would have imposed a lighter sentence, "or no jail at all," had he been guided only by Mr. Tonelli's guilty plea and the probation report.

But the judge said that rulings of the Second Circuit Court of Appeals had constrained him to consider also information that he had received while presiding over the trial of Henry Segal, the union's treasurer, who was indicted on the same charges. That trial is expected to go to the jury today.

Due Process at Issue

Since Mr. Tonelli had no chance to answer any charges against him raised at the Segal trial, Judge Weinstein said, it was possible his right to due process was violated.

"This raises a serious legal question," the judge said, and he expressed the hope that Mr. Tonelli's lawyer, Miles McDonald, would challenge the sentence.

cluding computers or photocopy machines) for private businesses, or just take things away in their pockets. In one ingenious theft at a Buffalo foundry, employees stole 129,000 pounds of lead by recasting it to fit their bodies.

Employee theft can be reduced by more careful applicant screening. Plainly, people with formal records of theft should not be placed in tempting situations. Polygraph tests are sometimes used, but many employees regard them as an intrusion. Mechanical devices such as magnetic detectors and videocameras can help, too. Improvement of job satisfaction is probably a better, more long-lasting approach. Studies do show that there is a close connection between job dissatisfaction and employee theft.[30]

Criminal law itself has not had much impact on dampening

[30] Thomas W. Mangione and Robert P. Quinn, "Job Satisfaction, Counterproductive Behavior, and Drug Use at Work," *Journal of Applied Psychology* 60 (1975): pp. 114-116.

To allow time for a challenge, Judge Weinstein delayed execution of the sentence for 120 days.

In addition to the three-year prison term, Judge Weinstein also imposed a $15,000 fine and three years of probation, dependent upon reimbursement to the union of $32,500. That sum is the amount involved in the count of the indictment to which Mr. Tonelli pleaded guilty.

"People in high office have to show high morality," Judge Weinstein said in sentencing Mr. Tonelli.

The labor leader burst into tears, and his lawyer said: "The President of the United States got an absolute pardon. To put this man in jail makes a mockery of justice."

"But Mr. Nixon was not before me," the judge replied.

Mr. Tonelli now is expected to face a civil trial for restitution of more of the $360,000 he was accused of embezzling from the union.

In praising the sentence, Thomas P. Puccio, head of the Organized Crime Strike Force in Brooklyn, said his office considered prosecution of labor racketeering important.

Mr. Tonelli, former chairman of the New York State Racing Commission, had been appointed to various agencies by three Presidents. He also was the representative of the United States at the 1975 meeting of the International Labor Organization in Geneva. His interests were varied enough to have earned him a knighthood from Pope Paul VI and the first Prime Minister's Medal awarded to an American by the State of Israel.

Source: The New York Times, November 21, 1978, p. B2.

employee theft. This may mean that better criminal laws dealing with the subject could be drafted, or it may mean that problems of apprehension and prosecution are too sensitive and complex to permit the criminal justice system to deal effectively with employee theft. The rate of prosecution of apprehended employee thieves is very low, probably well under 5 percent. Apparently most employee thieves "steal in the assurance that if caught they will merely be fined, not prosecuted."[31]

Companies fear bad publicity flowing from employee theft prosecutions. They also fear the risk of suits for libel, malicious prosecution, and false arrest. For some companies, the costs of criminal prosecution may be too high in terms of time, money, and effort. This kind of business perspective on employee theft means that such crimes, even when detected, tend to go unreported, and offenders move on to other jobs where they repeat such behavior. Unless appropriate legislation requires some sort of business prosecution or at least reporting of employee theft, it is difficult to see how criminal law can be helpful. At the least, other employers should have information about serious crimes committed by job applicants. Such a law should, to some extent, shield businesses from employee countersuits, while also protecting employees' reputations from careless accusations.

Employee theft may be either white-collar or blue-collar crime. It knows no class distinctions. It is a disease of industrial society. Soviet Russia also suffers from widespread employee thefts, although such thefts are considered offenses against the state. In all probability, new laws will be developed to deal with this social problem, even though laws cannot cure it. Attitudes about work must change, since laws can affect only calculations of the risk of punishment, not attitudes.

SUMMARY

Crimes of the marketplace abound in America. The perpetrators of these crimes may be private individuals or great corporations. Counterfeiting and forgery, while old crimes, have taken new forms in the age of the computer, the duplicating machine, and the credit card. Recently, new economic crimes have been created in

[31] David McClintick, "An Inside Job: More Workers Steal and Get Away with It," *Wall Street Journal,* February 5, 1970, p. 1.

order to create new responsibilities for the conduct of the marketplace. Consumer protection legislation has become a popular policy, supplementing criminal antitrust laws and other regulatory policies of federal government. There is a tendency to treat economic crimes as crimes of higher social status, to be differentiated from the more feared crimes of violence and stealth. The losses created by economic crimes are probably far greater than those of violence or stealth, but public attitudes toward economic crimes are far less fearful.

6

ADMINISTRATIVE CRIMES

Bureaucracy is the source of many rules and regulations that have the effect of law. In modern America virtually every citizen has encountered these rules and regulations, whether in filing income tax forms and business reports, claiming welfare benefits, or applying for a driver's license. Criminal sanctions are frequently attached to the violation of bureaucratically created law and, as the bureaucracy continues to expand, so the scope of what can be called *administrative crimes* also expands.

The American federal bureaucracy consists of over three million people, or about 3.5 percent of the entire civilian work force. This vast apparatus is a central feature of our highly regulated lives. The first great spurt in bureaucratic growth occurred at the end of the nineteenth century in response to popular demands for regulation of business corporations, especially the railroad industry. The Interstate Commerce Act of 1887 created the first national independent regulatory commission, the Interstate Commerce Commission, which has served as a model for such later agencies as the Federal Trade Commission (1915), the Federal Tariff Commission (1920), the Securities and Exchange Commission (1934), the National Labor Relations Board (1935), the Federal Communications Commission (1935), the Civil Aeronautics Board (1938), and many similar regulatory bodies, each supported by available criminal

Note the criminal powers assigned to the Federal Consumer Products Safety Commission

(b) The Commission shall also have the power—

(7) to—

(A) initiate, prosecute, defend, or appeal (other than to the Supreme Court of the United States), through its own legal representative and in the name of the Commission, any civil action if the Commission makes a written request to the Attorney General for representation in such civil action and the Attorney General does not within the 45-day period beginning on the date such request was made notify the Commission in writing that the Attorney General will represent the Commission in such civil action, and

(B) initiate, prosecute, or appeal, through its own legal representative, with the concurrence of the Attorney General or through the Attorney General, any criminal action,

sanctions against noncompliance with its administrative requirements. The Sherman Act of 1890 created modern antitrust policy and also led to an expansion of the federal bureaucracy. Similarly, every surge of national government activity has swelled the bureaucracy, a trend repeated by state governments in the past several decades. Together with these trends has come a great expansion of administratively defined crimes.

Administrative agencies usually have extensive powers of enforcement and control that go well beyond the authority found in ordinary criminal or civil courts. These agencies may act against individuals or groups. They may act retrospectively (against deeds committed in the past) or prospectively (against deeds they seek to prevent from being committed in the future). The source of the administrative sanction may be found in statutes or in the rules of the agency itself. Adjudication of the sanction may take place inside the agency, outside the agency, or, if Congress so desires, in the regular courts. However, criminal sanctions can be applied only through the courts, and they must be brought by the Justice Department on behalf of the agency involved.

Apart from criminal sanctions, those who run afoul of administrative agencies may suffer other types of penalties. Fines or other monetary penalties may be imposed; licenses may be revoked, sus-

---

for the purpose of enforcing the laws subject to its jurisdiction;

(8) to lease buildings or parts of buildings in the District of Columbia, without regard to the Act of March 3, 1877 (section 34 of Title 40), for the use of the Commission; and

(9) to delegate any of its functions or powers, other than the power to issue subpenas under paragraph (3), to any officer or employee of the Commission.

Noncompliance with subpena or Commission order; contempt

(c) Any United States district court within the jurisdiction of which any inquiry is carried on, may, upon petition by the Commission (subject to subsection (b) (7) of this section) or by the Attorney General, in case of refusal to obey a subpena or order of the Commission issued under subsection (b) of this section, issue an order requiring compliance therewith; and any failure to obey the order of the court may be punished by the court as a contempt thereof.

Source: 15 U.S.C. sec. 2076 (as of 1980).

pended, or altered; cease-and-desist orders may be issued that, if violated, can lead to contempt of court citations; goods may be confiscated or destroyed; benefits may be withheld until orders are complied with; and injunctions may be obtained through the courts. Criminal sanctions, which include the threat of imprisonment, are usually viewed as a last resort for administrative agencies. Only criminal sanctions require the formality of a full, due process, jury trial.

Administrative criminality exists by virtue of delegated powers derived from Congress or a state legislature. Technically, all criminality must be defined by legislatures, so administrative agencies cannot enact criminal statutes. Legislatures, however, have attached criminal sanctions to the violation of administrative rules and, in addition, sometimes subdelegated the power to define criminal offenses. Since subdelegation to administrative agencies is a familiar pattern in modern America, this kind of subdelegation has rarely been opposed, yet it raises real questions of separation of powers by the mixture of the legislative and executive functions. Nonetheless, the blending of legislative, executive, and judicial functions within the same bureaucratic agency has long since been accomplished. As a consequence, administratively defined crimes continue to expand in number with little resistance from the courts or the public. Administrative agencies have come to constitute an unacknowledged fourth branch of government, possessing the power to formulate, if not to adjudicate, criminal offenses. We must understand that administrative crimes are offenses only by virtue of the policies of bureaucracies or of legislatures supporting them. Often the acts involved lack the sense of wrongfulness that attaches to most other types of crime. Nonetheless the criminalizing of acts for bureaucratic purposes or through bureaucratic means still has exactly the same consequences as any other crime. Administrative crimes are crimes in the fullest sense of the word.

State administrative criminalization is even more prevalent than federal. One Texas agency provides a penal offense for the importation of boll weevils into that state. Overcriminalization of administrative crimes is a feature of state law only rarely noted.

The subject of administrative criminalization has been virtually unexplored in America. Yet state and federal statutes contain numerous proscriptions that are tacked on to essentially administrative measures. The use of the criminal sanction to obtain compliance with administrative policies is an everyday occurrence, but the social purposes served by defining unwanted behavior as criminally deviant have not been explored. In a rush to manage a range of behaviors not socially perceived as dangerous, certain behaviors have been labeled as criminal as a means of securing effective compliance with administrative policies. On the other hand, those businesses and individuals that help to shorten individual life spans by careless pollution of our environment may, in fact, cause more social harm than the burglar and the embezzler. Criminal law lacks a conceptual framework to explain and justify the absorption of administrative offenses. Furthermore, the decriminalization of a variety of behaviors such as alcoholism and drug addiction seems to run counter to the tide of new administrative criminalization.

It would be impossible to mention all or even most administratively defined crimes within the compass of a chapter. Their diversity and scope is so great that a mere survey of highlights is possible. Nowhere in the major studies of administrative law is any such survey available. The subject has been generally neglected by scholars of administrative law.[1] A glance at the federal law reveals

[1] The recent work of leading scholar Kenneth Culp Davis, *Administrative Law of The Seventies* (Rochester, N.Y.: Lawyer's Cooperative Publishing Co., 1976), makes no mention of the subject, although it is referred to briefly in his famous treatise.

Two techniques for controlling air pollution.

Notwithstanding any other provision of this chapter the director upon receipt of evidence that a particular pollution source or combination of sources is presenting an imminent and substantial endangerment to the health of persons, may request the attorney general to bring suit on behalf of the department in the appropriate superior court to immediately enjoin any contributor to the alleged pollution to stop the emission of contaminants causing such pollution or to take such other action as may be necessary. . . .

Misdemeanor; penalty

Any person who violates any provision of this article or any rule or regulation adopted pursuant to this article or any effective order of abatement issued pursuant to this article is guilty of a misdemeanor punishable by imposition of a fine of not less than fifty dollars or more than one thousand dollars per day for each day the violation continues. Each day of violation shall constitute a separate offense.

Source: Arizona Revised Statutes Annotated sec. 36-1719, sec. 36-1720.

---

a vast array of such offenses that make no particular sense except as support mechanisms for administrative policies. One typical administrative decision criminalizes the failure to file, with the Secretary of the Treasury, certain information regarding the selling, shipping, or distribution of 60,000 or more cigarettes. Failure to record the name, address, destination, vehicle license number, driver's license number, and signature of the recipient of the cigarettes would subject the violator to a fine of up to $100,000 and imprisonment up to 5 years.[2] Clearly, the administrative purpose is to limit the sale of untaxed cigarettes and also to make information available to state taxing authorities. The terrifying effect of these potential sanctions may be formidable, but how often are they invoked? Should the criminal process be burdened with such issues? This statute proscribes "knowing" violations. Is that the same as *mens rea*? Is it criminal intent? Who knows? At least contraband cigarettes are understandable items for possible criminalization. As we shall see, less tangible items, acts, and omissions are also subjects of administrative criminalization.

Properly conceived, the decision by a public prosecutor to institute a criminal proceeding is itself an act of administrative discretion. When a public prosecutor selects among available sanctions, decides to press charges, chooses a forum, and settles (or plea-bargains) a case, he or she performs many of the functions usually carried out by other bureaucrats. The discretion available to the prosecutor is as great as most bureaucrats have.[3] The public prosecutor, however, has more power than bureaucrats in that he/she has a virtual monopoly on the public prosecution of crime. When an act is defined as a crime, even though the definition essentially supports the activities of a bureaucratic agency, that agency may not institute criminal charges. For the federal government, only the Justice Department and the United States Attorney General may institute criminal charges. This funneling of the prosecution of administrative crimes through the public prosecutor means that the American administrator never carries through a criminal prosecution.[4] He or she merely recommends it. In effect, the administrator's function resembles the police officer's handling of ordinary crimes.

Administrative criminalizations test the limits of the fuzzy Lat-

[2] 18 U.S.C. sec. 2343 and 18 U.S.C. sec. 2344.

[3] See Kenneth Culp Davis, *Discretionary Justice* (Baton Rouge, La.: Louisiana State University Press, 1969), pp. 162–207.

[4] In England, however, many administrative agencies are empowered to institute their own criminal actions. The same is true in many other European nations.

in phrase *mens rea*. The mental element in crime—the intention to do a wrongful deed—is largely absent from administratively defined crimes, in the sense that a wrongdoer may simply be deviating from a particular list of administratively prescribed acts without meaning to cause harm.[5] Nonetheless, the culpability involved stems from the legislative determination to assist the bureaucracy in carrying on its tasks. Since legislatures have tended to delegate ever larger areas of policymaking to bureaucrats, there has been a great willingness to accompany this delegation with criminal sanctions, simply because that is an easy and even habitual way to regulate unwanted conduct.

Legislators sometimes forget that administrators have an extremely wide range of available sanctions. Indeed, the great advantage of the administrative process as a compliance mechanism is that inventive methods of changing and regulating behavior have been created, other than the fines or imprisonment known to the criminal law. Techniques such as assessment orders, penalty orders, confinement orders, deportation orders, cease and desist orders, liquidation, receivership, certification, licensing, permits, remission of penalties, quarantine, and a host of others have been devised by administrative agencies under their legislatively delegated authority.[6] Why, then, should administrative agencies so frequently rely upon criminal law?

Sometimes criminal sanctions seem the most effective deterrent to regulate unwanted behavior. Congress may permit an adminis-

[5] The most intelligent examination of these issues in many years is found in George P. Fletcher's *Rethinking Criminal Law* (Boston: Little, Brown & Co., 1978), pp. 395-408. Unfortunately Fletcher does not delve into the rationale for administrative crimes. A pity.

[6] See Dalmas H. Nelson, *Administrative Agencies of the U.S.A.* (Detroit: Wayne State University Press, 1964).

Many administrative crimes are linked to licensing.

Penalty for unlicensed operation of child welfare agency

Any child welfare agency that shall operate without a license issued by the Division for Children and Youth shall be guilty of a misdemeanor and shall be fined not less than $50 nor more than $200 for each such offense. Each day of operation without a license shall constitute a separate offense.

Source: Code of Georgia Annotated sec. 99-9902.

trative agency to formulate its own regulations and give those regulations the force of criminal law; for example, Congress has delegated to the Interstate Commerce Commission the authority to "formulate regulations for the safe transportation within the United States of explosives and other dangerous articles including radioactive materials."[7] Violation of these regulations may result in a fine of not more than $1,000 or up to 1 year's imprisonment. This legislation has been held to be valid delegation of congressional power,[8] even though it permits the commission to define criminal behavior by means of its regulations (or those of the Department of Transportation).

Courts have held that Congress is wholly competent to make the violation of an agency's rules and regulations a crime.[9] Perhaps the transportation of dangerous explosives should be criminalized, but it seems more sensible to seize dangerously transported goods than to criminalize their shipment. The best way to deal with the danger is to strike at its source—the explosives themselves. Seizure is a well-understood administrative practice that safeguards the public while it impinges on careless business practices. Is it likely that officers of a trucking company will be jailed for a violation of an

[7] 18 U.S.C. sec. 834 (a).

[8] United States v. Boyce Lines, 90 F. Supp. 996 (D.C. N.J. 1950). The regulations also apply to wholly intrastate shipments by interstate carriers. United States v. Oilfields Trucking Co., 549 F. 2d 646 (C.A. Cal., 1977). Actually, much of this power to issue such criminalizing regulations has been transferred from the Interstate Commerce Commission to the Department of Transportation, but the same principles apply.

[9] United States v. A.&P. Trucking Corp., 113 F. Supp. 549 (D.C. N.J., 1953).

The Supreme Court's view of administrative crimes.

From the beginning of the Government various acts have been passed conferring upon executive officers power to make rules and regulations—not for the government of their departments, but for administering the laws which did govern. None of these statutes could confer legislative power. But when Congress had legislated and indicated its will, it could give to those who were to act under such general provisions "power to fill up the details" by the establishment of administrative rules and regulations, the violation of which could be punished by fine or imprisonment fixed by Congress, or by penalties fixed by Congress or measured by the injury done.

Source: United States v. Grimaud, 220 U.S. 506, 517 (1910).

agency's regulations? Is a fine an effective deterrent if its cost is simply passed on the consumer? In spite of these policy objections, Congress and the state legislatures persist in creating administratively defined crimes, of which some are needed but many are useless.[10]

FISH AND GAME

Among the earliest uses of criminal law to enforce administrative regulations are the crime definitions intended to secure the enforcement of restrictions on the taking of fish and game. Doubtless, state legislatures can pass statutes that criminalize times and methods of hunting and fishing. Federal law can criminalize hunting, fishing, and trapping on federal lands. In this area, however, there has been substantial delegation of legislative power.

Federal law prohibits hunting, trapping, or capture of any fish or wild animal in violation of "rules and regulations promulgated by authority of law."[11] The transportation of wildlife taken in violation of state, national, or foreign laws is also penalized. This statute supports state as well as federal regulations, and makes such violation a matter of the federal criminal law, employing the interstate commerce power on behalf of state fish and game regulations.[12] Both commercial and noncommercial activity is covered. In effect this federal law incorporates many state fish and game regulations into the federal criminal law.

One of the troubling features of this criminalization of administrative processes is the lack of safeguards available to defendants. In the states, jurisdiction over prosecution for violations of fish and game regulations is left to justices of the peace or other lower-level magistrates. These relatively minor judges are able to reach swift, but not necessarily exact, decisions. Sometimes summary proceedings are used, and defendants are not entitled to a jury trial. The wisdom of this delegation of legislative power is dubious, especially since forfeitures, seizures, and license revocation may be more effective, and fairer, means of protecting wildlife.

[10] The only useful theoretical work on sanctions in the law is Richard Arens and Harold D. Lasswell, *In Defense of Public Order* (New York: Columbia University Press, 1961).

[11] 18 U.S.C. sec. 41.

[12] 18 U.S.C. sec. 43.

CONCEALMENT OR MUTILATION OF RECORDS AND REPORTS

A more appropriate definition of administratively derived crime concerns the concealment, removal, or mutilation of records, papers, or any documents filed with public officials. Since sound administration depends upon reliable records, the incrimination of tampering with those records is a necessary use of criminal sanctions.[13] Similarly, the neglect of a public officer to make required reports or keep required records also impedes good administration, and criminal sanctions may well be necessary.[14]

The falsification of important documents may be even more of a public danger. False entries, especially in the handling of moneys or securities, may severely impair the operation of government. Federal law makes federal employees subject to criminal sanctions for such false entries.[15] The law of criminal fraud could accomplish some of these same ends. In many instances falsification of government documents may amount to destruction of federal property, a separate and distinct offense.

For reasons of economic fairness the disclosure of records or information by certain public figures is also criminalized. These crime definitions are based upon a public policy need to conceal or withhold information on delicate questions. The offense consists in revealing information to persons other than those specifically authorized by statute. Thus, bank examiners should not disclose "names of borrowers or collateral for loans" to persons other than those few authorized to know.[16] The same is true for farm credit examiners[17] and certain other credit examiners.[18]

TAX CRIMES

Probably the most extensive area of administrative criminalization is in tax law enforcement. Criminal sanctions, or the threat of them, seem to encourage compliance with the complex requirements

[13] 18 U.S.C. sec. 2071.

[14] 18 U.S.C. sec. 2075.

[15] 18 U.S.C. sec. 2073.

[16] 18 U.S.C. sec. 1906.

[17] 18 U.S.C. sec. 1907.

[18] 18 U.S.C. sec. 1908.

of federal statutes and IRS regulations. The Internal Revenue Code is replete with criminal penalties for tax evasion, failures to report, failures to supply information, false statements, and failure to pay a tax. Interference with tax collection or administration is also penalized. The taxes involved include far more than the dreaded personal income tax; taxes on liquor, tobacco, filled cheese, machine guns, white phosphorous matches, wagering, and many other types of taxes must be paid at the risk of criminal penalties. Evidently many of these tax laws are not purely for the purpose of raising revenue, but are intended to discourage certain kinds of undesired practices. Nonetheless, the criminal law is used to strengthen administrative efficiency in tax collection.

A taxpayer is liable to the federal government in the same way a debtor is responsible for the payment of an obligation. Federal tax collection of the debts owed by taxpayers has been placed in the hands of the Internal Revenue Service. The methods of tax collection are purely administrative. The IRS may use such collection remedies as liens upon taxpayers' property, seizure and sale of property, and direct suits for the collection of taxes due. Criminal sanctions are also available, however, and invocation of civil sanctions does not exclude resort to criminal sanctions.[19]

The more important criminal penalties for tax law violation are found in the Internal Revenue Code itself, but they may be supplemented by other federal criminal statutes. Criminal penalties for tax law violations include fine and imprisonment. These violations may be classified as either misdemeanors or felonies, as with other crimes. However, a breach of a Treasury regulation is not criminal unless Congress makes it so.[20] Congress may criminalize any act that hinders tax collection, and any step in a transaction that leads to the hampering of tax collection may be penalized as well.

The major tax crimes are mainly attempts to evade or defeat a tax.[21] These criminalizations have been referred to as the climax of a variety of sanctions imposed by Congress to ensure the payment of taxes.[22] They are the gravest of tax offenses. *Willfulness* is the essential element of the offense, but the word is not easily defined. Apparently a willful attempt to evade a tax is not accidental or

[19] See Paul P. Lipton, "The Relationship Between The Civil and Criminal Penalties for Tax Frauds," *University of Illinois Law Forum* (1968), pp. 527-40.

[20] O'Brien v. United States, 51 F. 2d 193 (7th Cir., 1931).

[21] 26 U.S.C. sec. 7201.

[22] Spies v. United States, 317 U.S. 492 (1943).

inadvertent, nor is it based upon a genuine misunderstanding.[23] Reliance upon the advice of an attorney, accountant, or tax expert is a defense against a charge of attempting to evade an income tax.[24] In addition to willfulness, the government must also prove that there is a tax deficiency and/or that there has been some affirmative wrongful act by the defendant.

Congress has separately penalized the offense of willfully failing to make a tax return. The evasion of a tax and the failure to pay the tax are separate offenses in the Internal Revenue Code and may be charged separately, if appropriate to the facts.[25] A defendant might also be charged with perjury or false swearing as well as fraudulent filing. Despite the similarity of the acts involved, the courts have not invoked the double jeopardy clause to limit multiple

[23] United States v. Peterson, 338 F. 2d 595 (7th Cir., 1964).

[24] Lurding v. United States, 179 F. 2d 419 (6th Cir., 1950).

[25] Reynolds v. United States, 288 F. 2d 78 (5th Cir., 1961); Spies v. United States, 317 U.S. 492 (1943).

Converting a state tax offense into a federal crime.

§ 2343. Recordkeeping and inspection

(a) Any person who ships, sells, or distributes any quantity of cigarettes in excess of 60,000 in a single transaction shall maintain such information about the shipment, receipt, sale, and distribution of cigarettes as the Secretary may prescribe by rule or regulation. The Secretary may require such person to keep only—

(1) the name, address, destination (including street address), vehicle license number, driver's license number, signature of the person receiving such cigarettes, and the name of the purchaser;

(2) a declaration of the specific purpose of the receipt (personal use, resale, or delivery to another); and

(3) a declaration of the name and address of the recipient's principal in all cases when the recipient is acting as an agent.

Such information shall be contained on business records kept in the normal course of business. Nothing contained herein shall authorize the Secretary to require reporting under this section.

(b) Upon the consent of any person who ships, sells, or distributes any quantity of cigarettes in excess of 60,000 in a single transaction, or pursuant to a duly issued search warrant, the Secretary may enter the premises (including

criminal prosecutions.[26] Nor have the courts been able to provide a limiting definition of the meaning of an attempt to evade or defeat a tax.[27]

The Internal Revenue Code criminalizes the failure of a person to collect a tax as well as the failure to pay it. Business owners required to withhold taxes from employee wages must comply with the law or risk criminal penalties. Failure to collect such taxes and to account for them is a felony.[28] So income taxes, social security taxes, and similar taxes must be withheld. Excise taxes on admissions must be collected and paid over. Transportation, telephone, and safe-deposit taxes must be collected.[29] The federal excise tax on

[26] O'Brien v. United States, 51 F. 2d 193 (7th Cir., 1931), cert. denied 284 U.S. 673 (1931).

[27] See United States v. Bridell, 180 F. Supp. 268 (D.C. N.D. Ill., 1960) in which the court virtually abandons the attempt.

[28] 26 U.S.C. sec. 7202.

[29] Violation is a misdemeanor: 26 U.S.C. sec. 7215.

---

places of storage) of such person for the purpose of inspecting any records or information required to be maintained by such person under this chapter, and any cigarettes kept or stored by such person at such premises.
Added Pub. L. 95-575, § 1, Nov. 2, 1978, 92 Stat. 2464.

§ 2344. Penalties

(a) Whoever knowingly violates section 2342(a) of this title shall be fined not more than $100,000 or imprisoned not more than five years, or both.

(b) Whoever knowingly violates any rule or regulation promulgated under section 2343(a) or 2346 of this title or violates section 2342(b) of this title shall be fined not more than $5,000 or imprisoned not more than three years, or both.

(c) Any contraband cigarettes involved in any violation of the provisions of this chapter shall be subject to seizure and forfeiture, and all provisions of the Internal Revenue Code of 1954 relating to the seizure, forfeiture, and disposition of firearms, as defined in section 5845(a) of such Code, shall, so far as applicable, extend to seizures and forfeitures under the provisions of this chapter.
Added Pub. L. 95-575, § 1, Nov. 2, 1978, 92 Stat. 2464.

Source: 18 U.S.C. secs. 2343, 2344 (as of 1980).

wages must be not only collected but paid as well, a familiar trap for gamblers and bookies.

Interference with tax collection or administration is a crime. Force and the threat of force is an element of the crime, but corruption may replace the force requirement.[30] Persons who neglect to respond to a summons from the Internal Revenue Service are also committing a criminal offense because of their impeding the tax collection process. Books or papers must be produced before a hearing officer when a taxpayer is duly summoned, but the taxpayer may defend him- or herself from producing material on the ground that it is being sought for the improper purpose of using it in a criminal prosecution. Thus there is a thin line between an IRS hearing incident to tax collection and a hunting expedition for an eventual criminal prosecution.

There are many more tax crimes scattered through the Internal Revenue Code and the general criminal statutes. Many of them deal with specific taxes, such as the tax on gasoline and lubricating oil. The most important of these specific taxes are those on liquor, wines, and beer. Numerous criminal prosecutions are instituted for infractions of these laws, as well as for the taxes on tobacco, cigars, and cigarettes. In effect these kinds of taxes create a general purpose version of federal criminal law under the taxing process of Congress. They may be necessary to supplement state criminal law, or they may be perceived as an unneeded duplication of many state criminal laws.

BUSINESS REGULATIONS AND CRIMES

American business is surrounded by a complex web of federal and state laws intended to eliminate monopolies, restraint of trade, and unfair trade practices. Although ours is a capitalist economy, many acts of businesses have been criminalized, even when those acts enrich corporate treasuries and stockholders, rather than selfish business executives. Antitrust laws, both state and federal, contain criminal provisions. So do price discrimination laws, the FTC act, state unfair trade practice laws, and the laws concerning packaging, labeling, and advertising. Recently, consumer protection legislation has also incorporated criminal provisions. Since it is impossible to review all these laws in a few pages, the highlights of these administratively defined crimes will be examined here.

The passage of the federal Sherman Antitrust Act of 1890

[30] 26 U.S.C. sec. 7212.

marked the beginning of a still-unfolding process of the administrative correction of business abuses. In 1890 the fear of great monopolies was widespread. Congress passed the act in response to popular pressures against further concentration of business, making illegal "every contract, combination in the form of trust or otherwise, or conspiracy in restraint of trade. . . ." The meaning of this provision is still unclear, although its purpose is manifest. The Sherman Act is supposed to be a charter of economic liberty aimed at the preservation of free and unfettered business competition.[31] The pursuit of this policy has been inconsistent, as subsequent statutes and court decisions demonstrate.

Criminal sanctions are imposed for violations of the Sherman Act[32] and the subsequent Wilson Act,[33] Clayton Act,[34] and Robinson-Patman Act.[35] Criminal prosecutions must be brought by the Justice Department in the district where the crime was committed. Criminal conspiracy prosecutions, which are the most common type, may be initated in any district where the conspiracy was formed or carried out.

Every violation of the antitrust laws is a crime punishable by imprisonment for up to 1 year and a fine up to one million dollars, if the defendant is a corporation. The fine is $100,000 if a natural person is a defendant. Criminal proceedings are likely to be brought only when aggressively predatory conduct is evident[36] or when the many available administrative remedies do not work. As a result criminal sanctions are rarely sought. Experts have proposed that a system that could deny defendants any economic gains from their monopolistic practices would be a more effective deterrent than criminal sanctions.[37]

The Federal Trade Commission, one of the oldest federal regulatory agencies, is charged with regulating many business abuses, such as misbranding, mislabeling, unfair competition, and monopolistic practices in general. The FTC also has the power to investigate any business or corporation (other than banks or in-

[31] Northern Pacific Railroad Co. v. United States, 356 U.S. 1 (1958).

[32] 15 U.S.C. sec. 1-3.

[33] 15 U.S.C. sec. 8.

[34] 15 U.S.C. sec. 20.

[35] 15 U.S.C. sec. 13a.

[36] See United States v. American Tobacco Company, 221 U.S. 106 (1911).

[37] See Richard Posner, *Anti-Trust Law: An Economic Analysis* (Chicago: University of Chicago Press, 1976) and Richard Posner, *Economic Analysis of Law* (Boston: Little, Brown & Co., 1972).

terstate carriers) that engages in commerce. In spite of its broad-ranging authority the FTC has no criminal powers, unless its investigatory powers are flouted and its subpoenas ignored, in which cases it may obtain judicial support for its investigations by invoking criminal sanctions. Those who conceal, falsify, mutilate, or fail to keep business records for the use of the FTC are subject to fine and imprisonment.[38] For the most part, though, the FTC uses consent orders and other forms of voluntary compliance. Even activity that violates the FTC Act is subject not to a criminal sanction but to an administrative remedy, the cease and desist order.[39]

Some business activities are outside the jurisdiction of the FTC or the ICC, and these, for various reasons, are subject to criminal sanctions. For example, according to the Cigarette Labeling and Advertising Act, it is unlawful not to print on cigarette packages the legend, "Caution: Cigarette Smoking May be Hazardous to Your Health." Printing any other statement on a package regarding the relationship between safety and health is a misdemeanor punishable by a fine up to $10,000.[40]

Jewelry is also not regulated by the FTC. Falsely labeled or imprinted jewelry falls under the Jeweler's Hall-Mark Acts. Indicat-

[38] 15 U.S.C. sec. 50.

[39] 15 U.S.C. sec. 45 (6).

[40] 15 U.S.C. sec. 335.

Broad-based administrative crimes have been created out of traffic violations.

Penalties

Any person, firm or corporation failing to comply with any order or regulation made pursuant to any provision of this chapter shall be fined not more than one hundred dollars or imprisoned not more than thirty days or both, and shall be subject to the provisions of section 14-111. Any person, firm or corporation failing to comply with any traffic control signal, sign, marking or other device placed and maintained upon the highway, pursuant to any provision of this chapter, by the state traffic commission or the traffic authority of any city, town or borough shall be fined not more than fifty dollars, if no other penalty is provided by law.

Source: Connecticut General Statutes Annotated sec. 14-314.

ing that jewelry contains more silver or gold than it actually does is a criminal offense.[41]

A search through the statute books will disclose many similar examples of the criminalization of business activity which seem to be based upon accident rather than policy. These statutes seem to fall into a category of miscellaneous offenses, rather than being subject to the usual administrative remedies. They seem to be the result of effective interest group activity, not clearly designed administrative policy.

In the consumer protection area, criminal sanctions have been used more consciously and consistently. Violations of the regulations of the Department of Health and Welfare concerning hazardous substances are subject to fine and imprisonment.[42] Cigarette advertising is subject to DHW regulations and FTC reports. Violations of cigarette advertising regulations are subject to criminal penalties.[43] Flammable fabrics are regulated by the Department of Commerce, and to a limited extent by the FTC. Violators of the Flammable Fabrics Act are subject to fine and imprisonment.[44] However, in less dangerous areas of consumer protection, criminal sanctions are not attached to violations of administrative regulations. There are no criminal sanctions in support of the truth-in-lending law or the consumer credit legislation. Although vehicle safety regulations would seem closely related to public safety, justifying the use of criminal sanctions, there are none.[45] Automobile safety regulations are enforced by means of civil actions only.[46] An enforcement policy may be expedient but not wise.

THE GROWTH OF ADMINISTRATIVE CRIME

The power to set policy in criminal law rests primarily with Congress and the state legislatures, or so the classic criminal law theorists believed. The growth of administrative criminalization has taken place almost unnoticed and unremarked. Courts have not

[41] 15 U.S.C. secs. 293, 298.

[42] 15 U.S.C. sec. 1264.

[43] 15 U.S.C. sec. 1338.

[44] 15 U.S.C. sec. 1196.

[45] The improper sale of regrooved tires is subject merely to civil sanctions. 15 U.S.C. sec. 1424.

[46] 15 U.S.C. 1415. 88 stat. 1474 (1974).

strongly resisted the trend. The New York state legislature delegated to that state's alcoholic beverage control board the power to make rules that make violations of the board's regulations a misdemeanor, and New York state courts upheld the constitutionality of this broad concession of power to make criminal law.[47] Only a few state courts have been bold enough to declare such delegations unconstitutional,[48] a situation explained best by the general tendency of courts to permit broad legislative delegations of power to administrative agencies, rather than a desire to support the growth of administrative criminalization.

Professor Bernard Schwartz, attempting to justify administrative crimes, states, "The sanction behind delegated legislation is normally a penalty provided by the legislature."[49] Schwartz believes that there is a sharp distinction between allowing an administrative

[47] People v. Grant, 242 App. Div. 310, 275 N.Y.S. 74 (1934), affirmed, 267 N.Y. 508, 196 N.E. 553 (1935).

[48] See Lincoln Dairy v. Finigan, 170 Neb. 777,104 N.W. 2d 227 (1960). The court stated: "It is axiomatic that the power to define crimes and criminal offenses is in the legislature and it may not delegate such powers to an administrative agency."

[49] Bernard Schwartz, *An Introduction to American Administrative Law,* 2d ed. (Dobbs Ferry, N.Y.: Oceana Press, 1962), p. 51.

The California Table Grape Commission can create crimes.

Misdemeanor

It shall be a misdemeanor for:

(a) Any person to violate or aid in the violation of any provision of this chapter or any rule or regulation of the [California Table Grape] commission.

(b) Any person to willfully render or furnish a false or fraudulent report, statement or record required by the commission pursuant to the provisions of this chapter or any rules or regulations of the commission.

(c) Any person engaged in the shipping of table grapes or in the wholesale or retail trade thereof to fail or refuse to furnish to the commission or its duly authorized agents, upon request, information concerning the name and address of the person from whom he has received table grapes, regulated hereby, and the quantity of such commodity so received. (Added Stats.1967,c.1467, § 1.)

Source: California Code Annotated Agriculture sec. 65653.

agency to impose penalties by rules or regulations and the usual situation, in which the enabling statute provides that the violation of a regulation promulgated under it will be punished penally. Thus, for Schwartz, as long as the administrative agency cannot itself impose a criminal penalty, neither the Constitution nor his conscience is concerned. Schwartz is satisfied to have the administrators define the offenses, so long as they don't try to enforce them. Yet in a very real sense, many administrative agencies make criminal law policy with permission of the legislatures. Does this meet the common expectations about what a criminal law is supposed to be?

The Supreme Court has gone beyond Professor Schwartz. In 1977 the Court unanimously upheld a delegation by Congress that permitted administrators, without a jury, to find facts and to impose a penalty of up to $10,000 for a violation of the Occupational Safety and Health Act.[50] The fine in question was technically called a civil penalty. Neither the Sixth Amendment guarantee of a jury trial nor the Court-designed doctrines of delegation of legislative powers got much use in this decision. The Court simply brushed those problems aside.

Actually, federal law on this subject has been quite clear and consistent. Administrators may be delegated by Congress with the power to issue regulations whose violation makes a crime. That has

[50] Atlas Roofing Co. v. Occupational Safety and Health Review Commission, 430 U.S. 442 (1977).

NASA regulations incorporated into federal criminal law.

Whoever willfully shall violate, attempt to violate, or conspire to violate any regulation or order promulgated by the Administrator of the National Aeronautics and Space Administration for the protection or security of any laboratory, station, base, or other facility, or part thereof, or any aircraft, missile, spacecraft, or similar vehicle, or part thereof, or other property or equipment in the custody of the Administration, or any real or personal property or equipment in the custody of any contractor under any contract with the Administration or any subcontractor of any such contractor, shall be fined not more than $5,000, or imprisoned not more than one year, or both.
Added Pub.L. 85-568, Title III, § 304(c) (1), July 29, 1958, 72 Stat. 434.

Source: 18 U.S.C. sec. 799 (as of 1980).

---

been the law at least since 1911[51] and "the Supreme Court's view has not wavered a millimeter" since.[52]

The distinction between a so-called civil penalty and a crime is a hairline difference, but it is enough to give Congress the power to give away almost totally segments of its power to make sanctions, as long as the sanctions are not denoted criminal. As long as Congress provides a "distinctly civil procedure," a civil, not a criminal, sanction is created, and the penalty system is constitutionally acceptable.[53]

The nation's leading administrative law expert, Kenneth Culp Davis, has concluded that "nothing in the Constitution forbids administrative determination of criminal penalties, even in felony cases."[54] Professor Davis sees that parole boards, not judges, actually impose sentences under indeterminate sentence laws. He reminds us that police detain and imprison people every day, Constitution or no. But these are administrative actions, not administrative determination and definition of crime. Professor Davis seems to have missed the point that the delegation of the power to make criminal law is different from any other delegation, because it touches upon fundamental rights of defendants guaranteed by the Bill of Rights. A parole board may determine the length of a sentence; a police officer may detain a suspect; a board may fine a rule violator, but these are administrative actions pursuant to a law. The administrative crimes mentioned here involve much more; they exhibit administrative power to proscribe behavior and to subject it to penal sanctions.

Professor Davis seems to scorn state court decisions that promote the use of the delegation doctrine to limit or strike down legislative surrenders of power to make criminal law. But all the cases that Davis prefers involve the power of boards to impose monetary penalties. As we have seen, this is not the whole problem. Even if boards can, constitutionally, impose various stiff civil penalties, there is still a large area of administrative crimes that fall between the positions of Schwartz and Davis. Fundamentally, the issue is whether criminal sanctions are necessary to the administrative pro-

51 United States v. Grimaud, 220 U.S. 506 (1911).

52 Walter Gellhorn, "Administrative Prescription and Imposition of Penalties," *Washington University Law Quarterly,* 1970, p. 266.

53 Helvering v. Mitchell, 303 U.S. 391 (1938).

54 Kenneth Culp Davis, *Administrative Law Treatise,* vol. 1, 2d ed. (San Diego, Calif.: University of San Diego, 1978), p. 189.

cess. Do criminal sanctions for administrative purposes serve the general good? No general reply is possible. No simple formula will suffice. But the courts generally support this criminalization.

Consider, for example, the federal and state laws criminalizing behavior that would normally be quite innocent. Minor deviations from elaborate bookkeeping rules are made into administrative crimes. Does it work? Is cigarette smuggling managed effectively by converting minor deviations into criminal conduct? Seemingly, not at all.

Cigarette smuggling produces more than one million dollars a week in New York State. With a combined state and city tax in New York City of fourteen cents a pack, a lot of money can be made by evading tax collections. Professional criminals have regularly carried cigarettes from low-tax to high-tax states. The administrative tasks of cigarette tax collection are too overwhelming for any state agency, even though the Treasury Department's Bureau of Alcohol, Tobacco, and Firearms is now investigating cigarette smuggling by virtue of the recent federal criminalization of cigarette smuggling. This administrative supplement has proved insufficient. A newspaper investigation of cigarette tax collection in Pennsylvania revealed that the state tax collection machinery had been thoroughly corrupted. Administrators, police, and judges had been implicated,

---

An administrative civil rights crime.

Every person who denies to any other person because of race, creed or color, the full enjoyment of any of the accommodations, advantages, facilities or privileges of any place of public resort, accommodation, assemblage, or amusement, shall be guilty of a misdemeanor.

Source: State of Washington, RCW 9.91.010.

The inclusion of any question relative to an applicant's race or religion in any application blank or form for employment or license required to be filled in and submitted by an applicant to any department, board, commission, officer, agent, or employee of this state or the disclosure on any license of the race or religion of the licensee is hereby prohibited.

Any person who shall violate RCW 43.01.100 shall be guilty of a misdemeanor.

Source: State of Washington, RCW 43.01.100, RCW 43.01.110.

Administrative consequences of crime.

KLUCZYNSKI, Justice:

The Director of the Department of Registration and Education (Department) revoked three pharmacists' licenses to practice pharmacy after an administrative determination that they were guilty of "gross immorality" under the Pharmacy Practice Act (Ill.Rev.Stat.1973, ch. 91, par. 55.7–6, now Ill.Rev.Stat. 1977, ch. 111, par. 4019, as amended). The revocations were premised upon Federal convictions following the entry of pleas of guilty by Theodore Dolitsky, Sheldon Miller, and Aaron Finn to the Federal misdemeanor offense of offering and making a kickback or bribe in connection with the furnishing of drugs and pharmaceutical services for which payment is made in whole or in part out of Federal funds under an approved State medical assistance plan (42 U.S.C. sec.1396h(b)(1)(1976). The pharmacists filed three separate actions for administrative review in the circuit court of Cook County.

The complaints filed by Miller and Dolitsky were heard by Judge Richard L. Curry, who ruled that the term "gross immorality" is unconstitutionally vague; that the Federal misdemeanor offense to which Miller and Dolitsky pleaded guilty is not encompassed by the legislative proscription of "gross immorality"; and that the pharmacists did not receive a fair hearing before the State Board of Pharmacy since the entire 49-count indictment, although the pharmacists were convicted upon only one count following their guilty pleas. Judge Curry reversed the decision to revoke, and the Department filed the instant direct appeal under Rule 302(a) (58 Ill.2d R. 302(a)) on the ground that the circuit court had held section 7–6 of the Pharmacy Practice Act (Ill.Rev.Stat.1973, ch. 91, par. 55.7–6) invalid.

The complaint filed by Finn was heard by Judge Arthur L. Dunne, who found that the order of revocation was properly entered and affirmed the decision as not contrary to the manifest weight of the evidence or contrary to law. This court allowed Finn's motion for direct appeal under Rule 302(b) (58 Ill.2d R. 302(b)) and consolidated all three appeals.

The pharmacists' licenses were revoked following three separate hearings before the State Board of Pharmacy. At each hearing certified copies of the Federal convictions were introduced as evidence. Copies of the multicount indictments were attached to the complaints filed with the Board, and in the cases of Miller and Dolitsky, they were admitted into evidence over the objection of counsel. In each case the Board found that the pharmacist had been convicted of the Federal misdemeanor and concluded that the conviction of such an offense constituted "gross immorality" within the meaning of the Pharmacy Practice Act. The Board recommended to the Director of Registration and Education that the pharmacists' licenses be revoked. . . .

The term "practice of the profession of pharmacy," as defined in the Act, means "the compounding, dispensing, recommending or advising concerning contents and therapeutic values and uses, offering for sale or selling at retail, drugs, medicines or poisons, whether pursuant to prescriptions or orders of duly licensed physicians, dentists, veterinarians, or other allied medical practitioners, or in the absence and entirely independent of such prescriptions or orders, or otherwise whatsoever, or any other act, service operation or transaction incidental to or forming a part of any of the foregoing acts, *requiring, involving or employing the science or art of any branch of the pharmaceutical profession, study or training*." (Emphasis added.) (Ill.Rev.Stat.1973, ch 91, par. 55.3(d). The definition [emphasizes] the performance of acts requiring professional study and training in the science of pharmacy, rather than the business aspects of the practice of pharmacy.

The pharmacists and the Department place emphasis on *Gordon v. Department of Registration & Education* (1970), 130 Ill. App.2d 435, 264 N.E.2d 792, for the proposition that only convictions for misdemeanors which concern the practice of pharmacy constitute "gross immorality" within the intent and purpose of the Pharmacy Practice Act. The pharmacists argue that their misdemeanors did not concern the practice of pharmacy; the Department argues to the contrary. In *Gordon* the pharmacist pleaded *nolo contendere* in the United States district court to two charges of dispensing drugs without a prescription in violation of Federal law. The State Board of Pharmacy determined that two separate sales of legend drugs without a prescription on the same date to the same person indicated a woeful disregard for regulations and was contrary to the public interest. The *Gordon* court noted that "[t]here are, indeed, many misdemeanors which are not concerned with professional practice and conviction upon such may not be a concern of public interest or welfare." 130 Ill.App.2d 435, 439, 264 N.E.2d 792. 794.

[2] The payment of kickbacks or bribes is not concerned with the exercise of the professional skill of a pharmacist, the focus of the definition of the practice of pharmacy. Such conduct is related to matters extraneous to the central concern of the Pharmacy Practice Act, the protection of public health, safety, and welfare through regulation of the practice of pharmacy. A misdemeanor conviction for the payment of kickbacks or bribes is not "gross immorality" for purposes of pharmacy-license revocations.

Subsequent to the commission of the conduct which formed the basis for the pharmacists' Federal convictions, section 7–6 of the Pharmacy Practice Act was amended, effective August 27, 1975, to include fee splitting as a ground for license revocation (Ill.Rev.Stat.1975, ch. 91, par. 55.7–6, now Ill.Rev.Stat.1977, ch. 111, par. 4019). Fee splitting, as defined in section 10–1 of the Pharmacy Practice Act (Ill.Rev.Stat.1975, ch. 91, par. 55.10–1, now Ill.Rev.Stat.1977, ch. 111, par. 4032), encompasses the conduct which formed the basis for the plaintiff pharmacists' Federal misdemeanor convictions. Section 10–1 prohibits payments to employees, owners or managers of nursing homes of "any rebate, refund, discount, commission or other valuable consideration for, on account of, or based upon income received or resulting from the sale or furnishing * * * of drugs or devices, prescriptions or any other service to patients." The amendment expressly including fee splitting as a basis for revocation is a further indication that such conduct was not included in the general term "gross immorality" (see *People ex rel. Gibson v. Cannon* (1976), 65 Ill.2d 366, 373, 2 Ill.Dec. 737, 357 N.E.2d 1180) and cannot constitute a basis for the revocation of the plaintiff pharmacists' licenses.

We hold it was error to revoke the plaintiff pharmacists' licenses on the ground of "gross immorality" based upon their convictions of a Federal misdemeanor offense involving the payment of kickbacks or bribes. For this reason, the judgment reversing the revocation of Miller's and Dolitsky's licenses is affirmed.

Source: Miller v. Dept. of Registration and Education, 387 N.E. 2d 300 (Illinois, 1979). Reprinted by permission of West Publishing Company.

and the machinery for tax collection rendered impotent.[55] No amount of criminalization has reduced the incidence of smuggling; probably the only solution is uniform cigarette taxation that would remove all incentive for smuggling. Federal penalties to support state law collection merely hide the true problem—the unwillingness of tobacco-growing states to adopt adequate cigarette tax laws.

The legislature may delegate the power to an administrative agency to fill in the details of a legislative act. Are criminal sanctions merely details? Does the legislature have a more important and awesome power than that of defining a criminal offense and assigning criminal penalties? Vesting the regulations of an administrative agency with criminal sanctions appears to be acceptable to the Supreme Court, most state courts, and most law writers.[56]

An administratively defined crime is "not the outbirth of a particular unmoral conduct, but is characterized by disobedience to administrative duties."[57] The chief function of an administrative proscription is deterrence rather than retribution. Administrative

[55] Series in *Philadelphia Inquirer* of May 7 through May 11, 1979.

[56] The only serious article that disputes the legitimacy of most administrative crimes is Harlan S. Abrahams and John R. Snowden, "Separation of Powers and Administrative Crimes: A Study of Irreconcilables," *Southern Illinois University Law Journal,* 1976, pp. 1-150. Abrahams and Snowden contend that the creation of administrative crimes tends to violate the constitutional principle of separation of powers. While it is hard to accept their view of the exclusivity of legislative power to create criminal offenses, in view of long-standing practice to the contrary, they are quite right in their view of the flimsy distinction between civil and criminal sanctions.

[57] Edmund H. Schwenk, "The Administrative Crime, Its Creation and Punishment by Administrative Agencies," *Michigan Law Review* 42 (1943): p. 85.

definitions of crimes, where justifiable, must be based on some aim of obtaining compliance with administrative obligations, not punishment. Yet plain compulsion is simpler and usually easier for administrative agencies. The resort to criminal sanctions merely passes the buck, in many cases, to another administrative agency charged with prosecuting criminal offenses in the courts.

If the line between administratively defined crimes and ordinary (statute defined) crimes continues to be blurred, we shall erode the basic distinction between the concepts of crime and blameful behavior. Administrators should be concerned with present and future behavior, not past ill-deeds. If a criminal sanction compels an individual to comply with his or her administrative duty, then the administrative criminalization has served its function, but the legislature should not neglect its prime duty to establish the elements of the substantive criminal law. Courts will not usually compel legislatures to formulate the elements of criminal law. Instead there is only the dim realization that the presumed expertise of administrators does not always extend to the potent issue of proscribing unwanted behavior with criminal sanctions. As it is, "chaos abounds in the area of administrative crimes."[58]

SUMMARY

The growth of the American bureaucracy has been one of the most remarkable governmental events of the past 5 decades. Congress and the state legislatures have bestowed far-reaching powers upon bureaucratic agencies in an effort to regulate business, professions, labor, resource development, agriculture, health, and welfare. Sometimes criminal sanctions have been attached to infractions of rules that are essentially administrative. More rare has been the actual delegation of criminal law policy making to certain administrative agencies. Little is known about the empirical incidence of administratively defined crime, and less is known about the deterrent effects of such sanctions. Probably some administratively defined crimes could be eliminated from the statute books with little loss to the public, but the public appears to have no great concern for the problem.

[58] Abrahams and Snowden, op. cit., p. 148.

7

JUDICIAL CRIMES

The criminal justice system hinges on the effectiveness of courts as instruments for the implementation of criminal law. Without open, fair, impartial, unobstructed judicial deliberation, rational judgments are difficult if not impossible. There are many obstacles to a fair trial, some of them based upon the uncooperative or deceitful behavior of witnesses and parties. Jury-tampering sometimes occurs, too. These obstacles and other acts that hamper effective judicial deliberation have often been criminalized as a means of protecting the judicial process from improper influence.

In past centuries requirements for witness behavior were quite rigid. Under early English law only Christians were capable of serving as witnesses. Other religions were regarded as insufficient to assure the honesty or integrity of testimony. The courts today permit witnesses to make either oaths or affirmations at their swearing-in. Contemporary courts admit all relevant evidence, no matter what the source. Even atheists and convicts may be competent witnesses. These changes are reflected in the Federal Rules of Evidence, which abandon such traditional incapacities as religious belief, party interest, conviction of a crime, and mental defect.[1] On the other hand, persons who refuse to be sworn to give testimony may find themselves in contempt of court. Courts must possess the power to compel a recalcitrant witness to testify, or else their functions could be completely frustrated. Once it was believed that a sworn testimony was a contract between a witness and God to tell the truth. With the decline of faith in divine sanctions courts have learned to protect themselves from lies. Now legal penalties attach to lying and other offenses against the judicial process.

PERJURY

In common law, perjury was a witness's willful assertion of fact, opinion, belief, or knowledge that was known by the witness to be false and was intended to mislead the court or jury. The testimony must have been given in open court, following an oath or affirmation, or in a legal document (affidavit). The offense is now controlled by statutes that tend to be broader than the common law coverage. Many modern statutes penalize most forms of false swearing, even in matters not pending in court. Judicial and extrajudicial deceit has been criminalized in many states.

[1] Federal Rule of Evidence 601.

To be accused of perjury a person must have taken an oath or affirmation required by law. Oaths may be required by the military, by courts, or by other government agencies. A valid oath may be administered even to an illiterate person.[2] It is not necessary that oathtakers raise their hand, kiss the Bible, or make any other religious gesture. Clerks in court may administer valid oaths under the direction of the judge.

Perjury is widespread in America. One writer observed, "few crimes except fornication are more prevalent or carried off with greater impunity."[3] No one knows for sure, but perjury may occur in some form or other in about half of the cases tried in America.[4] In spite of the magnitude of the perjury problem and the harm caused the courts, fewer than 100 perjury prosecutions take place each year in this country.

One of the reasons for the paucity of perjury prosecutions is the technicalities that hamper proofs, especially the requirement that a valid perjury prosecution set forth the words of the alleged false statement. The perjury laws are unlike most criminal statutes, which do not depend upon exactness or precision in charging offenses. Perjured statements must also be material (or relevant) to an issue or a point of inquiry. This materiality requirement existed in common law and has been adopted by modern statutes and by the courts. Materiality of the perjured statement must be alleged in the indictment and proved in order to gain a conviction for perjury.[5]

Statutes can eliminate many of these problems of proving perjury. New York State has eliminated the materiality issue for third-degree perjury, while retaining it for first- and second-degree perjury.[6] Materiality is retained, however, in the basic federal perjury statute.[7] Some states disquality convicted perjurers from being witnesses in future litigation.[8] Whether these statutory changes

[2] United States v. Mallard, 40 F. 151 (D.C. S.C., 1889).

[3] Alfred D. Whitman, "A Proposed Solution to the Problem of Perjury in Our Courts," *Dickenson Law Review* 59 (1955): 127.

[4] See Harry Hibschman, "'You Do Solemnly Swear' or That Perjury Problem," *Journal of Criminal Law, Criminology and Police Science* 24 (1934): 901. Hibschman claims that perjury occurs in 75 percent of criminal cases and 90 percent of divorce cases.

[5] United States v. Gremillion, 464 F. 2d 901 (5th Cir., 1972); United States v. Friedman, 445 F. 2d 1220 (2d Cir., 1971).

[6] N.Y. Penal Law sec. 210.a5 (McKinney, 1967).

[7] 18 U.S.C. sec. 1621 (1970).

[8] Ky. Rev. Stat. Sec. 421.090 (197); Pa. Stat. Ann. ch. 28, sec. 253 (1958).

actually have a deterrent effect or not is unknown. Probably only vigorous prosecution of perjury would have such an effect. Prosecutors, however, rarely invoke perjury statutes, unless it is difficult to allege or prove a more serious offense, as in corruption cases, cases against organized crime, or the Watergate incident.[9]

Perjury statutes may also be used to supplement the administrative process. Federal laws make it a criminal offense to give "any false, fictitious or fraudulent statements or representations" in any matter within the jurisdiction of a department or agency of the United States.[10] This statute has been applied to false statements made to federal law enforcement officials.[11] The transformation of perjury into an administrative crime is clear in the Internal Revenue

[9] United States v. Krogh, 366 F. Supp. 1255 (D.D.C. 1973). Perjury charge against federal official who had given a sworn deposition in a proceeding after the Watergate grand jury inquiry.

[10] 18 U.S.C. sec. 1001 (1970).

[11] Note, "Criminal Liability for False Statements to Federal Law Enforcement Officials," *Virginia Law Review* 63 (1977): 451-470.

Note the detailed provisions of the basic federal false declarations statute.

§ 1623. False declarations before grand jury or court

(a) Whoever under oath (or in any declaration, certificate, verification, or statement under penalty of perjury as permitted under section 1746 of title 28, United States Code) in any proceeding before or ancillary to any court or grand jury of the United States knowingly makes any false material declaration or makes or uses any other information, including any book, paper, document, record, recording, or other material, knowing the same to contain any false material declaration, shall be fined not more than $10,000 or imprisoned not more than five years, or both.

(b) This section is applicable whether the conduct occurred within or without the United States.

(c) An indictment or information for violation of this section alleging that, in any proceedings before or ancillary to any court or grand jury of the United States, the defendant under oath has knowingly made two or more declarations, which are inconsistent to the degree that one of them is necessarily false, need not specify which declaration is false if—

(1) each declaration was material to the point in question, and

Code provisions for perjury in income tax matters.[12] Further expansion of the perjury doctrine is supported by the drafters of the Model Penal Code.[13]

SUBORNATION OF PERJURY

Subornation of perjury consists in procuring another to commit perjury. There can be no crime unless the perjury is actually committed. In a broader sense, subornation of perjury also includes instigating or inciting another to take a false oath or to be under oath.

Since subornation of perjury is an offense different from perjury, some of the requirements for proof are different. In Pennsylvania,

[12] IRC sec. 7206 (1) imposes a maximum punishment of three years imprisonment and a $5000 fine.

[13] Model Penal Code sec. 241.3 (Prop. Official Draft 1962) provides criminal sanctions for unsworn written statements made "with [the] purpose to mislead a public servant in performing his official function."

---

(2) each declaration was made within the period of the statute of limitations for the offense charged under this section.

In any prosecution under this section, the falsity of a declaration set forth in the indictment or information shall be established sufficient for conviction by proof that the defendant while under oath made irreconcilably contradictory declarations material to the point in question in any proceeding before or ancillary to any court or grand jury. It shall be a defense to an indictment or information made pursuant to the first sentence of this subsection that the defendant at the time he made each declaration believed the declaration was true.

(d) Where, in the same continuous court or grand jury proceeding in which a declaration is made, the person making the declaration admits such declaration to be false, such admission shall bar prosecution under this section if, at the time the admission is made, the declaration has not substantially affected the proceeding, or it has not become manifest that such falsity has been or will be exposed.

(e) Proof beyond a reasonable doubt under this section is sufficient for conviction. It shall not be necessary that such proof be made by any particular number of witnesses or by documentary or other type of evidence.

Source: 18 U.S.C. 1623 (as of 1980).

the law required the direct testimony of two witnesses to prove perjury; the proof needed for subornation of perjury was much less, and the witness requirement was dropped.[14] In most states subornation of perjury is declared by statute to be an offense separate from perjury. Usually statutes retain the requirement that the matter falsely sworn to is material to the proceeding or trial.

A futile attempt to commit subornation of perjury may itself constitute a crime. Attempt to suborn is a form of interference with the due course of justice. It is essential to the crime of attempted subornation that the accused knows that the testimony he or she wants the witness to provide is false. This corrupt intent on the part of the offender must be matched by the witness's belief that he or she is to give false testimony, since there can be no perjury otherwise. Again, there is a requirement that the testimony that the accused attempts to procure would be material to the proceeding.[15]

OBSTRUCTION OF JUSTICE

For many centuries acts that obstruct the due administration of justice have been criminalized. The efficiency of courts and even their integrity may be threatened by certain kinds of conduct. Since courts must attempt to arrive at the truth in a fair manner those who would hamper this effort must be controlled. On the other hand, some judges and some courts have been excessively sensitive to their dignity and power and have abused defendants or driven them into defiant acts. Nonetheless, common law and state or federal statutes all have some version of this crime, even though the crime may not be designated as obstructing justice. Under recent changes in the crime the offense has come to include elements that make it easier to indict organized crime figures who evade detection for other offenses.

Obstruction of justice is a criminal offense that sometimes overlaps with contempt of court. As a criminal offense, however, there must be a full hearing on a charge of obstruction of justice, while contempt proceedings may take place summarily, without trial. Attempting to influence a pending court proceeding may constitute either obstruction or contempt, depending upon the facts and the language of the controlling statute. Writing letters or publishing

[14] Commonwealth v. Mervin, 326 A. 2d 602; 230 Pa. Super. 552 (1974).

[15] State v. Howard, 137 Mo. 289, 38 S.W. 908 (1897).

newspaper articles in an effort to influence a judge's decision in a pending case could be one or the other offense.

The protection of the integrity of courts is placed at such a premium that picketing or parading in or near a courthouse in an effort to influence judges may be punished without violating the constitutionally protected rights of free speech or assembly.[16] It is also a federal crime to obstruct federal court orders.[17] Federal law also penalizes force or threats of force made against any witness.[18] Most states criminalize efforts to induce witnesses to give certain testimony or to absent themselves. This means that even if subornation of perjury is insufficiently demonstrated, a lesser charge for attempting to influence testimony may be appropriate. Getting a witness to leave the jurisdiction rather than testify at a trial is a clear example of obstruction of justice.

Acts intended to influence, intimidate, or injure witnesses, jurors, or court officers all fall under the heading of obstruction of justice. Destruction of incriminating documents may also be criminalized. Destruction of incriminating tape recordings (as the Watergate scandal suggests) may also be a form of obstruction of justice. Concealment of information needed by a tribunal or denial of the existence of the information may also amount to an obstruction of justice, since they make it difficult to ascertain the truth of a pending matter. Bribery of a witness may be a crime in itself under some statutes, but it may also be a type of obstruction of justice.

The concept of obstruction of justice has been expanded to cover events outside the courtroom and events that could not directly involve courts. Under federal law it is a crime to threaten witnesses or others before congressional hearings or administrative proceedings.[19] The same statute also penalizes those who willfully falsify documentary material demanded by various federal agencies. Presentation of false documents in response to an internal revenue subpoena violates another federal statute.[20] More recent federal statutes criminalize obstruction or delay of communications to a criminal investigator.[21] Success in the attempt to influence or intimidate is not a necessary element of the crime. Obviously, this

[16] Cox v. Louisiana, 379 U.S. 559 (1964).

[17] 18 U.S.C. sec. 1509.

[18] 18 U.S.C. sec. 1503.

[19] 18 U.S.C. sec. 1505.

[20] 12 U.S.C. sec. 1904.

[21] 18 U.S.C. sec. 1510.

expansive view of obstruction of justice is highly favorable to law enforcement officials, who need merely show that there was a pending investigation of a crime and that a person had information to provide for the investigation.

CONTEMPT

Contempt of court is sometimes confused with obstruction of justice. In many instances, the events that lead to the one charge could also be perceived as leading to the other. According to one view, contempt is neither a crime nor a misdemeanor.[22] Contempt is usually treated as *sui generis,* a unique aspect of judicial power concerned with preserving the authority, dignity, and decorum of the court. Practically, though, convictions for criminal contempt are indistinguishable from criminal convictions, and they affect a defendant in much the same way. The role of criminal contempt resembles the role of the criminal law generally—the protection of social and political institutions and the enforcement of their mandates. A defendant may be imprisoned for 6 months for perjury under the contempt power or for perjury under the criminal statutes, and the difference between the consequences may be nil.[23] As the Supreme Court once observed, "if contempts are not criminal, we are in error as to the most fundamental characteristic of crimes as that word has been understood in English speech."[24]

A distinction is made between criminal and civil contempt of court. Prosecution for criminal contempt is punitive. Defendants who disrupt a courtroom have committed criminal contempt, for which they will be judicially punished. Prosecution for civil contempt is remedial in nature. It is used to compel a party or a witness to comply with a request or order of the court. Thus, a spouse may be compelled to make alimony payments through a civil contempt citation. Serious disregard of a court order or an obstruction of justice could, however, be deemed criminal contempt, worthy of punishment. Typically a criminal contempt citation is for a definite, determinable sentence, while a civil contempt is revocable at the will of its subject, who can avoid the citation by complying with the court

[22] State v. Baker, 222 Iowa 903, 904; 270 N.W. 359, 360 (1936); appeal dismissed, 302 U.S. 769 (1938).

[23] Bloom v. Illinois, 391 U.S. 194, 201 (1968).

[24] Gompers v. United States, 233 U.S. 604, 610 (1914).

order. Hence the distinction between criminal and civil contempt may best be perceived after the fact.

Procedurally, criminal comtempt is treated quite differently from civil contempt. A criminal contempt committed outside the presence or the immediate vicinity of the court (an indirect contempt) is punishable only after a proper notice and hearing, with an opportunity for the accused to present a defense to the charge. A direct contempt, however, one committed in the actual presence of the court, may be punishable by the judge summarily, without a formal written accusation or hearing. Fine or imprisonment may be awarded as punishment, and persons convicted of criminal contempt may not purge themselves by undoing the wrong they did, as they may in cases of civil contempt. Civil contempt is an appropriate means of gaining remedial compliance in support of private rights and private parties, while criminal contempt is aimed at the protection of the government, the courts, and the public as a whole.

The distinction in the law of contempt between a direct and an indirect contempt is important.[25] Outbursts in a courtroom by any person present may constitute a direct contempt. Publishing prejudicial information in a newspaper may be indirect contempt. The distinction is salient because direct contempt can be punished by the judge summarily, without a jury, because of the immediacy of the need of protecting the court.[26] Indirect contempt can be heard in subsequent proceedings, especially since the events are not known personally by the judge. Still, there is a trend toward requiring a hearing before punishing any contemptuous behavior.[27]

The political trials of the 1960s saw an expanded use of the power of summary contempt. Lawyers and their clients often provoked judges into rash reactions in order to embarrass the legal system for political reasons. In a summary contempt proceeding the functions of judge, jury, and prosecutor are rolled into one person who "may proceed upon [his or her] own knowledge of the facts, and punish the offender, without further proof, and without issue or trial in any form."[28] The potential for judicial abuse of the contempt power is great, but the Supreme Court has imposed substantial con-

[25] This distinction goes back to old English statutes. See Halsbury's *Laws of England,* vol. 8 (3rd ed., 1969), pp. 2-3.

[26] Yates v. United States, 355 U.S. 66, 69 (1957).

[27] Harris v. United States, 382 U.S. 162 (1965).

[28] Ex parte Terry, 128 U.S. 289, 309 (1888).

stitutional limitations upon its exercise.[29] Today the right to a jury trial prohibits the trial judge from summarily imposing sentences in excess of 6 months for any one charge. If, however, the judge does not wait until the close of the trial to impose sentence, a particular trial might give rise to multiple summary contempt citations. Furthermore, a judge may be disqualified from trying contempt charges

[29] Summarized effectively in Robert Allen Sedler, "The Summary Contempt Power and the Constitution: The View From Without and Within," *New York University Law Review* 51 (1976): 34-92.

Chief Justice Burger restates the law of contempt and supports the judiciary.

The face-to-face refusal to comply with the court's order itself constituted an affront to the court,[8] and when that kind of refusal disrupts and frustrates an ongoing proceeding, as it did here, summary contempt must be available to vindicate the authority of the court as well as to provide the recalcitrant witness with some incentive to testify. *In re Chiles,* 22 Wall. 157, 168 (1875). Whether such incentive is necessary in a particular case is a matter the Rule wisely leaves to the discretion of the trial court.[9]

Our conclusion that summary contempt is available under the circumstances here is supported by the fact that Rule 42 has consistently been recognized to be no more than a restatement of the law existing when the Rule was adopted, *Bloom* v. *Illinois,* 391 U.S. 194, 209 (1968). . . .

[8]In order to constitute an affront to the dignity of the court the judge himself need not be personally insulted. Here the judge indicated he was not personally affronted by respondents' actions. He said: "I am not angry at Mr. Wilson because he refuses to testify. That is up to him." App. 14. He also said: "I don't consider [Bryan] to have a chip on his shoulder towards the Court or towards me."

[9]In *Shillitani* v. *United States,* 384 U.S. 364, 371 n. 9 (1966), we said:
"[T]he trial judge [should] first consider the feasibility of coercing testimony through the imposition of civil contempt. The judge should resort to criminal sanctions only after he determines, for good reason, that the civil remedy would be inappropriate."
Here, of course, that admonition carries little weight because at the time they acted contemptuously both respondents were incarcerated due to their own guilty pleas. Under the circumstances here the threat of immediate confinement for civil contempt would have provided little incentive for them to testify. Contrast, *Anglin* v. *Johnston,* 504 F. 2d 1165 (CA7 1974), cert. denied, 420 U.S. 962 (1975). Nevertheless, the careful trial judge made it clear to respondents that if they relented and obeyed his order he would consider reducing their sentences; and he also explained that he would consider other factors in deciding whether to reduce the sentences. *Supra,* at 312.

Source: United States vs. Wilson, 421 U.S. 309 at 316-316 (1975).

---

when he or she has become too personally embroiled in a controversy.

Contempt proceedings are not deemed criminal. As a result the provisions of the Fifth Amendment that normally protect accused persons do not apply. Grand jury indictment is unnecessary. In some states bail is unavailable to the contemnor (defendant accused of contempt). Often there is no appeal from contempt, although this varies from state to state. Habeas corpus may sometimes be unavailable to the contemnor. Jury trial, however, is not denied, except for summary contempts.[30] Thus, the consequences of defining contempt as noncriminal are obvious. The justification for such a categorization is not so obvious. A malicious or vindictive judge could employ the tactics of Judge Julius Hoffman in the "Chicago Seven" trials, in which Judge Hoffman held several of the defendants and their attorneys in multiple direct contempt in a hearing where the substantive charges themselves were flimsy.[31]

Increasingly judges are being expected to accept more misbehavior in their courtrooms. More judicial tolerance and less judicial sensitivity will result in fewer contempt citations. In one Pennsylvania case the Supreme Court held that where the alleged contempt consists of protracted vilification of the trial judge, the contemnor is entitled "to a public trial before a judge other than the one reviled by the contemnor."[32] Judges, however, may be prone to sympathize with an abused fellow judge. Such a requirement at least allows determination of guilt to be made in a more impartial manner and with an appearance of justice.

Civil contempt may be even more serious than criminal contempt. A civil contemnor is not entitled to plead his or her case before a jury. A sentence may be indefinite, not just 6 months in length. Newspaper reporters who refuse to supply the names of their informants at the request or subpoena of a court have sometimes been jailed for lengthy periods.

Probably a reevaluation of the law of contempt is in order. All contempt is effectively punitive in one way or another. It is virtually criminal. A more consistent and coherent approach to this broad judicial power is needed. Instead contempt law is expanding. Government agencies, seeking support for their decisions, have turned to the courts for assistance. Contempt law is being used to supple-

[30] Bloom v. United States, 391 U.S. 194 (1968).

[31] In re Dellinger, 461 F. 2d 389 (7th Cir. 1972); United States v. Seale, 461 F. 2d 345 (7th Cir. 1972).

[32] Mayberry v. Pennsylvania, 400 U.S. 455 (1971).

ment and amplify the decisions of more and more government agencies. Contempt law no longer protects just the judiciary; it extends to most levels of government.[33]

EMBRACERY

Embracery is the criminal offense of corruptly influencing a jury or juror. Attempt to influence, to corrupt, or induce them in any way is the essential element of the crime. There can be no attempted embracery since the crime itself is an attempt. The crime is complete when the attempt is made, regardless of the success of the attempt. Federal law penalizes an "endeavor" to influence a juror, which may be even less than an attempt.[34]

Embracery may constitute an obstruction of justice under some state statutes. Embracery usually constitutes contempt of court, as well. As in contempt of court, the success or failure of the attempt is irrelevant. Unlike contempt, an embracery charge is always criminal in character and effect. If money inducements are involved, a separate offense of bribery may have been committed, although the proof of bribery requires a promise or a gift or an acceptance of money or other things of value.

Embracery may consist of suggesting that a juror hang the jury. Letters, promises, threats, or persuasion are all forms of embracery. Urging others to intervene for the purpose of corruptly influencing the jury is also embracery.

Most embracery statutes apply to both criminal and civil proceedings. Grand juries are also covered by the offense. Some statutes have extended embracery beyond the courtroom to cover attempts to influence arbitrators and referees. Mainly the offense strikes at the heart of the fact-finding process and ought logically be applied to other fact finders as well as to jurors.

ESCAPE, RESCUE, AND PRISON BREAKING

Any departure from lawful custody may constitute the crime of escape. Force is not a necessary element, although some statutes refer to force in grading the offense. The flight of an accused seeking

[33] See Ronald Goldfarb, *Contempt of Court* (New York: Columbia University Press, 1963), pp. 144–151; for an enumeration of federal statutes which require agencies to use courts for contempt orders see note, *Duke Law Journal* 43 (1967): 640.

[34] United States v. Russell, 255 U.S. 138 (1920); Osborn v. United States, 385 U.S. 323, (1966), interpreting 18 U.S.C. sec. 1503.

to avoid arrest is probably obstruction of justice rather than escape, because custody is a necessary feature in escape law. Jumping bail is not usually escape because the accused has been released from custody lawfully. The purpose of escape law is to regain custody of the offender and to inhibit his or her freedom. Federal law punishes whoever escapes or attempts to escape from the custody of the attorney general, his or her designee, or any facility under the attorney general's direction. The same law penalizes those who improperly leave the custody of any court, judge, commissioner, or federal officer pursuant to a lawful arrest.[35] Inmates of federal prerelease guidance centers who left a facility by a system of signing in and out were guilty of escape under this statute when they failed to return at the designated hour.[36]

Sheriffs and jailers who permit persons in their custody to escape may be liable in a criminal prosecution. Negligence may suffice for this offense.[37] Safe and strict or close custody is required. Allowing a prisoner to go beyond the liberties permitted by law may amount to escape. Civil liability of custodians may also exist if they voluntarily or negligently permit an escape.

Rescue is the offense of aiding another person to escape from proper custody. It may be committed by the custodian or any third party, such as the escapee's faithful spouse. If one prisoner aids another to escape, he or she may have committed the crime of rescue. Some statutes make force a necessary element of this crime. Federal statutes also penalize the escape of those interred in a place of detention[38] and of prisoners of war or enemy aliens.[39]

Breaking from prison by force is sometimes a separate crime called prison breach or prison breaking. The gravity of the offense often depends upon the character of the offense for which the offender was sentenced as well as the degree of force involved. Escaping prison without force constitutes escape or lesser crime.

SUMMARY

The American system of criminal justice rests upon a foundation of a fair and honest trial. Perjury, false declarations, and obstructions of justice must be criminal offenses if the judicial pro-

[35] 18 U.S.C. sec. 751.

[36] McCullough v. United States, 369 F. 2d 548 (8th Cir., 1966).

[37] 18 U.S.C. sec. 755.

[38] 18 U.S.C. 756.

[39] 18 U.S.C. 757.

cess is to be protected from lies, distortions, and intimidation. The contempt powers of American courts, while not strictly part of the statutory law of crimes, are important adjuncts of the trial process. Even a president, as Richard Nixon discovered, must cooperate with court orders intended to expedite the criminal trial process. Other officials are held to an increasingly higher standard of conduct.

8

POLITICAL CRIMES

The term *political crime* has acquired a special meaning in democratic societies. The use of criminal law as a means of repressing political criticism is one of the oldest functions of the criminal law. Indeed, in communist countries where the crushing of non-Marxist groups is an accepted goal of law, both civil and criminal laws are used for that purpose. In America today, we often forget that repressive criminal laws can threaten civil liberty and "the political significance of criminal law has been almost forgotten."[1] But our lawmakers have been concerned with corruption of the political process and have begun to expand the criminal law beyond bribery to cover official oppression, destruction of government documents, falsification of documents, conflicts of interest, and other areas of improper official behavior. America does have repressive criminal laws that squelch unpopular groups and ideas, but government officials are increasingly being held accountable for their political misdeeds.

Political crimes in America include both remnants of earlier repressive legislation and a newer type of political offense, aimed at governmental officials themselves. No longer are political crimes concerned only with those who propound unpopular political ideas or who criticize the government. Increasingly the government itself is being held to higher standards of official conduct by means of criminal law. This modern American trend has not eliminated the threats to individual civil liberties inherent in the state's power to define its enemies and to pursue them, but America cannot be accused of ignoring governmental abuses of political power.

In most parts of the world *political crime* describes those activities that the state has criminalized in order to retain its hold on power. Essentially such political crimes are repressive in nature. Groups and individuals that threaten the government or are offensive to large numbers of people may be discouraged from continued agitation by having criminal sanctions applied to their deeds. Indeed, any society, democratic or otherwise, may choose to label a group of demonstrators as rioters and to apply criminal sanctions to turbulent behavior. It may be hard to distinguish among a genuine political threat to a country's security, reasonable regulation of large crowds, and suppression.

Political crimes can be perceived as "various formulas and techniques for controlling hostile minorities—whether small dissident groups or larger movements,"[2] or they may be defined more

[1] Jerome Hall, *General Principles of Criminal Law,* 2nd ed. (Indianapolis: Bobbs-Merrill, Inc., 1960), p. 64.

[2] Otto Kirchheimer, *Political Justice* (Princeton, N.J.: Princeton University Press, 1961).

broadly. The recent rise in terrorist activities, ostensibly for political purposes, raises the issue of the proper boundaries of the category of political crimes; in a more acute fashion, so did the issue of the proposed publication in *Progressive* magazine of the necessary elements for constructing a hydrogen bomb. The 1979 issuance of an injunction on publication by Federal District Court Judge Robert J. Warren was based on possible criminal violations of the Atomic Energy Act. The injunction, the first such prior restraint of the press in national history based upon national security, was grounded upon an extremely rare justification of ultimate political necessity. Although the injunction suppressed press freedom, the situation was not to be compared to events in Communist China, for example, in which at the same time a young worker was charged with being a counterrevolutionary, a crime punishable by death, for having put up wall posters calling for human rights and democracy.

TREASON

In 1351 the English Parliament passed the Statute of Treason, the essential source for the American law of treason. This highest of all crimes consisted in the fourteenth century of such elements as killing the king, queen, or the king's eldest son; violating the queen; counterfeiting the king's money; or slaying judges on duty. The chief modern vestige of the Statute of Treason is the phrase concerning adherence to the enemies of the government, which is still part of American law.

The English law of treason was often expanded to embrace all types of political offenses, but in America the adoption of our Constitution signaled a very restrictive view of treason, one which has great significance for American democracy. Unlike the earlier British practice, or for that matter, the policies of many of the modern states of the world, America did not define treason as consisting of disloyalty or political dissent. The American policy under the Constitution "was most consciously based on the fear of extension of the offense to penalize types of conduct familiar in the normal processes of the struggle for domestic political or economic power."[3]

The issue of defining treason in a restrictive manner was so significant that the definition was placed within the text of the original, unamended Constitution. The treason clause provides that

[3] James Hurst, *The Law of Treason in the United States* (Westport, Conn.: Greenwood Pub. Co., 1971).

"treason against the United States shall consist only in levying war against them, or in adhering to their enemies, giving them aid and comfort."[4] Two witnesses to the overt act of treason are required if the accused does not confess in open court. The punishment for treason is restricted to the individual who commits treason and may not extend to his or her family unless they also were participants in treasonable acts.

As a result of this constitutional clause political criticism of the government was permitted without fear of a treason charge. Courts did not expand the constitutional definition. There have been fewer than sixty treason prosecutions in American history. No one has ever been executed for treason. Executive pardons have been issued to many of those found guilty of treason.[5] For practical purposes, the treason charge has not been the principal means of safeguarding alleged state security. America has seen many efforts to punish political dissidents and to suppress their behavior. The prosecution of Eugene Debs, the Red Scare after World War I, the Billings-Mooney affair, the Sacco-Vanzetti trial, and the "Chicago Seven" trial of 1972—all are examples of the use of criminal law principally or partly for political purposes. None were treason trials. The only notorious treason trial in our history, that of Aaron Burr, was well deserved and well within the narrow boundaries of the American law of treason.

Treason, as a crime, requires a breach of allegiance. Nonresident aliens owe no duty to America and thus cannot commit treason. Former citizens residing outside the United States, for the same reason, cannot commit treason against the United States.[6] Resident aliens, however, do owe temporary allegiance to this country and could commit treason.[7] American citizens can commit treason whether residing here or elsewhere.

Treason is constitutionally defined as levying war against the United States; this means participation in a civil war or a foreign war against the United States. Armed American citizens who seize an American military emplacement may be committing treason when "mustered in military array for a treasonable purpose" since "every step which any one of them takes, by marching or otherwise, in part execution of this purpose is an overt act of treason in levying

[4] U.S. Constitution, Article III, Section 3.

[5] Hurst, *Law of Treason,* pp. 187-188.

[6] Ira Ikako Toguri D'Aqurio v. United States, 192 F 2d 338 (9th Cir. 1951).

[7] Carlisle v. United States, 83 U.S. 147 (1874).

war."[8] A conspiracy to use force to resist the execution of a federal law may amount to treason when committed for a national, disruptive purpose, according to older court rulings.[9] But it is doubtful whether modern courts would hold that armed efforts at draft resistance constituted treason.[10]

"Adhering to their enemies, giving them aid and confort" presents other treasonous possibilities. Selling critical military supplies to an enemy in wartime would constitute treason.[11] Purchasing an armed vessel for an enemy would be treason, too.[12] An American citizen who broadcasts demoralizing information to American troops in wartime would also be guilty of treason, especially if the broadcasts were transmitted from the enemy state.[13]

Treason might also be committed against a state government. State treason statutes cannot criminalize treason against the United States, since that is solely a federal offense. Treason against a state could be, at the same time, treason against the United States, if Congress permitted state criminalization. But the Supreme Court has held that Congress, through the Smith Act of 1940, has denied the states the power to punish the advocacy of the violent overthrow of the United States, even if it were intertwined with a similar advocacy of the overthrow of the state government.[14] Until Congress changes the effect of this ruling the treason that states may punish involves treason only against a particular state itself.

Federal law makes concealment and nondisclosure of the known treason of another a crime in itself.[15] This offense, rarely detected, requires "some affirmative act toward concealment of the felony," and "mere silence after knowledge of the commission of the crime" is not sufficient.[16] There are similar state statutes but very few cases have ever been brought under state law.

[8] United States v. Greiner, 26 Fed. Cas. 36, No. 15, 262 (1861).

[9] See charge to the Grand Jury, 30 Fed. Cas. 1015, No. 18,263 (1851).

[10] United States v. Vigol, Dall. 346,28 Fed. Cas. 376, No. 16,621 (1795) is the original case. It was followed in Druecker v. Salomon, 21 Wis. 621 (1867).

[11] Carlisle v. United States. 83 U.S. 147 (1874).

[12] United States v. Greathouse, 4 Sawy. 457,26 Fed. Cas. 18, No. 15,254 (1863).

[13] Ira Ikuko Toguri D'Aqurio v. United States, 192 F. 2d 338 (9th Cir., 1951).

[14] Pennsylvania v. Nelson, 350 U.S. 497 (1956).

[15] 18 U.S.C. sec. 2382.

[16] United States v. Farror, 38 F 2d 515,517 (D.C. Mass. 1930), affirmed 281 U.S. 624 (1930).

SEDITION

The objective of sedition may be similar to treason, that is, the subversion of the government and the open violation of its laws, but the offenses are different in their requisite elements. Sedition is a preliminary step to treason. Seditious behavior is preparatory to an injury to government. Sedition may be either a conspiracy aimed at the overthrow of government or a communication tending to promote disaffection for government and thereby tending toward the overthrow of government.[17]

Congress has the constitutional power to punish subversive activities.[18] Mere speech that criticizes government is, however, constitutionally protected by the First Amendment. The only example of a national statute directly aimed at the suppression of speech criticizing the government is the Alien and Sedition Laws of 1798. These laws were used to silence critics of the Adams administration, but their constitutionality was dubious and they were allowed to expire when the political climate changed during the Jefferson administration. The Espionage Act of 1917, amended by the Sedition Act of 1918, was also extremely broad. Under wartime stress almost any criticism of the government or the military was criminalized, and in addition the postmaster general was authorized to refuse to accept or deliver mail to anyone whom he suspected of violating the

[17] "The only offense of this general character which is known to our law is attempts by word, deed, or writing, to promote public disorder or to induce riot, rebellion or civil war, which acts are still considered seditions and may be overt acts, be treason." State v. Shepherd, 177 Mo. 205,222;76 S.W. 79,84 (1903).

[18] Ullman v. United States, 350 U.S. 422 (1955) holds that congressional power over national security is at least as broad as its power with respect to commerce.

A restraint on political activity in Florida.

876.36 Inciting insurrection

If any person shall incite an insurrection or sedition amongst any portion or class of the population of this state, or shall attempt by writing, speaking, or by any other means to incite such insurrection or sedition, the person so offending shall be guilty of a felony of the second degree, punishable as provided in § 775.082, § 775.083, or § 775.084.

Source: Florida Statutes Annotated.

Sedition Act. The Sedition Act of 1918 was repealed in 1921, and the Espionage Act amended again to incriminate the making or conveying of false statements with intent to interfere with the operation or success of the military or to promote the success of the enemy.

Current sedition law is based upon a series of acts passed since 1940, the best known being the Smith Act of 1940.[19] An Internal Security Act was passed in 1950,[20] together with a Subversive Activities Control Act.[21] In 1954 Congress approved the Communist Control Act[22] and in 1956 adopted an act requiring the registration of persons trained in espionage by foreign governments.[23] These are the basic sedition statutes, but their application is restricted by the liberties guaranteed in the Bill of Rights.

The Smith Act makes it a crime to knowingly or willfully advocate, abet, teach, or advise the "duty, necessity, desireability, or propriety of overthrowing or destroying the government of the United States or of any state . . . by force or violence." It also prohibits the publication or the distribution of material advocating such action as well as the organizing of "any society, group, or assembly of such persons who teach, advocate, or encourage" the overthrow of the government.

On its face the Smith Act seems to criminalize speech and assembly when a purpose to advance the overthrow of the government is manifest. The Supreme Court, however, has softened the impact of the act in various ways. In 1956 the Court held that the act is aimed not at advocacy of principles divorced from action, not at abstract political speeches, but at the advocacy and teaching of some "concrete action for the forcible overthrow of the government."[24] The membership in a subversive organization must be, according to the Court, a knowing membership in a group that advocates the violent overthrow of the government, and the membership must be active, not merely passive.[25] Moreover, some courts contend that active

[19] 41 Stat. 1359, ch. 136.

[20] 50 U.S.C. sec. 781

[21] 50 U.S.C. sec. 793.

[22] 50 U.S.C. sec. 841–844.

[23] 50 U.S.C. sec. 851 provides that every person who has knowledge of, or who has received instruction or assignment in, the espionage, counterespionage, or sabotage service or tactics of a foreign government or foreign political party, must register with the attorney general.

[24] Yates v. United States, 354 U.S. 298, 320 (1956).

[25] Scales v. United States, 367 U.S. 203 (1960).

membership in a subversive organization must be coupled with a personal intent to bring about the violent overthrow of the government as speedily as possible.[26] The Smith Act has been held not to violate the constitutional guarantees of free speech, free press, and free association.[27] Although it has been used mainly to prosecute members of the Communist party, it does not penalize simple, passive membership in the party.

The Subversive Activities Control Act of 1950 was based upon the declaration by Congress of a worldwide communist movement dedicated to espionage and subversion. But the act does not make mere membership in any communist organization, by itself, criminal. Instead Congress attempted to compel registration of Communist party members, a provision effectively stricken down by a Supreme Court decision resting upon the privilege against self-incrimination.[28] The 1954 Communist Control Act, in spite of its strong language, has not been much used, and the Smith Act, with amendments, remains the major piece of contemporary sedition legislation, available against communists or any other groups or individuals who seriously threaten national security. In practice, the Smith Act, too, is almost never the basis of a criminal prosecution because of its judicially restricted scope.

ESPIONAGE

In general, espionage, or spying, means obtaining information relating to the national defense and communicating it to a foreign nation, in the knowledge of its potential use to the injury of the United States.[29] Espionage is purely a federal crime since only the national government may wage war and protect the national security. It is unlawful to transmit documents, photographs, models, or similar information relating to national defense if the information could injure the United States or advantage a foreign nation. Transmitting such information to unauthorized individuals is espionage. Transmission to a foreign nation or a foreign military force is espionage punishable by death.[30]

[26] Hellman v. United States, 298 F. 2d 810 (9th Cir., 1962).

[27] Dennis v. United States, 341 U.S. 494 (1951); Scales v. United States, 367 U.S. 203 (1961).

[28] Albertson v. Subversive Activities Control Board, 382 U.S. 70 (1965).

[29] 18 U.S.C. sec. 792.

[30] 18 U.S.C. sec. 794.

Congress has broken down various aspects of espionage into separable offenses. Obtaining defense information without authorization[31] is a different offense from transmitting that same information.[32] Both offenses are distinct from the crime of treason, or so the courts have held.[33] Clearly the detailed specification of espionage offenses accomplishes many of the same ends as a treason statute, but without the great problems of proof.

No one can be convicted of espionage if the information in question was made available to the public by the government. If the information was lawfully available it can be lawfully transmitted. Furthermore, newspapers can publish material deemed secret, even if the person who obtained the information may have obtained it unlawfully. This is the significance of the landmark Pentagon Papers case, in which the United States government sought, and was refused, an injunction against two newspapers that published the contents of a government study that had been classified secret.[34] Such an injunction might have been issued, however, if the Supreme Court had been convinced of the threat to the national security.

It is not necessary that the United States be at war to invoke the espionage laws. The espionage laws make no distinctions among friendly, neutral, and unfriendly nations. Transmission to allies

[31] 18 U.S.C. sec. 793 (6).

[32] 18 U.S.C. sec. 794 (a).

[33] United States v. Drummond, 354 F. 2d 132 (2nd Cir., 1964), cert. denied, 384 U.S. 1013 (1965).

[34] New York Times Co. v. United States, 403 U.S. 713 (1971).

This basic act, not the Espionage Act, has been the main means of prosecuting spies.

(1) any person who acts as an agent, representative, employee, or servant, or any person who acts in any other capacity at the order, request, or under the direction or control, of a foreign principal or of a person any of whose activities are directly or indirectly supervised, directed, controlled, financed, or subsidized in whole or in major part by a foreign principal, and who directly or through any other person—

(i) engages within the United States in political activities for or in the interests of such foreign principal. . . .

Source: 18 U.S.C. sec. 611—The Foreign Agents Registration Act.

---

may constitute espionage, so long as there has been an injury to the United States or an advantage to a foreign nation.

Spies rarely are prosecuted under the espionage acts because of the high standards of proof required. Those believed to be spies may be prosecuted under the Foreign Agents Registration Act. This modest-seeming act can be used only against foreign nationals. While it may be a milder means of punishing spy activity than our spies might expect when caught overseas, the spy is at least exposed and removed from his or her activity.

SABOTAGE

Sabotage is usually a wartime offense. The criminalization of an interference with the national war effort is a necessary part of national defense. The crime of sabotage requires a specific intent to injure or interfere with the war effort of the United States or of an ally. But the concept of sabotage has been extended to include matters not found in Webster's dictionary. Under modern American statutes the willful manufacture or construction of defective war material or war facilities is also made a crime.[35] Sabotage has also been stretched to cover "national defense material" and "national defense premises,"[36] so an injury to a National Guard post might be included even if the injury occurred in peacetime.[37]

National defense interests rank so high that peacetime sabotage, like peacetime espionage, may be criminalized. Some observers contend that the penalties for espionage and sabotage are greater in America than elsewhere in the Western world.[38] In a nuclear age, however, the possibilities of peacetime sabotage just prior to a swift nuclear attack are ever present and sabotage of nuclear energy plants or civilian water supplies is a genuine risk. Even without a war, individual acts of terrorism may take the form of sabotage, a fact of life that the criminal law must acknowledge.

Another federal offense involves the destruction of government property. Since this offense requires a lower level of proof than

[35] 18 U.S.C. sec. 2154.

[36] 18 U.S.C. sec. 2156.

[37] See Gorin v. United States, 312 U.S. 19 (1941), and United States v. Achtenberg, 459 F. 2d 91 (8th Cir., 1972).

[38] See Harold W. Bank, "Espionage: The American Judicial Response," *American University Law Review* 21 (1972): 329-373.

sabotage does, the Justice Department often pursues sabotagelike conduct under this heading instead. During the late 1960s and early 1970s when popular antiwar sentiment took the form of direct action, the Destruction of Government Property Statute came in handy. Lately anti-nuclear power activists have been threatened with prosecution under this statute, although private power companies do not come under the umbrella of the statute.

The current version of a law found constitutionally defective in 1968, but reenacted by the California legislature anyway, as a means of punishing radical attitudes and behavior.

§ 11401. Offense; punishment

Any person who:

1. By spoken or written words or personal conduct advocates, teaches or aids and abets criminal syndicalism or the duty, necessity or propriety of committing crime, sabotage, violence or any unlawful method of terrorism as a means of accomplishing a change in industrial ownership or control, or effecting any political change; or

2. Willfully and deliberately by spoken or written words justifies or attempts to justify criminal syndicalism or the commission or attempt to commit crime, sabotage, violence or unlawful methods of terrorism with intent to approve, advocate or further the doctrine of criminal syndicalism; or

3. Prints, publishes, edits, issues or circulates or publicly displays any book, paper, pamphlet, document, poster or written or printed matter in any other form, containing or carrying written or printed advocacy, teaching, or aid and abetment of, or advising, criminal syndicalism; or

4. Organizes or assists in organizing, or is or knowingly becomes a member of, any organization, society, group or assemblage of persons organized or assembled to advocate, teach or aid and abet criminal syndicalism; or

5. Willfully by personal act or conduct, practices or commits any act advised, advocated, taught or aided and abetted by the doctrine or precept of criminal syndicalism, with intent to accomplish a change in industrial ownership or control, or effecting any political change;

Is guilty of a felony and punishable by imprisonment in the state prison*** (Amended by Stats. 1976, c. 1139, p. 5159, § 301, operative July 1, 1977.)

Source: Criminal Syndicalism Act, California Penal Code sec. 11401.

STATE SEDITION STATUTES

Many states have attempted to create sedition offenses similar to federal statutes. At first such statutes were upheld, but in the post-World War II era the constitutionality of state subversive control legislation has become suspect. Congress has preempted part of this field, but the states have not been entirely stripped of their powers to protect themselves. States may prosecute seditious activity against state or local government.[39] The Tenth Amendment to the Constitution does reserve to the states some residual powers to deal with sedition.[40]

State prosecution of political dissidents has been less prevalent in recent years than in the era between World War I and World War II. Criminal syndicalism statutes were enacted in twenty states from 1917 to 1920. Statutes have proscribed criminal anarchy and other subversive activities. A state criminal syndicalism or criminal anarchy statute is not unconstitutional unless it violates First Amendment rights or conflicting national powers to deal with subversion and sedition. Vagueness is also a constitutional infirmity.[41] Few state sedition statutes have survived the stringent scrutiny of the courts, but many remain on the books untested and unenforced.

Common law offenses may serve the same ends as a state sedition statute. Carrying a red flag in a parade may under some circumstances be punishable as a disturbance of the peace.[42] The duty of the state to uphold order and to prevent rioting may permit reasonable regulation of the display of political symbols. Whether or not the American Nazis can parade around Independence Hall in Philadelphia shouting defiance and death to Jews depends upon the threat to public safety such an event might cause. Even then, free speech and free expression may be valued above the municipality's interest in preserving order.

LOYALTY OATHS

Both federal and state laws require some individuals to make a loyalty oath asserting their lack of advocacy of sedition, subversive activities, or treason. States and the national government may re-

[39] People v. Epton, 19 NY 2d 496, 227 NE 2d 829 (1967).

[40] State v. Levitt, 246 Ind. 275, 203 NE 2d 821 (1965).

[41] See Re Harris, 20 Cal. App. 3d 632 (1971), which follows Brandenburg v. Ohio, 395 U.S. 444 (1969).

[42] People v. Burman, 154 Mich. 150, 117 NW 589 (1908).

An overbroad state sedition statute.

MR. JUSTICE STEWART delivered the opinion of the Court.

On December 27, 1963, several Texas law-enforcement officers presented themselves at the petitioner's San Antonio home for the purpose of searching it under authority of a warrant issued by a local magistrate. By the time they had finished, five hours later, they had seized some 2,000 of the petitioner's books, pamphlets, and papers. The question presented by this case is whether the search and seizure were constitutionally valid.

The warrant was issued under § 9 of Art. 6889–3A of the Revised Civil Statutes of Texas. That Article, enacted in 1955 and known as the Suppression Act, is a sweeping and many-faceted law which, among other things, outlaws the Communist Party and creates various individual criminal offenses, each punishable by imprisonment for up to 20 years. Section 9 authorizes the issuance of a warrant "for the purpose of searching for and seizing any books, records, pamphlets, cards, receipts, lists, memoranda, pictures, recordings, or any written instruments showing that a person or organization is violating or has violated any provision of this Act." The section sets forth various procedural requirements, among them that "if the premises to be searched constitute a private residence, such application for a search warrant shall be accompanied by the affidavits of two credible citizens."

The application for the warrant was filed in a Bexar County court by the Criminal District Attorney of that County. It recited that the applicant

> ". . . has good reason to believe and does believe that a certain place and premises in Bexar County, Texas, described as two white frame houses and one garage, located at the address of 1118 West Rosewood, in the City of San Antonio, Bexar County, Texas, and being the premises under the control and in charge of John William Stanford, Jr., is a place where books, records, pamphlets, cards, receipts, lists, memoranda, pictures, recordings and other written instruments concerning the Communist Party of Texas, and the operations of the Communist Party in Texas are unlawfully possessed and used in violation of Articles 6889–3[1] and 6889–3A, Revised Civil Statutes of the State of Texas, and that such belief of this officer is founded upon the following information:
>
> "That this officer has received information from two credible persons that the party named above has such books and records in his possession which are books and records of the Communist Party including party lists and dues payments, and in addition other items listed above. That such information is of recent origin and has been confirmed by recent mailings by Stanford on the 12th of December, 1963 of pro-Communist material."

[1]Article 6889–3 of the Revised Civil Statutes of Texas, enacted in 1951 and known as the Texas Communist Control Law, provides, among other things, that various people and organizations defined by the law who fail to register with the Texas Department of Public Safety are guilty of criminal offenses punishable by imprisonment of up to 10 years.

Attached to the application was an affidavit signed by two Assistant Attorneys General of Texas. The affidavit repeated the words of the application, except that the basis for the affiants' belief was stated to be as follows:

> "Recent mailings by Stanford on the 12th of December, 1963, of material from his home address, such material being identified as pro-Communist material and other information received in the course of investigation that Stanford has in his possession the books and records of the Texas Communist Party."

The district judge issued a warrant which specifically described the premises to be searched, recited the allegations of the applicant's and affiants' belief that the premises were "a place where books, records, pamphlets, cards, receipts, lists, memoranda, pictures, recordings and other written instruments concerning the Communist Party of Texas, and the operations of the Communist Party in Texas are unlawfully possessed and used in violation of Article 6889-3 and Article 6889-3A, Revised Civil Statutes of the State of Texas," and ordered the executing officers "to enter immediately and search the above described premises for such items listed above unlawfully possessed in violation of Article 6889-3 and Article 6889-3A, Revised Civil Statutes, State of Texas, and to take possession of same."

The warrant was executed by the two Assistant Attorneys General who had signed the affidavit, accompanied by a number of county officers. They went to the place described in the warrant, which was where the petitioner resided and carried on a mail order book business under the trade name "All Points of View."[2] The petitioner was not at home when the officers arrived, but his wife was, and she let the officers in after one of them had read the warrant to her.

After some delay occasioned by an unsuccessful effort to locate the petitioner in another part of town, the search began. Under the general supervision of one of the Assistant Attorneys General the officers spent more than four hours in gathering up about half the books they found in the house. Most of the material they took came from the stock in trade of the petitioner's business, but they took a number of books from his personal library as well. The books and pamphlets taken comprised approximately 300 separate titles, in addition to numerous issues of several different periodicals. Among the books taken were works by such diverse writers as Karl Marx, Jean Paul Sartre, Theodore Draper, Fidel Castro [and others].

We need not decide in the present case whether the description of the things to be seized would have been too generalized to pass constitutional muster, had the things been weapons, narcotics or "cases of whiskey." See *Steele* v. *United States No. 1,* 267 U.S. 498,504. The point is that it was not any

[2]The petitioner had obtained a certificate to transact business under this trade name in accordance with the Texas "Assumed Name Law."

contraband of that kind which was ordered to be seized, but literary material—"books, records, pamphlets, cards, receipts, lists, memoranda, pictures, recordings and other written instruments concerning the Communist Party of Texas, and the operations of the Communist Party in Texas." The indiscriminate sweep of that language is constitutionally intolerable. To hold otherwise would be false to the terms of the Fourth Amendment, false to its meaning, and false to its history.

Two centuries have passed since the historic decision in *Entick* v. *Carrington,* almost to the very day. The world has greatly changed, and the voice of nonconformity now sometimes speaks a tongue which Lord Camden might find hard to understand. But the Fourth and Fourteenth Amendments guarantee to John Stanford that no official of the State shall ransack his home and seize his books and papers under the unbridled authority of a general warrant—no less than the law 200 years ago shielded John Entick from the messengers of the King.

The order is vacated and the cause remanded for further proceedings not inconsistent with this opinion.

It is so ordered.

Source: Stanford v. Texas, 379 U.S. 476 (1965).

---

quire public employees and officers to swear to their loyalty. According to one estimate 14 million civilian workers and 3.5 million members of the armed forces are subject to some kind of loyalty oath.[43] A person who takes such an oath while belonging to an organization devoted to subversion and who intended to further the organization's subversive aims is guilty of a criminal offense.[44]

Loyalty oaths seem an ineffective way to deal with seditious activity. Requiring a spy to take an oath not to spy will be of little deterrent effect on espionage. Requiring loyal citizens to swear to their loyalty does not make them more loyal. No one has ever been convicted for falsely asserting loyalty.

Teachers and public school employees are the largest category of loyalty oath takers. Refusal to take an oath may be grounds for not employing an applicant for a position. Dismissal of an employee for refusal to take an oath, however, may not be warranted without proof of some sort of subversive intent. Plainly, there is a risk that subversives may gain employment in sensitive defense plants or in

[43] Note, "The National Security Interest and Civil Liberties," *Harvard Law Review* 85: 1160.

[44] Keyishian v. Board of Regents, 385 U.S. 589 (1967).

the halls of Congress, but how can a loyalty oath serve to regulate potential subversive activity by a public employee or a public official? More appropriate criminal penalties exist for actual subversive activities. Loyalty oaths seem a senseless adjunct to the criminal law, although they may serve some purpose in discouraging a few people from seeking public employment.

THE 1968 ANTI-RIOT ACT

A special category of political crime was created by the passage of the 1968 Federal Anti-Riot Act. The act was actually a rider to the 1968 Civil Rights Bill[45] and was enacted following the devastating riots of April 1968 that swept Washington, D.C., and other cities. The act intended to deal with large-scale civil disturbances, but it was poorly drafted in the heat of current controversy. Moreover, the act contains repressive features that challenge traditional American views about the proper objects of criminal law.[46] It was passed as a kind of lesser substitute for existing treason and sedition laws. The act is available for use in inhibiting political dissent, transforming riot into a political crime.

The act is unusually vague and seemingly criminalizes hundreds of pieces of behavior. In order to be charged the suspect must either travel in interstate or foreign commerce, or use any facility of interstate commerce (including mail, telephone, telegraph, radio, television), and during or afterwards do any overt act for a series of illegal purposes. The purposes include inciting, organizing, promoting, encouraging, or participating in a riot. Also criminalized are aiding and abetting any person in inciting, participating in, or carrying on a riot. Violent conduct in furtherance of a riot is also punished.[47] Attempts to commit this prohibited conduct are also prohibited in an even more complex section.[48]

Riot has long been a criminal offense. Violent acts committed during riots are subject to state criminal law. The federalization of riot vastly expands the crime to include acts only remotely con-

[45] Act of April 11, 1968, Pub. L. No. 90-284, 82 Stat. 73.

[46] See Marvin Zalman, "The Federal Anti-Riot Act and Political Crime: The Need for Criminal Law Theory," *Villanova Law Review* 20 (1975): 897-937.

[47] 18 U.S.C. sec. 2101 (a).

[48] 18 U.S.C. sec. 2101 (b).

nected to a riot. In fact no riot need ever occur to invoke the federal statute; organizing or promoting a riot by a telephone conversation, for example, is criminalized. Moreover, the act treats aiders and abettors just as harshly as principals. The act casts a broad net that could capture persons careless enough to discuss some future political demonstration with violent language. Even more peculiar is the requirement for specific intent that is unrelated to an eventual violent act or any preparation for such an act.

Thus far federal courts have upheld the constitutionality of the Anti-Riot Act. It has been found to be "obtuse and obscure"[49] but not unconstitutional. The First Amendment issue has been virtually ignored on the ground that it "does not protect rioting and the incitement for riot."[50] The act was heavily used a few years ago when political dissension was at its height. When employed against the so-called Chicago Seven for events growing out of the 1968 Democratic National Convention in Chicago, the act seemed a useful tool to discourage mass demonstrations and prevent the possibility of sporadic violence. Judicial acceptance of this vague statute is based upon the desire to prevent riots that "may well erupt out of an originally peaceful demonstration."[51] Future use may be less benign, however; future unpopular political regimes confronted with massive popular demonstrations of dissent can turn to the statute to discourage such dissent. Surely government has the obligation to keep order, but it must do so in a way that clearly draws boundaries between mass expressions of dissent and genuinely riotous behavior.

BRIBERY

Bribery is denoted a political crime because it usually involves public officials or official actions. Bribery is not a political offense because of the way in which it threatens the national security, nor does bribery endanger public order. Bribery is a quiet crime committed in seclusion, intended to interfere with the proper conduct of public office. As such it is one of a series of offenses that stain the

[49] United States v. Dellinger, 472 F. 2d 340,364 (7th Cir. 1972).

[50] National Mobilization Committee v. Foran, 297 F. Supp. 1, 4 (N.D. Ill. 1968), affirmed, 411 F. 2d 934 (9th Cir. 1969).

[51] United States v. Dellinger, 472 F. 2d 340 (7th Cir. 1972).

Words may constitute bribery.

WATERMAN, Circuit Judge:

Codefendants, Jacobs and Spieler, were charged, first, with conspiring to bribe an Internal Revenue Service agent to influence an IRS investigation and so to obstruct justice in violation of 18 U.S.C. §§ 201, 1503 (18 U.S.C. §§ 371, 2), and, second, with offering a bribe to the agent, 18 U.S.C. § 201.

They were tried by a jury which returned verdicts of guilty against both defendants on both counts. Jacobs received concurrent sentences of one year on each count. Spieler was given suspended concurrent one-year prison terms and placed on probation for one year. Jacobs was released on his own recognizance pending the outcome of this appeal.

On appeal from the judgments of conviction they both advance the following claims: (1) the evidence was insufficient to convict them for attempted bribery or for conspiracy to bribe; (2) certain portions of the court's charge to the jury constituted reversible error; and (3) the use, without first having obtained a warrant authorizing the use, of electronic transmitting and recording equipment to overhear and record conversations violated their rights under the Fourth Amendment. In addition, appellant Spieler contends that he was a victim of a government plan of entrapment, and, also, that the court improperly denied his motion for a new trial predicated on "newly discovered evidence." We affirm both convictions.

The fateful progression of events and circumstances that ultimately led to appellants' indictments began in 1966 when the Regional Inspector's Office of the Internal Revenue Service in New York City undertook an investigation into an alleged attempt by a Martin Siegel and a Harold Adler to bribe a Revenue Agent, Gerald Stone, in connection with an audit of the 1964 and 1965 federal income tax returns of television comedian Alan King. Siegel, who served as King's accountant, and Adler, who was a theatrical agent for King, were subsequently indicted by a grand jury in mid-1967. Appellant Spieler, an attorney, represented Siegel in that grand jury proceeding. Appellant Jacobs, a businessman working in Manhattan, was a friend of and sometimes a lender of money to Spieler. Brian Bruh, a Special Agent of the IRS Intelligence Division, who was the Government's principal witness at the Jacobs and Spieler trial, completes the cast of characters. Agent Bruh was friendly with Jacobs. They had lived near each other in Brooklyn and Bruh had occasionally commuted in Jacobs's car to and from work with Jacobs.

On April 4, 1967, Jacobs telephoned Agent Bruh and asked Bruh to meet him at his office the following morning. Bruh complied, and thus began a series of meetings between the two.

The jury found that the Government had proved beyond a reasonable doubt that the objective which Jacobs and Spieler sought to attain by contacting Bruh was to arrange a way to get Martin Siegel out of trouble with the law by enlisting the efforts of Bruh to that end and by the strategic placement of bribe monies to be raised through the efforts of Jacobs and Spieler. . . .

Appellants' challenge to the sufficiency of the evidence to convict them of attempted bribery rests on their contention that they never got beyond the stage of preparation to commit the offense and never made the alleged attempt. We do not agree.

To begin with, as was said in United States v. Manton, 107 F.2d 834, 839 (2 Cir. 1938), cert. denied, 309 U.S. 664, 60 S.Ct. 590, 84 L.Ed. 1012 (1940), "We must take that view of the evidence most favorable to the government and sustain the verdict of the jury if there be substantial evidence to support it. Hodge v. United States, 6 Cir., 13 F.2d 596; Fitzgerald v. United States, 6 Cir., 29 F.2d 881." See, e.g., United States v. Dardi, 330 F.2d 316, 325 (2 Cir.), cert. denied, 379 U.S. 845, 85 S.Ct. 50, 13 L.Ed.2d 50 (1964); United States v. Tutino, 269 F. 2d 488, 490 (2 Cir. 1959).

[**1,2**] The evil sought to be prevented by the deterrent effect of 18 U.S.C. § 201(b) is the aftermath suffered by the public when an official is corrupted and thereby perfidiously fails to perform his public service and duty. Thus the purpose of the statute is to discourage one from seeking an advantage by attempting to influence a public official to depart from conduct deemed essential to the public interest. As Judge Hastie aptly stated in United States v. Labovitz, 251 F.2d 393, 394 (3 Cir. 1958):

> It is a major concern of organized society that the community have the benefit of objective evaluation and unbiased judgment on the part of those who participate in the making of official decisions. Therefore, society deals sternly with bribery which would substitute the will of an interested person for the judgment of a public official as the controlling factor in official decision.

It therefore follows that Section 201(b) is violated even though the official offered a bribe is not corrupted, or the object of the bribe could not be attained, or it could make no difference if after the act were done it turned out that there had been actually no occasion to seek to influence any official conduct. See, e.g., Kemler v. United States, 133 F. 2d 235, 238 (1 Cir. 1943).

[**3–6**] It is also perfectly plain that the crime is consummated irrespective of whether an offer of an amount of money to influence an official's behavior is accepted by the official. Here the fact that Agent Bruh at the April 20 meeting between Jacobs and Bruh held out for more than $5,000 offered him has no bearing upon whether the offerors violated 18 U.S.C. § 201(b). It is also immaterial that Jacobs and Spieler were thwarted in their efforts to raise any money at all to pass on to Bruh. The crime was completed when Jacobs expressed an ability and a desire to pay Bruh $5,000 at their April 20 meeting. Jacobs was speaking for himself but he also was acting as Spieler's spokesman. This became abundantly clear by Spieler's admissions at the meeting of May 5 (see note 5 and accompanying text *supra*). The jury could well have found that Jacobs's statement of April 20 that Spieler had told him to "start with 5," (see note 4 *supra*) was a clearly expressed "opener" to Bruh that Jacobs *and* Spieler were ready, willing and able to close the deal at that amount, and was a statement designed to influence Bruh to accept $5,000 as a bribe for disposing of the case against Siegel.

Source: United States v. Jacobs, 431 F. 2d 754 (2d Cir. 1970). Reprinted by permission of West Publishing Company.

political process and impugn the integrity of our democratic government.[52] The essence of bribery is the prostitution of a public trust and a betrayal of the public interest.[53]

In the early common law, bribery consisted of the corruption of a judge or other judicial officer. Later the common law concept was extended to cover offering money to executive officers as well. Vote-buying was subsequently included under the offense. Today common law bribery includes all persons connected in any way with the government, whether as bribe givers or bribe takers.[54]

In most jurisdictions bribery is a statutory offense. While statutes vary, the coverage is generally at least as broad as the common law. In fact, bribery statutes sometimes cover persons other than public officials; for example, federal law now covers bribery of a juror.[55] Federal law also covers sports bribery, so that a jockey who attempts to fix a race falls within the statute.[56] Some states have created an offense known as commercial bribery which consists of bribing an employee with the intent to influence his or her relationship with the employer.[57]

Generally bribery consists of the giving or the taking of anything of value with intent to corrupt an official action of the receiver of the bribe. This is different from extortion, in which the receiver demands or coerces an illegal gift or fee, and from graft, in which the corrupt intent need not be proven.

In bribery, corrupt intent is essential, although both parties need not share in the corrupt intent. It is sufficient that the intent be in the mind of either the bribe taker or the bribe giver. Only the person who has the corrupt intent may be found guilty (in most

[52] One of the few thoughtful pieces on political crime is Herbert L. Packer, "Offenses Against the State," *Annals of the American Academy of Political Science* 339 (1962): 77–88. Parker believes there are two categories: offenses of government and offenses that affect the orderly and just administration of public business. He includes within the second category offenses such as bribery, graft, and corruption. Parker also suggests that beyond this area is "a large and uncertain area of pressure and persuasion by interest groups" and "the financing of election campaigns." Parker wonders whether criminal sanctions are effective in these latter areas.

[53] State v. Duncan, 153 Ind. 318,54 N.E. 1066 (1899).

[54] See Commonwealth v. Funk, 314 Ky. 282,234 S.W. 2d 957 (1950).

[55] 18 U.S.C. sec. 201(a), as amended by Pub. L. 91-405, 84 Stat. 853, September 22, 1970.

[56] United States v. Walsh, 544 F. 2d 156 (4th Cir., 1976), interpreting 18 U.S.C. sec. 224.

[57] See State v. Brewer, 258 NC 533,129 S.E. 2d 262 (1963).

states). Federal law requires corrupt intent on the part of the bribe giver. It is immaterial that the corrupt purpose of the bribe may have been unattainable.

Bribery may take the outward form of a political contribution, a personal loan, or a charitable donation. The form does not matter so long as the purpose of corruptly influencing a public official is present. This means that the bribe taker and the bribe giver need never meet or exchange money. A promise will do, even a promise delivered through an intermediary. Depending upon the language of the bribery statute, however, a specific corrupt understanding between the parties may be a necessary element. Federal law does not require such an understanding.

Attempts to bribe, solicitation to bribe, and conspiracy to bribe are separate criminal offenses, with different punishments provided for each. In a specific situation any or all of these offenses may be committed, because the elements of each offense are slightly different. An attempt to bribe may be no more than an expression of a desire to pay a bribe. Conspiracy to give or receive a bribe requires merely that two or more persons receive or ask for a bribe. Federal law may punish "whoever, directly or indirectly, corruptly asks, demands, exacts, solicits, seeks, accepts, receives, or agrees" to take something of value in exchange for testimony before a court or a congressional committee,[58] thus lumping together a number of bribery concepts into one, somewhat confusing, whole.

Certain kinds of questionable behavior may well be subject to bribery or an associated charge. Furnishing public officials with free meals, lodging, or travel may amount to bribery. Receiving money from contractors for official favors is bribery. Offering police officers money for faking a breathalizer test is bribery.[59] Trying to influence bank examiners may constitute bribery. Bribery covers a very wide range of possible conduct toward public officials, making enforcement difficult. Detection is even more difficult.

CORRUPT ACTIVITY

Public officers may be held criminally liable for various types of so-called corrupt practices. Criminal punishment might be in addition to such civil liability as disqualification for office or forfeiture of

[58] 18 U.S.C. 201 (e).

[59] See State v. Stanley, 19 NC App. 684,200 S.E. 2d 223 (1973).

When is judicial favoritism a crime?

JONES, Judge.

An indictment charging a Judge with official misconduct under subdivision 2 of section 195.00 of the Penal Law is insufficient, and accordingly should have been dismissed on timely application, where that indictment, for the purpose of defining the duty "clearly inherent in the nature of his office" which allegedly was violated, only incorporates by reference the provisions of the Code of Judicial Conduct. Moreover, the disciplining of Judges for violation of ethical standards not involving independently criminal conduct has been reserved by the State Constitution to proceedings instituted before the present Commission on Judicial Conduct and prior to that before the Court on the Judiciary.

Appellant, a Suffolk County District Court Judge, was indicted on April 26, 1976, and charged with three counts of official misconduct in violation of section 195.00 of the Penal Law. That section provides

> "A public servant is guilty of official misconduct when, with intent to obtain a benefit or to injure or deprive another person of a benefit:
>
> "1. He commits an act relating to his office but constituting an unauthorized exercise of his official functions, knowing that such act is unauthorized; or
>
> "2. He knowingly refrains from performing a duty which is imposed upon him by law or is clearly inherent in the nature to his office."

Two counts of the indictment were dismissed by the court at the close of the People's case. The remaining count, which was submitted to the jury, charged in pertinent part that appellant: "with the intent to obtain a benefit . . . knowingly refrained from performing a duty which is imposed upon her by law or is clearly inherent in the nature of her office, to wit, on December 24, 1974, in Suffolk County, in her capacity as District Court Judge, she improperly dismissed, for failure to prosecute, a Simplified Traffic Information received by . . . a personal friend, in violation of . . . the Code of Judicial Conduct, Canons 2 and 3." Submission of this count resulted in a hung jury. On retrial of this count a guilty verdict was returned. The Appellate Division affirmed appellant's conviction without opinion. We now reverse and dismiss the indictment.

At issue is the permissibility of the enforcement of the provisions of the Code of Judicial Conduct by resort to criminal prosecution. During the course of the proceedings at the first trial, and again prior to the second trial, appellant moved to dismiss the indictment on the ground that an indictment which only charges violations of canons of judicial ethics cannot support a criminal charge of official misconduct—that the "Canons of Ethics cannot be substituted for the Penal Law". The court denied appellant's motion, concluding that "[a]ssuming a specific *mens rea,* conduct in violation of the respective Canons constituting the code becomes a violation of law when it is done with intent to gain any benefit or advantage. . . . The inclusion by reference to . . . the Code of Judicial Conduct is accordingly appropriate". We disagree.

Subdivision 2 of section 195.00 of the Penal Law condemns, and this indictment charges, a breach, with the requisite intent, of a duty that is either imposed by law or clearly inherent in the nature of the office. The only definition or description in the indictment of the duty in question, however, is by cross-reference to Canons 2 and 3 of the Code of Judicial Conduct.

Source: People v. La Carruba, 389 N. E. 2d 799 (N.Y., 1979). Reprinted by permission of West Publishing Company.

office. If, as President Arthur once said, "a public office is a public trust," then those who betray their trust can expect both civil and criminal liability. Or sometimes, anyway.

The control of political corruption is very difficult. Malfeasance and misconduct in office were offenses known to the common law. Official oppression, falsification of public documents, acceptance of two or more public offices, and violation of official regulations are various kinds of behavior penalized by some federal and state statutes. Far more problems are created by conflict of interest legislation forbidding certain kinds of employment by public officials that might interfere with the unbiased discharge of their public duties. In fact, neither Congress nor the state legislatures have been able to draft conflict of interest legislation in a manner that would not cover harmless behavior as well as potentially harmful behavior.[60] Nevertheless, conflict of interest legislation may be one of the best means of dealing with subtle forms of official corruption.[61]

Special offenses have been carved out dealing explicitly with public officers. Officers in charge of public funds are usually criminally liable for failure to promptly deliver those funds when required to do so. Making a personal profit out of public funds entrusted to a public official is usually a crime. Of the special offenses that can be committed only by public officials, perhaps the most unusual and important incriminations are for acts "under color of state law" that deprive individuals of their constitutional rights without due process of law.[62] The unusual federal statute covering such offenses is intended to protect individuals against the actions of

[60] See A. K. Bolton, H.A. Owen, A. L. Evans, "Conflicts of Interests of Public Officers and Employees," *Georgia State Bar Journal* 13 (1976): 64-68.

[61] M. I. Span and P. Parent, "Conflict of Interest: A Totally Ignored Illinois Criminal Sanction Against Corruption in Government," *Chicago-Kent Law Review* 52 (1975): 64-81.

[62] 42 U.S.C. sec. 1983.

state officials that threaten the enjoyment of constitutional rights. Since this a federal crime, the federal courts rather than the state courts can scrutinize allegations of rights violations on the part of state public officials. The provision has been used against police officers while on duty and has even been directed at the governor of Ohio for his deployment of the National Guard in the disorders at Kent State University that resulted in several student deaths.[63] The general rule, however, is that all public officers—including police officers, judges, and governors—are not personally liable for acts done in the line of duty. If police officers or other public officials exceed what their duty requires, as in cases of police brutality, then their conduct falls under the appropriate heading of the criminal law, including even homicide.

Many corruption offenses are associated with the conduct of elections. Voter intimidation is clearly criminalized.[64] Under federal law the familiar dictatorial practice of placing troops at the polling places is outlawed.[65] Both state and federal laws proscribe voting frauds such as voting twice, impersonating a voter, false registration, permitting unqualified persons to vote, making a false ballot count, and making fraudulent returns of the election. New York's Boss Tweed used to gain his electoral victories through fraudulent means when he needed them. Convicts were paraded out of prison to the polls, ballot boxes stuffed, votes bought and sold. Presumably stiffer criminal laws now inhibit these familiar nineteenth century practices.

In the twentieth century election laws are more concerned with raising and expending electoral funds. Soliciting political contributions and reporting the sources of those contributions has become a favored technique for purifying American elections. Indeed the law of campaign financing and campaign regulation generally is still growing, with the criminal law used as a means of last resort to ensure the reduction of the political influence of wealthy groups and individuals. This use of the criminal law also raises some questions about the reasonable limits of criminal sanctions. The Federal Election Commission and its state counterparts are beginning to serve as responsible agencies for scrutinizing campaign expenditure, using disclosure of funding techniques instead of resorting to criminal sanctions.

[63] See Scheuer v. Rhodes, 416 U.S. 232 (1974).

[64] 18 U.S.C. sec. 594.

[65] 18 U.S.C. sec. 592.

ABUSE OF PROCESS, FALSE ARREST, FALSE IMPRISONMENT

One of the most oppressive actions of public officials is abuse of process. This perversion of a regularly issued civil or criminal process can be both a crime and a civil offense. For the civil offense, damages may be obtained for any losses caused by the abuse. The criminal offense is almost unknown, but the civil liability of the public officer remains an important safeguard against the perversion of court processes. The use of court orders to harass individuals, to procure money from them, to trick them, or to defraud them is an ancient abuse. Unfortunately it is rarely a crime, so victims are left to pursue their own remedies in a civil court, bearing the legal expenses that might be offset by a successful trial. This is an area that deserves the attention of state legislators contemplating correction of the arbitrary acts of law enforcement officials.

Malicious prosecution is a closely related offense that also is not usually criminalized. The malicious prosecution action is directed principally but not solely against the public official who deliberately institutes groundless criminal actions against individuals.[66] Courts frown on these suits, especially those based on prior criminal proceedings, because they do not wish to discourage vigorous public prosecution of crimes.[67] Again, there may be some public policy reason to criminalize malicious prosecution, rather than having the alleged victim bear sole responsibility for initiating an action.

False arrest and false imprisonment are two other offenses that are always civil and sometimes criminal. False arrest is the unlawful restraint by one person of the physical liberty of another person. False imprisonment is similar, but it requires a prolonged detention, holding, or restraint of another against his or her will. The two offenses are quite closely intertwined, and many false imprisonments involve false arrests.

Unlawful arrests or imprisonments need not involve jails or prisons. An arrest by a sheriff outside his or her jurisdiction may constitute false arrest and false imprisonment.[68] An abusive police or administrative investigation may amount to a false arrest or a false imprisonment when it exceeds proper and lawful bounds.[69]

[66] See Charles Stokes Co. v. O'Quinn, 178 F. 2d 372 (4th Cir., 1942).

[67] See Imbler v. Pachtman, 424 U.S. 409 (1975).

[68] Krug v. Ward, 77 Ill. 603 (1875).

[69] Ware v. Dunn, 80 Cal. App. 2d 936,183 P. 2d 128 (1947).

Improper confinement to a mental institution could give rise to the action.[70] Judicial officers are immune from these actions, as are other individuals named in statutes.

In a criminal prosecution for false imprisonment there must be a criminal intent. Therefore, unlike the situation in civil actions, the motive or intent of the defendant is a legitimate defense issue. If a police officer arrests an individual believing that a crime has been committed, good faith in the performance of police duties may be a defense against a false arrest or a false imprisonment criminal action. On the other hand, forcing an individual to remain in a parked car may well constitute the crime of false imprisonment.[71] The crime of false imprisonment is more regularly found among the states than either abuse of process, false arrest, or malicious prosecution. Perhaps the threat to physical integrity and to individual liberty is greatest in false imprisonment situations. Nonetheless, the offenses of abuse of process, malicious prosecution, false arrest, and false imprisonment all exhibit a politically repressive character.[72]

The term *political crime* has a broader, less repressive meaning in America than it has in nondemocratic states. While dictatorships jam their prisons with political prisoners, democracies attempt to discourage genuine threats to national security and to the safety of the general public. While overzealous American prosecutors may at times employ the criminal law to dampen the activity of political dissidents, this has been exceptional, except during periods of wartime or political hysteria. Instead the political law of crimes now extends to cover the deviant acts of government officials whose abuses disturb democratic order and decency. In spite of rhetoric to the contrary, there is little evidence to prove that American criminal laws are geared to the repression of minorities.[73]

[70] Only when there is some lack of jurisdiction by the committing body or some failure to comply with statutory requirements.

[71] People v. Zilbauer, 44 Cal. 2d 43,279 P. 2d 534 (1955). There is no federal crime of false imprisonment or false arrest.

[72] See Otto Kirchheimer, *Political Justice,* (Princeton: Princeton University Press, 1961), pp. 3-21, which sets some general guidelines and definitions.

[73] See Isaac D. Balbus, *The Dialectics of Legal Repression* (New York: Russell Sage Foundation, 1973), which develops a theory of legal repression in America based upon the response of the criminal courts to the black ghetto revolts of the mid-1960s. Balbus applies a Marxist analysis consistently but not convincingly in his effort to prove that political repression of blacks is a normal condition of American criminal law.

SUMMARY

In nondemocratic nations serious abuses of human rights are sometimes committed in the name of politics. Enemies of the regime are executed or imprisoned without trial. American democracy has been virtually free of these excesses. Governmental officials are in fact held accountable under the criminal laws for their infractions of public order. Treason and sedition are uncommon offenses in America, and peacetime prosecutions (save the Rosenberg atomic bomb conspiracy trial) are exceedingly unusual in modern America. Political repression has existed, as FBI efforts under Director J. Edgar Hoover vividly exemplify, but repression is not the same as criminal prosecution. Constitutional interpretations by the Supreme Court have narrowed the reach of sedition legislation, and the 1968 Anti-Riot Act remains the best available legislative weapon against active political dissidents. The political crimes of politicians, such as the 1979–1980 Abscam episode, have drawn more public attention than the suppression of political dissidents.

9

VICTIMLESS CRIMES

Once America made the consumption of alcoholic beverages a crime. The "noble experiment" of prohibition was aimed at stamping out the use of alcohol in every section of the country. The experiment failed. In fact, organized crime flourished as a supplier of illegal alcohol, and the forbidden consumption of alcohol became a much desired social activity. The failure of many well-meaning people to achieve this health benefit through the use of the criminal law remains an example of a poor use of the criminal law. Many present-day law reformers believe that Americans are still making similar vain effects to regulate private, voluntary behavior through criminal law. The crimes they identify as unnecessary are often denoted *victimless* crimes, a not very accurate label. Nonetheless, there is a specific group of familiar offenses which reformers are attempting to eliminate or *decriminalize*. For the sake of convenience, these are gathered together here as so-called victimless crimes.

There is some question about the very meaning of the term *victimless crime*. A crime seems to require a victim. Ordinary language suggests that crimes are offenses with identifiable objects—the victims. Yet there is a philosophical tradition in the English-speaking world that helps justify the notion of victimless crime. The nineteenth-century English philosopher John Stuart Mill explained that there were limits to the power of the state over individual behavior. Mill insisted that the state could not interfere with the individual's conduct of his or her own affairs. According to Mill the state could act against an individual only when it wished to prevent harm to others. Society had no legitimate interest in prescribing individual conduct unless others were affected by it. Mills's view lingers on in current libertarian thought. The crimes treated in this chapter are those that affect mainly the wrongdoer. The unresolved question for the criminal law is whether the state may step in when the principal victim is the wrongdoer. Put in other terms, the question is whether society has a legitimate concern with private choices.

There is no firm agreement as to which crimes are victimless. One expert lists only abortion, homosexuality, and drug addiction.[1] A second adds gambling, smoking marijuana, prostitution, and private fighting.[2] A leading criminal law scholar considers fornication, gambling, and narcotics offenses as victimless crimes, but also

[1] Edwin M. Schur, *Crimes Without Victims: Deviant Behavior and Public Policy* (Englewood Cliffs, N.J.: Prentice-Hall, Inc., 1965).

[2] Jerome Skolnick, "Coercion to Virtue: The Enforcement of Morals," *Southern California Law Review* 41 (1968): 588–641.

places bribery and espionage in the category.[3] Loitering, public drunkenness, and vagrancy have been denoted victimless.[4] In fact, the list is still expanded from time to time by law reformers, legislative bodies, and popular writers. The common features of these prevalent crimes are hard to identify, but there is still a prevalent mood among reformers to take some of these crimes off the criminal statute books. Actually many of these crimes do produce victims, even if they are willing or self-created victims.

Edwin Schur, a sociologist who has studied the question closely, defines victimless crimes as those that involve "the exchange between willing partners of strongly desired goods or services."[5] The consensual exchange between the parties seemingly renders the idea of victimization meaningless. Normally people do not knowingly injure themselves nor do they usually agree to do so. There is no need to punish people for doing things they enjoy or that they feel they need. Some say society has no genuine concern for such behavior, and that in the absence of victims or discernible harm, such offenses should be decriminalized.

In the real world, the prostitute's "john" will never complain about committing fornication. Adulterers do not feel injured when they do their deeds. Drunks may not always enjoy drinking, but they do not feel they are criminals. Gamblers thrive on their thrills, even if their families do not. Drug addicts are afflicted with their problem. Homosexuals usually do not feel they have a problem. Abortion is a questionable case. So, too, is private fighting. There may be harm produced by these behaviors, but the participants have volunteered, maybe even consented to the harm. Can voluntary participants be victims? Guilt and compulsion may be factors in lawbreaking, but are the good reasons for criminalizing behavior that is caused by personal problems?

The victimless crime definition is still unclear. It may be mere verbal trickery to argue that these offenses produce no victims because the participants do not feel victimized. Society has an interest in many kinds of behavior. If the legislature deems a particular

[3] Herbert L. Packer, *The Limits of the Criminal Sanction* (Stanford, Calif.: Stanford University Press, 1968), pp. 151-267.

[4] Norval Morris and Gordon Hawkins, *The Honest Politician's Guide to Crime Control* (Chicago: University of Chicago Press, 1970), pp. 3, 6, 13-15; and Norval Morris, "Crimes Without Victims: The Law Is a Busybody," *New York Times Magazine,* April 1, 1973, pp. 10-11, 58-62.

[5] Edwin M. Schur in Edwin M. Schur and Hugo Adam Bedau, *Victimless Crimes: Two Sides of a Controversy* (Englewood Cliffs, N.J.: Prentice-Hall, Inc., 1974), p. 111.

behavior criminal that means that society regards the behavior as harmful, even if the participants do not. A suicide pact is always criminal in our society. If, on the other hand, we wish to reform the criminal law by removing from it those offenses that involve public morality rather than physical harm, let us decriminalize deviant behavior that is relatively not very harmful. We should not, however, pretend that such behavior is harmless. Perhaps the state has no business forcing people to be decent and moral, but that philosophical issue is very difficult to manage. After all, "virtually the entire penal code expresses the community's ideas of morality, or at least of the most egregious immoralities."[6]

Many Americans regard abortion, gambling, homosexuality, prostitution, and narcotics offenses as socially undesirable. Whether such deviant behavior should be labeled criminal is ultimately a political question. Morality and law are intertwined. There is no reason why a popular majority cannot use the criminal law to control morally repugnant behavior. Perhaps the proponents of the concept of victimless crimes are obscuring their real purpose: the desire to tolerate more variant types of private behavior than have historically been acceptable to a majority. Perhaps minority life-styles deserve toleration, but that is a political issue. In a society undergoing rapid social change there may be a need to remove repressive criminal laws. That is a judgment for legislatures to make, and interest groups can make their views known through political channels.

Even if the vocabulary of victimless crimes is confused, the list of the current objects of decriminalization is clear enough. Abortion, drug addiction, gambling, public drunkenness, prostitution, homosexuality, fornication, and adultery are each candidates for decriminalization. A good political argument can be made for removing the criminal label from these activities. Professional criminals and organized crime would be less likely to exploit their underworld advantages if these offenses were decriminalized. The costs of law enforcement would be lowered. Disrespect for and open flouting of the law would decrease. We shall accept the list of marginal crimes and examine their current justification as crimes. As for drug addiction and vagrancy, the Supreme Court has made criminal sanctions unconstitutional.[7] The time is ripe for reconsideration of similar offenses.

[6] Louis B. Schwartz, "Morals Offenses and the Model Penal Code," *Columbia University Law Review* 63 (1962): 86.

[7] Robinson v. California, 370 U.S. 660 (1962) holds unconstitutional a ninety day sentence for the crime of "being addicted to the use of narcotics." Vagueness is a constitutional defect in most vagrancy statutes. Papachristou v. City of Jacksonville, 405 U.S. 156 (1972).

An almost official view of victimless crimes.

The absence of a complaining victim appears to mark many ineffective criminal laws. Any system of law enforcement must rely heavily upon the cooperation of those who are unwillingly victimized. When the conduct is consensual on both sides and particularly when it occurs in private, the normal techniques of law enforcement inevitably tend to be frustrated. The laws prohibiting certain consensual sexual relations, both heterosexual and homosexual, as well as the laws against abortion, drunkenness, gambling, and narcotics, display these characteristics in varying degrees.

Where the nature of the crime is such that there are added difficulties of detection and proof, a lack of strong enthusiasm for the criminal prosecution, plus a persistent demand to engage in the conduct, the potential effectiveness of the criminal process is further reduced.

The criminal prohibitions against some types of sexual behavior reflect an idealized moral code, not what a substantial percentage of the population, judged by their conduct, regard as beyond the margin of tolerability for the average fallible citizen. Consensual homosexuality, on the other hand, is repugnant to large segments of the community. But the general feeling that those who engage in such acts are psychologically disturbed rather than wicked, tends to sap enthusiasm for criminal prosecution. Prostitution is certainly not viewed as a tolerable form of behavior by the general community. Yet the existence of professionalized sex, not only in this country but historically in all cultures, availed of by otherwise reputable citizens in all walks of life, plus the mildness of the usual sanctions, are sure evidence that it is not regarded unequivocally as condemnable.

Abortion and gambling share these qualities in varying degrees. There are compelling reasons for liberalizing abortion laws to accommodate manifest health needs. Gambling attracts a legal response that is ambiguous on its face: Within the same jurisdiction some kinds of gambling are prohibited and some are permitted, on the basis of distinctions with scarcely any relevance to the moral quality of the participant's conduct. Narcotics use does commonly arouse sentiments of condemnation and fear. But the continued demand for drugs, generated by deep-rooted and complex social and psychological drives, and the sentiment that it should be treated as a sickness serve to limit the efficiency of criminal law enforcement.

In several instances the criminal process is directed at objectives quite different from deterring the outlawed conduct through surveillance, prosecution, and correction of offenders. The rule of law enforcement in the case of public drunkenness, for example, is to remove unsightly annoyances from the public streets, to protect the drunk against physical dangers, and to provide a respite for him from his self-destructive habits. In the case of family support laws its role is largely to ensure the performance of family obligations. With the insufficient fund check writer its role is often to collect debts in behalf of creditors. Obviously measuring effectiveness in traditional law enforcement terms is inappropriate in these cases. The issue is how well the use of the criminal process in these instances attains its special objectives. . . .

No doubt the criminal process is filling a need in these situations. It would seem, however, that civil processes or institutions designed to handle particular social problems would be more effective than the criminal process in many cases. The increasing demands of due process in all criminal proceedings, the requirements of appointment of counsel, prohibition of interrogation in certain circumstances, high standards with respect to waiver of constitutional rights, and others, add to the difficulty of enforcing the criminal law in many of the situations described in this chapter.

One substantial cost of overextended use of the criminal process is the risk of creating cynicism and indifference to the whole criminal law and its agencies of enforcement at a time when precisely the opposite is needed. This indifference tends to occur particularly where the criminal sanction is generally unenforced.

Source: President's Commission on Law Enforcement and the Administration of Justice, Task Force Report, *The Courts* (Washington, D.C.: Government Printing Office, 1967), p. 106.

ADULTERY AND FORNICATION

Fornication is probably America's most popular crime. Sociologists have discovered that more than two-thirds of the male population have indulged in fornication. Adultery is also prevalent, although statistics are not especially reliable. Certainly arrests for adultery or fornication are quite rare. For these reasons many experts have urged the decriminalization of adultery and fornication,[8] though many believe that sexual permissiveness will only increase after decriminalization.

Under common law, fornication was sexual intercourse between any unmarried woman and any male (whether married or not). Modern statutes usually define fornication as sexual intercourse between persons not married to each other. The crimes of adultery and fornication are often linked together, with the marital status of one of the parties the distinguishing feature.

Adultery is a statutory crime. The elements are: sexual intercourse and the fact that one of the participants is married to a person other than the other participant. This crime involves the mutual consent of the participants. The third party is deemed injured, and adultery is often a ground for divorce.

[8] Fornication statutes have been held to be unconstitutional invasions of privacy in some states. See Note, *Buffalo Law Review* 27 (1978): 395–409.

Many states no longer punish adultery or fornication. In place of these crimes there may be a statutory offense of illicit cohabitation. Given the growing popularity of that arrangement, pressures will be growing to decriminalize cohabitation. Perhaps all such offenses are better managed through religious or other social influences. The illicit cohabitation of unmarried individuals may be the kind of private behavior that is not a proper public concern.

There is one sidelight to adultery. Some states regard a wife's adultery as a provocation to commit manslaughter. In such states a murder charge may be reduced to manslaughter when adultery is involved. Some statutes go further and regard homicide committed when a wife is caught in the act of adultery as justified.

ABORTION

Abortion is viewed as a form of murder by some groups, but the modern trend is toward lessening the criminal aspects of abortion. Under common law, abortion consisted of an intentional procurement of the miscarriage of a pregnant women, with or without her consent, unless the act was done in an effort to save the life of the mother. After the fetus showed signs of life, abortion would be committed if it subsequently was killed. The legal irrelevance of women's consent aroused those groups concerned with women's rights. Today the chief issue in abortion legislation seems to have become an uneasy balance between the woman's right to control her own body, with a concomitant right to choose abortion, against the state's interest in preserving the life of the unborn child.

A fetus is not a life in being. Consequently, propaganda to the contrary, there is generally no possibility of regarding abortion as homicide. A few states have a broader view of a life in being that includes a fetus, but the purpose of such legislation is usually to punish those who assault the pregnant woman, not the woman herself.

Most modern abortion statutes criminalize the operation itself or the attempt to procure the miscarriage. A crime is committed whether or not the miscarriage results. There must be a specific intent to procure a miscarriage. Many statutes require corroboration of the act in addition to the testimony of the woman involved. Some states allow therapeutic abortions, but each state provides a somewhat different health justification.

There is some doubt about the constitutionality of abortion

statutes. In 1973, the Supreme Court decided that a state criminal abortion statute that provided for exceptions only to save the life of the mother, without regard to the stage of pregnancy, violated the due process clause of the Constitution.[9] According to the Court, during a period approximately the length of the first trimester of pregnancy an abortion decision must be left to the judgment of the pregnant woman and her attending physician. In a related decision the Court invalidated provisions of the Georgia abortion statute (based upon the Model Penal Code) that required that lawfully permitted abortions be performed in an accredited hospital, with the approval of a hospital committee on abortion, on the ground that this statute invaded the mother's area of choice during the first trimester.[10]

Partly because of the questionable constitutionality of abortion laws many state legislatures have moved toward decriminalization. Abortion is not treated as a crime in those states that have excluded from punishment voluntary terminations of pregnancy. The matter is still a heated political issue. Militant women's groups insist that women, having an unlimited right to use their own bodies, should be the sole agents of choice on the question of bearing children. Some militant pro-life activists insist that abortion laws are necessary to protect and preserve the life of the unborn child. State laws vary in the length of time during which abortion is criminal. A few have eliminated the crime of abortion altogether.

Even where abortion is still a crime, a woman generally may not be guilty of performing abortion upon herself. Neither can she be punished as an accomplice to the crime, unless a statute makes it a crime for a woman to solicit or submit to an abortion, or attempt to procure her own miscarriage.[11]

HOMOSEXUALITY

The law frowns upon improper sexual relationships. Heterosexuality within the monogamous marriage is the societal norm, and the criminal law sharply restricts other kinds of sexual relationships. Homosexuality has been deemed unnatural. The sodomy laws (which can refer to homosexual or heterosexual activity) prohibit homosexual acts, and police in some jurisdictions use these laws to harass homosexuals.

[9] Roe v. Wade, 410 U.S. 113 (1973).

[10] Doe v. Bolton, 410 U.S. 179 (1973).

[11] California Penal Code, sec. 275.

The Kinsey report and later surveys of American sexual behavior reveal that homosexuality is quite prevalent in American life. Indeed, homosexual political activity has emerged as a strong political force in California and elsewhere. Homosexual activists, male and female, have vigorously campaigned for their rights, claiming that the criminal law that declares them to be illegal deviants is an interference with their personal life-style, an intrusion into their privacy. Few states have modified their criminal law on the subject, but enforcement of these laws concerning sex deviance is increasingly lax.

In 1975 a group of male homosexuals brought a test case in a federal district court that challenged the constitutionality of the Virginia sodomy statute, as it was applied to consensual homosexual acts performed in private by adult males.[12] The case was heard by a three-judge panel, which voted two-to-one to sustain the statute. The majority opinion held that state legislation regulating sexual conduct is constitutionally suspect only when it "trespasses upon the privacy of the incidents of marriage, upon the sanctity of the home, or upon the nature of family life."[13] The Supreme Court later sustained this judgment, but failed to give any legal justification. Nonetheless the case did establish the proposition that state efforts to prohibit private, consensual homosexual conduct are constitutionally permissible.

The issue is one of sound public policy, not of constitutional rights. Does the state have a legitimate concern with regulating private, consensual homosexual behavior, or is the issue merely a concern for tolerating alternate life-styles? The matter has been hotly debated in New Jersey and other states undergoing revision and recodification of criminal law. Public expressions of homosexual activity may be offensive to a majority, but as long as that expression does not result in prohibited sexual activity the criminal law cannot reach it. The decriminalization of homosexuality may, however, result in a great increase in public display of homosexual affection. The real purpose of the criminal law in this area is probably not so much to punish private, consensual homosexual behavior as it is to discourage offensive public expressions of homosexual affection. Behind that may lie a fear of the contamination of children or of susceptible adults with the taint of homosexuality. These attitudes on the part of the heterosexual majority may be understand-

[12] Doe v. Commonwealth's Attorney, 403 F. Supp. 1199 (E. D. Va. 1975), aff'd. mem., 425 U.S. 901 (1976).

[13] 408 F. Supp. at 1200. (E.D. Va. 1975).

able, but do they provide a sufficient basis for criminalizing homosexuality?

Eighteen states have decriminalized sodomy. Four states expressly limit their prohibition of consensual sodomy to homosexual acts.[14] Currently, thirty-two states and the District of Columbia impose criminal penalties on consenting adults who engage in private homosexual activity. Two states have criminalized homosexual activity in detailed fashion.[15] The decriminalization of homosexual activity is no longer just a moral issue. It is a highly political one in which the forces of sexual toleration are ranged against those who seek to stem the tide of sexual permissiveness.

PROSTITUTION

Prostitution is one of America's most prevalent consensual crimes. While there is some disagreement about whether prostitution itself is a crime or whether it should be controlled under the laws concerning adultery, fornication, seduction, solicitation, lewd cohabitation, or vagrancy, our states do regard the engaging in sexual activity for a fee as a crime. Statutes differ over the status of the prostitute's customer, but under the impetus of pressure from women's groups statutes increasingly tend to regard the client and the prostitute as equal offenders. Prostitution laws are often enforced irregularly and variably, as every visitor to a big city bar well knows, but only in Nevada is prostitution legal. Elsewhere the crime, though common enough, is kept under a kind of discreet regulation by the police, who make sporadic arrests of prostitutes.

There is little evidence that prostitution can be suppressed by criminal laws, although it can be chased off the streets periodically. Apparently the law cannot eliminate prostitution. There might be less wasteful ways of using state and local funds than in pursuit of prostitution, an endless quest. Public solicitation and public sexual acts can be controlled under properly drawn disorderly conduct statutes. Why, then, should not discreet prostitution be decriminalized?

The drafters of the Model Penal Code considered these arguments and rejected them.[16] They contended that prostitutes were an

[14] Kansas Stat. Ann. sec. 21-3505 (1974); Kentucky Rev. Stat. Ann. sec. 510.100 (1975); Montana Rev. Codes Ann. sec. 94-2-101 (4), -5-505 (1976); Texas Penal Code Anno. sec. 21.06 (1974).

[15] Georgia Code Ann. sec. 26-2002 (1970); Wisconsin Stat. Ann. sec. 944.17 (1958).

[16] Model Penal Code, sec. 207.12, at p. 175 of the Tentative Draft No. 9, 1958.

important source of venereal disease, creating a public health problem. Prostitution, they believed, led to corruption of law enforcement and also led to "the maintenance of criminal organizations and parasitic elements living on the proceeds of prostitution . . . committed to promote the activity by finding new customers and new women to serve them."[17]

[17] Id.

Eliminating the "oldest profession" Nevada style.

Prostitution

6.12.010 Adoption. Public health, safety and welfare will be promoted by the adoption of the ordinance codified in this chapter licensing, regulating, and controlling prostitution within the county, and prohibiting any prostitution within the county except as conducted in accordance with the provisions of such ordinance.

6.12.020 Prostitution not an offense or nuisance. The operation of a house of prostitution within the county of Lyon in accordance with the provisions of this chapter does not constitute a public nuisance or an offense to public decency.

6.12.030 Unlawful when. A. It is unlawful for any person, firm or corporation to keep or operate any house of prostitution, house of ill fame or bawdy house of any description within the county of Lyon, except as herein provided in this chapter.

B. It is unlawful for any person to practice prostitution or to solicit business for a prostitute or to procure any person for the purpose of prostitution within the county of Lyon, except as herein provided in this chapter.

C. In the trial of any case arising under the provisions of subsection A. or B. of this section, evidence of general reputation shall be competent evidence as to the question of the ill fame of any house of prostitution and to the question of the ill fame of any woman alleged to be practicing prostitution.

. . .

6.12.070 License application—Filing and investigation. A. All license applications under the provisions of this chapter shall be filed with the county clerk, who shall present the same to the board at the time of the next regular session of the board of county commissioners.

B. Upon presentation of any license application to the board, the board shall refer such application to the county sheriff for investigation. The sheriff shall conduct a full investigation of all information contained in the license application . . .

Source: Lyon County, Nevada, Prostitution Ordinance, Chap. 6.12.

Doubtless, the crime of prostitution does involve these factors, but many of them are effects of the law itself rather than of the forbidden activity. These problems stem from the criminalization of prostitution more than from the conduct of the prostitutes. Some of these assertions are sexual myths. Prostitution does not contribute significantly to the spread of venereal disease, since over 80 percent of reported cases of disease were in the 15 to 30 age group, while most clients of prostitutes are in a much older age group.[18] Young people spread VD through voluntary sex acts. Prostitutes do not as a rule. Moreover, a presidential commission concluded that most prostitution is not controlled by organized crime.[19] If prostitution were legal there would be less need for pimps and police payoffs. Even though prostitutes may not be nice people and some of their friends might be criminals, those are different matters.

There are more than a half-million working prostitutes in America.[20] The police make 100,000 prostitution arrests annually. Police departments in large cities maintain vice squads that spend most of their time tracking down prostitutes. Once arrested the prostitute is usually released, but if jailed she (or he) simply returns

[18] For an extensive survey of this and related policy questions concerning prostitution, see Note, "Decriminalization of Prostitution: The Limits of the Criminal Law," *Oregon Law Review* 55 (1976): 553-566.

[19] President's Commission on Law Enforcement and Administration of Justice, *The Challenge of Crime in a Free Society* (Washington, D.C.: Government Printing Office, 1967), p. 189.

[20] A debatable figure, but see Note, *Oregon Law Review* 55 (1976): 561.

Who is the victim? Who is protected?

Patronizing a prostitute

(1) Patronizing a prostitute is either:

(*a*) Knowingly entering or remaining in a house of prostitution with intent to engage in sexual intercourse or any unlawful sexual act with a prostitute; or

(*b*) Knowingly hiring a prostitute to engage in sexual intercourse or any unlawful sexual act.

(2) Patronizing a prostitute is a class C misdemeanor. [L. 1969, ch. 180, § 21-3515; July 1, 1970.]

Source: Kansas Statutes Annotated sec 21-3515.

to the life of prostitution with a longer criminal record. Women prostitutes are repeatedly arrested for the crime and their criminal record merely makes access to a more decent life more difficult.

The decriminalization of prostitution need not mean the abandonment of public concern with the practice. Even Nevada confines prostitution to licensed premises. Administrative regulations might confine prostitution to particular sections of a city. Health inspections could be made mandatory. Public solicitation could still be an offense, if it were done in a notorious or disorderly fashion. We have learned to deal with obscenity by confining so-called adult book stores to shadier sections of town, away from the schools and playgrounds. The same could be done for prostitution. Again, the issue is essentially political. Whether the criminal law ought to be used to sustain a decaying code of sexual morality is a proper subject of political debate and discussion.

GAMBLING

People will bet on almost anything. If they choose to gamble, lottery tickets can be purchased, off-track betting can be enjoyed, and bingo can be played—somewhere in the United States—without fear of criminal punishment. Nevada is no longer alone in regulating and licensing professional gambling casinos. Atlantic City has become a gambling Mecca, while other states are considering permitting gambling casinos within their borders. In spite of all this permissiveness about gambling, however, in most states most forms of gambling are violations of criminal law.

There is an enormous inconsistency in public policy toward gambling. One can freely speculate in corn futures, stocks, or Krugerrands (gold coins) without violating criminal laws. But once a roulette wheel spins or a wager is placed on a sporting event there is a risk of violating one or another criminal law. Apart from the inconsistency, there is a question of the practical enforceability of the multitude of criminal laws touching upon gambling. As with other crimes discussed in this chapter, there is also a question of the wisdom of punishing a willing victim, a consenting adult who chooses to gamble.

A purchase of an insurance policy is, in a sense, a gamble as well as an investment. This is not, however, the kind of gambling contemplated by the criminal law. Courts differ a great deal over the meaning of such terms as gambling, betting, or wagering. Under various antigambling statutes the courts are often called upon to determine whether some particular activity is a game of chance, a game of skill, or a mixed game of chance and skill. Upon these distinctions may hinge the criminality or innocence of the conduct. Apparently, if the dominant element in a game is luck, then it is probably gambling, according to most courts. Even the fact that some players are highly experienced and knowledgeable at such a game does not detract from its essential character as gambling.[21]

[21] See Baedaro v. Caldwell, 156 Neb. 489,56 NW 2d 706 (1953).

A verdict on gambling.

We set out to understand what current anti-gambling laws mean to the criminal justice system. Our findings can be summarized fairly succinctly:

1. The laws against gambling in private are a symbolic gesture on the part of legislators; they are neither enforced or enforceable in any reasonable sense of the word.
2. Legislators have given police a relatively unattractive job, for which police can get little credit if they do a good job and considerable abuse if they fail.
3. The laws against public social gambling and commercial gambling probably are enforceable to the extent that other comparable laws are enforceable. The resources devoted to gambling law enforcement are very modest and the results, with a few notable exceptions, are modest as well. Most departments realistically strive for one of several models of limited enforcement.
4. Citizens are very likely to view non-enforcement of gambling laws as an indication of police corruption.
5. Regional, multi-service criminal organizations were reported to directly control all or a substantial portion of illegal commercial gambling operations in about half the cities. These cities were much more likely than others to have had publicly disclosed gambling-related corruption in the past. In the balance the cities, bookmaking and numbers were said to be run primarily by local, independent organizations that specialized in gambling. There had been no significant publicly disclosed gambling-related corruption in any of these cities in the past ten years.

Source: National Institute of Law Enforcement and Criminal Justice (LEAA), *Gambling Law Enforcement in Major American Cities* (Washington, D.C.: Government Printing Office, 1978).

Whatever we mean by gambling, the criminal law has become a major factor in regulating what has become the business of gambling. That business is now a concern of federal law enforcement officials. There is a great deal of state law on the subject of unlawful gambling, but the states, not the federal government, have punched holes in antigambling statutes to permit bingo, off-track betting, lotteries, and casinos. About one dollar of every three wagered in the United States is bet on legal games. This legal handle (wagered money) is for off-track betting in New York and Nevada, pari-mutuel jai alai betting in Nevada and Florida, casino games in New Jersey and Nevada, and even legalized commercial poker in Gardena, California. Illegal betting includes sports betting, horse race bookmaking, numbers, craps, blackjack, and football cards. Pari-mutuel betting at 150 horse race tracks in thirty states is quite legal.

Sportsbetting is illegal and is handled exclusively by bookmakers. The bettor usually wagers $11 to win $10, assuring the bookmaker a tidy profit. The bookmaker enhances his or her chances by assigning a point-spread handicap for stronger teams. Bookmaker odds and point spreads are often printed in the newspapers, although the sale and distribution of their sports card is a crime. Betting on the outcome of sports events is usually a crime, although a purely private wager may be permitted in many states.

Horse race bookmaking is a more than $5 billion business. Bookmakers on horse races compete directly with legal horse racing for the money take. Bookies offer more attractive bets and sometimes a better payoff than at the track, but they also extend credit to the bettors, a most attractive and dangerous practice offered only by these law violators.

The numbers game is illegal everywhere. In this game the bettor selects a three-digit number between 000 and 999. The winning number, by prearrangement, appears in an innocent designated place, usually a newspaper financial page. The payoff is at 500 or 600 to 1, less a tip of 10 percent to the numbers runner. The gross profit is between 40 and 50 percent. Overhead expenses for the illegal gambling operation include management costs, such as for runners, controllers, and business supplies. In larger criminal organizations there are also costs for payoffs of officials, lawyer's fees for those caught, and a large pool of cash to finance large winnings.[22]

[22] See *Legal Gambling in New York: A Discussion of Numbers and Sports Betting* (New York: Fund For the City of New York, 1972), pp. 31-33.

Lotteries are a special form of gambling. After Independence all thirteen original colonies established lotteries to raise revenue. Our oldest universities raised money by using the lottery wheel. By 1830 various lotteries were raising an estimated $60 million, five times the federal budget. But by 1900 lotteries had degenerated into crooked swindles and were generally outlawed. This was the law until New Hampshire renewed the public lottery in 1964. In 1969 New York established a lottery, followed by New Jersey, Pennsylvania, and others. Private lotteries may still run afoul of the criminal law. There is a growing resemblance between the techniques of the public lottery and the private, unlawful, numbers game.

Illegal gambling is a major American enterprise. The link between organized crime and illegal gambling is a strong enough to raise the matter of gambling control to the front ranks of public policy issues. Illegal gambling operations are often affiliated with large, diversified criminal syndicates. The syndicate provides protection from the law and security from competitors and "according to some observers, provides the initial investment for many large narcotic rings."[23]

Many advocates of the legalization of some forms of gambling contend that the present antigambling laws only provide a virtual monoply of this popular activity. Illegal gambling, they say, provides the funds that underwrite other illicit activities, such as narcotics, loan sharking, hijacking, and prostitution. Corruption of police and other public officials, say these reformers, stems from illegal gambling.

Legalization of gambling can be an effective means of denying some funds to the underworld, but experience shows that the state cannot provide many of the amenities of the private bookmakers.[24] Legal games, such as state-run lotteries and off-track betting, provide some revenues for state government, but they do not drive out their illicit counterparts. Legal gambling has been a popular remedy during the past 10 years, in the form of both government-run gambling operations and privately run operations subject to state regulation and taxes. Decriminalization, meaning the elimination of gambling offenses by repeal of current laws, is a much less popular measure, even though gambling seems to be an irrepressible American urge.

[23] David Beale and Clifford Goldman, *Easy Money, Report of The Task Force on Legalized Gambling* (New York: The Twentieth Century Fund, 1974), p. 61.

[24] Ibid., p. 11.

In a certain way, the legalization of gambling as an alternative to decriminalization is an experiment in crime control. No longer do the friends of on-track pari-mutuel horse racing pretend that racing merely improves the breed of horses. Sanctioned gambling in Nevada has existed since 1931, mostly as a revenue measure but partly as a crime control measure. Until recent crackdowns, underworld figures ran the big Nevada casinos, funneling money into the pockets of organized criminals. New Jersey has been trying, through stricter casino regulations, to avoid Nevada's mistakes. Pari-mutuel betting and state-regulated casinos are generally honest, but they still have not reduced the level of illegal gambling very much. Some claim that until the winnings from legal gambling are made tax exempt, illegal gambling will continue to flourish.[25] State lotteries have not had much impact upon illegal numbers games.

There is no federally run legalized gambling. Federal gambling laws are a hodge-podge of different statutes scattered over the statute books. The new federal criminal code bill tries to draw these together into a unified whole. In the 1950s Congress declared that control of illegal gambling by organized crime had become a major federal concern. A series of Revenue and Crime Control Acts were passed, expanding the federal role in this area. A special occupational tax of $50 per year was placed upon "each person who is engaged in the business of accepting wagers." The statute at the same time required professional bookmakers and gambling operations managers to register with the Internal Revenue Service and also to obtain an occupational tax stamp. The law was ill-conceived and unenforceable. Worse yet, it was unconstitutional.[26]

In 1970 the Organized Crime Control Act gave federal prosecutors the power to act against small-scale gambling operations. The same act gave the federal government power to pursue large-scale gambling operations even if they did not cross state lines.[27] This unusual expansion of federal jurisdiction shows a vigorous policy of repressing illegal gambling. More important than this statute and most other federal antigambling measures are the wager tax provisions of the Internal Revenue Code.[28] The code places a 10

[25] See remarks of Percy Sutton in ibid., pp. 18-21.

[26] Marchetti v. United States, 390 U.S. 39 (1968).

[27] Organized Crime Control Act of 1970, Pub. L. 91-452, sec. 801-811, 84 stat, 922. Originally, the gambling title was a separate bill, sec. 2022, 91st Cong., 1st sess. (1969).

[28] 26 U.S.C. sec. 4401.

percent tax on persons engaged in the business of accepting wagers. Players and operators must report profits or winnings, which are then subject to taxation. Legal and illegal gambling proceeds are subject to the tax and only pari-mutuel betting is exempted. The tax measures have been an effective deterrent because failure to pay the tax invites federal prosecution for evasion.

Public opinion on legalized gambling tends to waver. Many citizens fear the incursions of organized crime into state-run or state-licensed gambling activity. Others fear that gambling will attract new adherents if betting is made too available. Others view gambling as an essentially victimless crime akin to the consensual sex crimes mentioned previously. Decriminalization is favored by these people. The fact is that ignorance of state antigambling laws is widespread and enforcement is spotty. On May 3, 1979, the Hancock County (West Virginia) prosecutor was sentenced to 10 years in prison for failing to enforce antigambling laws in the county. That county is a rough and tumble steelmaking area where gambling is a way of life: Raffles, bingo games, and lotteries run by the Eagles Club, the VFW, and the volunteer fire company compete with slot machines, dice games, football parlays, bookmaking, and the numbers. All were illegal under West Virginia law. All went unpunished in Hancock County for many years. The new prosecutor in Hancock County said, "I never knew it was illegal to play policy numbers until I was 18 or 19."[29] Now he knows. Later in 1979 the West Virginia legislature met to consider decriminalizing some of these forms of gambling.

NARCOTIC AND DRUG USE

The most controversial of the victimless crimes are those concerned with the private, voluntary ingestion of illegal substances, especially heroin and marijuana but also amphetamines, barbiturates, and cocaine. The seller of these substances, who may or may not be a user, usually earns a profit. The profitable sale of the drug is almost always regarded as a proper object of criminal law, but the criminalization of consumption and possession of the drug has a more questionable purpose. Decriminalization of the latter activity is often the object of reformist activity.

Each of these substances has different biological properties.

[29] *Philadelphia Inquirer,* May 29, 1979, p. 3A.

Heroin seems to be highly addictive; once hooked, a user is unlikely to cease voluntarily. Marijuana use has a much more consensual character; there is little evidence of any addictive qualities although a psychological dependency sometimes arises. Hashish, mescaline, peyote, LSD, cocaine, and other popular drugs fall somewhere between heroin and marijuana in their addictive properties.

Drug use also has indirect consequences that are more far-reaching than the problem of addiction. In fact, consistent opiate use over a period of years need not pose a health problem at all.[30] Overdoses of certain drugs may produce serious harm, but many addicts (including Sigmund Freud) have used opiates consistently for years without undue health hazards. Drug addicts, however, are susceptible to hepatitis and tetanus from unsterile needles. Deaths from drugs may derive from impurities or from unusually concentrated doses. Both are risks of purchase on the underworld market place.

The most serious social consequence of drug addiction is the commission of other crimes to support the purchase of drugs. The habit is expensive, leading the addict to resort to more and more illegal activity as the craving grows. Dependence on opiates almost invariably produces heightened criminal activity. Legalization of narcotic use through state run clinics has been tried with mixed success.[31] No one knows whether providing addicts easier access to narcotics would reduce their criminal activity, though it seems likely. There has meanwhile been a proliferation of treatment programs and crackdowns on drug sales and use, but only a slight decline in addiction or addiction-related crime, as far as can be discerned.

The Supreme Court has declared that addiction to narcotics cannot be made a criminal offense. The Court majority found that drug addiction is an illness "comparable to leprosy, insanity, and the common cold" and that criminal punishment could not be inflicted for such an illness.[32] The dissenters in this opinion pointed out that addiction could not be separated from the use or possession of drugs, both of which form a constitutional boundary within which narcotic and drug use policy must be written.[33] Civil commitment procedures

[30] See Marie Nyswander, *The Drug Addict as a Patient* (New York: Grune and Stratton, 1965), p. 60.

[31] See Alfred R. Lindesmith, "The Narcotics Clinics," in *The Addict and The Law* (Bloomington, Ind.: Indiana University Press, 1965), pp. 135-161.

[32] Robinson v. California, 370 U.S. 660, 666-667 (1962).

[33] Ibid., pp. 679-689.

must be used for narcotics addicts, but there is no proof that civil commitment produces better results than criminal incarceration.[34]

The history of criminal policy toward drug use begins with the federal Harrison Act of 1914.[35] The effect of the Harrison Act was to allow doctors to administer controlled drugs to patients only for symptoms other than addiction. Doctors could not administer to or prescribe for addicts as such under any circumstances. Thus, addicts were cut off from all legal means of supply.

Since then state and federal laws have been passed criminalizing the use and possession of a variety of substances. In 1956 the Narcotic Control Act was passed, substantially raising minimum and maximum penalties for all drug offenses.[36] This act also required all persons who were addicts or users or had ever been convicted of a drug offense to register and obtain special certificates when leaving the United States.

In 1970 an omnibus measure was passed, entitled the Comprehensive Drug Abuse and Control Act of 1970.[37] This act consolidated all existing repressive federal measures and extended federal jurisdiction. The act reclassified all abusable substances into five schedules, with restrictions and penalties graded downward from the classification deemed most dangerous and the most likely to be abused. For some reason marijuana was placed in the most severe category. A new Uniform Controlled Dangerous Substances Act was also promulgated in 1970, prepared by the Department of Justice. The act, adopted by over forty state legisatures, is closely patterned on the federal categories and enforcement procedures. States still have their own versions of drug abuse statutes.

Decriminalization of drug use is not widely endorsed, except for marijuana. Harder drugs are less likely to be subjects of decriminalization at this time, in spite of the ineffectiveness of the drug control policies. Few experts favor eliminating possession of cocaine as a crime and even fewer favor liberal approaches to heroin, amphetamines, barbiturates, or hallucinogens.[38] Marijuana posses-

[34] See John C. Kramer, Richard A. Bass, and John Berecochea, "Civil Commitment for Addicts: The California Program," *American Journal of Psychiatry* 125 (1968): 816-824.

[35] P. L. 63-223,38 Stat. 785.

[36] P. L. 84-728,70 Stat. 567.

[37] P. L. 91-513, 84 Stat. 1236.

[38] See Eugenia T. Miller, Winsor Schmidt, and Kent S. Miller, "Decriminalizing Drugs: Variations in Endorsement Within Professional Roles," *Contemporary Drug Problems* 7 (1978): 181-201.

sion has been decriminalized to some extent in ten states so far, with many other states leaning in that direction. Differentiation among drugs is justifiable because "while legal sanctions may be of significant value to control alcoholics and heroin addicts they are of little value where marijuana users are concerned."[39] The only reason to retain criminal sanctions for marijuana use or possession is for moral impact. Social disapproval, not health reasons or crime related behavior, is the chief justification for retaining criminal sanctions for marijuana use and possession. There is a likelihood, however, that decriminalization of marijuana use will lead to increased consumption of the substance, at least in the short term. Doubtless the marijuana control laws will be the subject of experimentation for some time.[40]

DRUNKENNESS

There are between 4.5 million and 6.8 million alcoholics in America.[41] This is a medical fact of which the law takes little notice. Alcoholism may be a crime in itself or it may relate to the commissions of other crimes. In most states public intoxication and drunken driving are crimes. Police arrest statistics show that of 8 million arrests, about 1.2 million in 1975 were for drunkenness. Just under one million were for drunken driving and 692,000 were for disorderly conduct and vagrancy, crimes that often stem from drunkenness. Furthermore, heavy alcohol users are more frequently involved in serious crimes than are nondrinkers or light drinkers.[42] Many crimes are committed by individuals who are somewhat intoxicated. Alcohol and crime are linked, but "one cannot be sure that the alcohol-using offenders would not have committed some offense had they not been drinking."[43]

In some jurisdictions there are no laws prohibiting public drunk-

[39] Richard J. Bonnie, "Decriminalizing the Marijuana User: A Drafter's Guide," *University of Michigan Journal of Law Reform* 11 (1977): 25.

[40] Ibid., pp. 26-27.

[41] President's Commission on Law Enforcement and Administration of Justice, *Task Force Report: Drunkenness*, Appendix B (Washington, D.C.: Government Printing Office, 1967), pp. 29-49.

[42] John A. O'Donnell, Harwin L. Voss, Richard R. Clayton, Gerald T. Slatin, and Robin G. W. Room, *Young Men and Drugs—A Nationwide Survey* (Washington, D.C.: National Institute on Drug Abuse, Research Monograph No. 5, 1976), pp. 13-83.

[43] Richard Blum, "Mind Altering Drugs and Dangerous Behavior: Alcohol," in *Task Force Report: Drunkenness,* p. 43.

enness, but drunkennes that causes a breach of the peace is a criminal violation. Disorderly conduct statutes are often used to cope with drunkenness. Jail sentences range from 5 days to 6 months at a maximum, but most offenders are released after a day or two or after payment of a small fine. Most arrests for drunkenness involve skid row derelicts, although anyone who appears intoxicated in a public place may be arrested.

A typical skid row alcoholic who is arrested is a chronic inmate of the jails. These people are arrested and rearrested in a cycle that has been called the revolving door syndrome.[44] Some offenders are jailed hundreds of times. Such drunks may constitute almost half the jail population on any given day.

Some courts have deemed alcoholism an illness rather than a crime.[45] Criminalization of alcoholism was regarded as an unconstitutional form of "cruel and unusual punishment" until a Supreme Court decision in 1968, which upheld the conviction of a chronic alcoholic who had been charged with a crime of public alcoholism.[46] This narrow five-to-four decision is by no means the last word on the subject. There is a strong and growing tendency to treat alcoholism as a disease rather than a crime.

Several states have decriminalized the offense of public intoxication. Several commissions have recommended this step. The proposed Uniform Alcoholism and Intoxication Treatment Act is based upon the premise of decriminalization. One trend favors civil detoxification centers in place of jailing. Medical treatment is replacing incarceration. Hospitalization for a brief stay is becoming a preferred treatment for alcoholics caught in public.

Drunken driving remains a serious offense. More than half the nation's traffic fatalities are caused by people somewhat under the influence of alcohol. Arrests for drunken driving continue to approach the one million level. Vehicular homicide is often associated with drunkenness.

In spite of the trend toward decriminalization of public drunkenness, alcohol-related crime remains a problem. Alcohol use and criminal homicide are often linked.[47] Alcohol consumption may not

[44] D. J. Pittman and W. C. Gordon, *Revolving Door: A Study of The Chronic Police Case Inebriate* (New Brunswick, N.J.: Rutgers Center of Alcoholism Studies, 1958).

[45] Gaster v. District of Columbia, 361 F. 2d 50 (D.C. Cir., 1966); Driver v. Hinnant, 356 F. 2d 761 (4th Cir., 1966).

[46] Powell v. Texas, 392 U.S. 514 (1968).

[47] Marvin G. Wolfgang and R. B. Stran, "The Relationship Between Alcohol and Criminal Homicide," *Quarterly Journal of Studies on Alcoholism* 17 (1956): 411–426.

cause crime but it may reduce social inhibitions sufficiently to encourage criminal behavior. Since alcohol affects our personal control mechanisms, the voluntary use of alcohol must be considered a potential social danger. Decriminalization may take the skid row derelicts out of jails; it will not reduce the rate of alcohol-related crimes. Alcohol abuse is not merely an aesthetic or a moral problem. In some ill-understood fashion, alcohol use is a problem of great potential social harm. There are real victims of alcohol-induced behavior.

The problem of drunkenness is a fine example of the ambiguity of the concept of victimless crimes. Alcohol can be a benign drug, reducing tension and smoothing social intercourse, but when abused, can cause severe injury to family life and other important social interests. Compulsive alcoholism may well be a matter of public concern, just as suicide is. People can drink themselves to death, and the society that maintains a hands-off approach to such behavior aids in the alcoholic's slow suicide.

The same may be said of drug addiction but not of consensual sex crimes, since the health of the violator is not usually at stake. The societal interest in sex crimes is chiefly a moral, not a physical, concern. Marijuana use is on the border between a health and a moral issue, with the medical facts on marijuana use still uncertain. Gambling is different from either the sex crimes or drunkenness in that while morality is involved, the real issues are empirical ones, such as the link between certain forms of gambling and organized crime.[48] Each of the victimless crimes poses different social and political issues, and doctrinaire positions do little to assist in rational policy formation. Prohibition may have been an exercise in futility, but society has the obligation to set some boundaries even to ostensibly private behavior. What is still uncertain is whether regulation of permitted vice can realistically reduce the incidence of such "moral" offenses as gambling, drug use, and prostitution.

VICTIMLESS CRIMES: AN OVERVIEW

As stated at the outset, there are very few acts in which someone is not victimized. Gambling, prostitution, abortion, drug use, and homosexuality have social consequences, even when committed

[48] See Institute for Law and Social Research, *Victimless Crimes: A Description of Offenders* and *Their Prosecution in The District of Columbia* (Washington, D.C.: Institute for Law and Social Research, 1979), which emphasizes the high cost of processing gambling, prostitution and marijuana related offenses.

in private. Conflicts arise, however, because there is often a temptation for majorities to impose their moral views on a dissenting minority. Whether criminal law should be used to regulate morality has long been debated. Regardless of the merits of the debates, the vices of gambling, drug use, sexual liberalism or promiscuity, and drunkenness are hard to repress or correct. Criminal law may be inappropriate for such purposes.

The law in these areas is very much in flux. Drug users are regarded very differently from drug sellers or drug manufacturers, for those who trade upon the vices of other may properly be seen as more serious offenders than the actual deviant doers. Newer criminal statutes tend to render many victimless crimes as mere misdemeanors, while defining the commercial exploitation of individual vices as felonies. This seems a reasonable policy distinction, although it will not work for all so-called victimless crimes. Gambling casinos are big business (and big taxpayers), whereas homosexuality is not a massive commercial enterprise. Only in drug control does the commercial distinction work well.

Students of criminal law must closely examine the actual substantive law of victimless crimes within their own jurisdiction, always bearing in mind that the law in this area is politically sensitive and, hence, more susceptible than most criminal law to sporadic bursts of official zeal. Victimless crimes are prime examples of political incursions into criminal law. Few politicians can resist the desire to appear to improve the level of public morality. In this area of criminal law appearance may be more important than reality, posing genuine problems for police and prosecutors who must decide on the actual enforcement of the provisions of criminal law.

True decriminalization need not pose severe risks to society. Decriminalizing marijuana use is not tantamount to legalizing it. The substance itself can remain illegal, subject to seizure and confiscation. Possession or use can be distinguished from sale or shipment. Decriminalization does not bestow social approval on an act; legalization does. Many states have decriminalized possession of certain substances, while still making sale and transfer an offense, thus encouraging an illegal market. It might be more direct to seize and confiscate all such substances, criminalizing efforts to conceal or to smuggle the substance, but enforcement problems are enormous. Victimless crimes, especially those touching on private behavior, are difficult for police to detect, and the offenses are difficult for prosecutors to prove. The criminal law has great difficulty when it is used to correct private conduct.

SUMMARY

Behind the rhetoric about victimless crimes is the sense that criminal law should concentrate upon serious acts of deviance. Gambling, homosexuality, prostitution, narcotics use and, perhaps, abortion are serious moral problems, but not severe threats to the well-being of the American people. Whether criminal law can prop up a decaying or changing moral code is doubtful. Reformers all over the country are reexamining the basis of so-called victimless crimes. But there are no simple answers. Drug use may cause injury to an individual and to others with whom the users shares his or her life; the same is true of gambling and drunkenness. The resources of the criminal justice system are strained to the extreme. Elimination of some of these crimes and reduction of the penalties for others is at least expedient and in some sense wise.

10

DEFENSES

The principles of defense constitute one of the most essential features of criminal law. Criminal liability depends upon more than the actual occurrence of a harm or injury. The accused person must have engaged in a conscious, voluntary act or omitted to perform an act of which he or she is physically capable. The law cannot hope to deter involuntary movements or to compel people to do something of which they are incapable. Criminal conviction for involuntary acts requires some kind of wrongful conduct, whether it be intentional or merely negligent. Criminal defenses establish the outside perimeters of the criminal law. Those acts that could not have been avoided may be excused. Those acts that, though unlawful, are based upon some higher social policy or benefit may be justified, and hence serve as grounds for an acquittal.

Under special circumstances, each of the following may constitute an effective defense to a criminal prosecution: ignorance or mistake of fact, duress, entrapment, consent, self-defense, insanity, intoxication, and infancy. The best example of justification is the claim of public authority and law enforcement made by soldiers, police officers, and others professionally authorized to apply force. Defense of property or defense of others may in some places give rise to a justification to commit an act that otherwise would constitute a crime. Most crimes have related defenses that may be used to counter the state's effort to prove criminal wrongdoing. Almost every crime, including murder, may fail to lead to a criminal conviction if the correct defense is available and is asserted during a criminal trial.

The criminal law sometimes permits no defenses to be raised. Such crimes, called *strict liability offenses,* are exceptions to the general rules of criminal defenses. They obviously rest upon a belief that the ordinary principles of criminal responsibility should be put aside when there is an overriding social interest in deterring certain conduct. The very existence of strict liability exceptions underscores the importance of the various criminal defenses that generally operate to mitigate the strict application of criminal liability. Strict liability offenses require no culpable mental state. The elimination of the element of volition in defining a crime runs athwart the various doctrines of criminal defense and defeats their use, raising the policy issue of whether to consider the accused's attitude or to ignore it—an issue that can be resolved only in a legislature.

A claim of justification concedes "that the definition of the offense is satisfied" but challenges "whether the act is wrongful." A claim of excuse concedes "that the act is wrongful" but is used "to avoid the attribution of the act to the actor."[1] A justification is based on the alleged rightness of the act. An excuse is based on the particular position of the defendant at the time of the commission of the wrongful act. A person who claims as a defense that he or she needed to steal a loaf of bread to feed a starving family has still committed theft, an unjustifiable crime. The condition of poverty is an insufficient excuse, not allowed as a defense to a charge of theft. Whatever your private feelings may be on the subject, the law that creates defenses to criminal charges is rather well settled. Common sense, sympathy, or private sentiment may color the attitudes of jurors, but officially at least, the jury can consider only whether a defense fits established categories. If it does not, the defense fails and the defendant cannot avoid responsibility for committing the offense.

An excuse is a personal defense, available only to the individual involved. A justification is available to anyone. The reason is that a justification eliminates the criminality of the act in question. If the act is innocent no one can be punished. Self-defense is a good example. If someone injures another purely in self-defense (to be described subsequently) then a person who assists in the self-defense is not justified. The injury was unlawful, even if the perpetrator is excused from criminal liability.[2] Some jurisdictions actually regard self-defense as a justification, not merely an excuse. As a justification it provides a complete defense for all who assisted the self-defending person.[3]

Justification and excuse pose some of the most thorny moral problems in the law. To allow an individual to escape the normal consequences of lawbreaking is a risky business. Many well-meaning individuals break the law in the belief that they are serving a higher law. Draft evaders and civil rights demonstrators in the 1960s claimed that their lawbreaking was aimed at resisting an unjust war or a racist society. Society usually punishes civil disobedients, no matter how noble their claim. Persons may, however, justifiably break the law when necessity or duress impels them to do so. The most profound moral problem is presented when a person in an official capacity is ordered by a superior to commit a crime. Equally puzzling is the question of how to regard the criminal acts of an insane person. The law has answers to these problems, but the

[1] George P. Fletcher, *Rethinking Criminal Law* (Boston: Little, Brown and Co., 1978), p. 759. This is the most thoughtful book available on the subject.

[2] Developed in logical detail in ibid., pp. 762-769.

[3] See Model Penal Code, sec. 3.04. Compare with sec. 3.09, 3.06, and 3.11 (1).

legal doctrines are not always grounded on either logic or moral philosophy.

The Model Penal Code contains only one excuse—duress—which is defined very narrowly so as to require that the defendant's conduct be based upon a threat of unlawful force.[4] The Model Penal Code has not clearly addressed the problems surrounding excuses and justifications and this lapse has retarded legislative reforms in this important area.[5] A few state codes have attempted to specify the law concerning defenses but with mixed success. The state of Maine has devoted considerable attention to justification defenses.[6] Its code sets up specific forms of justification that make explicit some defenses scattered through the state's case law. In many instances prior to the enactment of the code, there had been no settled law on the subject. The clarification and articulation of criminal defenses seems a necessary step in the formulation of a sound criminal law policy.

STRICT LIABILITY, NO DEFENSES

Sound public policy may prohibit the commission of certain offenses altogether, without regard to any excuses or justification. For some crimes there is no defense. These offenses are placed in a category of strict liability under the law. For certain offenses against the public welfare a policy has emerged that allows a defendant no means of escaping liability.[7]

According to one view, strict liability offenses are essentially civil offenses. Fines are imposed virtually as an administrative matter, for example, in order to discourage the supplying of harmful drugs or foods. In this view, strict liability is noncriminal and imprisonment would be ruled out as a sanction. There is strict liability in some aspects of the criminal law, however. The Supreme Court has held drug manufacturers liable for introducing mislabeled bottles into interstate commerce, regardless of ignorance of the event or of

[4] Model Penal Code, sec. 2.09. Intoxication and insanity, among other defenses, are available, but not as full excuses.

[5] Comment, "Justification: The Impact of the Model Penal Code on Statutory Reform," *Columbia Law Review* 75 (1975): 914-961.

[6] Maine Revised Statutes Annotated, Title 17-A, sec. 101-108.

[7] See Wallace Sayre, "Public Welfare Offenses," *Columbia Law Review* 33 (1933): 55-83. Specific intent elements of crimes may be negated by ignorance.

mistaken acts.[8] Violations of the Food and Drug Act may result in a strict liability of those in a responsible relationship to the harmful goods.[9]

Few crimes are based upon strict liability of offenders. Individual fault and blameworthiness is involved both in the most important kinds of criminal activity and in minor offenses. Strict liability must be seen as an exception to the normal practice in American criminal law, which permits defendants to raise defenses as excuses and justifications. Crimes such as statutory rape are often treated as strict liability offenses, thus denying a defendant an opportunity to introduce the fact of ignorance of the victim's age. Only a few states, however, permit this defense,[10] although it is recommended by the Model Penal Code.[11]

Perhaps the leading example of strict liability in the criminal law is the doctrine that ignorance of the law is no excuse. There are in fact so many criminal laws that only experts can be said to be aware of most of them. Yet all persons are held to subject to the criminal laws, whether or not they know of them. To permit this defense might undermine the effectiveness of the criminal law since the application of the law would become dependent upon the state of the defendant's knowledge. Ignorance would be encouraged and the law would be defeated. A defendant may have truly believed that his or her conduct was morally, socially, and legally sound, but still may be held accountable under an obscure section of the criminal law. Refusal to take account of the subjective innocence of the defendant and the reasonableness of his or her lack of full awareness of the provisions of the criminal law amounts to an application of strict liability theory.[12] Curiously, unlawful military orders generate a valid defense as long as the defendant does not know the orders to be illegal. Why liability should be excused under unvalid orders and not under a mistake of law may not be easy to explain. Public policy simply provides that one kind of mistake is excused and the other is not.

[8] United States v. Dotterweich, 320 U.S. 277 (1943).

[9] United States v. Park, 421 U.S. 658 (1975).

[10] Illinois Ann. Stat. C. 38, sec. 11-4 (6); Indiana Stat. Ann. sec. 35-42-4-3 (e) (Suppl. 1977); Washington Rev. Code Ann. sec. 9.79. 160 (2).

[11] Model Penal Code, sec. 213.6 (1).

[12] See Fletcher, *Rethinking* [note 1, this chapter], pp. 730–736. Reasonableness of a mistake of law is sometimes regarded as sufficient to excuse *mens rea* requirement in a criminal offense. See Commonwealth v. Benesch, 290 Mass. 125 (1935).

IGNORANCE OR MISTAKE OF FACT

Generally ignorance of a fact is a valid defense, but the mistake must be reasonable and honestly made, and the conduct involved must be of a sort that would have been innocent if the facts were as they were supposed to be. There are instances in which a person shot another in the mistaken belief that a relative had been attacked.[13] A reasonable mistaken belief that one's own life or the life of a child is in danger is a valid defense. Mistakes of fact, not mistakes of law, can create valid defenses.

A mistake of fact is no defense if the fact involved would constitute no defense in itself. If A shoots X intending to shoot Y, A cannot claim mistake as a defense to a charge of assault or homicide. In such cases there is a criminal intent, whatever the mistake. The intent to commit a crime overcomes the mistake if the crime is carried to its conclusion.

A mistaken belief that is absurd is no defense. If A shoots X with a silver bullet in the mistaken belief that X is a vampire who can be thwarted only with such a bullet, the law will not admit such a defense. To do otherwise would permit the deranged and deluded to proffer their imaginary condition as a defense. Insanity itself might serve as a defense, but delusions cannot. Stupidity, foolishness, and gullibility are not defenses recognized in law. Aliens from other planets may be real, but earthlings are subject to the local version of the criminal law.

PUBLIC AUTHORITY AND LAW ENFORCEMENT

Acts committed pursuant to a valid public authority are not crimes. Acts that exceed or abuse the authorized exercise of power are not justifiable. Certain people are authorized to use force in the name of the state, for example, soldiers, police officers, and public executioners. Under more limited circumstances parents and school teachers are privileged to use some compulsion in order to promote the welfare of children. This privilege derives from the public interest in safeguarding children or in maintaining effective discipline and order. Other individuals who have similar privileges to use reasonable force pursuant to the exercise of their duties include wardens, ship captains, and hospital superintendents.[14]

[13] See State v. Nash, 88 N.C. 618 (1883).

[14] See Model Penal Code sec. 3.03, 3.07, and 3.08.

Acts committed in military service or in the National Guard may also be regarded as examples of this defense. In an old Pennsylvania case, a national guard was instructed to "shoot to kill" anyone who did not stop and identify him- or herself when asked to. The guardsman shot and killed an individual who repeatedly ignored the guardsman's requests to stop. When charged with manslaughter the guard successfully asserted as a defense the fact that he was authorized by military orders.[15] In 1970 four Kent State University students were shot and killed during political protest demonstrations. The incident severely tested the privilege of public au-

[15] Commonwealth ex. rel. Wadsworth v. Shortall, 206 Pennsylvania 165 (1903).

Two statutory defenses.

26-903 Use of force in defense of habitation

A person is justified in the threatening or using force against another when and to the extent that he reasonably believes that such threat or force is necessary to prevent or terminate such other's unlawful entry into or attack upon a habitation; however, he is justified in the use of force which is intended or likely to cause death or great bodily harm only if:

(1) The entry is made or attempted in a violent and tumultuous manner and he reasonably believes that the entry is attempted or made for the purpose of assaulting or offering personal violence to any person dwelling or being therein and that such force is necessary to prevent the assault or offer of personal violence; or

(2) He reasonably believes that the entry is made or attempted for the purpose of committing a felony therein and that such force is necessary to prevent the commission of the felony.

26-905 Entrapment as a defense

A person is not guilty of a crime if by entrapment his conduct is induced or solicited by a government officer or employee, or agent of either [,] for the purpose of obtaining evidence to be used in prosecuting the person for commission of the crime. Entrapment exists where the idea and intention of the commission of the crime originated with a government officer or employee, or with an agent of either, and he, by undue persuasion, incitement, or deceitful means, induced the accused to commit the act which the accused would not have committed except for the conduct of such officer.

Source: Code of Georgia Annotated.

thority as a defense, but the defense is still available, especially for conduct in wartime.

Police officers pose an even more severe test of the public authority defense. Allegations of police brutality abound in America's large cities. Blacks in particular have claimed that excessive exercise of force has been visited upon them. Suspects have even been killed under suspicious circumstances. Police do not have an unlimited right to employ force. They are generally entitled to use whatever force is reasonably required to apprehend or prevent the escape of any law violator. What is reasonable force? That depends upon the circumstances. One thing is clear: If the suspect could have been arrested by some method that avoided force or required only minimal force without risk to the arresting officer, then a serious use of force is not justifiable. Unfortunately no one can second-guess the police officer's perceptions, and there is a tendency on the part of juries to accept a police officer's claim of the danger presented by the arrest situation.

Deadly force is never justifiable to prevent misdemeanors and minor offenses. Police are not privileged to kill jaywalkers, speeders, drunks, or annoying vagrants. Deadly force is, however, usually permitted in arrests of suspects for more serious offenses. Progressive reformers would like to restrict the use of deadly force to arrests for felonies that themselves involve the use (or threat) of deadly force.[16] Most states do not agree, preferring to permit deadly force to be employed in the pursuit of all "dangerous felonies."[17] The issue is an important matter for police discipline and morale.

Private citizens also have some arrest powers. They are privileged to use force in the prevention of any felony, even if the felony is not directed at them. Private citizens act at their own peril in the use of force. They may be sued by an individual who, it turns out, has not committed an offense. On the other hand, private citizens may have available the defense of a reasonable mistake of fact regarding the commission of a dangerous felony.[18] The Model Penal Code states the more humane rule, by prohibiting the use of deadly force by private citizens altogether, unless citizens believe they are assisting a police officer.[19]

[16] See Model Penal Code, sec. 3.07 (2).

[17] Deadly force may generally be used in arresting felons. However, in attempting to prevent the commission of a crime most states limit the defense to dangerous felonies. See Commonwealth v. Emmons, 157 Penn. Sup. 495 (1945).

[18] Viliborhi v. State, 45 Ariz. 275 (1935).

[19] Model Penal Code, sec. 3.07 (2) (6) (ii) and 3.07 (4).

SELF-DEFENSE

As mentioned above, self-defense is more properly regarded as an excuse than a justification. The act committed is wrongful, but the defendant claims the defense in order to escape the consequences of the act. Self-defense is one of the most complex defenses. A successful plea of self-defense must demonstrate several elements. Moreover, if deadly force was employed in the offense, the defendant's burden of showing self-defense becomes much heavier.

Generally acts committed in defense of one's person are excusable. No criminal liability attaches to them if the acts were reasonable under the circumstances. The issue of reasonableness is usually a factual issue for the jury, to be resolved in terms of the jurors' perceptions of the conduct of average individuals under similar circumstances.[20] Some courts take a different view, regarding a person in distress and fear for his or her life as a less-than-reasonable person. Under this more modern doctrine, excitable but not irrational behavior may be excused.[21]

The right of third persons to claim self-defense when aiding the victim of an attack is not clearly settled. Intervening third parties may mistakenly believe that a person's actions are in self-defense, and by coming to the apparent victim's aid, they may cause injury to the apparent attacker. The ability of third parties to assert the claim of assisting the victim of self-defense depends upon whether the claim of self-defense is personal to the original victim. Since self-defense is usually an excuse and not a justification, it should not be available to third parties. Some states, however, permit third parties to use force when it is reasonably believed to be necessary under the circumstances.[22] A few states permit intervening third parties to use force only on behalf of those who stand in a special relationship to the intervenor, such as husband and wife, brother and sister, parent and child, and similar relationships, including, in a few places, employer and employee.

Defense of one's own property is a form of self-defense, but in a sharply diminished way. Mere trespasses on property do not justify taking a life, it is said. Yet a homeowner may not realize that a trespasser is not an armed burglar. Homeowners nonetheless may stand their ground in their own home and take life when necessary to protect themselves and their family or when such action seems

[20] See State v. Rummelhoff, 1 Wash. App. 192 (1969).

[21] See State v. Chiarello, 69 N.J. Super. 479, 174 A. 2d 506 (1961).

[22] N.Y. Penal Code sec. 35.15.

reasonably necessary to prevent the commission of a felon.[23] Outside the home this extension of self-defense rules does not apply. Crimes against property do not warrant the use of deadly force by private citizens except in most extraordinary circumstances. Even to use deadly force in defense of property in one's home requires a crime against the dwelling place that is quite serious. The modern view denies the right to use force in defense of a dwelling unless defendants reasonably believed themselves or their family to be threatened with death or serious bodily harm.[24]

When attacked directly an individual may not assert a claim of self-defense unless threatened with imminent deadly harm. The defendant must at least have an honest belief that he or she was in imminent danger. In most states a defendant is under a duty to retreat rather than use deadly force in self-defense. Defendants need not retreat if it would not be safe to do so or if they are in their own dwelling place.[25] The privilege of self-defense may not be asserted if the accused person was the aggressor in the incident. The determination of just who is the aggressor is an issue in many criminal cases. There is no easy solution to that issue, but it may be resolved by the collective wisdom and common experience of a jury. Many a fight is provoked by bitter words that quickly turn to violent gunplay or knifeplay, but the person who reaches first for a deadly weapon is usually seen as the aggressor. The law still will not countenance a later claim of self-defense by the initiator of violence.

DURESS, COMPULSION, OR COERCION

Courts often use the terms duress, compulsion, or coercion to describe a defense that excuses an accused's criminal behavior because of having been impelled by an external force or factor. The defense does not apply, in most jurisdictions, to homicide cases. In other cases, a defendant may claim that he or she committed the criminal act under duress, compulsion, or coercion applied by another person.

To be successful, a defense of duress must rest upon the defendant's reasonable belief that he(she) or a member of the immediate family is threatened with death or serious bodily harm. The boss of a

[23] See Flynn v. Commonwealth, 204 KY. 572, 264 S.W. 1111 (1924).

[24] Model Penal Code, sec. 3.06 (3) (d).

[25] Ibid., sec. 3.04 (2) (6).

Duress: An issue of fact.

STONE, J.

This case is before this court upon writ of error to the superior court of Grand Rapids, where the defendant was convicted upon his alleged plea of guilty of the robbery of a bank, being then and there armed with a revolver, and was sentenced to life imprisonment in the state prison at Jackson.

The defendant was born in Syria and is said to be 27 years of age. In July, 1919, he, with his family, moved from New York to Detroit, and he there engaged in the business of driving an automobile for hire. He owned his car and operated it as a public taxi. It is claimed by the defendant that on September 16, 1919, he was approached by certain parties in Detroit, who were entire strangers to him, who engaged his car and himself as driver to drive for them in the country at the rate of $3 per hour; that he knew nothing of the business of these men, nor where they were going; that there were originally six in the party that left Detroit, including himself; that they went to Grand Rapids; that on September 19, 1919, three of these men, namely Ally Hamden, Tofi Leon, and Tony Randazzo, being armed with revolvers, feloniously entered the Grandville Avenue branch of the Grand Rapids Savings Bank and there stole and carried away money and personal property consisting of bonds and other securities to the amount of $6,895.50, and one of the customers of the bank was then and there shot and killed by one of the robbers. Defendant claims that he had nothing to do with the robbery of the bank, and that he remained all of the time in his automobile.

[**2, 3**] A careful reading of the proceedings had in open court on the 24th day of September, as above set forth (which the court certifies are substantially correct, although not containing all that was said, yet correct as far as set forth), satisfies us that what occurred in open court on that occasion did not amount to a plea of guilty by the defendant. It is not a question merely when the plea of guilty was entered of record, but what was the condition of the case when the court and prosecuting attorney entered upon the colloquy there set forth? The answers of the defendant were so qualified and limited as to lead us to the opinion that what there took place was not the equivalent of, and did not amount to, a plea of guilty. Manifestly, if this defendant was acting under duress at the time, and prior to the robbery, such duress must affect to a greater or less degree his responsibility in the law for his acts. Counsel for the people cite the correct rule in their brief, which is found in 16 Corpus Juris at page 91, and is as follows:

> "An act which would otherwise constitute a crime may also be excused on the ground that it was done under compulsion or duress. The compulsion which will excuse a criminal act, however, must be present, imminent, and impending, and of such a nature as to induce a well-grounded apprehension of death or serious bodily harm if the act is not done. A threat of future injury is not enough. Such compulsion must

have arisen without the negligence or fault of the person who insists upon it as a defense."

[**4, 5**] The proceedings in open court both on the 23d and 24th of September were very unusual and anomalous. The statement made by the prosecutor on the 23d of September, "I understand some of you have taken a bigger part in it than others, but under the law of this state to aid and assist in the crime, and all who aid and assist, are responsible with the principal," was very unusual, and we think improper, language to be used by a public prosecutor in making arraignment in a court of justice. Equally unusual were the proceedings on the 24th. Bearing in mind that at that time the plea of not guilty was standing upon the records of the court, what right the prosecutor had to make any examination of the defendant in open court it is difficult to conceive, and yet the record shows that he started the investigation by this language: "Do you say you had a helping hand in robbing this bank down here on Grandville Avenue?" We desist from further discussion of this matter by saying that, in our opinion, the proceeding was prejudicial to the rights of the defendant, and what there occurred did not amount to an unqualified plea of guilty, and gave the court no power or authority to make the further examination which the record says he did make, all of which occurred before the plea of guilty was entered. We think that what occurred in open court on September 24th constituted reversible error.

Whether the defendant was responsible for his conduct on September 19th, and whether his actions on that occasion were voluntary, would be a fair question for a jury under all the circumstances of the case.

Source: People v. Merhige, 212 Michigan 601, 180 N.W.418 (1920). Reprinted by permission of West Publishing Company.

criminal gang may order a member to commit an offense "or else. . . ," but mere threat to the defendant's reputation, business, or property is insufficient to excuse criminal acts.

It must appear that the defendant's submission to the duress was reasonable under the circumstances. The defendant must show that there was no other reasonable alternative aside from committing the crime. If a defendant could have called the police or run away rather than commit the crime, the excuse fails. A proposed standard of conduct is that the threat must be one which "a person of reasonable firmness in the defendant's situation would have been unable to resist."[26] There was a case which excused a prisoner's escape from jail when he asserted as a defense the threats made against him. Once escaped, however, the prisoner was under an

[26] Ibid., sec. 2.09 (1).

obligation to report to authorities as soon as the threat was removed.[27]

Duress is not available as a defense in a murder charge, but it may be available for felony-murder. This means that if X is compelled by Y to go along on a robbery and Y kills someone in the course of the robbery, X will not be held accountable for the homicide. The excuse should also hold for the underlying crime as well. If, however, X joins a tough gang with a history of violent acts, X may not be able to assert this excuse after having willingly submitted to a situation in which coercion was probable.

The basis for the excuse of duress is the idea that someone who is compelled to commit a crime cannot form the requisite criminal intent, or even if one can, one's will is still impaired. Criminal responsibility depends upon acts of will. Under an earlier common law rule, wives are held to be not responsible for acts committed at the command of their husbands. Presumably wives were formerly obedient to the point of bending their wills. Nowadays wives are not excused from responsibility because of their husband's commands, because we expect women to have an independent will.[28]

Necessity is different from duress. The compulsion involved comes from an physical force of nature—a fire, flood, or storm—rather than from a third person. Necessity is available as a defense only when there is no reasonable alternative. A person may trespass on another's property to escape a natural disaster. A pharmacist may dispense drugs without a prescription in an emergency.[29] Nonetheless, necessity does not mean economic suffering. A mother cannot claim necessity when she steals money or food to save her starving children, since public assistance or charity are available to fend off starvation. Necessity is also not available as a defense to a charge of homicide, mayhem, treason, or rape, according to the law of most jurisdictions.

CONSENT

With certain crimes, consent of the victim may serve as an excuse. The consent must be given voluntarily. The consent must be given by a person who is legally competent to give it. Acts that go

[27] People v. Lovercamp. 43 Cal. App. 3d 823 (1974).

[28] Actually a few states retain the common law rule, called *coverture,* or keep it for misdemeanors only (California Penal Code, sec. 26). If the husband actually makes physical threats on his wife then the defense of compulsion may be available.

[29] See Comment, Model Penal Code, sec. 3.02.

Consent—the limits of fraternal abuse and of pledge's consent.

JAMES L. DOWSEY, Jr., Judge.

The trial of this case has proceeded for approximately two weeks. The prosecution has presented its case and rested. The indictment accuses the defendants of the crime of "hazing," in violation of Section 1030 of the Penal Law of the State of New York, committed as follows: "The defendants, Robert Lenti, Robert Pellegrino, Gaetano Aliseo and Frank Gannon, each aiding and abetting the other and acting in concert, and accompanied by juveniles, in the County of Nassau, State of New York, on or about the 4th day of April, 1964, did willfully and unlawfully engage in what is commonly called 'hazing', while attending an institution of learning in Union Free School District No. 11, Oceanside, County of Nassau, State of New York, to wit, the defendants, Robert Lenti, Robert Pellegrino, Gaetano Aliseo and Frank Gannon, each aiding and abetting the other and acting in concert, and accompanied by juveniles, during an installation of pledges in an initiation known as 'Hell Night', for the purpose of inducting certain pledges into a fraternal organization known as Omega Gamma Delta Fraternity, did willfully, wrongfully and knowingly assault Michael Kalogris, Daniel William Alexander, John Thomas Brennan, David Dennis and Richard Stewart by (sic) striking them about the body and face with clenched fists, open hands, forearms and feet."

The indictment also accuses the defendants of the crime of assault, in the third degree (five counts), in violation of Section 244 of the Penal Law, committed as follows: "The defendants, Robert Lenti, Robert Pellegrino, Gaetano Aliseo and Frank Gannon, each aiding and abetting the other and acting in concert, and accompanied by juveniles, in the County of Nassau, State of New York, on or about the 4th day of April, 1964, willfully, wrongfully, unlawfully and knowingly, assaulted Michael Kalogris, about the body and face with their clenched fists and open hands." . . .

The acts committed by the defendants and fellow members of this fraternity are not being condoned by this Court. In fact, this Court will pontificate to the extent whereby it will reveal its conscience is clearly shocked by the conduct these defendants and the members of this fraternity have exhibited; their conduct in the treatment of their contemporaries can only be characterized as sadistic, barbaric and immoral. The dangers inherent in hazing procedures and practices cannot be eliminated unless society, in close cooperation with school administrators, develop policies and attitudes that exhibit an awareness of the wrong and conscientious desire to eliminate it. Initially, a community effort should be set in motion to compel the legislature to pass a statute that is sufficiently clear in its term so that the acts prohibited are clearly defined and enforceable, and everyone is sufficiently advised in advance of the criminal activities to be condemned.

This entire problem of hazing must be looked at anew in terms of present fraternity practices. What is commonly referred to as "Hell Night", is well known and feared by most of the parents and responsible school authorities of this country. It is a practice and custom which a mature society should not allow its young people to engage in. It has no educational value or significance; on the contrary, it is conduct that is shameful, degrading and despicable. To assist in an intelligent attempt to aid legislators, educators and parents to band together to promulgate legislation to properly restrict and restrain hazing activities, this Court makes the following recommendations:

The present statute may be retained in its present form without changes, which is as follows: Section 1030—Penal Law; "It shall be unlawful for any person to engage in or aid or abet what is commonly called hazing, in or while attending any of the colleges, public schools or other institutions of learning in this state, and whoever participates in the same shall be deemed guilty of a misdemeanor, and upon conviction shall be fined not less than ten dollars nor more than one hundred dollars, or imprisonment not less than thirty days nor more than one year, or both at the discretion of the court. Whenever any tattooing or permanent disfigurement of the body, limbs or features of any person may result from such hazing, by the use of nitrate of silver or any like substance, it shall be held to be a crime of the degree of mayhem, and any person guilty of the same shall, upon conviction, be punished by imprisonment for not less than three nor more than fifteen years."

Source: People v. Lenti, 260 N.Y.S. 2d 284 (1965). Reprinted by permission of West Publishing Company.

---

beyond the range of the consent are not privileged. A defendant may not claim any more than was specifically agreed to by the victim.

Consent is no defense to the prosecution of certain crimes deemed important to public order or morals. There can be no consent to homicide, mayhem, breaches of the peace, or acts that tend to corrupt public morals. These limitations upon consent are based on a public interest greater than the motives of the parties. Certain acts are not to be done, regardless of the consent of the parties, because the state may, for good reason, want to prohibit certain offensive conduct. The principles here are not consistent. Consent is generally a defense to larceny, burglary, and arson. But would it be good public policy to allow people to consent to having their homes burned down?[30]

To be effective, consent must be free of fraud. There are complex rules governing consent gained through fraud. Fraud *in the factum* vitiates consent. This kind of fraud is present when victims do not understand what they have consented to. A person who signs a

[30] See ibid., sec. 2.11 (2), which provides that consent is a defense to conduct that "causes or threatens bodily harm" if the harm is not serious or if the conduct and the harm are "reasonably forseeable hazards of joint participation in a lawful athletic contest or competitive sport."

blank piece of paper may believe it to be harmless, but when it is made into a promissory note it becomes a fraud that disposes of any claim of voluntary consent. A gynecologist or sex therapist who has intercourse with a patient cannot claim consent unless the victim understood that what she or he was receiving was not normal medical treatment. There is also a similar concept of fraud in the inducement in which there has been some deception to obtain the consent of the victim. In this situation the consent to a collateral (different) matter may not be vitiated. If a person wants to test-drive a car and a car dealer consents, the person who uses the car may not later be charged with the crime of joyriding since the fact that the dealer was deceived is really immaterial.[31]

Condonation, or forgiveness by the victim after the crime has been committed, is not consent. An injured party cannot ratify a crime. A crime is a harm to the whole society. Once it is committed the retroactive approval of the victim cannot be treated as consent because the act has been completed and the harm obtained. Rape is rape, and the victim cannot avoid a criminal prosecution of the perpetrator, although the victim's unwillingness to testify may frustrate the prosecution. In any event, an agreement not to prosecute a crime may constitute a crime in itself. Even if a thief repays a victim the act comes too late to excuse the offense. A few states have provided an exception to this general rule in the case of private property wrongs or misdemeanors. A statute may permit condonation under these circumstances.[32]

The consent of a victim may negate an element of an offense or it may preclude the infliction of the harm that was the intended area of statutory protection. Either kind of consent is sufficient as a defense. The issue of consent does raise major problems of proof, though. If the victim is drunk, high on narcotics, or simply impressionable, a strong-willed and determined person may induce consent. Although consent based upon the impairment of the victim's judgment or faculties is ineffective as a defense, as long as force and fraud are not used the matter of the victim's consent can be a factual matter that is difficult for a jury to determine.

ENTRAPMENT

A law enforcement officer may, by excess of zeal, induce or encourage a crime. When that happens an alleged offender may be acquitted in a subsequent criminal trial if he or she can show (usu-

[31] People v. Cook, 228 Cal. App. 2d 716 (1964).

[32] California Penal Code, sec. 1378.

Entrapment—a necessary weapon against crime?

CAMERON, Circuit Judge (dissenting).

I agree with the contention of the United States here that the evidence does not tend to establish entrapment as that term has been usually accepted by this Court. Cf. Accardi v. United States, 1958, 5 Cir., 257 F.2d 168, 172; Vamvas v. United States, 1926, 5 Cir., 13 F.2d 347, 348: and Park v. United States, 1960, 5 Cir., 283 F.2d 253, 254. What we said in the last mentioned case sums up the rule recognized by this Court: "Nothing here established that the agents lured and induced the commission of the offense rather than affording an opportunity to persons of ready willingness and complaisance to enter into the unlawful transaction."

The majority, in reality, reverses this case because of the ignoble part assigned by the Government to the informer Moye. The sole basis of the reversal is that Moye was working on a contingent fee basis.[1] He was paid a nominal salary and furnished gasoline and was to receive $200.00 if he made a purchase from one of these defendants leading to his conviction and $100.00 if he made a like purchase from the other.

In the majority's view, the very fact of hiring an informer on a contingency is ignoble. Such a holding would rob the Government of one of its most effective weapons in detecting crime and bringing to the bar of justice those who commit it.

For decades the use of informers has been accepted as a proper means of enforcement of the criminal law. It is recognized by all as one of the most important means. And, in practically all instances, the informer is in reality on a contingent basis.

The method chiefly used in apprehending sellers of narcotics, for instance, is the employment of addicts to make the purchases from suspects in the presence of federal officers who are secreted or in disguise. Every such informer knows that his day to day arrangement with the Government will continue only if he delivers the goods. The addict is given barely enough money to live on and supply his need for narcotics for a few days. In most cases, the Government agents are after one or more individuals to whom the informer is sent. If the addict succeeds in landing some of the criminals the Government is after, he is well paid and his services will continue. If he does not, he is dropped. As far as I know, the courts have accepted such practices as permissible. The same attitude has prevailed in connection with informers in the apprehension of liquor law violators.

Those who represent persons charged with crime have for ages made impassioned pleas—mostly to juries—that the hiring of informers, in many

[1]The basis for the reversal which the majority apparently accept is thus stated in the appellants' brief:

"We respectfully urge that all entrapments accomplished by an informer working for a contingent financial fee should be outlawed as being incurably afoul of public policy and not to be permitted under our form of government."

cases friends of the victims being sought, is dirty business. Crime itself is dirty business, and the universal experience of law enforcement officers is that the use of informers is necessary to the enforcement of law.

Not only the court but the Congress has put its stamp of approval, under conditions like those present here, on the employment of informers in the enforcement of the Internal Revenue Laws. Cf. Internal Revenue Code, 1954, § 7623. It is common knowledge that, based upon that statute, those charged with the responsibility of collecting the government revenues make it a practice of rewarding, contingently, individuals who "squeal" on those from whom sums are collected through information furnished by the "squealer." It is commonly accepted that the one who informs is given ten percent of the take. By § 7214(a) of the Code, the discretion is given to a court imposing sentence on a revenue agent or employee convicted as the result of information furnished by an informer, to award the informer a portion of the fine imposed not in excess of one-half thereof.

At a time when crime of all sorts is so definitely on the increase, I am not willing to weaken the hand of the law by interfering with a practice as well established as the one here under examination. Juries generally take into account the interest of every witness who testifies before them. What we are really dealing with here is the weight of the testimony of an interested witness employed as an informer. The juries can be counted upon to make proper discount in crediting the testimony of an informer employed on a contingent basis. It is their function to determine the extent of the discount. I do not think we ought to take such a witness off of the stand entirely. I respectfully dissent.

Rehearing denied; CAMERON, Circuit Judge, dissenting.

Source: Dissent of Circuit Judge Cameron in Williamson v. United States, 311 F. 2d 441, 445-446 (3d Cir., 1963). Reprinted by permission of West Publishing Company.

---

ally by a preponderance of the evidence) that the conduct was actually in response to the actions or invitations of a law enforcement official. Causation is the problem in entrapment. Did the actions of the law enforcement official directly result in the criminal offense? If not, and if the infraction might also have taken place in the absence of the policeman's conduct, then entrapment will fail as a defense.

Entrapment is generally not available as a defense for serious crimes involving physical injury to others, such as rape or murder. Typically entrapment is claimed with offenses such as narcotics offenses and prostitution in which law enforcement officials seek to present themselves as victims or participants in lawbreaking in order to expose secretive criminal practices. The usual rule is that a defendant has been entrapped if he or she committed, on the instigation of a law enforcement official, an act that he or she would not otherwise have been predisposed to commit.[33] A few courts will permit entrapment to be asserted merely if there was reprehensible police conduct even though the defendant might have committed the crime anyway.[34] This minority view is based upon a keen judicial concern with controlling police, since the defendant's state of mind is made immaterial. Most state courts hold that a police officer may not commit a crime in order to induce another to commit an offense. Entrapment is plain in such a case.

A police officer may make a valid arrest leading to a conviction by pretending to be a criminal. He or she may join a gang without raising the risk of engaging in the entrapment, but may not act as an accomplice to the crime or commit the crime himself or herself. A police officer may not instigate the plan, but may participate in the commission of the offense if that is done without any criminal intent. The whole matter is risky for the police officer, who may, for the sake of convincing others of his or her genuine criminal attitudes and experience, come close to leading the way towards a criminal act, which of course is entrapment.

Other public employees besides police officers may commit entrapment. Informers, private detectives, or police agents may also create an entrapment situation. A line is drawn between law enforcement persons on one side and strictly private citizens on the other. Entrapment can never be based upon the conduct of a private person who is unconnected with law enforcement.

The underlying policy of entrapment is to prevent the unnecessary commission of crime. Police frequently entrap an offender who they believe to be a frequent lawbreaker but on whom they have had difficulty getting evidence. Police commit entrapment out of frustration more than malice. They may believe that their public duties should be made easier by forcing the law breaker into the open. Policy have used "granny squads" of men dressed as older women in order to attract muggers who prefer weak older women as safe targets. When the mugger finds out, with surprise, that he or she has attacked a vigorous male police officer, the mugger may later claim entrapment, but acting as a decoy is permissible police conduct. Acting as a drug addict to uncover narcotics sellers is another police ploy. In all such cases there is the possibility that the police officer may actively incite the crime; then there probably is an en-

[33] Sorrells v. United States, 282 U.S. 435 (1930); Sherman v. United States, 356 U.S. 369 (1957).

[34] See State v. Boccelli, 105 Ariz. 495 (1970).

trapment. Procedurally, there is considerable dispute over who must prove or disprove entrapment. In the federal courts the burden of proof regarding entrapment rests upon the government, which must establish beyond a reasonable doubt that no entrapment exists once the defendant has introduced evidence to show entrapment.[35] Most states adopt a different rule, exemplified in the Model Penal Code, which requires the defendant to establish entrapment by a preponderance of the evidence.[36] The difference in the procedural use of the defense reflects very different policy considerations concerning the balance between police conduct and wrongdoing. Entrapment remains a defense that rests upon subtle psychological states and the temptations affecting those states.

INTOXICATION

While drunkenness is increasingly not regarded as a crime, offenses committed under the influence of alcohol are usually regarded as crimes unless excused or unless the degree of the offense is reduced. A distinction is usually made between voluntary and involuntary intoxication. If someone is forced to get drunk (which seems a rare event) then intoxication may be a defense. Being tricked into taking drugs or drinking too much liquor will also constitute involuntary intoxication. On the other hand, most of us are, when intoxicated, voluntary victims of that condition. The general rule has been that voluntary intoxication is not a defense to any crime.

Voluntary intoxication be may introduced as a factor in a case to reduce a crime to a lower degree, but voluntary intoxication rarely leads to a total acquittal. Evidence of intoxication may be admissible only to negate a "particular purpose, motive, or intent" that is necessary "to constitute a particular species or degree of crime."[37] Voluntary intoxication from drugs or alcohol is no defense where only a general intent is required.[38] A person who experiments with hallucinogenic drugs will not be excused from criminal responsibility if he or she kills someone while in a drugged state. Such a person may, however, be guilty of a lesser degree of homicide because of a deranged mental state. A murder charge may be reduced to second degree or even manslaughter when a killing is caused by a

[35] See Kadis v. United States, 323 F. 2d 370 (1st Cir. 1967).

[36] Model Penal Code, sec. 2.13 (2).

[37] California Penal Code, sec. 22.

[38] See Frank v. State, 118 So. 219 (Fla. 1960).

drugged or drunken person, but not if the killer got intoxicated to build up courage to commit the act.

Courts have struggled valiantly with supposed differences between general and specific intent, since the availability of intoxication as a defense hinges upon the distinction. Intoxication is no defense to assault, battery, assault with a deadly weapon, or any other crime lacking a specific intent. Where malice, knowledge, or some other specific mental element[39] is required, intoxication may provide a defense, though not a total excuse. Larceny may fall into either the general or specific intent category, depending upon the language of the statue. There is often no clear meaning in the statute to suggest what kind of mental element is needed. Perhaps courts should not take this distinction too seriously anyway, since its chief function is not to acquit a defendant but merely to encourage (or deny) the possibility of a compromise verdict, a kind of verdict jurors often find desirable. Much of this talk about general and specific intent is highly artificial and may obscure the real policy issue of whether people who get themselves drunk should be able to claim the benefit of their folly. Perhaps it would be better to punish separately acts committed while voluntarily intoxicated, rather than to juggle legal doctrines to produce a negotiated verdict.

The status of being addicted to alcohol or drugs cannot be criminalized. According to the Supreme Court the Eighth Amendment's cruel and unusual punishment clause forbids making narcotics addiction a crime.[40] The court reasoned that narcotics addiction was a condition beyond the control of the addict and could no more be a crime than could being mentally ill or being afflicted with a venereal disease. Chronic alcoholism also appears to be a status or condition that cannot, in itself, be made a crime, although public intoxication remains an offense.[41] For addicts the defense of intoxication seems much more valid since their actions are not really under their own control.

INSANITY

Insane persons have much less control over their actions than intoxicated persons. For this reason insanity is a better defense against a criminal charge than is intoxication. Actually persons are

[39] In a burglary case intoxication may be admissible to negate the intent to commit that felony; People v. Ruiz, 265 Cal. App. 2d 766, 71 Cal. Reptr. 519 (1968).

[40] Robinson v. California, 370 U.S. 660 (1962).

[41] Powell v. Texas, 392 U.S. 514 (1968).

Insanity is not a complete defense.

R. B. BURNS, Judge.

Defendant was charged with the first-degree murder of his wife. M.C.L. § 750.316; M.S.A. § 28.548. Defendant presented an insanity defense at his bench trial. The trial court found him guilty of second-degree murder, M.C.L. § 750.317; M.S.A. § 28.549, but mentally ill, M.C.L. § 768.36; M.S.A. § 28.1059. Defendant appeals.

Evidence presented at trial indicates that defendant stabbed his wife to death, and then attempted suicide by stabbing himself three times. From defendant's testimony and corroborating evidence it could be inferred that defendant believed his wife was possessed by a demon and that, when he stabbed her, he believed that she was already dead, and that he was attempting to cut the demon out and restore her to life. A psychiatrist who testified for the defense concluded that defendant was suffering from acute schizophrenia at the time of the incident and had been insane. Two psychiatrists, called by the prosecution in rebuttal, expressed contrary opinions.

The primary thrust of defendant's argument on appeal is factual: that the trial court erred in finding defendant sane at the time of the homicide. The argument rests in part on several erroneous arguments concerning the law, raised in related issues. Thus, we will first discuss the related issues before reaching the primary issue on appeal.

Defendant argues that he was prejudiced in the presentation of his defense by the trial court's failure to grant his pretrial motion to dismiss the charge of first-degree murder because the trial court was inclined thereby to reach a compromise verdict. Defendant relies upon the preliminary examination and trial transcripts to argue that the evidence of mental illness was compelling and asserts that a person who is mentally ill is incapable of "willful, deliberate and premeditated killing". M.C.L. § 750.316; M.S.A. § 28.548.

[1, 2] The issue of whether there was sufficient evidence to hold defendant for trial for first-degree murder was one addressed to the magistrate's discretion and reviewable only for abuse of discretion. *People v. Karcher,* 322 Mich. 158, 162–163, 33 N.W.2d 744, 746 (1948). Review is limited to the preliminary examination transcript; testimony taken at trial cannot be considered. *People v. Walker,* 385 Mich. 565, 572, 189 N.W.2d 234, 237 (1971). While there was evidence presented at the preliminary examination from which it could be inferred that defendant was mentally ill at the time of the offense, there was also evidence from which it could be inferred that the killing was willful, deliberate and premeditated. It does not necessarily follow that a person with a "substantial disorder of thought or mood which significantly impairs judgment, behavior, capacity to recognize reality, or ability to cope with the ordinary demands of life", M.C.L. § 330.1400a; M.S.A. § 14.800(400a), is incapable of deliberation and premeditation. We find no abuse of discretion.

[3] Defendant argues that he should have been acquitted of second-degree murder because the trial court found that he was mentally ill at the time of the offense. The incorrect premise underlying this argument is that one who is mentally ill is incapable of forming the *mens rea* of murder. Mental illness and malice aforethought are not mutually exclusive mental conditions. While mental illness may factually negate a finding of malice aforethought in a particular case, see *People v. Lynch,* 47 Mich.App. 8, 208 N.W.2d 656 (1973), it does not follow as a matter of law that a finding of mental illness necessitates a finding of not guilty of murder.

Source: People v. Ramsey, 280 N.W.2d 565 (Michigan, 1979). Reprinted by permission of West Publishing Company.

simply not criminally responsible for any of their acts if they are so insane as to be incapable of having a criminal intent. Unlike intoxication, insanity is a complete defense. Insanity may not be asserted to reduce the degree of an offense, since the defendant is either responsible or not. If insane, a defendant is entitled to an acquittal by reason of insanity. Such a verdict may lead to civil committment for an indefinite period, so insanity does not mean that the offender will go free to walk the streets.

Insanity is sometimes regarded as a special class and sometimes regarded as an excuse for a particular act. Insanity may be regarded as akin to infancy, signifying that the accused lacks the mental capacity to commit a criminal act. Treating insanity as an excuse means that it is in the same category as duress or self-defense; a criminal deed is assumed to have occurred, but proof is required that the act was motivated by insanity. If insanity is merely an excuse, the government must first prove its case before the jury can consider the defense of insanity.[42] If insanity is a condition of mental impairment and incompetency, then a criminal court may virtually lack jurisdiction altogether, with the issue of insanity essentially a civil and administrative matter. Once lunatics—along with witches, infants, and wild beasts—were considered to have no criminal responsibility. The trend nowadays is toward treating insanity as an excuse, not a permanent infirmity or condition.

Insanity is seldom obvious. There is some doubt whether it is even a scientific category. Psychologists and psychiatrists are familiar with terms such as psychosis or paranoia, but these terms are not

[42] See jury instructions, Brawner v. United States, 471 F. 2d 969,1008 (D.C. Cir. 1972): "You are not to consider this defense unless you have first found that the government has proved beyond a reasonable doubt each element of the offense."

useful to the law or acceptable to courts. Medical parlance and legal parlance are quite different and serve different purposes. Medical terms refer to sickness in a context of treatment. Insanity in law is a concept of legal and moral responsibility, a quite different notion with different consequences.

Society has a right to be protected against the acts of insane persons. Whether the criminal courts are equipped to make sound judgments on insanity is questionable, but the need for social protection may be greater than the need for accuracy in diagnosis. Value judgments are implicit in a determination of insanity, however shrouded it is by the use of such phrases as mental disease, mental disturbance, or irresistible impulse. Since no one is wholly sane, the decision that someone is permanently or temporarily insane is frequently based upon the views of laymen about the boundaries of rational behavior.

The oldest current test for insanity is the M'Naghten rule, derived from an English case decided in 1843. After the acquittal of Daniel M'Naghten, Lord Chief Justice Tindal of the House of Lords made a single condition, human reason, the determining factor in resolving the question of sanity. The rule is not based upon the general mental condition of the defendant, but upon whether he or she knew that the particular act was wrong.[43] Thus insanity is treated as an excuse, not a condition of mind.

The question under the M'Naghten rule is simply whether the defendant knew that the particular act in question was wrong. Then a defendant may be found not guilty of a crime by reason of insanity because he or she suffered from a defect of reason or from a disease of the mind at the time of the act in question. The rule may be invoked when defendants do not know the nature and quality of the act, or they know the nature and quality of the act but did not know the act was wrong. The cause of insanity is immaterial. Whether caused by heredity, injury, protracted illness, or environment, the state of a person's reason at the time of an act is what counts.

An insane delusion is also encompassed by the M'Naghten rule. If appropriate, the judge can charge the jury in language such as this:

> If you find that the defendant was acting under a delusion at the time of his act, but was not otherwise insane, his action should be evaluated as if the facts of his delusion were true and he should be convicted if, under the facts of his delusion, his act would be an offense [that is, he

[43] Many lawyers and judges mistakenly believe that the M'Naghten rule refers to a general condition of insanity.

> (or she) could tell right from wrong in spite of the delusion]. [Author's application of the rule of the M'Naghten case]

Under this test, if a person kills another while suffering from a delusion that the victim was out to kill oneself, the killer would be insane because of a mistaken belief in self-defense. There must be proof that the accused acted under the delusion, and there must be some evidence of a mental disease or defect.

The M'Naghten rule is the sole test for insanity in most states. In fourteen states it is supplemented by another test, called *irresistible impulse.* The charge to the jury for an irresistible impulse would include the requirement that the defendant was compelled by such an impulse, even though he or she knew it was wrong, owing to a mental disease or defect that prevented the person from controlling his/her actions. There are instances in which the defendant knew the difference between right and wrong but still could not stop from doing wrong. That is an irresistible impulse. Will, the governing power of the mind, was beyond the defendant's control at the time of the act. This test, while based upon a somewhat primitive psychology, is more in accordance with professional understanding of human behavior than is the general M'Naghten rule.

The M'Naghten rule has been criticized as too restrictive and too old-fashioned. The rule is based upon nineteenth-century notions of mental capacity and rationality. To satisfy the rule requires complete impairment of the defendant's mental capacity, a situation quite uncommon in mental illness. Emotional disturbance may take many shapes, and the capacity to distinguish right from wrong is not very meaningful in terms of mental disease. Using the rule reduces medical matters to legal terms. Doctors are hard put to talk about right and wrong since this is not their mode of discourse, nor is it the usual problem in mental illness.

There is a more modern test of insanity known as the Durham rule, which is followed in New Hampshire. Under this rule defendants may be found not guilty by reason of insanity if they were suffering from a mental disease or defect, and their act was a product of that disease or defect. The reason for the rule is the belief that there is no adequate legal test for insanity anyway, so the issue is best left to a jury after it has heard the testimony of medical experts. Mental disease is defined under this test as "any abnormal condition of the mind which substantially affects mental or emotional processes and substantially impairs behavior controls."[44] Experts and lay persons may disagree about the existence of legal insanity, and

[44] McDonald v. United States, 312 F. 2d 847 (D.C. Cir. 1962).

in the end the jury must decide insanity as though it were a fact. The Durham test places a great burden on the jury while providing little guidance. The Durham rule is the law in only two states.

The federal courts and a few states have adopted a still more modern test, that of the Model Penal Code. The Code provides:

> (1) A person is not responsible for criminal conduct if at the time of such conduct as a result of mental disease or defect he lacks substantial capacity either to appreciate the criminality [wrongfulness] of his conduct or to conform his conduct to the requirements of the law.[45]

This rule emphasizes a lack of substantial capacity. This makes it less harsh than the M'Naghten rule because there need be no showing of a total mental incapacity.[46] This rule or test is less vague than the Durham rule and it covers the situation of defendants who lack effective control over their behavior, regardless of their intellectual or emotional understanding. The jury's role, while difficult, is more modest under the Model Penal Code.

Certain kinds of mental disturbance are not regarded as legal insanity. Uncontrollable sexual passion, such as that depicted in novels and movies, is not regarded as insanity. Some people are lucid on most subjects and deranged on others. They may be subject to partial delusions or fixations. They may be ordinarily rational but convinced that God or the devil orders them about at times. This mental condition simply does not fit the usual rules.

A few courts take the view that mental disorder may result in dimished capacity or diminished responsibility. Under this view mental disorder is not so much a defense to the crime as it is a condition bearing upon the requisite criminal intent.[47] This doctrine would lead to the general/specific intent problem encountered in the topic of intoxication. It would in fact be hard to distinguish mental disease from intoxication.

Some reformers would abolish the whole idea of an insanity defense. Is there really a difference between being wicked and being mentally ill?[48] If Thomas Szasz is correct, can we be sure that there is such a thing as mental illness.[49] The insanity defense is often

[45] Sec. 4.01.

[46] Blake v. United States, 407 F. 2d 908 (5th Cir. 1969).

[47] See dissent in Fisher v. United States, 328 U.S. 463 (1946).

[48] See Justice Weintraub's opinion in State v. Lucas, 30 N.J. 37, 82, A. 2d 50, 74 (1959).

[49] Thomas Szasz, *Law, Liberty and Psychiatry* (New York: Macmillan & Co., 1963).

abused, although people really do act irresponsibly. Since criminal law is grounded on the idea of personal responsibility for individual actions, the insanity defense challenges the most fundamental aspects of criminal law. The law must have compassion for the weak but it must also be concerned with protection of society against impulsive dangerous acts.

THE BORDERLAND: POSSESSORY OFFENSES

If criminal liability rests upon volitional conduct, then criminal defenses serve to preserve the integrity of the criminal law. While strict liability offenses are an exception to this generally accepted view of criminal law, other exceptions are beginning to appear. A whole new class of offenses based upon possession, a rather passive condition, has been enacted. These possessory type offenses are not strict liability offenses, yet defendants found with contraband or heroin dust in their pockets are not able to raise the traditional defenses to excuse their criminality. The possessory offenses are described in such a way as to criminalize behavior without actually using strict liability concepts, while still denying defendants a substantial ground for excusing themselves.

Some deny that possession is an act. Courts, wrestling with the conceptual difficulties involved, have often refined the definition of possession. One court defined possession as "intentional control and dominion"[50] over stolen property, meaning merely that the defendant was aware of possession. But under such a view, which is common enough, the state does not have to prove that the defendant had guilty knowledge and knew the goods held were stolen. Such a definition seems to make criminal defenses unavailing. Ignorance or duress cannot be claimed.

The advantage of the possessory type crime is that it makes the crime easy to prove. If the possession of brass knuckles is a crime then a defendant cannot be excused by claiming that they were a family heirloom.[51] The possession of burglar tools has been made a crime in many states, thus saving the state the trouble of waiting for the tools to be used. The intention to use the tools need not be proved. Judges are made nervous by these abridgments of the usual

[50] State v. DiRienzo, 53 N.J. 360, 369-370 (1909).

[51] People v. Ferguson, 12a Cal. App. 300, 18 P. 2d 741 (1933).

categories of criminal liability, but only rarely do they strike down such statutes.

Firearm possession may be inherently dangerous. Statutes that prohibit the possession of certain weapons rest upon a well-conceived public policy to control the latent danger of firearms in the home or office. The possession of narcotics is criminalized for another reason: Narcotics transactions are difficult and expensive to detect, while possession is easily shown.

Much less defensible, as public policy, is a statute that prohibits the possession of lottery tickets or of obscene materials. Both kinds of objects could present some risk of harm to the public, but that risk hardly justifies the punishment of mere (possibly innocent) possession.

Police and prosecutors tend to be fond of possessory type offenses because they make law enforcement so much simpler. Legislators are often tempted by these arguments. Legislators should remember, however, that strict liability offenses deny criminal defenses and possessory offenses curtail them. If we are to preserve a consistent, principled approach to criminal responsibility in America, criminal defenses should be preserved as much as possible.

SUMMARY

The criminal law recognizes a number of defenses that are somewhat at variance with familiar tenets of ethics or religion. There are several ways in which persons may be partly or wholly excused for their wrongful conduct. Courts have fashioned many of these legal doctrines, which are more stringent than those of most moral philosophers. Duress, self-defense, insanity, and ignorance are less useful as defenses in a court of law than they might be in a dining room discussion. The law in this area may be somewhat out of line with popular contemporary expectations, but legislatures have altered these original common law rules only a little. In an age of widespread criminality, there is little enthusiasm for relaxation of the fairly high standards of legal responsibility established by the law of criminal defense. However medically unsound the law concerning the insanity defense, the prosecutors, judges, and legislators prefer to retain older principles rather than to exchange them for the legal uncertainties of modern medical knowledge.

11

AGENTS AND PARTIES

PRINCIPALS AND ACCESSORIES

Who is responsible for crime? How far does guilt extend? According to the common law guilty parties to felonious acts were either principals or accessories. Principals were those who directly and actually perpetrated the crime. All other parties were, in some fashion, accessories. This crude scheme assumed that there was only one criminal event and that guilt attached to all persons associated with that event, as long as they had *mens rea,* criminal intention. This common law scheme was further refined so that the punishments meted out to offenders were graded according to their degree of culpability. Culpability depended upon the degree of criminal responsibility for the act.

This neat common law approach suffered from several deficiencies. First, it did not cover all criminal offenses, only felonies. Second, highly artificial distinctions arose between principals in the first and second degrees and between accessories before and after the fact. Third, statutes began to blur the categories and to apply the same punishments to different categories. Finally, the common law rules were bent and stretched out of shape on issues such as the category of a person who incites another to commit a crime or a person who conspires with others to plan the commission of a crime.

The policy purposes that supported the common law distinctions have largely disappeared, but the language of the common law has been retained. At the time of the development of the criminal law of parties all felonies carried the death penalty potential. As the death penalty was gradually removed from most crimes the law of parties was not adjusted to meet new conditions. State criminal laws still refer to the common law terms even though the policy towards offenders has radically changed. This means that the interpretation of state statutes referring to principals or accessories is subject to con-

---

How do you "relieve" or "comfort" an "offender"?

§ 3. Accessory after the fact

Whoever, knowing that an offense against the United States has been committed, receives, relieves, comforts or assists the offender in order to hinder or prevent his apprehension, trial or punishment, is an accessory after the fact.

Source: 18 U.S.C. 3.

---

siderations derived from outmoded common law categories. Most modern statutes make no distinctions in punishment between principals and accessories.

The basic common law distinction between kinds of principals was made in terms of first and second degree responsibility. Principals in the first degree were those who committed the crimes themselves, either with their own hands or by compelling an innocent person to commit their felonious deed. Principals in the second degree were those who assisted (abetted) the commission of the crime or who incited the commission of a crime. A principal in the second degree need not be physically present at the crime scene. For that reason the driver of a getaway car is principal in the second degree to a bank robbery even though he was sitting in the car while his partners were robbing the bank.

There were, under common law, different types of accessories. An accessory at the fact was one who aided or abetted the perpetrator in the commission of a crime. Obviously this type was often factually close to the principal in the second degree. There was also an accessory before the fact who is not present at the crime at all, but incites it or assists in it. An example is the bank employee who gives the robbers the combination to the vault prior to the robbery. Then there was the accessory after the fact, a person who usually assists the perpetrator in escaping from the authorities. Hindering an arrest or prosecution also makes a person an accessory after the fact. Under the common law the rule was that no one could be an accessory after the fact to a misdemeanor. This is still the law today.

There always was a strong connection between the law of parties and the substantive law of crimes. Under the common law all parties to the crime of treason were regarded as principals—perpetrators—regardless of their degree of involvement. The crime of misprison is withholding information as to a felon's guilt. The crime of compounding a crime consists of accepting money (or gifts) for concealing a felony. Nowadays it is often hard to distinguish among commission of substantive crimes and responsibility as a secondary party for the commission of a felony. Individuals may be held accountable for conduct fairly remote from the actual commission of an offense.

VICARIOUS LIABILITY

Under some conditions individuals and groups may be held criminally liable even though they took no actual part in the crime.

There are two major instances of party liability without being an actual participant. These are employer liability for certain offenses of employees and some types of corporate liability for acts of top management.

Employer criminal liability for acts of employees derives from the common law doctrine of *respondeat superior,* which means that employers have the power to control the acts of their employees, who act as their virtual agents. Only crimes in which no *mens rea* is required may result in vicarious employer liability. So traffic offenses and liquor violations may be held to be acts for which an employer is criminally liable, even without the employer's doing anything. The employee's criminal act must have been done within the course and scope of his or her employment. Then the employer will be liable even without having expressly requested or authorized

---

One of the most direct statutes on the subject.

§ 5–2. When Accountability Exists

A person is legally accountable for the conduct of another when:

(a) Having a mental state described by the statute defining the offense, he causes another to perform the conduct, and the other person in fact or by reason of legal incapacity lacks such a mental state; or

(b) The statute defining the offense makes him so accountable; or

(c) Either before or during the commission of an offense, and with the intent to promote or facilitate such commission, he solicits, aids, abets, agrees or attempts to aid, such other person in the planning or commission of the offense. However, a person is not so accountable, unless the statute defining the offense provides otherwise, if:

(1) He is a victim of the offense committed; or
(2) The offense is so defined that his conduct was inevitably incident to its commission; or
(3) Before the commission of the offense, he terminates his effort to promote or facilitate such commission, and does one of the following: wholly deprives his prior efforts of effectiveness in such commission, or gives timely warning to the proper law enforcement authorities, or otherwise makes proper effort to prevent the commission of the offense.

Laws 1961, p. 1983, § 5-2, eff. Jan. 1, 1962.

Source: Illinois Statutes Annotated.

---

the criminal act. There is some dispute over whether the employer should be liable for criminal acts committed contrary to orders.[1]

Employers will not be imprisoned for acts committed by their employees, but they may be fined or suffer some kind of forfeiture. Employers are not criminally liable for acts of their employees that go beyond their duties and responsibilities as employees.

Corporations may be liable for the acts of their directors or chief executives in the same way. Corporations are punishable by fine. Corporations may not suffer a death penalty, but they may have their charters revoked in extreme cases of officer criminality.

Corporations are more criminally liable than employers, generally. Even offenses requiring a general criminal intent may apply to corporations. Thus, if a responsible corporate officer commits theft for a corporate purpose within the scope of employment, the corporation is criminally liable.[2] Furthermore, even if the crime requires a specific intent the corporation is liable,[3] unless the corporation has exercised due diligence to prevent commission of the offense. Corporations obviously cannot commit murder, rape, assault even if their officers may have committed those violent offenses.

Statutes may impose on officers a responsibility to meet certain health, sanitary, or safety standards. Failure of supervisors to meet these standards may make them criminally liable if they do not correct violations. They may be under a legal duty to seek out such violations.[4]

SPECIAL DEFENSES OF ACCOMPLICES AND OTHER IMPLICATED PARTIES

Parties may escape liability for crimes committed by others under certain circumstances. As indicated previously, employers are not liable for acts of employees that go beyond the scope of their employment. Abandonment of a criminal plan or withdrawal from a collective criminal act may result in an escape of criminal liability.

If someone agrees to burn another's house in order for the

[1] Overland Cotton Mill Co. v. People, 32 Colo. 263 (1904) makes the employer liable; Commonwealth v. Morakis, 208 Pa. Super. 180 (1966) holds employers blameless.

[2] W. T. Grant Co. v. Superior Court, 23 Cal. App. 3d 284 (1972).

[3] New York Central and Hudson Railroad v. United States, 212 U.S. 481 (1908).

[4] United States v. Park, 421 U.S. 658 (1974).

homeowner to collect insurance, both parties are guilty of arson. But if the homeowner changes his or her mind and tells the firebug not to burn the house, then the homeowner escapes criminal liability even if the house is illegally burned. The homeowner has abandoned the criminal plan in sufficient time if he or she effectively communicates the change of intention.[5]

People who assist (abet) another person to commit a crime must do more than announce the abandonment of criminal activity. They must also make a substantial effort to withdraw the assistance. Withdrawal is more than abandonment. Abettors must try to get back weapons or burglar tools or any other items with which they provided assistance to a partner in crime. The Model Penal Code suggests that abettors should also give timely warning to the police or otherwise make a "proper effort to prevent the commission of the offense."[6]

SOLICITATION

Modern statutes often criminalize the act of encouraging others to commit a crime. The crime is completed when a request, a command, an enticement, or any other inducement to another to commit a crime takes place. Solicitation is another type of inchoate crime, but it is treated here because it is so close to the law of party criminal liability.

Those states in which solicitation is proscribed by statute usually punish the solicitation of any crime. The common law view of solicitation was much more narrow, covering only felonies or misdemeanors that obstructed justice, threatened the public welfare, or created a breach of the peace.

Solicitation may come close to the area of First Amendment freedoms. A public speaker who calls for the use of force or violence may be fomenting a riot if he or she is addressing a mob ripe for action. On the other hand, a speaker who advocates violence in general without any sense of immediacy may be protected by the First Amendment. State statutes may not proscribe abstract advocacy of the use of force.[7]

[5] State v. Peterson, 213 Minn. 56 (1942).

[6] Model Penal Code, sec. 206 (6) (c).

[7] Brandenburg v. Ohio, 395 U.S. 444 (1969).

CONSPIRACY

Criminal conspiracy is one of the most legitimate and justifiable kinds of crime if the social fabric of society is threatened by the formation of criminal groups bent upon disruption, violence, and destruction. At the same time it can be a potent means of political suppression. From the 1890s until the 1920s criminal conspiracy charges were invoked by the governments to discourage the formation of labor unions. Criminal conspiracy charges became a favored means of antiradical activity under the Nixon administration. Attorney General John Mitchell (later jailed for his activities in the Watergate conspiracy) exploited the limits of conspiracy law in an effort to dampen the ardor of anti-Vietnam War protesters. Leaders of such protests were prosecuted, sometimes on flimsy evidence, for conspiracy to create violence. A dramatic example was the 1969 Chicago conspiracy trial that grew out of the violence at the 1968 Democratic National Convention.

Conspiracy is a combination of two or more people for the purpose of committing a criminal act. Under the common law it was a misdemeanor for two or more persons to agree to accomplish an unlawful purpose or a lawful act by unlawful means (force, threat, extortion). Modern statutes tend to confine conspiracy to criminal acts or to other specifically defined offenses. While the common law conspiracy doctrine was much broader than modern statutes, conspiracies today are generally serious crimes (felonies).

Conspiracy requires the presence of an actual criminal intention plus a specific intent to commit the unlawful act. Each conspirator must know that the ultimate act is unlawful. Ignorance or a mistake of law on the part of an alleged conspirator is a valid defense to a conspiracy charge.

The conspirators' motives are immaterial. Burning draft cards is an unlawful destruction of government property. Those who advocated this gesture of opposition to the Vietnam War were guilty of criminal conspiracy regardless of the purity of their beliefs.[8]

Conspiracy is easy for the prosecution to prove because the basic element is the forming of the agreement to commit the unlawful act.[9] The agreement can be proved either by inference or by showing that an express statement was made. The conduct of the parties may supply sufficient evidence of joining the conspiracy.

[8] United States v. Berrigan, 417 F. 2d 1002 (4th Cir., 1969).

[9] State v. Carbone, 10 N.J. 329 (1952).

From the most famous conspiracy trial of the century.

OPENING STATEMENT ON BEHALF OF THE GOVERNMENT BY MR. SCHULTZ

Mr. Schultz: . . . The Government, ladies and gentlemen of the jury, will prove in this case, the case which you will witness as jurors, an overall plan of the eight defendants in this case which was to encourage numerous people to come to the city of Chicago, people who planned legitimate protest during the Democratic National Convention which was held in Chicago in August of 1968, from August 26 through August 29, 1968. They planned to bring these people into Chicago to protest, legitimately protest, as I said, creat[ing] a situation in this city where these people would come to Chicago, would riot . . . [T]he defendants, in perpetrating this offense, they, the defendants, crossed state lines themselves, at least six of them, with intent to incite this riot.

. . .

[WITHOUT THE PRESENCE OF THE JURY]

The Court: This will be but a minute, Mr. Marshal. Who is the last defendant you named?

Mr. Schultz: Mr. Hayden.

The Court: Hayden. Who was the one before?

Mr. Schultz: Davis, and prior to that was Dellinger.

The Court: The one that shook his fist in the direction of the jury?

Mr. Hayden: That is my customary greeting, your Honor.

The Court: It may be your customary greeting but we do not allow shaking of fists in this courtroom. I made that clear.

Mr. Hayden: It implied no disrespect for the jury; it is my customary greeting.

The Court: Regardless of what it implies, sir, there will be no fist shaking and I caution you not to repeat it.

. . .

[Mr. Schultz continuing with his opening statement—ed.]

Mr. Schultz: . . . The Defendants Dellinger, Davis and Hayden joined with five other defendants who are charged in this case in their venture to succeed in their plans to create the riots in Chicago during the time the Democratic National Convention was convened here.

Two of these defendants, the Defendant Abbie Hoffman who sits—who is just standing for you, ladies and gentlemen—

The Court: The jury is directed to disregard the kiss thrown by the Defendant Hoffman and the defendant is directed not to do that sort of thing again.

. . .

Mr. Schultz: . . . Ladies and gentlemen of the jury, the Government will prove that each of these eight men assumed specific roles in it and they united and that the eight conspired together to encourage people to riot during the Convention. We will prove that the plans to incite the riot were basically in three steps. The first step was to use the unpopularity of the war in Vietnam as a method to urge people to come to Chicago during that Convention for purposes of protest. The first was to bring the people here.

The second step was to incite these people who came to Chicago, to incite these people against the Police Department, the city officials, the National Guard and the military, and against the Convention itself, so that these people would physically resist and defy the orders of the police and the military.

So the second step, we will prove, was to incite, and the third step was to create a situation where the demonstrators who had come to Chicago and who were conditioned to physically resist the police would meet and would confront the police in the streets of Chicago so that at this confrontation a riot would occur. . . .

. .

First they demanded, when these people arrived in Chicago, to sleep in Lincoln Park. At one point they were talking in terms of up to or exceeding 500,000 people who were coming to Chicago to sleep in Lincoln Park and they demanded free portable sanitation facilities, they demanded free kitchens and free medical facilities.

The second demand, non-negotiable demand which was made by those defendants I just mentioned was for a march to the International Amphitheatre where the Democratic National Convention was taking place. They said they were going to have a march of up to or exceeding 200,000 people. Although they were told that the United States Secret Service which was charged with the protection of the President of the United States, the Vice President of the United States and the candidates for nomination—although they were told that the Secret Service said that a permit could not be authorized because of the danger to the security of these individuals, the President and the Vice President and the candidates, the defendants demanded a permit for a march. . . .

So, ladies and gentlemen, of the jury, the Government will prove with regard to the permits that I have just mentioned that the defendants incited the crowd to demand sleeping in Lincoln Park and to demand that march to the Amphitheatre so that when the police ordered the crowd out of Lincoln Park at curfew and when the police stopped the march, the crowd, having been incited, would fight the police and there would be a riot.

. .

. . . The Government will not prove that all eight defendants met together at one time, but the Government will prove that on some occasions two or three of the defendants would meet together; on other occasions four would meet; on some occasions five of them would meet together to discuss these actions, and on several occasions six of the defendants met together to discuss their plans. . . .

In sum, then, ladies and gentlemen, the Government will prove that the eight defendants charged here conspired together to use interstate commerce and the facilities of interstate commerce to incite and to further a riot in Chicago; that they conspired to use incendiary devices to further that riot, and they conspired to have people interfere with law enforcement officers, policemen, military men, Secret Service men engaged in their duties; and that the defendants committed what are called overt acts in furtherance of the conspiracy—that is, they took steps, they did things to accomplish this plan, this conspiracy. . . .

. . .

The Court: Is it the desire of any lawyer of a defendant to make an opening statement?

Mr. Kunstler: It is, your Honor.

The Court: All right. You may proceed, sir.

Mr. Kunstler: Your Honor, it is 12:30.

The Court: I know, I am watching the clock. You leave the—What does that man say—you leave the time-watching to me—on the radio or TV—leave the driving to me. Mr. Kunstler, I will watch the clock for you.

Mr. Kuntsler: Your Honor, will you permit us to complete the opening statements?

The Court: I will determine the time when we recess, sir. I don't need your help on that. There are some things I might need your help on; not that.

. . .

OPENING STATEMENT ON BEHALF OF CERTAIN DEFENDANTS BY MR. KUNSTLER

Now the Government has given you its table of contents. I will present to you in general what the defense hopes to show is the true book. We hope to prove before you that the evidence submitted by the defendants will show that this prosecution which you are hearing is the result of two motives on the part of the Government—

Mr. Schultz: Objection as to any motives of the prosecution, if the Court please.

Mr. Kunstler: Your Honor, it is a proper defense to show motive.

The Court: I sustain the objection. You may speak to the guilt or innocence of your clients, not to the motive of the Government.

Mr. Kunstler: Your Honor, I always thought that—

Mr. Schultz: Objection to any colloquies, and arguments, your Honor.

The Court: I sustain the objection, regardless of what you have always thought, Mr. Kunstler.

. . .

Mr. Kunstler: The evidence will show as far as the defendants are concerned that they, like many other citizens of the United States, numbering in the many thousands, came to Chicago in the summer of 1968 to protest in the finest American tradition outside and in the vicinity of the Convention, the National Convention of the party in power. They came to protest the continuation of a war in South Vietnam which was then and had been for many years past within the jurisdiction of the party in power which happened to be the Democratic Party at that time. . . .

There was, as you will recall, and the evidence will so indicate, a turmoil within the Democratic Party itself as to whether it would enact a peace plan, as part of its platform. This, too, would be influenced by demonstrators. The possibility of this plank was what motivated many of the demonstrators to come to Chicago. The possibility of influencing delegates to that National Convention to take an affirmative strong stand against a continuation of this bloody and unjustified war, as they considered it to be along with millions of persons was one of the prime purposes of their coming to Chicago. . . .

At the same time as they were making plans to stage this demonstration and seeking every legal means in which to do so, the seeking of permits would be significant, permits in the seeking of facilities to put their plans into operation in a meaningful and peaceful way.

. .

At the same time as all of this was going on, the evidence will show that there were forces in this city and in the national Government who were absolutely determined to prevent this type of protest, who had reached a conclusion that such a protest had to be stopped by the—the same phrase used by Mr. Schultz—by all means necessary, including the physical violence perpetrated on demonstrators. These plans were gathering in Washington and they were gathering here in this city, and long before a single demonstrator had set foot in the city of Chicago in the summer of 1968, the determination had been made that these demonstrations would be diffused, they would be dissipated, they would essentially be destroyed as effective demonstrations against primarily the continuation of the war in South Vietnam. . . .

We will demonstrate that free speech died here in the streets under those clubs and that the bodies of these demonstrators were the sacrifices to its death. . . .

. .

. . . [T]he defense will show that the real conspiracy in this case is the conspiracy to which I have alluded, the conspiracy to curtail and prevent the demonstrations against the war in Vietnam and related issues that these defendants and other people, thousands, who came here were determined to present to the delegates of a political party and the party in power meeting in Chicago; that the real conspiracy was against these defendants. But we are going to show that the real conspiracy is not against these defendants as individuals because they are unimportant as individuals; the real attempt was—the real attack was on the rights of everybody, all of us American citizens, all, to protest under the First Amendment to the Constitution, to protest against a war that was brutalizing us all, and to protest in a meaningful fashion, and that the determination was made that that protest would be dissolved in the blood of the protesters; that that protest would die in the streets of Chicago, and that that protest would be dissipated and nullified by police officers under the guise of protecting property or protecting law and order or protecting other people. . . .

Dissent died here for a moment during that Democratic National Convention. What happens in this case may determine whether it is moribund.

Source: Verbatim transcript in United States of America v. David Dellinger, Rennard C. Davis, Thomas E. Hayden, Abbott H. Hoffman, Jerry C. Rubin, Lee Weiner, John R. Froines, and Bobby G. Seale.

The group nature of conspiracy used to be the chief criminal feature. The conspiracy doctrine was used to discourage dangerous groups from disturbing the society. Conspiracy itself was seen as an evil regardless of the outcome of the conspiracy. Most modern statutes, however, require the commission of an overt act of some kind.

Parties to the conspiracy need not know each other. It is only necessary that each conspirator have the requisite *mens rea*. Corporations can be conspirators when acting through their officers or directors.

Certain offenses can be punished either as conspiracies or as substantive offenses. Illegal gambling can be a conspiracy. A legislature can also make gambling itself a separate offense without violating the double jeopardy clause.[10]

If the conspired crime is completed the parties can be tried both for conspiracy and for the completed crime. They may be liable as principals or accessories for the completed crime, but they are equally liable as conspirators for their crime of conspiracy.

A conspirator may abandon the conspiracy. He or she must communicate the withdrawal to every other conspirator in sufficient time to permit them to consider whether they should continue by themselves. The withdrawing conspirator cannot escape prosecution for the original conspiracy itself. Abandonment or withdrawal only matters if the substantive crime is actually committed. Then the withdrawing conspirator may be held blameless for the commission of the crime.

Modern law still fears conspiracy. That is why most states make conspiracy a felony rather than a misdemeanor. A collective agreement to commit a crime is regarded still as a greater threat to society than crimes committed by a lone individual. Since the substantive crime may be charged separately from the conspiracy, modern conspiracy law gives the prosecutor a double opportunity to secure a guilty verdict. This makes conspiracy law a source of enhanced power to the state, especially in its dealings with organized crime.

Some states reflect a growing fear of forceful conspiracies. The basic federal antiriot law remains a most potent weapon against violence or against unpopular groups. This law states that,

> whoever travels in interstate or foreign commerce, including, but not limited to, the mail, telegraph, telephone, radio, or television with

[10] Iannelli v. United States, 420 U.S. 770 (1974).

A brief explication of federal conspiracy law that places limits upon federal conspiracy prosecutions.

MESKILL, Circuit Judge:

The material facts of this unusual conspiracy case are not in dispute. Morris D. Brooks, the appellant's alleged co-conspirator, made false entries in the accounts payable records at the Manhattan Postal Service headquarters where he worked and thereby obtained eight checks totalling over $180,000. The checks were drawn on the United States Treasury and were payable to individuals having no claim to payment from the Postal Service. Brooks was caught and indicted for conspiracy to defraud the United States, 18 U.S.C. § 371. He was also charged with eight counts of falsifying postal records in violation of 18 U.S.C. § 2073. After pleading guilty to conspiracy and to one count of making false entries, he testified against the appellant. Brooks was sentenced to five years imprisonment, but execution of the sentence was suspended, and he was placed on probation for five years.

Appellant, Rabbi Elyakim G. Rosenblatt was the Dean of the Rabbinical College of Queens. At Brooks' request, he "laundered" the eight checks through the college's bank account, and kept roughly ten percent of the face value of the checks for his services. Rosenblatt was indicted, along with Brooks, for conspiracy to defraud the United States. After pleading not guilty, he was tried and convicted by a jury and sentenced to six months imprisonment and a fine of $8,000.

Our difficulty with Rosenblatt's conviction arises from the lack of any agreement between him and Brooks concerning the type of fraud in which they were engaged. It is clear that Brooks was defrauding the United States by obtaining payment for government checks which he had caused to be printed without authorization. The government stipulated, however, that Rosenblatt did not know the truth about Brooks' activities. Brooks led him to believe that the checks were valid. He told Rosenblatt that the purpose of the laundering operation was to help some payees evade taxes and to help other payees conceal kickbacks on government contracts. In other words, both men agreed to defraud the United States, but neither agreed on the type of fraud. On this appeal, Rosenblatt argues that under 18 U.S.C. § 371 a conspiracy to defraud the United States must be grounded upon agreement on some common scheme or plan. He maintains that proof of an argument to defraud, without further qualification as to the nature of the fraud, is insufficient to support a conviction under § 371. We agree and reverse the conviction.

THE LACK OF AGREEMENT

[1] A conspiracy is an "agreement *among* the conspirators." *United States v. Falcone,* 311 U.S. 205, 210, 61 S.Ct. 204, 85 L.Ed. 128 (1940) (emphasis added). A "meeting of minds" is required. *Krulewitch v. United States,* 336 U.S. 440, 448, 69 S.Ct. 716, 93 L.Ed. 790 (1949) (Jackson, J., concurring).

"[U]nless at least two people commit [the act of agreeing], no one does. When one of two persons merely pretends to agree, the other party, whatever he may believe, is in fact not conspiring with anyone." Developments in the Law—Criminal Conspiracy, 72 Harv.L.Rev. 920, 926 (1959) [hereinafter cited as Developments]; see *Sears v. United States,* 343 F.2d 139 (5th Cir. 1965) (no conspiracy with government informant who secretly intends to frustrate the conspiracy); *Delaney v. State,* 164 Tenn. 432, 51 S.W.2d 485 (1932) (no conspiracy with person who feigns agreement).

[2] The law of conspiracy requires agreement as to the "object" of the conspiracy. Developments 929–33. This does not mean that the conspirators must be shown to have agreed on the details of their criminal enterprise, but it does mean that the "essential nature of the plan" must be shown. *Blumenthal v. United States,* 332 U.S. 539, 557, 68 S.Ct. 248, 92 L.Ed. 154 (1947).

The problem of identifying the "essential nature" of the conspirators' plan often arises in cases in which knowledge is in issue. An examination of those cases sheds some light on the degree of specificity that is required as to the agreement. In *Ingram v. United States,* 360 U.S. 672, 79 S.Ct. 1314, 3 L.Ed.2d 1503 (1959), two individuals who had assisted in the operation of a lottery that was illegal under state law were convicted of conspiracy to evade federal wagering taxes for which their employers were liable. The Supreme Court reversed because there had been no evidence that the individuals knew of the tax liability. Absent such knowledge, tax evasion could not have been one of the objectives of their conspiracy, and the convictions could not stand. In contrast, the convictions of the employers for conspiracy to evade taxes were upheld. Similarly, in *United States v. Gallishaw,* 428 F.2d 760 (2d Cir. 1970), the defendant was convicted after a trial judge charged the jury that he could be convicted of conspiracy to rob a bank if he had rented a machine gun to another individual "with the knowledge 'that there was a conspiracy to do something wrong and to use the gun to violate the law.'" *Id.* at 762. This Court reversed. We said that "at the very least" the government was required to show "that he knew that a bank was to be robbed." *Id.* at 763. We explained that the defendant "had to know what kind of criminal conduct was in fact contemplated." *Id.* at 763 n. 1; *cf. United States v. Calabro,* 467 F.2d 973, 982 (2d Cir. 1972), *cert. denied,* 410 U.S. 926, 93 S.Ct. 1357, 35 L.Ed.2d 587 (1973) (supplier of false identification must have known that it would be used in a transaction involving forged bonds in order to be guilty as an aider and abettor; generalized suspicion of illegal use would not suffice). Thus, it is clear that a general agreement to engage in unspecified criminal conduct is insufficient to identify the essential nature of the conspiratorial plan.

Proof of the essential nature of the plan is required because "the gist of the offense remains the agreement, and it is therefore essential to determine what kind of agreement or understanding existed as to each defendant." *United States v. Borelli,* 336 F.2d 376, 384 (2d Cir. 1964), *cert. denied,* 379 U.S. 960, 85 S.Ct. 647, 13 L.Ed.2d 555 (1965). The importance of making this determination cannot be overstated. "[A]greement is the essential evil at which the crime of conspiracy is directed" and it "remains the essential element of the crime." *Iannelli v. United States,* 420 U.S. 770, 777 n. 10, 95 S.Ct. 1284, 1290, 43 L.Ed.2d 616 (1975). "Nobody is liable in conspiracy except for the fair import of the concerted purpose or agreement as he understands it." *United States v. Peoni,* 100 F.2d 401, 403 (2d Cir. 1938). A conspirator's liability for substantive crimes committed by his co-conspirators depends on whether the crimes were committed "in furtherance of the unlawful agreement or conspiracy." *Pinkerton v. United States,* 328 U.S. 640, 645, 66 S.Ct. 1180, 1183, 90 L.Ed. 1489 (1946). Similarly, the admissibility against a defendant of a co-conspirator's declaration depends on whether the declaration was made "during the course and in furtherance of the conspiracy." Fed.R.Evid. 801(d)(2)(E). This determination can be made only after the scope of the agreement has been defined. The question of whether single or multiple conspiracies have been pled or proved depends on the nature of the agreement. *United States v. Dardi,* 330 F.2d 316, 327 (2d Cir.), *cert. denied*, 379 U.S. 845, 85 S.Ct. 50, 13 L.Ed.2d 50 (1964). Because overt acts are acts "to effect the *object* of the conspiracy," 18 U.S.C. § 371 (emphasis added), they are defined by reference to the conspiratorial agreement. *United States v. Bayer,* 331 U.S. 532, 542, 67 S.Ct. 1394, 91 L.Ed. 1654 (1947). In addition, when questions arise concerning matters such as venue, *Hyde v. United States*, 225 U.S. 347, 32 S.Ct. 793, 56 L.Ed. 1114 (1912), or the statute of limitations, *Grunewald v. United States,* 353 U.S. 391, 396–97, 77 S.Ct. 963, 1 L.Ed.2d. 931 (1957), which depend on the formation of the agreement or the occurrence of overt acts, it becomes "crucial," *id.* at 397, 77 S.Ct. 963, to determine the scope of the conspiratorial agreement. *See Bridges v. United States,* 346 U.S. 209, 224, 73 S.Ct. 1055, 97 L.Ed. 1557 (1953) (statute of limitations). Finally, the punishment that may be imposed under § 371, for a conspiracy to commit an offense against the United States, depends on whether the "object" of the conspiracy is a felony or a misdemeanor. In order to make this determination, specificity with respect to the "object" of the conspiracy is essential.

It is clear that, under the general rules of conspiracy, Rosenblatt could not have been validly convicted of conspiracy to make false entries on postal records, 18 U.S.C. § 2073, the substantive crime with which Brooks was charged, because he had no knowledge of such a plan; he neither intended nor agreed to commit that offense, or any other offense of which Brooks might have been guilty. . . .

[4] In this case the government neither pled nor proved an agreement on the essential nature of the fraud. Accordingly, Rosenblatt's conviction is reversed, and the case is remanded with instructions to dismiss the indictment.

Source: United States v. Rosenblatt, 554 F.2d 36 (2d Cir. 1977). Reprinted by permission of West Publishing Company.

> intent (A) to incite a riot; or (B) to organize, promote, encourage, participate in, or carry on a riot; or (C) to commit any act of violence or furtherance of a riot; or (D) to aid or abet any person in inciting or participating in or carrying on a riot or committing any act of violence in furtherance of a riot; and who either during the course of any such travel or use or thereafter performs or attempts to perform any overt act for any purpose specified . . . shall be fined not more than $10,000, or imprisoned not more than five years, or both [(The Rap Brown law) 18 U.S.C. Sec. 2101].

Under this section and two other parts of the United States Code, the Chicago conspiracy trial was prosecuted. David Dellinger, Rennie Davis, Tom Hayden, Abbie Hoffman, Jerry Rubin, Lee Weiner, John Froines, and Bobby Seale were charged with crossing state lines with intent to cause a riot.

Political conspiracy seems to be a common offense in the United States, in spite of our committment to free speech. Convictions of American Communists for conspiracy to incite the violent overthrow of the government have been upheld.[11] Justice Jackson once said that "the Constitution does not make conspiracy a civil right."[12] Proof of a political conspiracy must, however, be of a higher standard than in other kinds of conspiracy cases. There must be clear proof of the defendant's personal adherence to the alleged political type conspiracy.[13] In most other conspiracies mere membership in the conspiring group is sufficient to establish criminal complicity.[14]

[11] Dennis v. United States, 341 U.S. 494 (1951).

[12] Ibid., p. 572.

[13] United States v. Spock, 416 F. 2d 165 (1st Cir., 1969).

[14] Pinkerton v. United States, 328 U.S. 640 (1946). This position of broad accountability of conspirators is rejected by the Model Penal Code.

Who is criminally liable for what under this statute?

Whenever two or more persons assemble together to do an unlawful act, and separate without doing or advancing toward it, or do a lawful act in a violent, boisterous, or tumultuous manner, such assembly is an unlawful assembly.

Source: Unlawful Assembly—California Penal Code sec. 407, definition changed in 1969.

Conspiracy has often become a catchall category. The crime has been dubbed the prosecutor's darling. Legislatures have increasingly enacted broad sweeping conspiracy statutes in order to snare more offenders more easily. Some state statutes forbid conspiracies to commit any act injurious to the public health, to public morals, or to trade or commerce or for the perversion or obstruction of justice or of the due administration of law. One such statute was held to be unconstitutionally vague unless it could be narrowed by state court interpretation.[15]

Conspiracy covers criminal and noncriminal offenses. Courts have been unwilling to restrict the notion of conspiracy to unlawful criminal acts. As a result the act of criminality that conspiracy law regulates is the formation of the conspiracy, not the final act. Conspiracy may involve civil offenses or even nonoffenses, if the legislature pleases. The conception of a criminal conspiracy for noncriminal acts seems to reveal clearly that merely forming a group may constitute antisocial behavior. Criminal law is stretched to its limits in the idea of criminal conspiracy. What could be broader than the language of the basic federal conspiracy statute?

> If two or more persons conspire either to commit any offense against the United States, or to defraud the United States, or any agency thereof in any manner or for any purpose, and one or more of such persons do any act to effect the object of the conspiracy, each shall be fined not more than $10,000, or imprisoned not more than five years, or both.[16]

SUMMARY

The criminal law concerning agents and parties is undergoing considerable change. Common law categories are being replaced by different notions of individual and collective responsibility. Vicarious liability has become increasingly popular, extending criminal responsibility to individuals who are ignorant of the particular offense. Criminal conspiracy statutes permit a broad net of criminal

[15] Musser v. Utah, 333 U.S. 95 (1948). This case involved a conviction on a charge of counseling, advising, and practicing polygamy.

[16] 18 U.S.C. sec. 371. The statute clearly reaches noncriminal conduct as well as criminal conduct. See United States v. Hutto, 256 U.S. 524 (1921). On the fraud aspect, see A. Goldstein, "Conspiracy to Defraud the United States," *Yale Law Journal* 68 (1959): 405-435.

responsibility to be cast, if the government chooses to pursue groups for the conspiracy to commit a substantive offense as well as the actual commission of the offense. This area of law deserves clarification. Some states have attempted to define legal accountability for crimes in precise but general language. Such statutes make it easier to determine the extent of legal accountability and they avoid some of the inconsistencies found in the case law on the subject.

12

REFORM AND CHANGE IN CRIMINAL LAW

IMPROVING OR REFORMING CRIMINAL LAW

Criminal law is always imperfect and often unsatisfactory. No attempt to prescribe rules for human behavior is ever satisfactory, as the divergent codes of moral behavior subscribed to by various religions clearly demonstrate. But criminal laws, unlike moral rules, are publicly enforceable standards of behavior. It is sad that agreement about what behavior should be criminalized and what penalties should be meted out for infractions is lacking in American society. Legislators, keen to placate the voting public, tend to pass ever increasing numbers of criminal statutes and to step up the punishments that flow from infractions. Americans are disturbed by crime but do not agree as to the best means of reducing or eliminating it. As a result criminal laws seem to tumble out of our legislatures with great frequency and little reflection. Although there is some movement towards decriminalization of certain behavior, the general tendency is towards proliferation of criminal laws. In America more is often confused with better. Fortunately there are enlightened groups in our society that have resisted thoughtless enactment of criminal offenses. Reform and improvement begin with reflection and theory.

All criminal laws are composed of three elements. There must be a definition of the substantive elements of the crime, to establish precisely what behaviors are proscribed. There must be a specification of penalties that flow from infractions of the criminal law. Finally, there must be some outlines of the principles of criminal responsibility, including the mental states that accompany wrongdoing. All criminal laws in America include these elements. The relationship among the elements is, however, often incoherent or even contradictory. Relatively minor offenses, such as marijuana use, may be accompanied by severe penalties, while white-collar frauds and deceptions that harm large numbers of people often receive lesser penalties. The phrases used to describe *mens rea,* criminal states of mind, may vary considerably from one offense to another. These inconsistencies and contradictions may reflect a considered public policy about the best means to discourage unwanted behavior or they may represent historical events long past or the accidental byproduct of hasty legislation. Reform of criminal law requires that these matters be reviewed periodically to ensure that the criminal law is all of a piece and is directed at control of unwanted behavior in accordance with standards of fairness and consistency.

Reform and improvement has been a recurrent theme in crimi-

A judicial view of free will in the criminal law.

LEVENTHAL, Circuit Judge:

The principal issues raised on this appeal from a conviction for second degree murder and carrying a dangerous weapon relate to appellant's defense of insanity. After the case was argued to a division of the court, the court *sua sponte* ordered rehearing en banc. . . .

We have decided to adopt the ALI rule as the doctrine excluding responsibility for mental disease or defect, for application prospectively to trials begun after this date. . . .

The ALI's [American Law Institute—Ed.] formulation retains the core requirement of a meaningful relationship between the mental illness and the incident charged. The language in the ALI rule is sufficiently in the common ken that its use in the courtroom, or in preparation for trial, permits a reasonable three-way communication—between (a) the law-trained, judges and lawyers; (b) the experts and (c) the jurymen—without insisting on a vocabulary that is either stilted or stultified, or conducive to a testimonial mystique permitting expert dominance and encroachment on the jury's function. There is no indication in the available literature that any such untoward development has attended the reasonably widespread adoption of the ALI rule in the Federal courts and a substantial number of state courts.

A number of proposals in the journals recommend that the insanity defense be abolished together. This is advocated in the amicus brief of the National District Attorneys Association as both desirable and lawful. The amicus brief of [the] American Psychiatric Association concludes it would be desirable, with appropriate safeguards, but would require a constitutional amendment. That a constitutional amendment would be required is also the conclusion of others, generally in opposition to the proposal.

This proposal has been put forward by responsible judges for consideration, with the objective of reserving psychiatric overview for the phase of the criminal process concerned with disposition of the person determined to have been the actor. However, we are convinced that the proposal cannot properly be imposed by judicial fiat.

The courts have emphasized over the centuries that "free will" is the postulate of responsibility under our jurisprudence. 4 Blackstone's Commentaries 27. The concept of "belief in freedom of the human will and a consequent ability and duty of the normal individual to choose between good and evil" is a core concept that is "universal and persistent in mature systems of law." Morissette v. United States, 342 U.S. 246, 250, 72 S. Ct. 240, 243, 96 L.Ed. 288 (1952). Criminal responsibility is assessed when through "free will" a man elects to do evil. And while, as noted in *Morissette,* the legislature has dispensed with mental element in some statutory offenses, in furtherance of a paramount need of the community, these instances mark the exception and not the rule, and only in the most limited instances has the mental element been omitted by the legislature as a requisite for an offense that was a crime at common law.

The concept of lack of "free will" is both the root of origin of the insanity defense and the line of its growth. This cherished principle is not undercut by difficulties, or differences of view, as to how best to express the free will concept in the light of the expansion of medical knowledge. We do not concur in the view of the National District Attorneys Association that the insanity defense should be abandoned judicially, either because it is at too great a variance with popular conceptions of guilt or fails "to show proper respect for the personality of the criminal [who] is liable to resent pathology more than punishment."

These concepts may be measured along with other ingredients in a legislative re-examination of settled doctrines of criminal responsibility, root, stock and branch. Such a reassessment, one that seeks to probe and appraise the society's processes and values, is for the legislative branch, assuming no constitutional bar. The judicial role is limited, in Justice Holmes's figure, to action that is molecular, with the restraint inherent in taking relatively small steps, leaving to the other branches of government whatever progress must be made with seven-league leaps. Such judicial restraint is particularly necessary when a proposal requires, as a mandatory ingredient, the kind of devotion of resources, personnel and techniques that can be accomplished only through whole-hearted legislative commitment.

Source: United States v. Brawner, 471 F.2d 969 (D.C. Cir. 1972). Reprinted by permission of West Publishing Company.

---

nal law. A few great legal thinkers have led the way. Blackstone, Foster, and East helped form the English version of criminal law.[1] Romilly, Brougham, Peel, and Greaves also made their contributions. In nineteenth-century England Jeremy Bentham was preeminent. In twentieth-century America, three legal philosophers are outstanding for their theoretical contributions to American criminal law: Herbert Wechsler, Herbert Packer, and Jerome Hall. A fourth should probably be added, Fletcher, whose recent work has stirred acclaim. These men have each helped shape and form our understanding of the goals and purposes of criminal law. Whatever coherence there may be in American criminal law is attributable to the thought, writing, and direct efforts of Wechsler, Packer, and Hall. They sought to reduce confusion and to aid justice by constructing a rational system of criminal law. To a remarkable degree American criminal law has responded to their insights, even though a good deal of incoherence and irrationality still remain.

Jerome Hall has asserted that the objectives of criminal law

[1] Bruce Ashworth, "The Making of English Criminal Law, Blackstone, Foster, East," *Criminal Law Review* (1978): 389ff.

reform are "(a) to preserve what is sound in the criminal code and jurisprudence, (b) to improve that law, and (c) to organize the statutes...."[2] Law reform requires refinement, clarification, and the resolution of ambiguities. This is by no means a task unique to America. English criminal law is undergoing review under the English Criminal Law Reform Committee. The Law Reform Commission of Canada is continuing its efforts. West Germany just adopted a new Penal Code in 1975. We have our Model Penal Code, produced by the American Law Institute and still highly influential. In America, however, criminal law reform tends to be sporadic, occurring every 30 or 40 years or so. Unlike the custom in many other countries there is no continuing effort at revision and reform of American criminal law. Jerome Hall concludes, "improvement of the criminal law should be a permanent ongoing enterprise and detailed records should be kept."[3] For these reasons reformers of criminal law should keep in touch with the work of specialists if they are to keep our criminal law responsive and responsible.

We are in the midst of a period of furious activity aimed at the reform, or at least the improvement, of American criminal law. State after state has undertaken the task. The federal criminal law is in the midst of a major overhaul. This is a fertile time to take stock of American criminal law and to evaluate the work of those who seek to reform it. Any evaluation will be tentative, but we appear to want some fresh starts in criminal law policy. Reform is in the air, although it may not be in our hearts or minds.

Tough stands on crime are politically fashionable. The reported crime rate is on the increase. Yet on January 1, 1977, the United States had an imprisonment rate of 244 per 100,000 population, the highest rate in the so-called free world. Sweden's imprisonment rate is 32 per 100,000 population, Denmark's 22 per 100,000 and the Netherlands' 18. Something is wrong with our criminal law if we put more people behind bars than do other industrialized democracies, while our crime rate continues to mount. Reform of criminal law is needed.

REFORMING CRIMINAL LAW IN AMERICA

Much has been said and written about the central problem of crime in America. Conservatives and liberals alike share a deep concern with the prevalence of crime, especially violent crime.

[2] Jerome Hall, "Theory and Reform of Criminal Law," *Hastings Law Quarterly* 29 (1978): 898.

[3] Ibid., p. 918.

Charles E. Silberman believes that it is necessary to change the way Americans think about criminals and crime.[4] He believes that the crime problem, especially violent crime, is partly a black problem and that to ameliorate the crime problem we must create varying disincentives to criminal activity. Many criminals are not simply bad people. They do act bad not because of their genes but because of a general breakdown in social contact mechanisms, especially within the black community. The violent crime problem that most deeply concerns Silberman can only be met by attempting to contain blacks' perfectly understandable rage against American racism. Much of Silberman's thesis is daring because it discusses some of the racial aspects of deviant behavior, a subject often considered too delicate for public discussion. Blacks are disproportionately arrested, convicted, and incarcerated in America. Silberman suggests why this is so.

Silberman's argument is that American racism is the chief cause of our alarming rate of criminal violence. He admits that a criminal substructure has sprung up to provide a pathway for ghetto children to attain middle-class affluence. He notes, however, that much criminal violence is not profitable, and that crime really does not pay, for most repeating criminals eventually get caught. How would criminal law cope with the decay of family life, with racist attitudes, with senseless violence, with the prevalence of violence directed by blacks against other blacks? If our prison population is much too black, can we change criminal laws or procedures in such a way as to correct racial imbalance in criminal punishment? Only in minor ways. The crime problem—or at least the problem of violent crime—runs too deep in our society to be corrected by reform or manipulation of the criminal law.

Nor can Silberman suggest ways to reform criminal laws that would reduce the high incidence of juvenile offenders. In 1976, 40 percent of arrests for FBI indexed crimes were for offenses committed by persons under 17. We may change our views of the role of juvenile courts, but this seems unlikely to reduce the incidence of juvenile crime. As New York State has done, we may change the criminal law so as to criminalize acts that were previously noncrimes because of the age of the offenders. The latter reform, of course, merely increases the statistical crime rate while labeling more juvenile offenders as criminals.

Most American critics of the criminal law are hard-liners, call-

[4] Charles Silberman, *Criminal Violence, Criminal Justice* (New York: Random House, 1978), p. IX.

Criminal law reform as of April 1979.

Status of Substantive Penal Law Revision*

I. REVISED CODES, EFFECTIVE DATES (36)

ALA. CODE tit. 13A (1978 Special Pamphlet: Criminal Code); 5/17/1978.
ALAS. STAT. tit. 11 (Oct. 1978 Pamphlet); 1/1/1980.
ARIZ. REV. STAT. ANN. tit. 13 (1978 Special Pamphlet: Criminal Code); 10/1/1978.
ARK. STAT. ANN. tit. 41 (1977 Replacement Vol. 4); 1/1/1976.
COLO. REV. STAT. ANN. tit. 18 (1973); 7/1/1972.
CONN. GEN. STAT. tit. 53a (1977); 10/1/1971.
DEL. CODE ANN. tit. 11 (1974); 7/1/1973.
FLA. STAT. ANN. tit. 44 (1976); 7/1/1975.
GA. CODE ANN. tit. 26 (1977); 7/1/1969.
HAW. REV. STAT. tit. 37 (1976 Replacement Vol. 7A); 1/1/1973.
ILL. ANN. STAT. ch. 38. § 1-1 (Smith-Hurd 1972); 1/1/1962.
ILL. UNIFIED CODE OF CORRECTIONS, ILL. ANN. STAT. ch. 38 § 1001-1-1 (Smith-Hurd 1973); 1/1/1973.
IND. CODE ANN. tit. 35 (Burns Supp. 1977); 10/1/1977.
IOWA CODE ANN. chs. 701—732 (Criminal Code): chs. 901—909 (Corrections Code) (West, 1978 Special Pamphlet); 1/1/1978.
KAN. STAT. ANN. ch. 21 (1974); 7/1/1970.
KY. REV. STAT. ANN. ch. 500 (1975 Replacement Vol. 16); 1/1/1975.
LA. REV. STAT. ANN. tit. 14 (West 1974); 1942.
ME. REV. STAT. ANN. tit. 17-A (West, 1978 Pamphlet); 5/1/1976.
MINN. STAT. ANN. ch. 609 (West 1953); 9/1/1963.
MO. ANN.STAT. tit. 38 (Vernon, 1979 Special Pamphlet: Criminal Code); 1/1/1979.
MONT. REV. CODES ANN. tit. 94 (Special Pamphlet: Criminal Code of 1973 [1977]); 1/1/1974.
NEB. REV. STAT. ch. 28 (1978 Cum. Supp.); 1/1/1979.
N.H. REV. STAT. ANN. tit. 62 (1974); 11/1/1973.
N.J. CODE OF CRIMINAL JUSTICE, ch. 95, 1978 N.J. Sess. L. Serv. 279 (West) (to be codified as N.J. STAT. ANN. tit. 2C); 9/1/1979.
N.M. STAT. ANN. ch. 40A (1972 Second Replacement Vol. 6); 7/1/1963.
N.Y. PENAL LAW (McKinney 1975); 9/1/1967.
N.D. CENT. CODE tit. 12.1 (1976 Replacement Vol. 2); 7/1/1975.
OHIO REV. CODE ANN. tit. 29 (Baldwin 1974 Replacement Unit); 1/1/1974.
ORE. REV. STAT. tit. 16 (1977 Replacement Part); 1/1/1972.
PA. CONS. STAT. ANN. tit. 18 (Purdon 1973); 6/6/1973.
P.R. LAWS ANN. tit. 33 (1977 Cum. Pocket Supp.); 1/22/1975.
S.D.C.L. ANN. rev. tit. 22 (1978 Supp.); 4/1/1977.
TEX. PENAL CODE ANN. (Vernon 1974); 1/1/1974.
UTAH CODE ANN. tit. 76 (1975 Supp.); 7/1/1973.

VA. CODE tit. 18.2 (1975 Replacement Vol. 4); 10/1/1975.
WASH. REV. CODE ANN. tit. 9A (1977); 7/1/1976.
WIS. STAT. ANN. tit. 45 (1958); 7/1/1956.

II. CURRENT SUBSTANTIVE PENAL CODE REVISION PROJECTS:

A. REVISION COMPLETED: NOT YET ENACTED: (6)

District of Columbia (Basic Criminal Code being considered by D.C. City Council)
Maryland (Part of Proposed Code enacted: S.B. 1153 [consolidation & revision of theft and related offenses] enacted 4/8/1978; effective 7/1/1979) (Remainder of Proposed Code being brought up to date for possible submission to Legislature in 1980)
Massachusetts (Special Legislative Committee preparing new bill)
Michigan (State Bar Criminal Code Committee submitted revision of 1967 Proposed Code to Legislature March 1979; Legislative Service Bureau to draft bill for introduction in House of Representatives)
United States (95th Cong.: S. 1437 passed by Senate Jan. 1978; S. 1437. H.R. 6869 & H.R. 2311 died in House Judiciary Subcommittee) (96th Cong.: new bills being prepared in Senate & House)
West. Virginia (Proposed Code, printed in bill form with commentary, to be studied by Subcommittee on Criminal Laws: hearings to be held prior to introduction in 1980 Legislature)

B. REVISION WELL UNDER WAY: (1)

North Carolina (misc. correctional provisions enacted 1977, effective 7/1/1978; Ch. 15A [Criminal Procedure Act], Arts. 78, 80–85)

C. REVISION AT VARYING PRELIMINARY STAGES: (1)

Wyoming

D. CONTEMPLATING REVISION: (1)

Mississippi

III. REVISION COMPLETED BUT ABORTIVE: (6)

IV. NO OVER-ALL REVISION PLANNED: (2)

Nevada (recodification with minor changes enacted 1967). Rhode Island.

*As of April 1978 (53 jurisdictions). This chart was prepared and is maintained by Rhoda Lee Bauch.

Source: Annual Report, American Law Institute, New York, 1979. Reprinted by permission.

ing for harsher, swifter, and more certain punishment. Such reforms are favored by Van den Haag[5] and Wilson.[6] Similar critics take an economic view of crime, believing that most offenders make a rational calculation of the rewards of crime against the price, in fines and jail time, imposed by the state. Thus, as the cost of crime increases by stepping up the penalties, the rate of commission should decrease, according to this view.[7] This view has been persuasively argued before legislative bodies concerned with criminal law reform.[8] Remember, though, that the substantive criminal law may not be so critical for crime control, if this view is correct, as are the procedures of the criminal justice system. Perpetrators must be caught, convicted, and punished if they are to lose their economic gamble.[9] Criminal procedure rules, police, prosecutors, and judicial practices may have more to do with the probability of paying for crime than do the substantive provisions of the criminal law.

One of the favorite recent reforms of American criminal law is determinate sentencing legislation. In recent years doubts have been raised about the use of criminal sentences for the purpose of rehabilitating convicted persons. In place of extensive discretion in sentencing offenders, some states have sharply limited indeterminate sentencing. Some states have openly rejected the rehabilitative ideal in favor of a policy of definite punishment linked to the commission of substantive crimes. California penal law states that

> The Legislature finds and declares that the purpose is best served by terms proportionate to the seriousness of the offense with provisions for uniformity in the sentences of offenders committing the same offense under similar circumstances.[10]

In most states crimes are not linked directly to fixed sentences, but considerable discretion is permitted to judges and parole boards. Some discretion remains in California, but imprisonment and sub-

[5] Ernest Van Den Haag, *Punishing Criminals* (New York: Basic Books, 1975).

[6] James Q. Wilson, *Thinking About Crime* (New York: Random House, 1977).

[7] Richard Posner, *Economic Analysis of Law,* 2nd ed. (Boston: Little, Brown and Company, 1977). Section 7, 1-2. Many others could be mentioned.

[8] See California Assembly Committee on Criminal Procedure, Progress Report, *Deterrent Effects of Criminal Sanctions* (1968).

[9] See Franklin E. Zimring and Gordon J. Hawkins, *Deterrence: The Legal Threat in Crime Control* (Chicago: University of Chicago Press, 1973).

[10] California Penal Code, sec. 1170 (a) (1).

stantive crimes are directly tied to each other. Whether this is reform or regression is still in doubt.[11]

One of the controversies among reformers of criminal law is just what kind of crime most needs revision and clearer definition. Most citizens conceive of violent crimes and crimes affecting property as the core of the crime problem. The adoption of determinate sentencing policies is largely based upon a desire to deter potential offenders in those two areas of criminal activity. Yet organized crime is responsible for a large number of offenses and organized crime often resembles legitimate business. Indeed, there sometimes is a connection between crimes committed by shady businesses and the unsavory practices of organized criminal elements.

We must also consider official crimes, that is, offenses commit-

[11] National Institute of Law Enforcement and Criminal Justice (L.E.A.A.), *Determinate Sentencing: Reform or Regression,* (Washington, D.C.: Government Printing Office, 1977). Arizona, Indiana, Illinois, Maryland and New Mexico also have adopted some form of determinate sentence.

The American Bar Association's view of the proper role of the legislature in establishing criminal sentences.

Part II. Statutory Structure

STANDARD 18-2.1. GENERAL PRINCIPLES: ROLE OF THE LEGISLATURE

(a) The proper role of the legislature with respect to sentencing is a limited one. All crimes should be classified by it for the purpose of sentencing into a small number of categories which reflect substantial differences in gravity. For each such category, the legislature should specify the sentencing alternatives available for offenses which fall within it. The penal codes of each jurisdiction should be revised where necessary to accomplish this.

(b) The legislature should provide sentencing authorities with a range of alternatives, including nonincarcerative sanctions and gradations of supervisory, supportive, and custodial facilities, so as to permit an appropriate sentence in each individual case consistent with standards 18-2.2 and 18-3.2.

(c) The legislature should not specify a mandatory sentence for any sentencing category or for any particular offense.

(d) The legislature should establish a guideline drafting agency authorized to develop more detailed sentencing criteria and standards and to promulgate presumptive sentencing ranges in order to curtail unwarranted sentencing disparities. Standards addressed to such an agency are set forth in standards 18-3.1 to 18-3.5.

(e) Both the legislature and sentencing authorities should recognize that in many instances prison sentences which are now authorized, and sometimes

ted by government officials in violation of the laws. These types of crimes are part of the American crime problem and must be examined by those concerned with the improvement of criminal law.

The phenomenon of organized crime in America may pose the greatest threat to the social system. Crimes of violence and crimes against property have been committed with familiar frequency throughout American history, but the growth of professional organized crime as a virtual industry is a product of a mass, urbanized, impersonal society.

Organized crime in major American cities involves crimes of force and violence, but its economic mainstay is in illegal services such as narcotics, loansharking, gambling, pornography, and prostitution. Some of these crimes are regarded as minor offenses, but in the total context of the crime industry the profits of one sector feed into another. In New Jersey, one of the hotbeds of organized crime, recent revisions of the criminal code have been introduced that are directly addressed to controlling organized crime. A special statu-

---

required, are significantly higher than are needed in the vast majority of cases in order adequately to protect the interests of the public. For most offenses, the maximum prison term authorized ought not to exceed ten years and normally should not exceed five years. Longer sentences should be reserved for particularly serious offenses committed by particularly dangerous offenders, but such sentences should only be authorized or imposed in accordance with specific criteria established by the legislature and its guideline drafting agency and should require a specific finding of dangerousness based on repetitive criminality in accordance with standards 18-2.5(c) and 18-4.4 and reached under the special procedures required by 18-6.5. . . .

STANDARD 18-2.2 GENERAL PRINCIPLE: LEAST RESTRICTIVE ALTERNATIVE

(a) The sentence imposed in each case should call for the minimum sanction which is consistent with the protection of the public and the gravity of the crime. In determining the gravity of the offense and the public's need for protection, sentencing authorities best serve the public interest and the appearance of justice when they give serious consideration to the goal of sentencing equality and the need to avoid unwarranted disparities.

(b) It would be appropriate for the legislature to codify such a principle in its delegation of authority to the guideline drafting agency and to sentencing authorities generally.

Source: American Bar Association, *Sentencing Alternatives and Standards,* Project on Minimum Standards for Criminal Justice (Chicago: American Bar Association, 1981). Reprinted by permission.

tory section dealing with such crimes was introduced. Fencing stolen goods, labor racketeering, and new theft laws have also been added to the criminal code in an attempt to meet the threat of organized crime.

The connection between organized crime and legitimate business has become so close that new criminal laws have been drafted to criminalize improper entry of racketeers into businesses. Federal statutes make it unlawful

> for any person who has received any income derived, directly or indirectly, from a pattern of racketeering activity or through collection of an unlawful debt . . . to use or invest, directly or indirectly any part of such income, or the proceeds of such income, in acquisition of any interest in, or the establishment or operation of any enterprise which is engaged in or the activities of which affect, interstate or foreign commerce.[12]

This provision enables law enforcement officials to obtain prosecution of organized crime figures at the point at which they invest the profits of their ill-gotten gains. It also proscribes activity which is superficially innocent in order to prevent the spread of organized crime into legitimate business. We shall see if this approach really works.

Organized crime has also infected the government. Secret payments by organized crime to politicians may have reached the presidential levels during the Nixon administration, and have long been prevalent in the nation's cities and counties. In New York City organized crime's influence on city government has been personalized and individual mobsters have had access to individual politicians and judges. The administration of criminal justice has sometimes been compromised and indictments against organized crime defendants are sometimes dismissed rather easily. Organized crime is deeply involved in illegal gambling, making payoffs to police and prosecutors part of the cost of doing business.[13] Whether adequate laws can be drafted to deal with subtle forms of corruption is doubtful, but certainly our public officials can be held to a higher standard of conduct through properly drafted criminal laws.

The issue of reform of criminal law is ultimately a political issue. The criminal law is so thoroughly statutory that the only hope for reform is by means of legislation. In 1930 legal philosopher Ros-

[12] 18 U.S.C. sec. 1962 (a).

[13] See Jack Newfield and Paul Dubrul, "The Political Economy of Organized Crime," in Jerome Skolnick and Elliot Currie, eds., *Crisis in American Institutions,* 4th ed. (Boston: Little, Brown, 1979), pp. 514–526.

coe Pound noted the "close connection of criminal law with politics in a democratic government [that] leads to a tendency to put an over-heavy burden upon the criminal law."[14] Pound observed that many unhappy features of our society lie too deep to be reached by criminal legislation. Some of our problems are due to the statutes themselves while "many more have been aggravated by statutes."[15] The central problem of the reform of criminal law is to identify those futile and counterproductive criminal statutes, to change or eliminate them, and to make laws that are socially responsive and effective. The task for true reform, Pound believes, is "to discover how and how far the criminal law actually secures the social interests which we expect it to secure."[16] The task is best performed in our colleges, universities, and law schools. We can only hope that the political forces that dominate criminal law formulation will be guided, as they have been after the drafting of the Model Penal Code, by a sense of what is wise rather than what is expedient.

CODIFICATION AS REFORM

The idea of a code of law that would embrace all basic elements of law in a single, rational, coherent, consistent framework goes back to the Code Napoléon of 1804. European codification has a long, distinctive history and development. No serious codification proposal was made in the United States until David Dudley Field drafted a civil code for the state of New York in the late nineteenth century. The Field code launched a debate over the desirability of adopting a comprehensive general code for all American law, but that prospect is exceedingly dim. Instead particular areas of the law underwent codification long before the Model Penal Code was produced.

In America codification has been piecemeal, from one substantive area to another. Codifications of negotiable instrument law and sales law took place in the early decades of the twentieth century. The high point of codification in America was reached in the middle of the twentieth century with the drafting of the Uniform Commercial Code. As the popularity of codification grew in the commercial law area, its feasibility for use in the criminal law was considered.

[14] Roscoe Pound, *Criminal Justice in America* (New York: Henry Holt and Co., 1930), pp. 66-67.

[15] Ibid., p. 67.

[16] Ibid., p. 212.

This was the beginning of the process that led to the preparation of the Model Penal Code.

The history of European codification is quite irrelevant to American experience. Codification in America has had a different meaning, different sources, and has produced different results. The very meaning of the term *criminal code* has been different for America than for Europe. Now that the American Law Institute's Model Penal Code has captured the imagination of law reformers many assume that codification is in itself reform. Indeed, it may be; often it is not. One expert has defined a true code as a

> pre-emptive, systematic, and comprehensive enactment of a whole field of law. It is pre-emptive in that it displaces all other law in its subject area save only that which the code excepts. It is systematic in that all its parts arranged in an orderly fashion and stated with a consistent terminology, form an interlocking, integrated body, revealing its own plan and containing its own methodology. It is comprehensive in that it is sufficiently inclusive and independent to enable it to be administered in accordance with its own basic policies.[17]

These conditions are rarely met in American criminal codes.

In fact, American criminal codes are generally not so comprehensive. Some terms and doctrines imbedded in the prior criminal statutes are sometimes omitted from the criminal code, requiring courts to reach back to precode rulings.[18] The proposed federal criminal code fails to define the general *mens rea* element in crimes. This may lead to precode judicial interpretations.

[17] William Hawkland, "Uniform Commercial 'Code' Methodology," *University of Illinois Law Forum* (1970): 292.

[18] See People v. White, 67 Ill. 2d 107, 365 N.E. 2d 337 (1977).

A true code.

A true code is a pre-emptive, systematic, and comprehensive enactment of a whole field of law. It is pre-emptive in that it displaces all other law in its subject area save only that which the code excepts. It is systematic in that all of its parts, arranged in an orderly fashion and stated with a consistent terminology, form an interlocking, integrated body, revealing its own plan and containing its own methodology. It is comprehensive in that it is sufficiently inclusive and independent to enable it to be administered in accordance with its own basic policies.

Source: William Hawkland, "Uniform Commercial Code Methodology," *University of Illinois Law Forum* (1962), p. 292.

There is a well-established American practice of calling any compilation of existing criminal statutes a code. Unless it is clearly understood that a new criminal code contains an interrelated and consistent body of principles of criminal law there will be a strong judicial tendency to revert to American habit and to read a particular section of the code in terms of judicial precedents rather than in the light of the whole body of the criminal code.

Code drafters need to have some legislative latitude if a true criminal code is to be produced. They must not merely compile the existing state of the criminal law. They cannot merely weed out quaint and archaic criminal statutes. The drafters must be empowered to interweave the provisions of the criminal law to form a consistent, integrated document. The construction of a true code would of necessity change certain familiar judicial precedents, and even some long-established statutes, in the process of integration. Whether legislatures will permit such sweeping changes depends upon the political climate, but the drafters have no constituency and have to resort to comments and recommendations to convey their expectations. Whether drafters' comments have any legal effect depends upon the willingness of courts to embrace them.

Organized, rational, integrated criminal codes can be a major instrument of reform. They can at least help avoid uncertainty, inconsistency, and excessive technicality. But a criminal code may do the opposite whenever political factors become paramount and whenever expert recommendations are shelved in favor of interest group satisfaction. In Europe most criminal codes were drafted by legal scholars, with few changes by the legislatures. Such a process would benefit American reform. Scholars can be wrong, but they are more likely to be logical and less likely to be concerned with image manipulation in dealing with the so-called crime problem than are most politicians.[19]

THE MODEL PENAL CODE

The major instrument of criminal law reform today is the Model Penal Code. The code is the work of the American Law Institute and legal scholars who labored long on the project. The institute was founded in 1923 and its founders were heartily opposed to codification. Their major activities for decades were directed at saving the

[19] See Jerry E. Norton, "Criminal Law Codification: Three Hazards," *Loyola University Law Journal* 10 (1978): 61–74.

common law. This was to be done by freezing common law, the essential principles derived from case law, into a set of restatements of the law. Judges and professors tried to arrange the common law principles into some kind of pattern. They intended not to suggest new legislation but merely to present logical, orderly principles from already existing case law. These restatements "were almost virgin of any notion that rules had social or economic consequence."[20]

The restatements (which are still being produced) examined the major law fields: contracts, trusts, property, torts, agency, corporations, and conflicts of law. Criminal law, which had become increasingly scattered, was at first neglected. Fortunately for the reform of criminal law a major figure emerged to dominate the production of the institute's statement on criminal law, Herbert Wechsler. The vision and reach of the Model Penal Code is due to his leadership. The code was forward-looking and receptive to the mood for reform.[21] It was not a mere summation of the best thought on the subject. It was not a restatement.

The American Law Institute intended to examine the validity of the then current substantive classification of criminal offenses in America. The institute assumed that the economic and industrial development of modern society might require the reclassification of offenses. New offenses might need to be added. Outmoded offenses might be discarded. In 1950 the institute received a substantial grant from the Rockefeller Foundation, a grant that sustained 10 years of research, 13 tentative drafts, and a final draft in 1962. The purpose of the grant was "to crystallize for the benefit of the legal profession and the public the best thought up to now in this difficult and neglected field" so that the product would "affect the thinking about criminal law for the next fifty years."[22] This and more was accomplished.

The drafters of the Model Penal Code were fortunate in that they were relatively "free from immediate political demands,"[23] a

[20] Lawrence A. Friedman, *A History of American Law* (New York: Simon and Schuster, 1973), p. 582.

[21] Professor Herbert Wechsler was Chief Reporter. Louis B. Schwartz was another Reporter. Morris Ploscowe and Paul W. Tappan were Associate Reporters. These were the key positions.

[22] Quoted in Herbert F. Goodrich and Paul A. Wolkin, *The Story of the American Law Institute* (St. Paul, Minn.: American Law Institute Publishers, 1961), p. 25.

[23] Herbert Wechsler, "A Thoughtful Code of Substantive Law," *Journal of Criminal Law, Criminology and Police Science* 45 (1955): 525.

factor much appreciated by Herbert Wechsler, the main moving force for the code. Since the code was being prepared for the examination of all the states, changes could be made according to what the draftsmen thought best rather than in response to the limitations and obstacles of a single jurisdiction. Also, as Wechsler emphasized, there was a varying content of substantive criminal law among the states that demanded evaluation and selection. A restatement approach was rejected as undesireable.[24] The Model Penal Code would differ from other American codification efforts in its elimination of statutes that were "often accidental in their coverage."[25] Wechsler rekindled the "reformist zeal of the early Benthamite codification movement."[26]

The proposals for the criminal law contained in parts I, III, and IV of the completed Model Penal Code were based largely upon Professor Wechsler's formulations. Part II of the completed code was originally drafted by Professor Louis Schwartz. As with all such collective products, many experts influenced the final language, but there is little doubt about the chief sources of the Model Penal Code.[27] This code has nearly revolutionized legal thinking about criminal law. The code has influenced every drafter of American criminal law and served as a dominant influence in many American states.

The Code has four main parts: (I) General Provisions, (II) Definition of Specific Crimes, (III) Treatment and Correction, and (IV) Organization of Correction.

Parts I and II are of most interest for criminal law policy. Part I sets forth the principles that govern the scope and nature of criminal liability. Topics include the mental elements of culpability, causality and strict liability, complicity, defense, and justifications for criminal conduct. Inchoate crimes are discussed at length in Part I: attempts, solicitation, and conspiracy to commit substantive offenses. Part I also attempts a major innovation, the specification of the type of disposition that should follow from a criminal conviction. A classification scheme is established that differentiates among offenses, making only three graded distinctions among major crimes.

[24] Herbert Wechsler, "The Model Penal Code and the Codification of American Criminal Law," in Roger Hood, ed., *Crime, Criminology, and Public Policy* (New York: Free Press, 1975), pp. 420-421.

[25] Wechsler, "Thoughtful Code," p. 526.

[26] Sanford H. Kadish, "Codifiers of the Criminal Law: Wechsler's Predecessors," *Columbia University Law Review* 78 (1978): 1138.

[27] See statement of R. Ammi Cotter, President, American Law Institute, in *Columbia Law Review* 78 (1978): 955-961.

Part II was drafted in the light of the classificatory scheme of Part I. The specific crimes are related to Part I's distinctions as an aid to policy makers and to the sentencing process. Several topics were omitted from Part II: narcotics, motor vehicle offenses, alcoholic beverage control, gambling offenses, and offenses against trade and tax laws. These offenses are treated in this book as either administrative crimes or victimless crimes, and it is no coincidence that the drafters of the Model Penal Code chose to leave them out.[28] Part II does contain full treatment of violent crimes, sex offenses, property offenses, political offenses (called offenses against public administration), and certain crimes involving marriage and the family.

The Model Penal Code is an effort to criminalize systematically only conduct that "unjustifiably and inexcusably inflicts or threatens substantial harm to individual or public interest."[29] It is not designed merely to express pious sentiments or empty moral concern. The code rejects the idea that the mental element of crime can be overlooked, and its definition of *mens rea* is enormously influential. The code begins with the explicit declaration that "a person is not guilty of an offense unless his liability is based on conduct which includes a voluntary act or the omission to perform an act of which he is physically capable."[30] Excluded from the category of voluntary acts is a reflex or convulsion, movements during sleep or consciousness, or any "movement that otherwise is not a product of the effort or determination of the actor, either conscious or habitual."[31] This is one of the largest single contributions of the Model Penal Code. American law abounds in *mens rea* terminology, such as general intent, specific intent, malice, willfulness, recklessness, wantonness, scienter, and a host of other words used to describe mental activity deemed criminal. Clarification of this highly confused and central area of criminal law was a much needed reform. The code reduces the mental element of crimes to four concepts: purpose, knowledge, recklessness, and negligence.[32] Most criminal laws have not yet caught up with the code.

[28] Actually, Wechsler wrote that the omission was due "either . . . to lack of time or in the view that they are better treated in a regulatory statute placed outside the Penal Code." Herbert Wechsler, "Codification of Criminal Law in the United States: The Model Penal Code," *Columbia Law Review* 68 (1968): 1429.

[29] Model Penal Code, sec. 1.02 (1) (a).

[30] Sec. 2.01 (1).

[31] Sec. 2.01 (2) (d).

[32] Sec. 2.02 (1).

According to Section 2.02 of the Model Penal Code "a person is not guilty of an offense unless he acted purposely, knowingly, recklessly or negligently." In subdivisions (4) through (10) the code explores, with little detail, the interrelationships between *purposely, knowingly, recklessly,* and *negligently,* indicating briefly just how and when the requirements for these elements are satisfied. There is some difficulty in grasping the precise degrees of intention expressed by these adverbs, but they form the basis for the gradation of criminal offense categories found throughout the code.

A trial judge working with an offspring of the code must examine language like this, taken from Section 2.02 (2) (a)-(b) of the Model Penal Code:

> (2) *Kinds of Culpability Defined.*
>
> (a) *Purposely.*
>
> A person acts purposely with respect to a material element of an offense when:
>
> (i) if the element involves the nature of his conduct or a result thereof, it is his conscious object to engage in conduct of that nature or to cause such a result; and
>
> (ii) if the element involves the attendant circumstances, he is aware of the existence of such circumstances or he believes or hopes that they exist.
>
> (b) *Knowingly.*
>
> A person acts knowingly with respect to a material element of an offense when:
>
> (i) if the element involves the nature of his conduct or the attendant circumstances, he is aware that his conduct is of that nature or that such circumstances exist; and
>
> (ii) if the element involves a result of his conduct he is aware that it is practically certain that his conduct will cause such a result.

The Model Penal Code is generally opposed to criminal responsibility without criminal intent or purpose. Strict liability, that is, liability for conduct regardless of the intention, is seen as sometimes necessary for effective regulation, but strict liability runs counter to the prevailing philosophy of the code, which is to assign criminal responsibility only to acts involving a criminal state of mind. Fines and forfeitures are deemed appropriate means of civil regulation, but if imprisonment is involved then there is a crime and there must be a mental element shown. The code boldly declares that a violation "does not constitute a crime,"[33] and a violation is an offense that

[33] Sec. 1.04 (5).

does not involve the possibility of imprisonment. All administrative crimes, as we have called them, must be redrafted if they are to conform to the Model Penal Code, because the code provides that there can be no imprisonment without proof of criminal culpability, including a mental element of wrongfulness.[34]

There are numerous other ways in which the Model Penal Code departs from established criminal law. Space does not permit a full exposition of these proposed reforms. A few examples are provided in the accompanying material of this chapter. What should be remembered about the Model Penal Code, so far as substantive crimes are concerned, is the drafters' intention to "safeguard conduct that is without fault from condemnation as criminal [and] to differentiate on reasonable grounds between serious and minor offenses."[35]

THE FEDERAL CRIMINAL CODE

In late 1980 the new Federal Criminal Code was struggling through Congress. This comprehensive revision of the federal criminal laws has taken over 10 years to produce. The nation has never had a thorough, logical criminal code. Even though the United States Code contained most of the criminal laws in Title 18 there were many criminal laws scattered throughout the rest of the code. The previous code had been compiled in 1948[36] but it had not attempted to combine or consolidate offenses nor to produce a coherent body of federal criminal law. That was finally attempted in 1980, but in spite of the support of President Carter and key leaders of Congress, this vital reform seemed close to defeat.

The 1948 code was filled with inconsistencies and anomalies. For example, larceny was atomized into twenty different, often overlapping statutes, some of which were outside Title 18, the basic criminal code. Federal jurisdiction was broad and sometimes reached intrastate commerce, but each type of larceny was surrounded with different meanings and the reach of federal larceny law was actually determined by federal prosecuting officials and the courts. The scope and extent of federal jurisdiction over larceny was unclear, as it was for most federal crimes. This meant that the reach of the federal government over such crimes was uncertain, even if

[34] Sec. 2.05 (2).

[35] Sec. 1.02 (1).

[36] Act June 25, 1948, 62. Stat. 683.

the constitutional power over federal crimes was potentially very broad.[37] Other crimes were also subject to similar inconsistencies and anomalies.

The old code suffered from inconsistent and opaque definitions of crimes. The essential elements of familiar crimes were largely undefined, leaving the actual formulation of policy to the courts, which had to make sense out of a mixture of statutes. Even the judge-made decisions became inconsistent and contradictory. This lead to a system of judge-shopping in which procedural considerations ranked highly. Sentencing provisions were also inconsistent, a condition which also encouraged judge-shopping.[38]

The National Commission on Reform of Federal Criminal Laws was established in 1966 with a mission of restructuring federal criminal law. By 1966 Title 18 had over 5000 separate sections, making the existing code virtually unworkable and certainly unjust. In 1971 the commission, chaired by former California Governor Edmund G. (Pat) Brown, issued its final recommendations. The Brown Commission Report recommended a specific, broad, comprehensive framework for a new federal criminal code. The report was submitted to President Nixon, who called for a prompt study, review, and evaluation of the report.

In spite of its innovative and reformist features the Brown Commission Report was immediately opposed by the influential National Association of Attorneys General, who contended that the draft "works not a revision and rearrangement of the federal criminal code or its reform in light of recent developments of case law, but rather a wholesale expansion of federal police power and a wholesale destruction of state responsibility and state autonomy."[39] Revision and reform of the federal criminal law became a political issue.

The Nixon administration had its own notion of reform. Although the Brown Commission had produced a draft code resembling the Model Penal Code the Nixon administration had something much sterner in mind. In 1973 the Nixon administration submitted its own proposals, which were joined into something called Senate Bill 1 (S.1). This bill contained many repressive features,

[37] See *Hearings, Subcommittee on Criminal Laws and Procedures of the Committee on the Judiciary, U.S. Senate, 92nd Congress, 1st Session (1971), Part I (The Brown Report)*, p. 11.

[38] Ibid., p. 12.

[39] Ibid., p. 7.

most notably a section known as the "Official Secrets Act" that was directed against disclosures of classified or defense information and to the regulation of political dissidence. Freedom of the press would have been curtailed and the powers of federal investigative agencies and of federal prosecutors vastly expanded. S.1 raised a storm of protest. Reform of the criminal code had become merged with Nixon's war on crime and his war on radicals. S.1 died in committee, but the taint of politics remained.

Finally, Senators Kennedy and McClellan worked out a new bill, Senate Bill 1437, which represents a major series of compromises between adherents of the old S.1 and more liberal opponents. The result is a version of law reform that departs from the Brown Commission broad-gauge approach and from the S.1 politicized approach. Yet the proposed code is a bitter pill for many who had hoped to get reform without new expansions of federal power and new curtailment of individual rights.

The proposed new criminal code replaces 1614 pages of statutes with 130 pages. For the first time all the penal statutes are grouped together in an orderly, rational arrangement. All the felonies are in one title of the United States Code, obsolete laws have been dropped, and trivial laws have been eliminated. The requirements of federal jurisdiction are clearly stated. The mental states required to support a criminal charge have been drastically reduced in number. Sentencing disparity has been restricted by curtailing the sentencing discretion available to federal judges.

The federal code contains many new features. White-collar crime is more clearly dealt with. Commercial bribery, consumer fraud, insurance fraud, and improper sales schemes are all criminalized, while grossly usurious loans are prohibited. New election law offenses, including a Watergate dirty-tricks statute, have been enacted. The law on bribery, corruption, and tax evasion has been strengthened and toughened. Gambling, prostitution, and obscenity offenses have been reduced somewhat. The penalty for simple possession or free transfer of marijuana has been reduced to a simple fine. Wiretapping statutes have been narrowed. Conspiracy now requires an overt act in all instances, and a renunciation defense is permitted. These are all major changes in the substantive law. Riot coverage is narrowed somewhat. Penalties for state crimes that are prosecutable federally are dropped to a misdemeanor level.[40]

[40] See Ronald L. Gainer, "Proposed Code Is More Systematized, More Ordered, Far Clearer than Present Law," *The Center Magazine,* March/April 1979, pp. 12–15.

Many scholars find the new criminal code still unduly repressive. The American Civil Liberties Union expressed fears about First Amendment freedoms that they felt would be threatened by the new law. The expansion of federal jurisdiction carries with it the potential of criminalizing political criticism. The conspiracy provision, in particular, has drawn the fire of libertarians because "the new conspiracy law abolishes the traditional requirement that a conspirator must intend to commit the underlying offense,"[41] thus arming the FBI with new anticonspiracy powers. Certainly the provision on facilitating a crime broadens our usual concepts by saying that one is guilty of a crime if, knowing that another is committing a crime, one facilitates or aids that person in committing a crime. But facilitating and aiding are not defined. The law would create a new catchall crime that expands the reach of criminal responsibility.

Nonetheless most groups accept the need for a new federal criminal code. The code is less than it might have been because of the political struggles and compromises that attended its enactment. The criminal conspiracy, attempt, and solicitation statutes retain some of the worst features of the old inchoate crimes, offenses in which no actual harm results. But we now may have a sentencing commission that establishes sentencing guidelines for federal judges. We may have a coherent federal criminal law, even if it is less than ideal. As a leading scholar observed:

> Undoubtedly one will not find purity in the code. This is not the American Law Institute. This is not a group of academics. This is a group of practical senators trying to do their best, and it has produced a camel. But it has produced our camel, not their camel.[42]

THE NEW JERSEY CRIMINAL CODE

In September 1979 the nation's newest and in many respects most comprehensive criminal code went into effect in the state of New Jersey. The code is based upon the work of the New Jersey Criminal Law Revision Commission, which was heavily influenced by the Model Penal Code and by revisions in New York State, Il-

[41] John H. F. Shattuck, "Criminal Law Is Expanded at the Expense of Civil Liberties," in ibid., p. 25.

[42] Alan Dershowitz, "As a Pragmatist I Support This Bill," in ibid., p. 23.

linois, Wisconsin, Michigan, California, and Connecticut. The study draft of the Federal Criminal Code also provided a source of criminal law policy.[43] The commission's report contained a specific redrafting of New Jersey Criminal Law. While the legislature changed many parts of the proposed revisions in the final report, the code as enacted reflects most of the principal features of the commission's report. Several matters were not considered: corrections reform, capital punishment, narcotics legislation, and some other matters reserved by the legislature. The code as enacted represents, nevertheless, the most ambitious codification of criminal law yet undertaken in America, and as such it deserves special attention.

The general objectives of the New Jersey Code of Criminal Justice are clearly stated in the basic statute. This approach in itself was a departure for the New Jersey legislature which had, like most

[43] New Jersey Criminal Law Revision Commission, *Final Report* (Newark, N.J.: 1971) I: X–XI.

The basic criminal law policy of New Jersey.

Section 2C:1–2. Purposes; Principles of Construction.

a. The general purposes of the provisions governing the definition of offenses are:

(1) to forbid, prevent, and condemn conduct that unjustifiably and inexcusably inflicts or threatens substantial harm to individual or public interests;

(2) to insure the public safety by preventing the commission of offenses through the deterrent influence of the sentences authorized, the rehabilitation of those convicted, and their confinement when required in the interests of public protection·

(3) to subject to public control persons whose conduct indicates that they are disposed to commit offenses;

(4) to give fair warning of the nature of the conduct proscribed and of the sentences authorized upon conviction;

(5) to differentiate on reasonable grounds between serious and minor offenses; and

(6) to define adequately the act and mental state which constitute each offense, and limit the condemnation of conduct as criminal when it is without fault.

---

legislatures, left to the courts the formulation of general principles governing the criminal law. The general purposes of the definition of criminal offenses in New Jersey are:

1. To forbid, prevent, and condemn conduct that unjustifiably and inexcusably inflicts or threatens substantial harm to individual or public interests;
2. To insure the public safety by preventing the commission of offenses through the deterrent influence of the sentences authorized, the rehabilitation of those convicted, and their confinement when required in the interests of public protection;
3. To subject to public control persons whose conduct indicates that they are disposed to commit offenses;
4. To give fair warning of the nature of the conduct proscribed and of the sentences authorized upon conviction;
5. To differentiate on reasonable grounds between serious and minor offenses; and

---

b. The general purposes of the provisions governing the sentencing of offenders are:

(1) to prevent and condemn the commission of offenses;

(2) to promote the correction and rehabilitation of offenders;

(3) to insure the public safety by preventing the commission of offenses through the deterrent influence of sentences imposed and the confinement of offenders when required in the interest of public protection;

(4) to safeguard offenders against excessive, disproportionate or arbitrary punishment;

(5) to give fair warning of the nature of the sentences that may be imposed on conviction of an offense;

(6) to differentiate among offenders with a view to a just individualization in their treatment; and

(7) to advance the use of generally accepted scientific methods and knowledge in sentencing offenders.

c. The provisions of the Code shall be construed according to the fair import of their terms but when the language is susceptible of differing constructions it shall be interpreted to further the general purposes stated in this Section and the special purposes of the particular provision involved.

Source: New Jersey Code of Criminal Justice, 1979.

6. To define adequately the act and mental state which constitute each offense, and limit the condemnation of conduct as criminal when it is without fault.[44]

While these purposes and principles of construction do contain some self-contradictory features, they are actually exemplified in the code itself.

The New Jersey Code was the product of 10 years of labor by lawyers, politicians, and the state attorneys general. The code replaces a scattered group of statutes with a comprehensive statute containing many new substantive and procedural requirements. All common law crimes are abolished, although the rules concerning contempt of court are retained. Local laws and ordinances that conflict with the code are preempted (nullified) by it.

Criminal culpability is now determined by only five categories of mental states or conditions. The prosecution must prove that a person acted either purposely, knowingly, recklessly, negligently, or that he "violated a statute imposing strict liability."[45] This language strongly resembles the Model Penal Code and the Federal Penal Code, though not in its use of *purposely* and in its treatment of strict liability offenses (offenses without fault). Section 2C:2-2, one of the keystones of the code, eliminates the use of such terms as *unlawfully, maliciously,* or *intentionally*. Possession, however, is criminalized as an act in which the "possessor knowingly procured or received the thing possessed or was aware of his control thereof for a sufficient period to have been able to terminate his possession."[46] This definition stretches the code's general philosophy of requiring a voluntary act or omission to constitute a criminal offense, but not as far as it has been stretched in other states. It is significant that New Jersey chose not to adopt the Model Penal Code's provision that would eliminate a conviction that leads to imprisonment unless the convicted offense contained a mental element of culpability.[47]

The New Jersey Code crystallizes the law concerning criminal defenses, excuses, and justification. It adds a new defense (for New Jersey) of distress, which had been barely implicit in a few cases. The law concerning the consent defense is restructured in such a way as to prohibit the consent defense for conduct involving serious

[44] New Jersey Code of Criminal Justice 2C:1-2.

[45] New Jersey Code of Criminal Justice 2C:2-2.

[46] New Jersey Code of Criminal Justice 2C:2-1c.

[47] Model Penal Code sec. 2.05.

bodily harm. Entrapment is available as a defense whenever the police officer "induces or encourages" the criminal activity and his or her conduct "as a direct result, causes"[48] that activity, a test much less likely to deter police abuses than the rule of the Model Penal Code. The New Jersey Code directly follows the lead of the Model Penal Code by giving the assignment judge the power to dismiss a prosecution if the defendant's conduct was within a "customary license or tolerance" not "expressly negated by the person whose interest was infringed nor inconsistent with the purpose of the law defining the offense."[49] The judge may also dismiss a prosecution of an offense deemed "too trivial to warrant the condemnation of conviction." This provision, although it permits appeal by the prosecutor, has been bitterly opposed by some law enforcement groups because it allows assignment judges to substitute their judgment as to the need to bring the charges for those of the grand jury and the prosecutors.

The New Jersey Code, unlike the Model Penal Code, retains the M'Naghten test for insanity, described in Chapter 10 of this book. The New Jersey Code is progressive, however, in its codification of the criteria that must be considered before determining whether an individual is competent to stand trial. A detailed examination of the defendant is to be conducted.[50] The New Jersey Code also introduces the defense of voluntary renunciation for the accomplice to a criminal offense.[51] This borrowing from the Model Penal Code represents a liberalization of the New Jersey law on the subject. Renunciation as a defense in criminal attempts[52] is another innovation in New Jersey law derived from the Model Penal Code. The law on conspiracy is also quite new and is heavily influenced by the Model Penal Code.[53]

The New Jersey Code generally retains most familiar crimes many ways familiar to students of the Model Penal Code. The traditional felony-murder rule is altered, permitting the defendants to prove that they did not cause a death and that they had no reasonable ground to believe that any other participant intended to engage

[48] New Jersey Code of Criminal Justice, 2C:2-12.

[49] New Jersey Code of Criminal Justice, 2C:2-11.

[50] New Jersey Code of Criminal Justice, 2C:4-4.

[51] New Jersey Code of Criminal Justice, 2C:2-6.

[52] New Jersey Code of Criminal Justice, 2C:5-1.

[53] New Jersey Code of Criminal Justice, 2C:5-2; 2C:5-4.

in conduct likely to result in death or serious injury.[54] Purposefully aiding suicide is a new offense created by the code's drafters.[55] A new offense entitled "terroristic threats"[56] lumps together a number of earlier New Jersey statutes. The law concerning sexual offenses was changed drastically, abandoning familiar terms such as *rape* and *sodomy* in favor of the more comprehensive term *sexual assault,*[57] a change which arouse the ire of many citizens and church groups. The term *sodomy* was not restored to the final version of the statute, but disputes shifted to the legal age for consent to sexual acts.

The New Jersey Code generally retains most familiar crimes known to earlier New Jersey law, although the definition of those crimes is changed to keep them consistent with the required five mental elements of culpability. Theft laws are drastically modernized and combined. White-collar crimes are more extensively defined and described than they have been under most state laws. A whole new body of law is created surrounding bribery and corruption of the political process. Perjury law is clarified. Misconduct in office and abuse of office are clearly proscribed. Gambling laws are simplified and players are differentiated from bookmakers and promoters of gambling.[58]

The most interesting provisions of the code are those dealing with sentencing, which represent a complete revision of the existing law in New Jersey. The code establishes a gradation of crimes and offenses based upon a legislatively determined judgment as to the gravity of each offense. The degrees of the offenses supposedly correspond to the moral (and legal) culpability of the offender. Crimes are divided into four categories, according to the degree of seriousness of the offense. The statute sets forth authorized ordinary terms of imprisonment. Sentences for first degree, 5 to 10 years; second degree, 3 to 5 years; third degree, 1 to 3 years; fourth degree, up to 12 months.[59] Three types of individuals may be subject to additional time in prison: persistent offenders previously convicted at least twice within 10 years for the same kind of offense; professional criminals who rely

[54] New Jersey Code of Criminal Justice, 2C;11-3 (a) (3) (a), (b), (c), (d).

[55] New Jersey Code of Criminal Justice, 2C:11-6.

[56] New Jersey Code of Criminal Justice, 2C:12-3.

[57] New Jersey Code of Criminal Justice, 2C:14-2.

[58] Bookmakers are treated sternly. Acceptance of three or more bets in any 2-week period is a crime subject to a maximum fine of $15,000 (2C:37-2(6).

[59] New Jersey Code of Criminal Justice, 2C:43-6.

on criminal activity as the major source of their livelihood; and defendants convicted of crimes for hire.[60] Disorderly persons may be sentenced to no more than 6 months in jail.

Sentencing, parole, and pretrial intervention are no longer subject to wide judicial discretion. This code reduces the span of judicial choice. A sentencing commission has also been established to set forth even more definitive criteria and standards to aid sentencing courts. Beyond that the legislature has set up presumptive sentences for each degree of crime. Even if the sentencing court varies from the fixed presumptive sentence it may do so only within the boundary set by the code, which is one degree lower for any offense. Even this is subject to the appeal of the prosecuting attorney, who may complain of a "manifestly lenient sentence."[61] The drafters of the Model Penal Code oppose fixed mandatory sentences of imprisonment. New Jersey has invented a scheme of flexible fixed terms of imprisonment, subject to the possibility of suspension of sentence for most crimes.[62] The scheme is complex and represents an uneasy compromise with those who would toughen it. The code is riddled with such compromises, which may, in the end, injure the symmetry of its essential design.

The code's numerous progressive features place the state in the forefront of criminal law reform, but it cannot be fairly labeled liberal or conservative. Public input largely concerned emotional issues such as sexual offenses and abortion. More than most, this code was the product of lawyers and law-enforcement officials who were politically neutral. Even then, political compromises had to be made to secure passage of the code.

TRENDS IN CRIMINAL LAW DEVELOPMENT

The New Jersey Code contains a consolidation of theft offenses. Previously distinct property crimes—larceny, embezzlement, false pretense, cheat, extortion, blackmail, fraudulent conversion, and receiving stolen property—are brought together under one unifying conception of involuntary transfer of property. Traditional historical distinctions, grounded on the common law or on nineteenth-century legislative enactments, are discarded in favor of a streamlined,

[60] New Jersey Code of Criminal Justice, 2C:43-7.

[61] New Jersey Code of Criminal Justice, 2C:44-1.

[62] New Jersey Code of Criminal Justice, 2C:43-2.

simplified set of definitions so general as to break down historical boundaries between traditional offenses. Criminal law, which had slowly evolved to meet changing social needs and changing perceptions of human behavior, has now become reconstructed in many states into highly rational though historically dubious categories of criminal conduct. History, once the source of most definitions of crime, has become less potent, less significant in the formulation of criminal law. This tendency proceeds at a different pace in different American jurisdictions, but the tendency to define crime broadly in ways unfamiliar to the nineteenth century seems prevalent everywhere. The separate purposes that led to the definition of such crimes as embezzlement, extortion, and fraud are being overlooked in favor of a new policy of merging the offenses into the single concept of involuntary transfer of property.

This trend to merge old offenses into newer, broader categories was spurned by the drafters of the Model Penal Code.[63] Reformed theft statutes may create substantive consolidation (as in New Jersey and the Model Penal Code) or procedural consolidation. A procedural consolidation permits several crimes to be joined in the same indictment, so that a defendant could be charged with both larceny and embezzlement, with the prosecutor waiting until the case is sent to the jury before electing the proper crime. A substantive consolidation may entail some resort to earlier definitions derived from older statutes or the common law in order to specify for the defendant the specific acts of wrongdoing. A bill of particulars is usually available to the defendant under a substantive consolidation of theft offenses. Thus the common law is not dead, but serves as a reservoir of familiar descriptions of crime. Defendants prosecuted under consolidated theft statutes cannot escape conviction merely because the prosecutor chose the wrong category of theft as his/her theory of prosecution. Theft, of whatever variety, is the modern offense in many jurisdictions. States differ, however, as to the number of crimes subsumed under the heading of theft, few having gone as far as New Jersey, which includes frauds, extortion, threat, and receiving stolen goods.

Consolidation or merger of sex offenses is much less common. The same logic that impels the combination of theft offenses suggests that crimes relating to sexual conduct exemplify a single kind of proscribed behavior. Fornication, adultery, homosexuality, deviate sexual behavior, and rape may be regarded as sufficiently

[63] Model Penal Code, sec. 223.1.

similar to be treated under one heading. Few states have chosen this path as yet, but the anomalies in this area of criminal conduct are favorite targets of reformers, suggesting that there is a growing elite (not yet a public) awareness of the need to separate serious offenses in this area from conduct that is immoral but not necessarily criminal. Changing sex codes also point in this direction, as tolerance of diverse patterns of sexual behavior grows. The sorting out process that comes with consolidation has led to considerable legislative debate over this sensitive issue, and some consolidation and decriminalization has taken place.

The Model Penal Code as originally drafted contained a provision outlawing illicit cohabitation or intercourse. This provision was ultimately deleted, decriminalizing this kind of behavior. Many states no longer criminalize adultery and fornication, and few prosecutions take place in those states that retain these offenses. Liberal reformers of laws concerning sexual offenses favor the decriminalization of private sexual acts between consenting adults. The policy "to exclude from the criminal law all sexual practices not involving force, adult corruption of minors, or public offense is based on the grounds that no harm to the secular interests of the community is involved in a typical sex practice in private between consenting adults."[64] Whether or not the state has a legitimate concern with private adult sexual practices is a determination that hinges upon one's view of the proper limits of criminal law when it impinges upon sexual morality. There is a discernable trend towards eliminating such offenses from the criminal code, although homosexuality continues to offend many persons' sensibilities. It is perhaps better to concentrate official concern on involuntary sexual conduct, especially rape and corruption of youth, than to pretend that the law can regulate kinds of behavior that may well be undetectable.

Criminal law is increasingly concerned with the problem of sentence disparity. Drastically dissimilar punishment for similar offenses may not be as prevalent as rumored, but many reformers of criminal law are concerned with reducing the extent of sentence disparity. Making the punishment fit the crime concerned Gilbert and Sullivan's Mikado and it still concerns all reformers of criminal law. But what does *fit* mean in this context? Does it mean identical sentences for all who commit the same offense? No one goes this far at present, but there is a marked trend toward reducing judicial

[64] New Jersey Criminal Law Revision Commission, *Final Report* (Newark, N.J., 1971) 2:196.

discretion in sentencing and toward imposing mandatory average sentences matched to particular crimes. Most convicted felons are in fact still placed on probation or given some form of suspended sentence.

Comprehensive criminal sentencing legislation ranks high on the agenda of reform. Present law generally lacks guidelines or criteria to be considered by the sentencing judge. But the days of unfettered judicial discretion in sentencing are ending as the realization has dawned that "the almost wholly unchecked and sweeping powers [of judges] are terrifying and intolerable for a society that professes devotion to the rule of law."[65]

The new Federal Criminal Code and most modern codes attempt to correct this potential abuse of power. Sentencing limitations, however, may also become sharply punitive, incarcerating more and more individuals for even longer terms than at present. Reformers should not lose sight of the fact that even without sentencing reform, American judges impose the longest sentences and the harshest penalties in the Western democratic world. New sentencing guidelines may be repressive as well as reformative depending on the precise terms of their formulation.

There is a continuing trend away from regarding certain offenders as bad persons toward treating them as patients. The therapeutic model of criminal law has led to the passage of sexual psychopath laws, a process described by criminologist Edwin H. Sutherland.[66] These laws generally provide that persons diagnosed as sexual psychopaths may be confined for an indefinite period in a state hospital for the insane. These statutes, which are politically quite popular, do not distinguish violent from nonviolent acts or serious offenses from unimportant ones. These statutes rely upon a psychiatric diagnosis of the subject's mental condition rather than upon the actual wrongful conduct. They adopt a medical model, making release from confinement for sexual psychopaths dependent upon an improvement in their condition and/or a decrease in their dangerousness as assessed by medical or psychological staff. The statutes depart from traditional criminal law in many ways, granting vast discretion to medical professionals within very vague legislative

[65] Marvin E. Frankel, *Criminal Sentences: Law Without Order* (New York: Hill and Wang, 1973), p. 5.

[66] Edwin H. Sutherland, "The Diffusion of Sexual Psychopath Laws," *American Journal of Sociology* 56 (1950): 142–148.

guidelines. Almost half the states have such laws, continuing a trend begun in 1911.[67]

There is growing suspicion about the effectiveness of the therapeutic model, especially when no real treatment is provided those who are hospitalized. Doctors may not be able to detect when a patient is truly well enough to reenter society. Long repressed urges may spring out when the patient returns to an old life. In mental illness cures are rarely clearcut and predicting the future behavior of violent persons is almost impossible. Moreover, doctors may not agree on who is ill and who is well, so release may depend upon chance as much as genuine cure. In the light of all these conditions there is a growing doubt about the usefulness of a therapeutic or medical model for dealing with violent behavior.

If criminal law is on the retreat in the area of sex crimes, the same may be said of the use of criminal sanctions against alcoholism and drug addiction. These, too, tend to be regarded more as medical problems than as matters appropriate to the criminal justice system. True, public drunkenness and drug use are still regarded as offenses of some importance. Drug selling is the subject of increasingly harsh punishment. On the other hand, those unfortunates who suffer from a chronic dependency on drugs and alcohol may, in the more modern view, be better treated in a hospital than in a prison. In 1968 Congress passed a District of Columbia Alcoholics Rehabilitation Act that repealed criminal penalties and involuntary civil commitment of chronic alcoholics and provided instead for treatment facilities. Pursuant to the act various detoxification centers were established and hospital beds provided. Narcotics addicts are sometimes treated in a similar fashion, although fewer states are willing to provide treatment centers for addicts. A national commission staff report advocates treating alcoholics and addicts in similar fashion, releasing them from institutional care as soon as they are no longer a danger to themselves or to society.[68] Because of the personality weaknesses and dependency of the exalcoholic and exaddict, continuing support and therapy might be needed for several years after treatment.

Many other crimes are being eliminated from the statute books because of the belief that there are too many criminal laws in

[67] The Briggs Act, Mass. Acts and Resolves, ch. 595, sec. 1-12.

[68] Staff Report to the National Commission on the Causes and Prevention of Violence, *Law and Order Reconsidered* (Washington, D.C.: Government Printing Office, 1969), pp. 551-570.

America and that too many trivial harms or events have been criminalized. Professor Sanford H. Kadish has called it a "crisis of over-criminalization."[69] He reminds us that authorizing a criminal conviction for a person who fails to use a required textbook or criminalizing the failure of a teacher to carry a first aid kit on a field trip are both improper or excessive uses of the criminal sanction. Morals offenses are more disputable, but much debate surrounds the issue of reducing or eliminating criminality in areas of sexual behavior once deemed vital but now more lightly regarded. Excessive application of the criminal sanction has also been condemned by a presidential commission.[70] Drafters of new criminal codes have generally attempted to weed out antiquated and unenforced criminal laws. They have also attempted to curtail the criminalization of conduct creating little or no harm (excepting conspiracy and attempt statutes). Overcriminalization has in many ways come to be recognized as a serious problem in the administration of criminal law, causing a convergence of the reform efforts of many law enforcement groups. The area denoted administrative crimes, however, remains overcriminalized with little sign of improvement, in spite of the Model Penal Code's view that many of these crimes could be eliminated.

At the same time that decriminalization is advancing in many areas of criminal law there has been a growth in the use of criminal law to improve the political process. The use of criminal sanctions to purify the political process is not entirely new to the American scene, but had never reached the extent of the present wave of criminal statutes defining official corruption, bribery, and intimidation in ever-broader dimensions, reaching many areas previously considered seamy politics but legitimate behavior.

Electoral frauds and offenses associated with the electoral process have long been part of the criminal law.[71] Political contributions and their solicitation by public officials have been made a

[69] Sanford H. Kadish, "The Crisis of Overcriminalization," *Annals of the American Academy of Political and Social Science* 374 (1967): 158-170.

[70] President's Commission on Law Enforcement and the Administration of Justice, *Task Force Report: The Courts* (Washington, D.C.: Government Printing Office, 1967), pp. 97-107.

[71] Old Federal Code: 18 U.S.C. sec. 241 (vote fraud); 18 U.S.C. sec. 597 (vote bribery). Other provisions incriminated subversion of the electoral process, such as ballot box stuffing, tampering with machines, corrupting election officials, suppressing absentee ballots, offenses which are also found detailed in state election codes and criminal laws.

crime in the past few decades.[72] The offense of official bribery has been expanded in many jurisdictions. Under the federal criminal code it is unlawful for a public servant to solicit, accept, or agree to accept money or its equivalent for advice, assistance, or promotion of a claim. The code criminalizes payments to public officials or party officials in order to obtain public office or even endorsement for public office, reaching behavior customarily accepted in inner party circles. Federal jurisdiction is also extended over offenses of official bribery in violation of state and local bribery and extortion laws. Gifts to public officials may now be crimes in many states.

Organized crime has also been a favorite target of recent criminal legislation. The new federal criminal code contains a section that penalizes leadership of criminal organizations. The section potentially criminalizes those who organize, control, finance, or otherwise manage a racketeering syndicate. Trafficking in drugs and engaging in a gambling business are two typical offenses usually committed by organized crime that are being treated as serious offenses in many jurisdictions in order to reduce the appeal of these offenses to the crime industry. In a few jurisdictions monies derived from the profits of organized crime are tainted and the expenditure of the receipts is treated as a crime in a stretched and strained fashion designed to attack organized crime.

In 1970 the federal government launched a new campaign against organized crime by enacting the Organized Crime Control Act[73] as a part of President Nixon's program to deal with the crime problem. The policy of the act was to seek the eradication of organized crime. The act elevates what is usually considered as local criminal activity to the level of a federal offense by finding a pattern of racketeering activity. Racketeering activity is criminalized by the statute and made subject to civil sanctions. Racketeering is a new federal criminal offense that consists of two previously committed substantive criminal offenses under federal or state law. The state offenses are of the type usually employed by organized criminals: murder, kidnapping, gambling, arson, robbery, bribery, extortion, drug and narcotics offenses. As long as a defendant has engaged in these acts (or has threatened them) twice within 10 years he or she may be charged with racketeering, even if the government cannot show a link with organized crime. Congress revealed its lack of regard for traditional criminal offenses in dealing with organized

[72] 18 U.S.C. sec. 602, 603, and 607.

[73] 18 U.S.C. sec. 1961-1968.

crime when it enacted this broad-gauge, awkward statute. The RICO statute, as it has become known (*R*acketeer *I*nfluenced and *C*orrupt *O*rganizations), is the most sweeping criminal statute ever passed by Congress,[74] incorporating twenty-four separate kinds of federal crimes and eight state felonies. The penalties for racketeering activity are often more severe than the penalties for the underlying crimes. Many states have enacted little-RICO statutes, as well. The frustration of combatting organized crime has led to a blunderbuss approach.

Corporate crime is another category of offense virtually unknown in the nineteenth century but developed and expanded in the twentieth century. The modern corporation is a central feature of modern American life. Regulation of corporate behavior has been a familiar concern of social reformers for 50 or 60 years. Criminal sanctions, however, were usually not regarded as an important means of regulation until the past decade. In recent years, "in areas ranging from tax, securities, and antitrust to the newer fields of environmental control, safety regulation, and the prevention of 'corrupt practices,' the federal government has come to rely more and more on the deterrent effect of criminal punishment to shape corporate actions."[75] Corporate crimes multiply in the statute books and

[74] See Jeff Atkinson, "Racketeer Influenced and Corrupt Organizations," 18 U.S.C. secs. 1961-68: Broadest of the Federal Criminal Statutes," *Journal of Criminal Law and Criminology* 69 (1978): 1-18.

[75] Note, "Developments in the Law—Corporate Crime," *Harvard Law Review* 92 (1979): 1229.

Another new-technology crime.

Transportation, sale, or receipt of phonograph records bearing forged or counterfeit labels

Whoever knowingly and with fraudulent intent transports, causes to be transported, receives, sells, or offers for sale in interstate or foreign commerce any phonograph record, disk, wire, tape, film, or other article on which sounds are recorded, to which or upon which is stamped, pasted, or affixed any forged or counterfeited label, knowing the label to have been falsely made, forged, or counterfeited, shall be fined not more than $1,000 or imprisoned not more than one year, or both.

Source: 18 U.S.C. sec. 2318.

responsibility for criminal acts of the corporation has been extended downwards to corporate agents and upwards, under some statutes, to corporate board rooms. Furthermore, the Justice Department has instituted criminal prosecutions against corporations with greater frequency under the Carter presidency than it has done since New Deal days.[76]

The increasing tendency to community control over corporate behavior through criminal sanctions has been especially prevalent in the enforcement of environmental protection. Pollution has become a crime. Air pollution, water pollution, and even noise pollution have been criminalized, often regardless of fault. Previously safety was used to justify criminal sanctions against those who manufactured dangerous drugs or produced unfit food. During the early New Deal, criminal sanctions were used against corporations as a means of economic regulation and this use has continued and expanded in recent years. While commentators debate whether deterrence, incapacitation, rehabilitation, or retribution supply an adequate justification or purpose for corporate criminal liability, legislators continue to turn to the use of criminal sanctions to supplement civil sanctions in controlling corporate behavior.

Why should there be increased concern with corporate crime, organized crime, and crimes by public officials at the same time that decriminalization of traditional offenses is taking place? No simple explanation will suffice. Yet the fact that collective kinds of crime are increasing is not unrelated to the fact that individual blameworthiness is decreasing. Citizens are convinced that the major evils of our society are to be attributed more to big business, big crime, and crooked politicians than to the acts of deviant individuals. Indeed, deviance in the criminal law is in the process of being redefined. If illegal drug use is much less serious than being in the business of marketing illegal drugs, and gambling is much less serious than being in the gambling business, then the capacity to do large-scale harm may be more significant than small-scale harm. We have not abandoned our horror or burglary, theft, and assault, but many citizens are also alarmed at widespread injury through nuclear radiation or poorly manufactured goods. Citizens nowadays expect a higher standard of conduct by their politicians and business leaders, and the criminal laws have come to reflect these shifts in public attitudes. Whether or not criminal sanctions can make

[76] Attorney General Griffin Bell indicated this conscious policy in a speech to the Harvard Law Review on March 19, 1977. In addition, cases have been increasingly referred to the Justice Department for criminal prosecution by regulatory agencies.

corporate leaders or politicians more responsible remains to be seen. Whether organized crime can be checked by powerful legislation also remains to be seen.

There appears to be a healthy trend towards the elimination of penal sanctions for less serious conduct and the introduction of new kinds of crimes to meet the challenges of modern technology. Some reformers, pursuing this approach, favor the eventual decriminalization of traffic offenses, providing civil type penalties in place of criminal penalties. Meanwhile, computer crimes, skyjacking, terrorism, and similar contemporary offenses have entered the criminal law. Many legislatures are adopting a more rational and more modern approach to criminal law in response to modern technology.

Whatever the future may hold for the development of criminal law in America there is sufficient dissatisfaction with the current condition of criminal law to continue reformist ferment for many years. Recidivism remains a major problem in crime, and the deterrent aspects of criminal law will receive closer scrutiny. Nowadays

Modern government is so vulnerable to terrorism that drastic measures have been seriously proposed to cope with it.

Standard 5.7 Content of Emergency Legislation

Emergency legislation should provide for the exercise, in specified contingencies, by the chief executive or some other designated official, of extraordinary powers to meet the threat of disorder and the disruption of society through mass disturbances; the dislocation of vital services; or acts of extraordinary violence of a terroristic or politically inspired nature that cannot be controlled or contained by ordinary means.

Such powers, conferred for the restoration of order, should include:

1. Proclamation of a curfew, with restrictions on movement and association during certain hours and in specially designated areas;
2. Prohibition of certain conduct, which although not ordinarily prohibited by law, is considered inflammatory and likely to provoke disorder or to aggravate an already disorderly situation;
3. Control of access to and from and movement within certain specified areas;
4. Evacuation and relocation of persons normally residing in certain specified areas who are threatened by disorders or terrorist activity;
5. Restrictions on communication with and communication within certain specially designated areas;

there is less of a tendency to excuse criminal conduct as a result of an unfortunate upbringing and a hostile environment. Legislators are losing faith in rehabilitation and therapeutic techniques in the control of crime. Although there is little evidence that prisons, halfway houses, and other institutional forms really do much for the rehabilitation of the offenders, there is at least the realization that keeping some people in prison prevents a certain amount of criminal activity by keeping potential criminals off the street. In sum, the general drift is toward penalties and away from punishment. Surer, shorter, swifter penalties proportioned to the offense seems a favored reform. Criminal law is beginning to learn some lessons from psychology, especially the newer approaches to learning theory. But beyond the question of teaching criminals a lesson lies the need for social order and control. In these fast-changing times criminal law is being employed increasingly to introduce greater control over a turbulent society. At some point control approaches repression. We have not come close to reaching that point.

---

6. Restrictions on the use of certain specified private property during certain times in designated areas;
7. Requirements of stipulated means of carrying identification during certain times in designated areas; and
8. Prohibition of the possession, sale, transfer, or consumption of certain articles or substances capable of being used for the commission of acts of violence or in stimulation of or preparation for such acts.

Because of the breadth of such extraordinary emergency powers and the threat to ordinary, individual liberties that they represent, the law should provide that they be exercised for a fixed time, preferably for not more than 30 days, after which an extension should be granted by the legislature, on the petition of the executive, only if cause is shown. Legislatures should be alert to any exercise of such emergency powers contrary to the spirit and intent of the legislation and should guard against the unwarranted creation of permanent laws and practices developing out of their exercise. The ordinary review by the courts of the exercise of the emergency powers authorized by such legislation should be rigorously preserved.

Source: National Advisory Committee on Criminal Justice Standards and Goals, *Disorders and Terrorism* (Washington, D.C.: Government Printing Office, 1976).

SUMMARY

The recent history of attempts to forge a federal criminal code suggests that criminal law is much embroiled with politics. The ambitions of major national political figures have been a cause of the slow pace of development of that code and the numerous major changes in its provisions. On the state level the many codifications of criminal law also have been caught up in interparty bickering and political grandstanding. Yet criminal law is less politically salient than tax law or agricultural subsidies, so the infighting is less intense, and the headlines are reserved for a few hot subjects such as abortion, homosexuality, and obscenity. Few interest groups operate in the arena of criminal law, and their political clout is small. Many changes in criminal law are under way nonetheless, and a major reform movement has gained important successes in the rationalization of American state criminal law. American legislatures appear to realize that harsh and inconsistent criminal laws are not effective, and they are groping for something better or at least for a fresh approach to criminal law.

Afterword

As 1980 drew to a close the fate of the federal criminal code was settled. Sadly, in spite of years of research and legislative effort, this important reform of criminal law was never finally voted upon. The 96th Congress had made more progress than any other toward revising federal criminal laws, but the impact of the November presidential elections was so great that the fragile compromises that formed the basis for the code were rent asunder.

Prospects for passage of the code appeared bright prior to the election because of extensive bargaining over key provisions by legislative leaders. Senator Edward Kennedy (Mass.) led the Democratic forces, and Senator Strom Thurmond (S.C.) represented Republican viewpoints. However, the fall Senate triumph of the GOP stiffened the attitudes of conservative Republicans, especially Senators McClure of Idaho and Helms of North Carolina. McClure's protracted opposition in the lame duck session of Congress following the election resulted in a delay that spelled the death of the code during the final days of the session.

Passage of the new federal criminal code was delayed by other factors that helped kill it. Senator Kennedy had a bill (S. 1722) ready for floor action early in 1980, but turned his attention to his bid for the presidential nomination. In addition, interest group dissatisfaction slowed down action. The American Civil Liberties Union opposed the Senate bill and gave only qualified support to the House measure (H.R. 6915). On the other end of the political spectrum, conservative religious groups criticized provisions on sex crimes, civil rights offenses, pornography, prostitution, and drug penalties. Between the left and right, business and labor groups also became involved in writing provisions to their liking. The Justice Department, the chief administrative champion of the code, received no special support from its chief, the president.

The lesson to be learned from the story of the federal criminal code is that major reform of criminal law requires clear-cut leadership and compromise between Democrats and Republicans. In spite of the many pitfalls which the code had escaped, it fell victim to the heavy Republican victory of 1980. Doubtless we shall see Republican changes in the federal criminal law, incorporating such favored notions as the death penalty, but no criminal code revision can be expected until tempers cool and criminal law is insulated from ideological factors and forces. A criminal code is not just a partisan affair; it requires general agreement among the law enforcement community, the legislative leaders, and the legal profession. It must satisfy the interest groups, but it need not placate them. Criminal law is too important a matter to become a political football. Instead it is an end product of informed political compromise.

Appendix A: Finding the Law

American criminal law varies greatly from one jurisdiction to another. No text can accurately encompass all the criminal laws to be found in America. As a practical matter law enforcement officals need a close familiarity with the criminal law of the state in which they work. Federal officials are usually unfamiliar with state criminal law. As a consequence current knowledge of American criminal law requires some skill at locating and examining the criminal law of a particular jurisdiction. In an age of rapid change in the criminal law there is even a greater need to develop an ability to find the criminal law.

FEDERAL AND STATE LAWS

These are normally issued individually in pamphlet form and collected at the end of the year or the legislative session into bound volumes. For the federal government, these books are called *Statutes at Large*. Individual new federal laws are kept in binders with the *Statutes at Large*. At the state level bound volumes of laws are referred to generally as *Session Laws*.

The Statutes at Large and the Session Laws are not the most convenient sources for existing statutory law because they supply the texts of laws in chronological order with no regard for the topics the laws deal with. There are also sets of books that contain current laws for the federal government and of individual states. A good example of a law code is the *New Jersey Statutes Annotated*, grouped together as the New Jersey Code of Criminal Justice. The codes are especially useful, because they arrange laws by subject and contain detailed indexes. Every state has a code that groups criminal laws together, but sometimes criminal laws are scattered over different code volumes.

Law codes are kept up to date by pocket parts, supplements inserted into the backs of the books, and by pamphlets. Codes are extremely helpful since not only do they collect the currently valid laws, they also contain references to court decisions that interpret statutes and/or sections of laws. Usually the best way to research statute law is to determine which codes you will need to use: the United States Code (or United States Code Annotated) or one or more state codes. Then study the indexes and refer to supplements (including pocket parts) as needed.

LOCAL ORDINANCES

Municipalities and other units of government possess limited delegated powers over minor crimes. These crimes are defined in county or municipal ordinances available at the county seat or the city hall. Sometimes large law libraries have copies of these laws, but they are hard to find. Recent enactments may be available only in the minutes of the appropriate local governing body.

COURT REPORTERS

Texts of federal court and administrative agency opinions and of major state courts are published in series called reporters. The cases appear in chronological order, so it is not easy to use the reporters unless you have found the citations to particular cases or administrative rulings in other sources, such as digests or treatises.

United States Supreme Court decisions are published in three editions: *United States Reports; United States Supreme Court Reports, Lawyer's Edition;* and the *Supreme Court Reporter*.

It is important to note that the text of the decisions themselves does not differ from edition to edition. Therefore, it will simply waste your time to read a decision in all three editions. Probably, the most useful edition is the *Supreme Court Reports, Lawyer's Edition,* since it contains annotations, West key notes, and many references to other sources of information, such as the *American Law Reports* and *American Jurisprudence.*

Lower federal court decisions are published primarily in two series issued by the West Publishing Company: Circuit Court of Appeals opinions in the *Federal Reporter* and District Court decisions in the *Federal Supplement.* Earlier decisions appear in a series called *Federal Cases.* Some district court decisions are never included in the *Federal Supplement* and are not published elsewhere. The *Federal Reporter* also contains decisions from the Court of Claims and the Court of Customs and Patent Appeals.

State court reports are usually published volume by volume by individual states and reprinted in the *Regional Reporters* published by West Publishing Company. As often happens in the law, the commercial editions are more useful and more often used than the official reports put out by the states. Surprising as it may seem, the regional reporters are issued more frequently than the official volumes and often contain cases that are never published by the official reports. The regional reporters are so good, in fact, that some states have given up publishing their own court reports and rely on West. These states are:

State	Regional Reporter
Alaska	Pacific
Florida	Southern
Kentucky	Southwestern
Louisiana Appeals	Southern
Maine	Atlantic
Mississippi	Southern
Missouri	Southwestern
North Dakota	Northwestern
Oklahoma	Pacific
Texas	Southwestern
Wyoming	Pacific

Nevertheless, the official state reports are not without their importance for the student. For one thing, if you are writing a paper that includes one or more citations to state cases, you must include both the West *Regional Reporter* and the official citations. Fortunately there are books that provide the necessary information for switching from one system to the other. Probably the most convenient source is the appropriate citator.

ADMINISTRATIVE REGULATIONS

Administrative regulations are an increasingly important source of information, because of the greater efforts of the federal government and of the states to regulate economic and social behavior. At the federal level, regulations are collected in the *Code of Federal Regulations*. All the regulations issued by an agency such as the Coast Guard or the Social Security Administration and which are in force are gathered together. Most administrative regulations lack criminal aspects.

To be sure that you are really up to date in checking currently valid federal regulations, you must also use the *Federal Register*. This is a daily publication that resembles a tabloid newspaper. There are monthly indexes and annual indexes; also, and very important, there are tables showing which sections of the *Code of Federal Regulations* are affected by new regulations published in the *Federal Register*. These are in each issue and in the monthly and annual indexes.

Until recently research on state administrative law was difficult, because of the lack of up-to-date sets of regulations. This situation is being remedied by the issuance of looseleaf binders containing codes of administrative regulations by many of the individual states.

PERIODICAL ARTICLES

Articles in law journals are often extremely helpful to the student who is researching a topic, since many relevant cases will be cited and discussed. The most important periodical index for the law student is the *Index to Legal Periodicals*. Most of each volume of the index is taken up with listing journal articles by subject. Author names are also included in this section. The major problem with the *Index to Legal Periodicals* is that rather broad terms are used for indexing purposes. Therefore, you must read through the titles of a number of articles to find those pertinent to your research. To facilitate locating index terms, it helps to skim the List of Subject Headings with cross references in all bound cumulations. "Criminal law" and "criminal procedure" are useful headings.

There are two other sections to the index. One is a case table. Cases about which law journal articles have been written are listed in alphabetical order by the first party to the case. Following the citation, there will be a listing of law journal articles, comments, and notes, with exact citations to law journals. The last section of *Index to Legal Periodicals* is a listing of book reviews.

LEGAL DICTIONARIES AND ENCYCLOPEDIAS

Students and other nonlawyers often have difficulty understanding the meaning of legal terminology. For simple definitions either of two books will be helpful: *Black's Law Dictionary* and *Ballentine's Law Dictionary*, both handy quick references and both reasonably accurate. Beware of overly simple definitions. For greater accuracy use what lawyers use: *Words and Phrases,* a multivolumed reference work that provides detailed, annotated, and updated meanings of legal terms.

Legal encylopedias are useful for obtaining an overview of large expanses of the law. There are two major encyclopedias: *American Jurisprudence* and *Corpus Juris Secundum*. Neither multivolumed work describes the law of any state or of the federal government; instead, the editors attempt to survey the general doctrines of the law in a systematic fashion. These encylopedias are kept up-to-date by the inclusion of supplemental pocket parts at the rear of each volume. "Criminal law" is a major subject heading in both encylopedias. These encyclopedias are a good starting point for those unfamiliar with particular aspects of the criminal law, although the entries are hard to read and require close attention.

SOME SHORTCUTS

Current criminal statutes are usually available in a condensed version. Typically, handbooks for law enforcement officers are prepared by county prosecutors or by the state attorney general. These condensations must be accurate because they are actually the basis for arrests, since police officers are trained in their duties by the use of these manuals. These handbooks or manuals nonetheless often neglect complex white-collar crimes, corruption offenses, frauds, and administrative crimes. These manuals moreover are not an authoritative statement of the law, merely a set of simplified restatements.

Many states have digests of the criminal law prepared by lawyers for a single jurisdiction. These summaries are usually found in larger law libraries and may be purchased commercially. Since such books are often used for reference by practicing attorneys they tend to be highly reliable, but they may quickly become outdated.

More general compilations of the current criminal laws are also available commercially. The Bureau of National Affairs publishes the excellent *Criminal Law Reporter* that keeps track of recent court decisions, federal and state. Duane Nedrud's annual *Criminal Law* does the same in an easily accessible manner.

Other research tips will be suggested by a good law librarian or a public documents librarian. Often the state library maintains current information on pending criminal legislation. Appropriate committee reports of Congress and the state legislatures also can be useful for summaries or as indicators of change in the criminal law.

Glossary of Legal Terms

accomplice. An individual who voluntarily and knowingly assists another in committing an offense.

accused. The generic name applied to the defendant in a criminal case.

acquittal. A final determination, after trial, that the accused is not guilty of the offense charged.

action. A proceeding in a court by which one party seeks to protect or enforce his or her rights.

actor. The person who does an act or commits an offense.

adversary proceeding. A proceeding in which the opposing sides have the opportunity to present their evidence and arguments.

affidavit. A written or printed declaration or statement of facts, under oath, by the party making it and taken before an officer having authority to administer such an oath.

allegation. A statement of fact (assertion) in a pleading of what one expects to prove.

allocution. The court's inquiry of a convicted person as to whether he or she has anything to say on one's own behalf before sentence is imposed.

amicus curiae. Literally, a friend of the court. A person who has no right to appear in a suit but is allowed to introduce argument, authority or evidence to ensure that the court receives all relevant information.

appeal. The removal of a case from a lower court to a higher court for the purpose of obtaining a review of the legality of the proceedings in the lower court.

appellant. The party who makes an appeal from one court to another.

appellate jurisdiction. The authority of a court to review the decision of a lower court; the power to hear cases appealed from a lower court.

appellee. The party against whom an appeal is taken.

arraign. To bring a prisoner before the court to answer the indictment or information. In practice, sometimes used also to refer to the appearance of the accused before a magistrate, at the point of first appearance.

arrest. The taking of a person into custody for the purpose of charging the person with a crime or having the person answer to a charge already brought.

arrest warrant. A court order authorizing a police officer to arrest a particular person or persons.

asportation. The removal of things from one place to another, which in some states is a required element of the offense of larceny.

attempt. An overt act, beyond mere preparation, moving directly toward the actual commission of a substantive crime and for which criminal liability may be imposed.

bail. The term *bail* is used to refer to any condition that must be fulfilled to obtain the accused's release pending a judicial proceeding, not just the posting of property as security.

bail bond. A document that obligates a person to forfeit a certain sum of money if the accused fails to appear as promised in obtaining release on bail. The bond is an alternative to posting the money itself. The persons who issue the bond and suffer the forfeiture are known as *sureties.*

bench. A reference to the court or to the judges composing the court. A trial before a judge alone, sitting without a jury, is known as a bench trial.

bench warrant. An order issued by the court itself, or from the bench, for the arrest of a person; it is not based as is an arrest warrant on a probable cause showing that a person has committed a crime, but only on the person's failure to appear in court as directed.

beyond a reasonable doubt. Proof to the degree required by law to permit the jury to convict in a criminal case.

bill of attainder. A legislative act that directs that punishment be imposed on a particular person without giving the person an opportunity to contest his or her guilt in a judicial trial.

bindover. The decision of the preliminary hearing judge holding that there is sufficient evidence to send the case on (bind it over) to the next stage in the proceeding.

brief. A written or printed document prepared by a lawyer that serves as the basis of the argument he or she is prepared to make in a appellate court. A brief contains the basic legal contentions of the party that provides legal authorities justifying the appeal (or its denial).

burden of proof. The obligation to introduce evidence establishing a fact so clearly as to meet the legal standard of proof.

calendar. As used in connection with judicial administration, a court calendar is a listing of the various cases filed in a court and the order in which they will be heard. Also referred to as the court's *docket.*

capital crime. Any crime punishable by death.

capital punishment. The use of the death penalty (i.e., execution) as the punishment for the commission of a particular crime.

cause of action. (1) The facts or circumstances that, if established, would justify a court in rendering a judgement on the merits of the case; (2) also sometimes used synonymously with *suit, action,* or *case.*

certiorari, writ of. An order (writ) directed by a superior court to an inferior court asking that the record of a case be sent up for review by the superior court. This is the common method for obtaining a review of a case by the United States Supreme Court.

challenge. As used in connection with the selection of jurors, the objection of counsel to the acceptance of a prospective person as juror. If the objection is based on a showing of bias, it is described as a challenge for cause.

change of venue. The removal of an action begun in one county or district to another county or district for trial.

charge (to a jury). Instructions given by the judge to the jury concerning points or questions involved in a case.

circumstantial evidence. All evidence of an indirect nature; the existence of a principal fact is inferred from circumstances.

civil action. A private lawsuit brought to obtain redress for some wrong in a manner other than by imposing punishment.

common law. The system of law under which courts have authority to create new standards through their rulings in cases, and future cases are decided on the basis of rulings in past cases. Statutes may eliminate or change the common law rules. Common law is based on case precedents.

complaint. In criminal law, a charge, preferred before a magistrate having jurisdiction, that a person named has committed a specified offense. Usually the first document filed in court charging the offense.

conclusions of fact. A series of stated conclusions from the facts, a result of reasoning from the facts that is set forth in the opinion to show how the court reached its decision.

conclusion of law. The conclusions drawn by court in a case that along with the facts make up the basis of the decision, which follows the court's conclusions of facts.

contempt of court. Any act that is allegedly calculated to embarrass, hinder, or obstruct the court in the administration of justice, or which is calculated to lessen its authority or dignity. The failure to obey a lawful directive of the court to engage no longer in certain activities is one type of contempt.

contraband. Any object that it is unlawful for a private individual to possess.

corpus delecti. The body of the crime; the essential elements of the criminal act; the substantial fact that a crime has been committed. The actual commission by someone of the offense charged.

count. The several parts of an indictment or information each charging a distinct offense. Often used synonymously with the word *charge*.

crime. Generally, a violation of the penal law of a state; a felony or misdemeanor as contrasted with offenses (or sometimes summary offenses) such as violations of traffic laws.

culpable. Blameworthy; subject to criminal liability.

damages. A monetary compensation which may be awarded in a civil suit for loss or injury suffered.

decree. The judgment of the court; a declaration of the court announcing the legal consequences of the facts found.

de facto. In fact, actually, pertains to a condition that exists. See *de jure*.

defendant. The party against whom relief or recovery is sought in an action or suit. In criminal law, the party charged with a crime.

definite sentence. A sentence that provides for a specific term of incarceration; also referred to as a flat-time, fixed-time, or determinate sentence.

de jure. By right; lawful; legitimate; pertains to a condition that should by law exist. See *de facto*.

delinquent child. A person of no more than a specified age who has violated any law or ordinance or, in some jurisdictions, is deemed incorrigible; a person who has been adjudicated a delinquent by a juvenile court.

de novo. Anew, afresh. A trial *de novo* is a retrial of a case, usually before a higher court.

detainer. A kind of hold order filed against an incarcerated person by another state or jurisdiction that seeks to take him or her into custody to answer to another criminal charge whenever he or she is released from his or her current imprisonment.

dicta. Something said in an opinion that is not necessary to the decision of the case.

dissent. The explicit disagreement by one or more judges of a court with the decision passed by the majority upon a case before them.

en banc. The whole bench of appellate judges hear the case. In federal courts of appeal, a panel of three judges usually hears a case. Some courts divide into units of several judges sitting together.

evidence. Any species of proof, presented at the trial, for the purpose of inducing belief in the minds of the court or jury.

exclusionary rule. The rule that excludes from the trial of an accused evidence illegally seized or obtained.

ex rel. By or on the information of. Used in case title to designate the person at whose instance the government or public official is acting.

ex parte. On one side only; by or for one party; done for, in behalf of, or on the application, of one party only.

ex post facto law. A law passed after the commission of an act which retrospectively changes the legal consequences by making the act criminal or increasing the criminal penalty for its commission. Prohibited by the U.S. Constitution.

federalism. The national government and the state governments, each within its assigned sphere, operate directly upon all persons and property within their territorial limits. Each has a complete governing apparatus, legislative, executive, and judiciary. The Constitution divides authority between the national and state governments.

federal question. A case that contains an issue involving the United States Constitution, treaties, or statutes presents a federal question.

felony. Generally an offense punishable by death or imprisonment in the penitentiary (or, as defined in some states, any term of imprisonment in excess of one year). A crime of graver nature than those designated as a misdemeanor.

fruits of a crime. Material objects acquired by means of and in consequence of the commission of a crime, and sometimes constituting the subject matter of the crime.

grading of offenses. Grading refers to the legislative assignment of punishment within a hierarchy of penalties.

grand jury. A jury selected from the community with the authority to conduct its own investigation into possible crimes and with the obligation to review cases presented by the prosecutor to determine if there is sufficient evidence to charge the accused with a crime. The charging instrument issued by the grand jury, if it decides the evidence is sufficient, is called an indictment.

grand larceny. Larceny deemed more serious than ordinary larceny.

habeas corpus, writ of. A writ, issued by a judge, that directs a person (a sheriff, a police official) detaining in custody a second person to produce the latter before a judge. The function of this writ is to release a detained person from unlawful imprisonment, and it has been used to challenge wrongful decisions of state courts.

harmless error. An error committed by the trial court that is viewed as not affecting the substantial rights of the appellant and therefore not requiring reversal of the trial court's judgment.

hearsay. Evidence not proceeding from the personal knowledge of the witness, but from the mere repetition of what he or she has heard others say.

holding. The actual decision of a court; what the court held in a case. Cf. **dicta.**

homicide. The killing on one human being by another.

hung jury. A jury so irreconcilably divided in opinion that it cannot agree upon any verdict.

inadmissible evidence. That which, under the rules of evidence, cannot be received for consideration in making a legal determination. Sometimes called incompetent evidence.

in camera. A case heard when the public is excluded and only persons concerned in the case are admitted.

incarceration. As used in the criminal law, *incarceration* refers to imprisonment in a prison, jail, or similar correctional facility.

indeterminate sentence. A sentence setting a minimum term and a maximum term of imprisonment (e.g., "not less than 3 years nor more than 10 years"), with the parole authority determining the exact point of release within the minimum and maximum limits.

index crimes. The specific crimes used by the Federal Bureau of Investigation in reporting the incidence of crime in the United States in the Uniform Crime Reports.

indictment. An accusation in writing handed down by a grand jury, charging that a person therein named has been guilty of a crime.

infamous crimes. A crime that entails infamy upon one who has committed it; crimes punishable by imprisonment in the state prison or penitentiary. At common law, all felonies were considered to be infamous crimes.

inferior courts. A term sometimes used to refer to magistrate courts (i.e., courts of limited jurisdiction).

information. A charging instrument, similar in form and effect to an indictment except that it is issued by the prosecuting attorney rather than the grand jury.

in forma pauperis. In the form of a pauper; as a poor person or indigent. Permission to bring legal action without the payment of required fees for writs, transcripts, and the like.

infraction. The name given in many jurisdictions to minor offenses, usually punishable by fine but no incarceration.

injunction. A judicial writ prohibiting an individual or organization from performing some specified action. Issued by a court of equity.

in re. In the matter of; concerning. This is the usual method of entitling a judicial proceeding in which there are no adversary parties. For this reason, used in the title of cases in a juvenile court.

insanity. A defect of reason caused by a disease of the mind in a person such that he or she did not know at the time of an act that the act was wrong, and/or did not know the nature and quality of the act, according to a prevailing legal doctrine now under scrutiny.

inter alia. Among other things.

inquest. A proceeding, often conducted by a coroner, to determine whether a death could have been caused by criminal homicide.

judgment. In general, the official decision of a court of justice upon the respective rights and claims of the parties to the action or suit therein litigated and submitted to its determination. In a criminal case, a judgment is comprised of a conviction and the sentence imposed thereon.

judgment notwithstanding verdict. A decision by a judge made after a jury verdict that reverses that verdict and enters judgment for the other party notwithstanding the jury verdict.

jurisdiction. The authority of a court to take a certain action. It refers to the authority to hear and decide a particular case. If a court lacks jurisdiction it may not consider a case.

jury. A group of persons summoned and sworn to decide on facts at issue. The use of the word *jury* by itself refers to the petit (i.e., trial) jury rather than the grand jury. Jury verdicts are conclusive of facts.

legal. Conforming to the law; according to a law; required or permitted by law; not forbidden or discountenanced by law; good and effectual law.

legal fiction. An assumption or doctrine of law that something is true or that a state of facts exists that has never taken place.

legislation. Legislation is rules of general application, enacted by a law-making body. Most often the term is used to refer to a statute.

lesser included offense. When it is deemed impossible to commit a particular crime without also committing, by the same conduct, another offense of lesser grade, the latter is, with respect to the former, a "lesser included offense." For example, a person who commits armed robbery also commits the crime of robbery itself. The elements of robbery are a part of armed robbery. Thus, robbery is a lesser included offense of armed robbery.

limitation of actions. In criminal law, the time after the commission of the offense within which the indictment must be presented or the information filed. The statute setting that time limit is called a statute of limitations.

local criminal courts. A popular name for magistrate courts, particularly when the court is a municipal court rather than a county court.

mala in se. Wrong in themselves; acts immoral or wrong in themselves.

mala prohibita. Crimes *mala prohibita* embrace actions prohibited by statute as infringing on other's rights, though no moral wrongdoing is involved. Absolute liability is imposed by such offenses.

malfeasance. The doing of an act that a person ought not to do; often used in the sense of misfeasance.

malice. A supposed intention to do harm without lawful justification or excuse; not necessarily the same as personal hate, spite, or ill will.

malice aforethought. A deliberate and premeditated intention to commit an unlawful act, as in murders.

mens rea. The mental element required for criminal liability. The required *mens rea* varies from crime to crime, but requires a mental element suggesting a wrongful purpose. Literally, a guilty mind.

minor. A person or infant who is under the age of legal competence; under twenty-one in some states and under eighteen in others.

misdemeanor. Any crime that does not fall within the state definition for felony; usually an offense punishable by imprisonment of one year or less and imprisonment only in a jail (as opposed to a penitentiary). Not used as terminology in all states.

moral turpitude. An act of vileness or depravity in the private and social duties that a person owes to fellow persons, or to society in general, contrary to the accepted and customary rule of right and duty between persons.

murder. The highest degree of culpable homicide. Unlike manslaughter, which is the lowest degree of homicide.

narcotic offenses. Those offenses relating to narcotic drugs, such as unlawful possession, sale, or use.

negligence. The failure to do something that a reasonable and prudent person would do, or the unintentional doing of something that such a person would not do, which constitutes the proximate cause of actual injury to another. The standard of care involved is an issue for factual determination, usually by a jury.

nolle prosequi. A motion of the prosecutor stating that he or she wishes to drop the prosecution and have the charges dismissed. A declaration that he or she will not further prosecute the case.

nolo contendere. A pleading by the defendant, having the impact of a guilty plea in permitting a judgment of conviction to be entered by the court and sentence to be imposed, but not admitting guilt. Literally, a declaration that the defendant will not contest the charge.

objection. Lawyer's act of taking exception to some statement or procedure at trial.

ordinance. An enactment of an authorized subdivision of the state, such as a city or a county, that has both penal and civil aspects, depending on the nature of the ordinance.

original jurisdiction. Jurisdiction in the first instance, commonly used to refer to trial jurisdiction as compared to appellate jurisdiction.

overrule. To annul an earlier decision by depriving the rule upon which it was based, as well as the case itself, of all authority as precedent. Cf. *reversal.*

pardon. An exercise of the executive power of the government to grant mercy by excusing an individual from the legal consequences (particularly the punishment) that follow from commission of a crime.

parens patriae. The doctrine that the juvenile court treats the child as a kind and loving father. Also refers generally to the judicial exercise of protective powers over children, the insane, or the incompetent.

parole. The release of a prisoner from imprisonment, but not from the legal custody of the state, for rehabilitation outside of prison walls under such conditions and supervision as the Board of Parole may determine.

party to a suit. Person or group of persons undertaking a court action.

penitentiary. A correctional facility for housing persons convicted of felony offenses.

per curiam. An opinion of the court that is authored by the justices collectively in the name of all the members.

petitioner. The party who presents a petition to a court asking (praying) for relief (in the form of an injunction, for example). The party against whom relief is prayed, or who opposes the prayer of the petition, is called the respondent.

petit jury. A trial jury as distinguished from a grand jury.

plaintiff. The party who sues another in a civil action to obtain a relief for injuries to his or her rights. The state serves as the complainant in all criminal cases.

plea of guilty. A confession of guilt in open court.

plea of not guilty. A plea of defendant that denies guilt as to the offense charged and puts the state to the proof of its charge.

precedent. A judicial decision that is taken as binding authority for the settlement of future similar cases arising in the same court or in other courts of lower rank within the same jurisdiction (or a superior federal court in cases decided by state courts).

preponderance of the evidence. Greater weight of evidence: the preponderance of the evidence rests with the evidence that produces the stronger impression and is more convincing as to its truth when weighed against the evidence in opposition.

presumptive sentencing. A sentencing system under which a particular sentence is presumed to be typical for a particular offense. A trial judge is allowed to depart from that typical sentence, within limited ranges, upon finding present certain mitigating factors or aggravating factors that may decrease or increase the sentence.

probable cause. This is an apparent state of facts that would induce a reasonably intelligent and prudent person to believe, in a criminal case, that the suspected person had committed the crime in question. More than suspicion, less than certainty. Usually required to support an arrest.

probation. The release of a convicted defendant by a court under conditions imposed by the court for a specified period of time, with the court reserving the right to impose a sentence of imprisonment if the probationer violates the conditions it imposed.

proximate cause. That which, in a natural and continuous sequence, unbroken by any independent intervening cause, produces the injury, and without which the result would not have occurred.

public defender. An official in the employment of the government who is responsible for representing indigent persons accused of crime.

ratio decidendi. The primary explanation or logical basis for the decision.

recidivism. Repeated acts of criminal conduct by an individual.

record. A written or taped account of all of the acts and proceedings in an action or suit in a court of record.

remand. A judicial order to send a case back to a lower court with instructions to carry out the judgment of the higher court.

remedy. Vindication of a claim of right. A legal procedure by which a right is enforced or the violation of a right is prevented or compensated.

res judicata. The legal principle that a right, question, or fact once put in issue and adjudged by a court of competent jurisdiction cannot be disputed in a subsequent suit between the same parties, thus preventing a repetition of disputes already judicially settled.

respondent. The party who is the defendant on an appeal.

reversal. The annulling or changing of an earlier decision because of some error or irregularity.

scienter. Knowingly, with guilty knowledge. An element of *mens rea.*

sentence. The judgment, formally pronounced by the court after defendant's conviction, setting forth the punishment to be inflicted.

separation of powers. The separation of governmental powers into three separate and independent branches—legislative, executive and judicial—a fundamental characteristic of both federal and state governments in the United States.

standing. The requisite qualifications to bring a legal action or to raise a certain legal objection.

stare decisis. The adherence to decided cases; when a court has once laid down a principle of law as applicable to a certain state of facts, it will adhere to that principle and apply it to all future cases where facts are substantially similar. Employed extensively in England and America.

statutory law. See *legislation.*

statutory rape. Carnal knowledge of a female child below the age fixed by statute. The child lacks the legal capacity to consent so the crime can be committed where no force is used and child consents in fact. A form of absolute criminal liability.

strict liability. Liability without fault, a crime without either wrongful intent or negligence on the part of the defendant. Defendant's intent and motive are immaterial.

***sua sponte*.** An action taken by a court on its own authority.

summary judgment. A decision by a judge rendered solely on the basis of affidavits or arguments submitted by one or both parties seeking to set forth all facts pertinent to decide the case. If there are no facts at issue the judge may issue judgment on the law.

summons. A legal order of a court directing a person to appear in court to answer certain charges.

suspect. A person who is suspected of having committed an offense, or who is believed to have committed an offense, but has not been formally charged with the offense or arrested.

theft. A popular name for larceny and now an expanded category of crime in some states.

tort. A private civil wrong or injury; a legal wrong committed upon the person or property, independent of contract violation, that is redressed in a civil court. The facts may also contribute the basis for a criminal action.

transcript of record. The printed record as prepared for review of a case by a higher court. The words *transcript* and *record on appeal* are used interchangeably by appellate courts.

vacating the judgment. The elimination or nullification of a judgment already entered because the original or appellate court is convinced the original judgment was in some way wrong or defective.

vandalism. Willful or malicious destruction, injury, or defacement of property without consent of the owner or person having custody or control. An offense defined in various ways by different states.

venue. Designates the particular county or city in which a court with jurisdiction may hear the case. In criminal cases this ordinarily is the county or city in which the offense occurred.

verdict. The formal decision or finding made by a jury, reported to the judge. A finding on issues submitted to a jury.

vicarious liability. Legal responsibility imposed upon one person because of the act or failure to act by another, such as one's employee or agent. Knowledge of the act is not necessary.

victimless crime. A crime in which the victim is a willing participant or to which the victim has consented, such as abortion and gambling. Some argue that society is not especially harmed by such conduct, hence it ought not to be criminalized.

voir dire. Literally, to speak the truth. The preliminary examination of a prospective juror as to competency, interest in the case, bias, etc.

waive. To abandon or throw away; in modern law, to abandon or surrender a claim, a privilege, a right, or the opportunity to take advantage of some defect, irregularity, or wrong.

wanton conduct. A reckless disregard of others' rights where injury is a probable consequence. More serious than negligent conduct.

warrant. A written order of the court (usually a magistrate) directing a peace officer to arrest a certain person (arrest warrant) or to search a certain place (search warrant).

writ of error. A common law writ issued by an appellate court to review a decision of a lower court upon appellant's contention that errors were committed by the lower court. This method of appeal is a matter of right for the appellant.

Criminal Law: A Working Bibliography

The literature of criminal law is vast, but certain books and articles should really be closely read by serious students and professionals. This annotated list contains entries that truly supplement the materials presented in the text.

Amir, Menachem. *Patterns in Forcible Rape*. Chicago: University of Chicago Press, 1971.

An empirical examination of rape that is supported by sophisticated methodology.

Andeneas, Johannes. *Punishment and Deterrence*. Ann Arbor: University of Michigan Press, 1974.

A major speculative work on the theory of criminal punishment and deterrence.

Anderson, Ronald A. *Wharton's Criminal Law and Procedure*. Rochester, N.Y.: The Lawyer's Cooperative Publishing Co., 1957.

Somewhat dated but essentially sound five-volume reference work.

Block, Richard. *Violent Crime*. Lexington, Mass.: Lexington Books, 1977.

Emphasizes dramatically different crime and victimization rates among various ethnic and age groups.

Bureau of National Affairs. *Criminal Law Reporter*. Washington, D.C.: continuing dates.

This is the best quick source for current reference concerning court cases and legislative developments in criminal law. This looseleaf service is necessary for all professional offices.

Cardozo, Benjamin. *The Growth of the Law*. New Haven, Conn.: Yale University Press, 1924.

The significance of precedent in the development of legal doctrines is ably explained by this eminent jurist.

Clark, Ramsey. *Crime in America*. New York: Simon and Schuster, 1970.

A prime example of social reformist approaches to criminal justice.

Cloward, Richard A., and Ohlin, Lloyd E. *Delinquency and Opportunity*. New York: Free Press, 1960.

Provides convincing explanations for some types of deviant behavior and also defines criminal activity in a way that is followed in this book.

Conklin, John E. *Robbery and the Criminal Justice System*. Philadelphia: J. P. Lippincott Co., 1972.

A blend of sociological insight and criminal law.

Doleschal, Eugene "Crime—some popular beliefs," *Crime and Delinquency* 25 (1979): 1-8.

A brief reminder, in one of our best journals, that American crime rates fluctuate, that our systems is more punitive than most other nations', and that the crimes of the affluent cause the greatest financial loss.

Fletcher, George. *Rethinking Criminal Law*. Boston: Little, Brown and Co., 1978.

Analyzes the bases of specific offenses, such as theft, larceny, embezzlement, and burglary; reexamines some assumptions about homicide; and considers wrong-doing as a whole.

Garofalo, James. *Public Opinion About Crime: The Attitudes of Victims and Nonvictims in Selected Cities*. Washington, D.C.: Government Printing Office, 1977.

An important study of victims and of general public attitudes.

Goldstein, Abraham S. *The Insanity Defense*. New Haven, Conn.: Yale University Press, 1967.

A wise and balanced treatment of a difficult and controversial subject.

Hall, Jerome. *General Principles of the Criminal Law*. Indianapolis: The Bobbs-Merrill Co., 1960.

A philosophical and jurisprudential summary of underlying principles in criminal law still much used by lawyers, judges, and law professors.

Hall, Jerome. *Theft, Law, and Society*. 2nd ed. Indianapolis: The Bobbs-Merrill Co., 1952.

Describes the derivation and purposes of the crimes against property in a thoughtful, original fashion.

Harris, Richard. *Justice*. New York: Avon Books, 1969.

The pursuit of political dissidents by the Nixon administration and John Mitchell's Justice Department is described in harrowing detail.

Hurst, James W. *Law and Social Order in the United States*. Ithaca, N.Y.: Cornell University Press, 1977.

A valuable historical survey of American law, including criminal law.

La Fave, Wayne, and Scott, Austin W. *Handbook of Criminal Law*. St. Paul, Minn.: West Publishing Co., 1972.

A hornbook or standardized, but thorough, interpretation of most of the major elements of substantive criminal law.

Levi, Edward H. *An Introduction to Legal Reasoning*. Chicago: University of Chicago Press, 1948.

As the title suggests, this is an effort, probably the most successful effort, to describe and explain the reasoning processes of judges in the American legal system.

Lieberman, Jethro K. *How the Government Breaks the Law*. Baltimore: Penguin Books, 1973.

A popularized but valuable account of a variety of political crime.

Lowe, G. Nobles, and Shargel, Harry D. *Legal and Other Aspects of Terrorism*. New York: Practicing Law Institute, 1979.

This hard-to-find volume is an excellent compilation of legal texts and essays concerning this important area of criminal activity.

National Commission on the Causes and Prevention of Violence. *Final Report*. New York: Praeger Publishers, Inc., 1970.

A leading official source.

Note, "Recent Statutory Developments in the Definition of Forcible Rape," *Virginia Law Review* 61 (1975): 1500–1535.

Useful summation.

Orloski, Richard J. *Criminal Law*. Chicago: Nelson-Hall Publishers, 1977.

Subtitled "An Indictment," this book has good chapters on failing to define crimes, on victimless crimes, and on abortion, among other matters.

Packer, Herbert. *The Limits of the Criminal Sanction*. Palo Alto, Calif.: Stanford University Press, 1968.

Describes two models of the criminal process: crime control and due process. The two models suggest divergent policies towards criminal behavior.

Perkins, Rollin M. *Criminal Law*. Mineola, N.Y.: Foundation Press, 1969.

In its various editions this has been one of the most widely adopted law school texts in criminal law.

Petersilia, John; Greenwood, Peter W.; and Lavin, Marvin. *Criminal Careers of Habitual Felons*. Santa Monica, Calif.: Rand Corporation, 1977.

A study of forty-nine imprisoned armed robbers indicates that most get away with their crime, but expect to get caught once in a while as a risk of their profession.

Pound, Roscoe. *Jurisprudence*. St. Paul, Minn.: West Publishing Co., 1959.

A major work by America's leading legal philosopher sets forth basic postulates for American law.

President's Commission on Law Enforcement and Administration of Justice. *Challenge of Crime in a Free Society*. Washington, D.C.: Government Printing Office, 1967.

The point of departure for many criminal law reforms of the past dozen years.

President's Commission on Law Enforcement and Administration of Justice. Task Force Report, *Organized Crime*. Washington, D.C.: Government Printing Office, 1967.

Contains important descriptions and a coherent strategy to deal with organized crime.

Quinney, Richard. *The Social Reality of Crime.* Boston: Little, Brown and Co., 1970.

In this and other books Quinney opens a Marxist approach to American criminal law, seeing that law as an expression of class dominance and control.

Roebuck, Julian, and Weeber, Stanley C. *Political Crime in the United States: Analyzing Crime by and Against Government.* New York: Praeger Publishers, 1978.

Adopts an expansive definition of political crime to include crimes by corporations as well as crimes by government. This approach allows consideration of evasion and collusion by government and business interests working together.

Sayre, Francis B. "Public Welfare," *Columbia Law Review* 33 (1933): 55-88.

Still the best description of administratively defined crimes without fault.

Schur, Edwin M. *Crimes Without Victims.* Englewood Cliffs, N.J.: Prentice-Hall, Inc., 1965.

Helped popularize and explain the concept of victimless crimes.

Schwartz, Louis. "The Wechslerian Revolution in Criminal Law and Administration," *Columbia Law Review* 78 (1978): 1159-1170.

Describes the critical contributions of Herbert Wechsler to the development of American criminal law.

Silberman, Charles. *Criminal Violence, Criminal Justice.* New York: Random House, 1978.

Criminal violence has been a recurrent phenomenon in American history, but now a disproportionate share is black crime. Why?

Skolnick, Jerome H. *Justice Without Trial.* New York: John Wiley & Sons, Inc., 1966.

A sociological critique of criminal justice, with valuable chapters on the penalty structure and police attitudes towards criminal law.

Sutherland, Edwin H. *White-Collar Crime.* New York: Holt, Rinehart and Winston, 1961.

An eminent sociologist who helped form the concept of white-collar crime, Sutherland has authored other important works, including a leading text in criminology.

Sykes, Gresham. *Crime and Society.* New York: Random House, 1967.

A major work blending history, sociology, and criminology.

Turk, Austin I. *Criminality and Legal Order.* Chicago: Rand McNally, 1969.

A useful overview of criminology with an emphasis on establishing criminal categories.

Wilson, James Q. *Thinking About Crime.* New York: Basic Books, 1975.

A highly influential book that attacks criminological approaches to crime causation in favor of a more direct crime control approach.

Wolfgang, Marvin, and Cohen, Bernard. *Crime and Race.* New York: Institute of Human Relations, 1970.

In spite of its title, a fairly hopeful book that aims at treating root causes of crime. Wolfgang has become somewhat less hopeful in recent years.

Table of Cases

Index